Personal Finance For Dummies, 3rd Edition

Eric Tyson's Keys to Personal Financial Success

- **Take charge of your finances.** Procrastinating is detrimental to your long-term financial health. Don't wait for a crisis or major life event to get your act together. Read this book and start implementing now!

- **Don't buy consumer items (cars, clothing, vacations, and so on) that lose value over time on credit.** Use debt only to make investments in things that gain value, such as real estate, a business, or an education.

- **Use credit cards only for convenience, not for carrying debt.** If you have a tendency to run up credit card debt, then get rid of your cards and use only cash, checks, and debit cards.

- **Live within your means and don't try to keep up with your coworkers, neighbors, and peers.** Many who engage in conspicuous consumption are borrowing against their future; some end up bankrupt.

- **Save and invest at least 5 to 10 percent of your income.** Preferably, invest through a retirement savings account to reduce your taxes and ensure your future financial independence.

- **Understand and use your employee benefits.** If you're self-employed, find out the best investment and insurance options available to you, and use them.

- **Research before you buy.** Never purchase a financial product or service on the basis of an advertisement or salesperson's solicitation.

- **Avoid financial products that carry high commissions and expenses.** Companies that sell their products through aggressive sales techniques generally have the worst financial products and the highest commissions.

- **Don't purchase any financial product that you do not understand.** Ask questions and compare what you're being offered to the best sources recommended in this book.

- **Invest the majority of your long-term money in ownership vehicles that have appreciation potential, such as stocks, real estate, and your own business.** When you invest in bonds or bank accounts, you are simply lending your money to others and will earn a return that probably won't keep you ahead of inflation and taxes.

- **Avoid making emotionally based financial decisions.** For example, investors who panic and sell their stock holdings after a major market correction miss a buying opportunity. Be especially careful in making important financial decisions after a major life change such as a divorce, job loss, or death in your family.

Personal Finance For Dummies, 3rd Edition

Cheat Sheet

- **Make investing decisions based upon your needs and the long-term fundamentals of what you are buying.** Ignore the predictive advice offered by financial prognosticators — nobody has a working crystal ball. Don't make knee-jerk decisions based on news headlines.

- **Own your home.** In the long run, owning is more cost-effective than renting, unless you have a terrific rent-control deal. But don't buy until you can stay put for a number of years.

- **Purchase broad insurance coverage to protect against financial catastrophes.** Eliminate insurance for small potential losses.

- **If you're married, make time to discuss joint goals, issues, and concerns.** Be accepting of your partner's money personality; learn to compromise and manage as a team.

- **Prepare for life changes.** The better you are at living within your means and anticipating life changes, the better off you will be financially and emotionally.

- **Read publications that have high quality standards and that aren't afraid to take a stand and recommend what's in your best interests.**

- **Prioritize your financial goals and start working toward them.** Be patient. Focus on your accomplishments and learn from your past mistakes.

- **Hire yourself first. You are the best financial person that you can hire.** If you need help making a major decision, hire conflict-free advisors who charge a fee for their time. Work in partnership with advisors — don't abdicate control.

- **Invest in yourself and others. Invest in your education, your health, and your relationships with family and friends.** Having a lot of money isn't worth much if you don't have your health and people with whom to share your life. Give your time and money to causes that better our society and world.

Copyright © 2000 Eric Tyson
All rights reserved.
Cheat Sheet $2.95 value. Item 5231-7.
For more information about IDG Books,
call 1-800-762-2974.

For Dummies™: Bestselling Book Series for Beginners

Praise for Eric Tyson

Here's what critics and readers have said about Eric Tyson's previous national best-sellers:

"Eric Tyson For President!!! Thanks for such a wonderful guide. With a clear, no-nonsense approach to . . . investing for the long haul, Tyson's book says it all without being the least bit long-winded. Pick up a copy today. It'll be your wisest investment ever!!!'

> — Jim Beggs, VA

"*Personal Finance For Dummies* is the perfect book for people who feel guilty about inadequately managing their money but are intimidated by all of the publications out there. It's a painless way to learn how to take control. My college-aged daughters even enjoyed reading it!"

> — Karen Tofte, producer, National Public Radio's
> *Sound Money*

"I own many finance and investment books — this is by far the best!"

> — Mike Dodge, Baltimore, MD

"Among my favorite financial guides are . . . Eric Tyson's *Personal Finance For Dummies*."

> — Jonathan Clements, *The Wall Street Journal*

"The book was well-written, concise, inspirational, excellent for common-folk, and doesn't send you running for a dictionary."

> — Brian O'Connor, Bogota, NJ

"Smart advice for dummies . . . skip the tomes . . . and buy *Personal Finance For Dummies,* which rewards your candor with advice and comfort."

> — Temma Ehrenfeld, *Newsweek*

"Superb reference! Led to my being offered a job as a mortgage originator. [The] bank said I was the 'most informed buyer' they ever sat with!!!"

> — K.A. Carney, Greensburg, PA

"A nice, easy-to-use format allowed me to skip useless data and glean only the information relevant to me."

— Steven A. Baffy, Trenton, MI

"Best new personal finance book."

— Michael Pellecchia, syndicated columnist

"I thoroughly enjoyed the honest, matter-of-fact, straightforward manner in which the book was written. I am grateful to you for providing me with a valuable resource for one of life's great drudgeries."

— Sven Hagen, Atlanta, GA

"Eric Tyson . . . seems the perfect writer for a ...*For Dummies* book. He doesn't tell you what to do or consider doing without explaining the why's and how's — and the booby traps to avoid — in plain English. . . . It will lead you through the thickets of your own finances as painlessly as I can imagine."

— Clarence Peterson, *Chicago Tribune*

"Great book!"

— Cheryl Eichelkraut, Phoenix, AZ

"The best book I've ever bought!"

— David Clarke, Chicago, IL

"This book was written for real people."

— Lisa Timco, Westland, MI

"*Personal Finance For Dummies* is, by far, the best book I have read on financial planning. It is a simplified volume of information that provides tremendous insight and guidance into the world of investing and other money issues."

— Althea Thompson, producer,
PBS Nightly Business Report

". . . amazingly you were even able to add humor to such a topic."

— Steve Stachling, Wausau, WI

"This book provides easy-to-understand personal financial information and advice for those without great wealth or knowledge in this area. Practitioners like Eric Tyson, who care about the well-being of middle-income people, are rare in today's society."

> — Joel Hyatt, founder, Hyatt Legal Services, one of the nation's largest general-practice personal legal service firms

". . . very understandable, informative, and enjoyable. . . . This should be required reading for every senior!"

> — Barbara Greub, River Falls, WI

"*Personal Finance For Dummies* is a sane and useful guide that will be of benefit to anyone seeking a careful and prudent method of managing their financial world."

> — John Robbins, founder of EarthSave, author of *May All Be Fed*

"Very informative, lighthearted. . . . I read it cover to cover."

> — Lou Furry, Northampton, PA

"Worth getting. Scores of all-purpose money-management books reach bookstores every year, but only once every couple of years does a stand-out personal finance primer come along. *Personal Finance For Dummies,* by financial counselor and columnist Eric Tyson, provides detailed, action-oriented advice on everyday financial questions. . . . Tyson's style is readable and unintimidating."

> — Kristin Davis, *Kiplinger's Personal Finance Magazine*

"The organization of this book is superb! I could go right to the topics of immediate interest and find clearly written and informative material. The author answered questions that I didn't even know."

> — Lorraine Verboort, Beaverton, OR

"I was able to locate all items that I was interested in by the index. . . . Great!"

> — Robert Linardo, Nas Lemoore, CA

"For those named in the title, such as myself, *Personal Finance For Dummies* is a godsend. It's bright, funny, and it can save you money, too."

— Jerome Crowe, reporter, *Los Angeles Times*

"Simple and understandable and enjoyable!"

— Jeanette Johnson, Soldotna, AK

"Eric Tyson has brought his financial experience, investment knowledge, and down-to-earth writing style to create an *outstanding* book on mutual funds for all investors — and an *essential* book for new investors. . . in short, a classic. . . ."

— Jack Bogle, former CEO, The Vanguard Group

"Understandable to anyone."

— Pam Smith, Tehachapi, CA

"Confused by finances and taxes? Eric Tyson has written *Personal Finance For Dummies,* a friendly, easy-to-follow guide to smart money strategies."

— Deb Lawler, anchor, WBZ radio, Boston, MA

". . . by far the best book I've read about the U.S. tax system and personal financial planning."

— Seva Baykin, Brisbane, CA

"This is a great book. It's understandable. Other financial books are too technical and this one really is different."

— Shad Johnson, producer, Business Radio Network

"Down-to-earth, straightforward information. It was as if Mr. Tyson was a close friend of mine who really cared about me."

— Arnold L., Monterey Park, CA

"An invaluable, easy-to-read financial help book that should be in every family's library."

— Stan Schaffer, reporter, *The Morning Call,* Allentown, PA

"I purchased copies for each of my children."

— M.G. Sher, Marblehead, MA

"I liked his holistic view. He placed money management in perspective to life's important considerations. Invaluable! I'd like to give a copy to each of my sons just starting their 1st jobs."

— Robin Ketchum, Norfolk, CT

"Fantastic. I wish I had it 20 years ago. I'll make sure my children get one."

— C.H. Day, Richmond, VA

"Presents complicated issues with simplicity, clarity, and a touch of humor."

— *The Times-Picayune,* New Orleans, LA

"This book is the first on finances that I have ever read that makes sense to me."

— Tony Toledo, Salem, MA

"Straightforward, readable. . . Tyson is an authoritative writer. . . ."

— *The Orange County Register*

"*Personal Finance For Dummies* is a great book. It addresses everything and helps me feel secure about my finances."

— Phyllis Haber, Kansas City, MO

". . . among tax advice books is far and away the best. *Taxes For Dummies* is fun to read and teaches about the tax system itself. The book also provides excellent advice about dealing with mistakes — created by you or the Internal Revenue Service. And it talks about fitting taxes into your daily financial planning. In other words, it's a book you can use after April 15, as well as before."

— Kathy M. Kristof, *Los Angeles Times*

"*Taxes For Dummies* helped us save $500 on our tax return."

— Bob and Diane Hayman, Mishawaka, IN

"Smart chapters — not just thumbnail sketches — for filling out forms."

— Susan Tompor, Gannett News Service

"Finally, a book about finance that I can understand!"

— Michael K. Owens, Knoxville, TN

"*Taxes For Dummies* will make tax preparation less traumatic. . . . It is a book that answers — in plain English, and sometimes with humor — many puzzling questions that arise on the most commonly used tax forms."

— Stanley Angrist, *The Wall Street Journal*

"I should never have brought this book into work — everyone wants to borrow it!"

— Maria Zografos, San Francisco, CA

". . . a witty, irreverent reference . . . And since laughter is good medicine, it most definitely is what it claims. But its focus on humor does not undermine its merit as a research tool. While the guide could be used just to answer individual questions, its friendly format is such fun that you may end up reading Eric Tyson's book from cover to cover. No kidding."

— *The Times-Picayune,* New Orleans, LA

"This book answered so many questions. Truly, I was completely illiterate financially — now I am becoming the family guru."

— Jean M., Holt, MO

"There are plenty of books out there that do the job, but if you're looking for one which explains the tax laws using plain English, with a dash of a sense of humor, *Taxes For Dummies* is highly recommended. . . . *Taxes For Dummies* is the ideal guide for getting you through the Ides of April."

— Bill Peschel, *The Herald*

"It's great! It moves you to a mindset that allows you to control your finances — instead of them controlling you."

— Sabrina Karl, Madison, WI

"Dummies is a primer for those who are tired of making bad choices — or no choices at all — with their money."

— Barbara Tierney, *Smart Money* by
The Wall Street Journal

"This book should be taught in every high school and college in America. Most people, like me, wait until they're in trouble before they get help."

— Gary Rzepka, APO AP Japan

More ...For Dummies™ Titles by Eric Tyson

Investing For Dummies™

Mutual Funds For Dummies™

Taxes For Dummies™
(co-authored with David Silverman)

Home Buying/House Selling/Mortgages For Dummies™
(co-authored with Ray Brown)

Small Business For Dummies™
(co-authored with Jim Schell)

TM

References for the Rest of Us!™

BESTSELLING BOOK SERIES

Do you find that traditional reference books are overloaded with technical details and advice you'll never use? Do you postpone important life decisions because you just don't want to deal with them? Then our *...For Dummies*® business and general reference book series is for you.

...For Dummies business and general reference books are written for those frustrated and hard-working souls who know they aren't dumb, but find that the myriad of personal and business issues and the accompanying horror stories make them feel helpless. *...For Dummies* books use a lighthearted approach, a down-to-earth style, and even cartoons and humorous icons to dispel fears and build confidence. Lighthearted but not lightweight, these books are perfect survival guides to solve your everyday personal and business problems.

> *"More than a publishing phenomenon, 'Dummies' is a sign of the times."*
>
> — The New York Times

> *"A world of detailed and authoritative information is packed into them..."*
>
> — U.S. News and World Report

> *"...you won't go wrong buying them."*
>
> — Walter Mossberg, Wall Street Journal, on IDG Books' ...For Dummies books

Already, millions of satisfied readers agree. They have made *...For Dummies* the #1 introductory level computer book series and a best-selling business book series. They have written asking for more. So, if you're looking for the best and easiest way to learn about business and other general reference topics, look to *...For Dummies* to give you a helping hand.

1/99

Personal Finance
FOR
DUMMIES®
3RD EDITION

by Eric Tyson, M.B.A.

Financial Counselor, Syndicated Columnist,
and Author of Five National Best-Sellers, including
Investing For Dummies and Mutual Funds For Dummies

IDG Books Worldwide, Inc.
An International Data Group Company

Foster City, CA ◆ Chicago, IL ◆ Indianapolis, IN ◆ New York, NY

Personal Finance For Dummies,® 3rd Edition

Published by
IDG Books Worldwide, Inc.
An International Data Group Company
919 E. Hillsdale Blvd.
Suite 400
Foster City, CA 94404
www.idgbooks.com (IDG Books Worldwide Web site)
www.dummies.com (Dummies Press Web site)

Library of Congress Catalog Card No.: 99-68615

ISBN: 0-7645-5231-7

Printed in the United States of America

10 9 8 7 6 5 4 3 2 1

3O/QR/QS/QQ/IN

Distributed in the United States by IDG Books Worldwide, Inc.

Distributed by CDG Books Canada Inc. for Canada; by Transworld Publishers Limited in the United Kingdom; by IDG Norge Books for Norway; by IDG Sweden Books for Sweden; by IDG Books Australia Publishing Corporation Pty. Ltd. for Australia and New Zealand; by TransQuest Publishers Pte Ltd. for Singapore, Malaysia, Thailand, Indonesia, and Hong Kong; by Gotop Information Inc. for Taiwan; by ICG Muse, Inc. for Japan; by Intersoft for South Africa; by Eyrolles for France; by International Thomson Publishing for Germany, Austria and Switzerland; by Distribuidora Cuspide for Argentina; by LR International for Brazil; by Galileo Libros for Chile; by Ediciones ZETA S.C.R. Ltda. for Peru; by WS Computer Publishing Corporation, Inc., for the Philippines; by Contemporanea de Ediciones for Venezuela; by Express Computer Distributors for the Caribbean and West Indies; by Micronesia Media Distributor, Inc. for Micronesia; by Chips Computadoras S.A. de C.V. for Mexico; by Editorial Norma de Panama S.A. for Panama; by American Bookshops for Finland.

For general information on IDG Books Worldwide's books in the U.S., please call our Consumer Customer Service department at 800-762-2974. For reseller information, including discounts and premium sales, please call our Reseller Customer Service department at 800-434-3422.

For information on where to purchase IDG Books Worldwide's books outside the U.S., please contact our International Sales department at 317-596-5530 or fax 317-572-4002.

For consumer information on foreign language translations, please contact our Customer Service department at 1-800-434-3422, fax 317-572-4002, or e-mail rights@idgbooks.com.

For information on licensing foreign or domestic rights, please phone +1-650-653-7098.

For sales inquiries and special prices for bulk quantities, please contact our Sales department at 800-762-2974 or write to the address above.

For information on using IDG Books Worldwide's books in the classroom or for ordering examination copies, please contact our Educational Sales department at 800-434-2086 or fax 317-572-4005.

For press review copies, author interviews, or other publicity information, please contact our Public Relations department at 650-653-7000 or fax 650-653-7500.

For authorization to photocopy items for corporate, personal, or educational use, please contact Copyright Clearance Center, 222 Rosewood Drive, Danvers, MA 01923, or fax 978-750-4470.

is a registered trademark under exclusive
license to IDG Books Worldwide, Inc.
from International Data Group, Inc.

About the Author

Eric Tyson first became interested in money matters nearly three decades ago. After his father was laid off during the 1973 recession and received some retirement money from Philco-Ford, Eric worked with his dad to make investing decisions with the money. A couple of years later, Eric won his high school's science fair with a project on what influences the stock market. Dr. Martin Zweig, who provided some guidance, awarded Eric a one-year subscription to the *Zweig Forecast,* a famous investment newsletter. Of course, Eric's mom and dad share some credit with Martin for Eric's victory.

After toiling away for a number of years as a management consultant to Fortune 500 financial-service firms, Eric finally figured out how to pursue his dream. He took his inside knowledge of the banking, investment, and insurance industries and committed himself to making personal financial management accessible to us all.

Today, Eric is an internationally acclaimed and best-selling personal finance book author, syndicated columnist, and speaker. He has worked with and taught people from all financial situations, so he knows the financial concerns and questions of real folks just like you. Despite being handicapped by an M.B.A. from the Stanford Graduate School of Business and a B.S. in Economics and Biology from Yale University, Eric remains a master at "keeping it simple."

An accomplished personal finance writer, his "Investor's Guide" syndicated column, distributed by King Features, is read by millions nationally, and he was an award-winning columnist for the *San Francisco Examiner.* He is the author of five national best-selling financial books in the ...*For Dummies* series on personal finance, investing, mutual funds, home buying (co-author), and taxes (co-author).

Eric's work has been featured and quoted in hundreds of local and national publications including *Newsweek, The Wall Street Journal, Los Angeles Times, Chicago Tribune, Forbes, Kiplinger's Personal Finance Magazine, Parenting, Money, Family Money, Bottom Line/Personal,* and on NBC'S *Today Show,* ABC, CNBC, *PBS Nightly Business Report,* CNN, and FOX-TV, and on CBS national radio, NPR *Sound Money,* Bloomberg Business Radio, and Business Radio Network.

ABOUT IDG BOOKS WORLDWIDE

Welcome to the world of IDG Books Worldwide.

IDG Books Worldwide, Inc., is a subsidiary of International Data Group, the world's largest publisher of computer-related information and the leading global provider of information services on information technology. IDG was founded more than 30 years ago by Patrick J. McGovern and now employs more than 9,000 people worldwide. IDG publishes more than 290 computer publications in over 75 countries. More than 90 million people read one or more IDG publications each month.

Launched in 1990, IDG Books Worldwide is today the #1 publisher of best-selling computer books in the United States. We are proud to have received eight awards from the Computer Press Association in recognition of editorial excellence and three from Computer Currents' First Annual Readers' Choice Awards. Our best-selling ...*For Dummies*® series has more than 50 million copies in print with translations in 31 languages. IDG Books Worldwide, through a joint venture with IDG's Hi-Tech Beijing, became the first U.S. publisher to publish a computer book in the People's Republic of China. In record time, IDG Books Worldwide has become the first choice for millions of readers around the world who want to learn how to better manage their businesses.

Our mission is simple: Every one of our books is designed to bring extra value and skill-building instructions to the reader. Our books are written by experts who understand and care about our readers. The knowledge base of our editorial staff comes from years of experience in publishing, education, and journalism — experience we use to produce books to carry us into the new millennium. In short, we care about books, so we attract the best people. We devote special attention to details such as audience, interior design, use of icons, and illustrations. And because we use an efficient process of authoring, editing, and desktop publishing our books electronically, we can spend more time ensuring superior content and less time on the technicalities of making books.

You can count on our commitment to deliver high-quality books at competitive prices on topics you want to read about. At IDG Books Worldwide, we continue in the IDG tradition of delivering quality for more than 30 years. You'll find no better book on a subject than one from IDG Books Worldwide.

John Kilcullen
Chairman and CEO
IDG Books Worldwide, Inc.

Steven Berkowitz
President and Publisher
IDG Books Worldwide, Inc.

*Eighth Annual
Computer Press
Awards ≥ 1992*

*Ninth Annual
Computer Press
Awards ≥ 1993*

*Tenth Annual
Computer Press
Awards ≥ 1994*

*Eleventh Annual
Computer Press
Awards ≥ 1995*

1/24/99

Dedication

This book is hereby and irrevocably dedicated to my family and friends, as well as to my counseling clients and customers, who ultimately have taught me everything that I know about how to explain financial terms and strategies so that all of us may benefit.

Author's Acknowledgments

Being an entrepreneur involves endless challenges, and without the support and input of my good friends and mentors Peter Mazonson, Jim Collins, and my best friend and wife, Judy, I couldn't have accomplished what I have.

I hold many people accountable for my perverse and maniacal interest in figuring out the financial services industry and money matters, but most of the blame falls on my loving parents, Charles and Paulina, who taught me most of what I know that's been of use in the real world.

I'd also like to thank Michael Bloom, Chris Dominguez, Maggie McCall, David Ish, Paul Kozak, Chris Treadway, Sally St. Lawrence, K.T. Rabin, Will Hearst III, Ray Brown, Susan Wolf, Rich Caramella, Lisa Baker, Renn Vera, Maureen Taylor, Jerry Jacob, Robert Crum, Duc Nguyen, and Maria Carmicino, and all the good folks at King Features for believing in and supporting my writing and teaching.

Many thanks to all the people who provided insightful comments on this book, especially financial planner Robert Urban with Bingham Osborn & Scarborough in the San Francisco Bay area and Barton Francis, Mike van den Akker, Gretchen Morgenson, Craig Litman, Gerri Detweiler, Mark White, Alan Bush, Nancy Coolidge, and Chris Jensen.

And thanks to all the wonderful people at IDG Books on the front line and behind the scenes, especially John Kilcullen, who had the vision, foresight, and courage to do this book, Kathy Welton, and Mark Butler. I'd especially like to thank my creative and talented project editor, Wendy Hatch. I'd also like to thank Justin Wells and Judy Lee for other thoughtful suggestions and willingness to help me meet difficult deadlines.

Publisher's Acknowledgments

We're proud of this book; please register your comments through our IDG Books Worldwide Online Registration Form located at http://my2cents.dummies.com.

Some of the people who helped bring this book to market include the following:

Acquisitions and Editorial

Project Editor: Wendy Hatch

Acquisitions Editor: Mark Butler

Technical Editor: William R. Urban

Editorial Coordinator: Michelle Hacker

Editorial Assistant: Beth Parlon

Production

Project Coordinator: E. Shawn Aylsworth

Layout and Graphics: Joseph Bucki, Jill Piscitelli, Janet Seib, Brian Torwelle, Erin Zeltner

Proofreaders: Laura Albert, Corey Bowen, John Greenough, Marianne Santy, Joel Showalter

Indexer: Ty Koontz

General and Administrative

IDG Books Worldwide, Inc.: John Kilcullen, CEO; Steven Berkowitz, President and Publisher

IDG Books Technology Publishing Group: Richard Swadley, Senior Vice President and Publisher; Walter Bruce III, Vice President and Associate Publisher; Joseph Wikert, Associate Publisher; Mary Bednarek, Branded Product Development Director; Mary Corder, Editorial Director; Barry Pruett, Publishing Manager; Michelle Baxter, Publishing Manager

IDG Books Consumer Publishing Group: Roland Elgey, Senior Vice President and Publisher; Kathleen A. Welton, Vice President and Publisher; Kevin Thornton, Acquisitions Manager; Kristin A. Cocks, Editorial Director

IDG Books Internet Publishing Group: Brenda McLaughlin, Senior Vice President and Publisher; Diane Graves Steele, Vice President and Associate Publisher; Sofia Marchant, Online Marketing Manager

IDG Books Production for Dummies Press: Debbie Stailey, Associate Director of Production; Cindy L. Phipps, Manager of Project Coordination, Production Proofreading, and Indexing; Tony Augsburger, Manager of Prepress, Reprints, and Systems; Laura Carpenter, Production Control Manager; Shelley Lea, Supervisor of Graphics and Design; Debbie J. Gates, Production Systems Specialist; Robert Springer, Supervisor of Proofreading; Kathie Schutte, Production Supervisor

Dummies Packaging and Book Design: Patty Page, Manager, Promotions Marketing

◆

The publisher would like to give special thanks to Patrick J. McGovern, without whom this book would not have been possible.

◆

Contents at a Glance

Cartoons at a Glance

By Rich Tennant

Fax: 978-546-7747
E-mail: richtennant@the5thwave.com
World Wide Web: www.the5thwave.com

Table of Contents

Part III: Investing Crash Course 145

Chapter 8: Important Investment Concepts 147

Chapter 9: Investment Vehicles 175

Introduction

Welcome to *Personal Finance For Dummies,* 3rd Edition. For a number of years, I dreamed of writing a personal finance book that would be different. The book would describe in a down-to-earth and friendly way the important concepts that you need to know in order to manage your money. It would give specific answers to financial questions where it could, and where it couldn't give the answers, it would suggest the best resources to turn to.

As fate would have it, my path crossed that of IDG Books. The *...For Dummies* approach is how I had conceived my personal finance book; I just didn't know it at the time!

More than one million copies of the first and second editions of this book are in print, and as you can see from the quotes in the front of this edition, readers and reviewers alike were pleased with the previous editions. However, I and the good folks at IDG don't rest on our laurels. So what you hold in your hands reflects more hard work to bring you the freshest material to address your personal financial quandaries.

Why This Book?

Many Americans are financially illiterate. If you are, it's probably not your fault. Personal Finance 101 is not offered in our schools — not in high school, not even in the best colleges and graduate schools. It should be. (Of course, if it were, I wouldn't be able to write fun and useful books such as this — or maybe they would use this book in the course!)

There are some common financial problems and mistakes — procrastinating and lack of planning, wasteful spending, falling prey to financial salespeople and pitches, failing to do sufficient research before making important financial decisions, and so on — and different people keep making those same mistakes over and over. This book, like a good friend, can whop you upside the head to keep you from falling into the same traps.

Unfair as it seems, many of these traps await you when you are actually seeking help. The world is filled with biased and bad financial advice. As a practicing financial counselor, I see and hear about the consequences of this poor advice. Of course, every profession has bad apples, but too many people calling themselves "financial planners" have conflicts of interest and inadequate competence.

All too often, financial advice ignores the big picture and focuses narrowly on investing. Because money is not an end in itself but part of your whole life, this book helps connect your financial goals and problems to the rest of your life. You need a broad understanding of personal finance to include all areas of your financial life: spending, taxes, saving, insurance, and planning for major goals like education, buying a home, and retirement.

Even if you understand the financial basics, thinking about your finances in a holistic way can be difficult. Sometimes you're too close to the situation to be objective. Like the organization of your desk or files (or disorganization, as the case may be), your finances may reflect the history of your life more than they reflect a comprehensive plan for your future.

You are likely a busy person and don't have enough hours in your day to get things done. Thus, you want to know how to diagnose your financial situation quickly (and painlessly) and determine what you should do next. Unfortunately, after figuring out which financial strategies make sense for you, choosing specific financial products in the marketplace can be a nightmare. You have literally thousands of investment, insurance, and loan options to choose from. Talk about information overload!

To complicate matters, you probably hear about most products through advertising that can be misleading, if not downright false. Of course, some ethical and useful firms advertise, but so do those that are more interested in converting your hard-earned income and savings into their profits. And they may not be here tomorrow when you need them.

You want to know the best places to go for your circumstances, so I filled this book with specific, tried-and-proven product recommendations. I also suggest how and where to turn next if you need more information and help.

Uses for This Book

You can use this book in one of three ways:

- ✔ If you want to find out about a specific topic, such as getting out of high-interest consumer debt, planning for major goals, or investing, you can flip to that section and get your answers quickly.

- ✔ If you want a crash course in personal finance, read this book cover-to-cover. Reading the whole book helps to solidify major financial concepts and gets you thinking about your finances in a more comprehensive way.

- ✔ If you're tired of picking up scattered piles of bills, receipts, and junk mail every time the kids chase the cat around the den, you can use this book as a paperweight!

Seriously, though, this book is basic enough for a novice to get his or her arms around thorny financial issues. But advanced readers will be challenged as well to think about their finances in a new way and identify areas for improvement. Check out the table of contents for a chapter-by-chapter rundown of what's in this book. You can also look up a specific topic in the index. Or you can turn the page and start at the beginning: Chapter 1.

The Big Picture

This book is organized into five parts, each covering a major area of your personal finances. The chapters within each part cover specific topics in detail. You can read each chapter and part without having to read what comes before, which is useful if you have better things to do with your free time. This book also makes for great reading anywhere you might be sitting for a length of time (perhaps the bathroom). You may be referred occasionally to somewhere else in the book for more details on a particular subject. Here is a summary of what you find in each part.

Part I: Where Do You Go from Here?

This part explains how to diagnose your current financial health and explores common reasons for any missing links in your personal finance knowledge. We all have dreams and goals, so in this part, I also encourage you to think about what your financial aspirations are and to figure out how much you should be saving if you want to retire someday or accomplish other important goals.

Part II: Saving More, Spending Less

Most people don't have gobs of extra cash. Therefore, this part shows you how to figure out where all your dollars are going and how to reduce your spending. Chapter 5 is devoted to helping you get out from under the burden of high-interest consumer debt, such as credit card debt. I also provide specifics for reducing your tax burden.

Part III: Investing Crash Course

Earning and saving money is hard work, so you should be careful when it comes to investing what you have worked so hard to save (or waited so long to inherit!). Learning investment basics helps you pick investments wisely and understand investment risks, returns, and a whole lot more. I explain all the major and best investment options. I recommend specific strategies and investments for both inside and outside of tax-sheltered retirement accounts. I also discuss buying, selling, and investing in real estate as well as other wealth-building investments.

Part IV: Protecting What You've Got

Insurance is an important part of financial life. Unfortunately, for most people, it is a thoroughly overwhelming and dreadfully boring topic. But perhaps I can pique your interest in this esoteric topic by telling you that you're probably paying more than you should for insurance and you probably don't have the right coverages for your situation. This part tells you all you ever wanted to know (okay, fine — all you *never* wanted to know but probably should know anyway) about how to buy the right insurance at the best price.

Part V: Where to Go for More Help

As you build your financial knowledge, more questions and issues may arise. In this part, I discuss where to go and what to avoid, should you be in the market for more financial information and advice. In this part, I discuss hiring a financial planner as well as investigating resources in print, on the air, and online.

Part VI: The Part of Tens

These chapters of ten somethings can help you manage major life changes or help you keep money in its proper perspective with the rest of your life.

Glossary

The world of money is filled with jargon, so you'll be happy to know that this book includes a comprehensive glossary of financial terms that you'll often hear tossed around but seldom hear properly explained.

Icons Used in This Book

 This nerdy guy (who is rumored to bear some resemblance to a senior official at IDG Books!) appears beside discussions that aren't critical if you just want to learn basic concepts and get answers to your financial questions. You can safely ignore these sections, but reading them will deepen and enhance your personal financial knowledge. This stuff can also come in handy if you're ever on a game show or find yourself stuck on an elevator with a financial geek.

 This target flags strategy recommendations for making the most of your money (for example, paying off your credit card debt with your lottery winnings).

 This icon highlights the best financial products in investment, insurance, and so on to implement strategy recommendations (for example, calling Ethical Bank & Trust for low-interest rate loans).

 This icon is a friendly reminder of information discussed elsewhere in the book or stuff you'll definitely want to remember.

 This icon marks things to avoid and common mistakes people make in managing their finances.

 This icon alerts you to scams and scoundrels that prey on the unsuspecting.

 This icon highlights when you should consider doing some additional research. Don't worry — I explain what to look for and look out for.

Part I
Where Do You Go from Here?

The 5th Wave — By Rich Tennant

"You bought what? You know we're on a budget. Now take Hughes Electric back to General Motors and see if you can get your money back."

In this part . . .

1 discuss the concepts that underlie sensible personal financial management. You also find out why you didn't know all these concepts before now (and whom to blame). Here, you'll undergo a (gentle) financial physical exam to diagnose your current economic health. I also cover how to plan for and accomplish your financial goals.

Chapter 1

Figuring Your Financial Fitness

· ·

· ·

"**I**'ve made just about every financial mistake there is to make," lamented a student in my personal finance course. The student, who had an anxious yet depressed look, seemed to be asking me for forgiveness.

This is when it first dawned on me that as grown-up children — referred to as adults — we're not really allowed to make mistakes. If you mangle your car in an accident because you weren't paying attention or get fired from a job because of poor attendance and performance, you feel awful.

With financial matters, however, the fact that you've made a mistake may not be as obvious as twisted metal or a pink slip and no more paycheck. Some mistakes take months, years, even decades to manifest themselves. Even then, some people don't realize the foolishness of their ways.

Few people like to be made to feel stupid or told that they're doing something wrong. And what you do with your money is a quite personal and confidential matter. I've endeavored not to be paternalistic in this book but to provide guidance and advice that is in your best interest. You don't have to take it all — pick what works best for you and understand the pros and cons of your options. But from this day forward, please don't make the easily avoidable mistakes nor overlook the sound strategies that I discuss throughout this book.

If you're young, congratulations for being so forward-thinking as to realize the immense value of investing now in your personal financial education. You'll reap the rewards for many decades to come. But even if you're not so young, you surely have many years to make the most of what money you currently have and will earn (and may even inherit!) in the future.

Throughout our journey together, I hope to challenge and even change the way you think about money, about making important personal financial decisions — sometimes even about the meaning of life. No, I'm not a philosopher, but I do know that money, for better but more often for worse, is connected to many other parts of our lives.

Common Financial Problems

How financially healthy are you? You may already know the bad news. Or perhaps things aren't quite as bad as they seem.

When was the last time you sat down surrounded by all of your personal and financial documents and took stock of your overall financial situation, including reviewing your spending, savings, future goals, and insurance? If you're like most people, you've either never done this exercise or did so a long time ago.

Financial problems, like many medical problems, are best detected early (clean living doesn't hurt, either). Here are some common personal financial problems I've seen in my work as a financial counselor:

- **Not planning.** Human beings were born to procrastinate. That's why there are deadlines — and deadline extensions. With your finances, unfortunately, you have no deadlines, and you may think you have unlimited extensions! You can allow your credit card debt to accumulate or leave your savings sitting in lousy investments for years. You can pay higher taxes, leave gaps in your retirement and insurance coverage, and overpay for financial products. Of course, planning your finances isn't as much fun as planning a vacation, but doing the former will help you take more of the latter.

- **Overspending.** The average American saves less than 5 percent of his after-tax income (in contrast to those in other industrialized countries, where the savings rate is two to three times that in America). Simple arithmetic helps you determine that savings is the difference between what you earn and what you spend (assuming you're not spending more than you're earning!). To increase your savings, you either have to work more (yuck!), know a wealthy family who wants to leave its fortune to you, or spend less. For most of us, the thrifty approach is the key to building savings and wealth.

✔ **Buying with consumer credit.** Even with the benefit of today's lower interest rates, carrying a balance month-to-month on your credit card or buying a car on credit means that even more of your future earnings are earmarked for debt repayment. Buying on credit encourages you to spend more than you can really afford.

✔ **Delaying saving for retirement.** Most people say they want to retire by their mid-60s or sooner. But in order to accomplish this financially, most people need to save a reasonable chunk (around 10 percent) of their incomes starting sooner rather than later. The longer you wait to start saving for retirement, the harder it will be to reach your goal. And you'll pay much more in taxes to boot if you don't take advantage of the tax benefits of investing through particular retirement accounts.

✔ **Falling prey to financial sales pitches.** Great deals that can't wait for a little reflection or a second opinion are often disasters waiting to happen. A sucker may be born every minute, but a slick salesperson is born every second! Steer clear of those who pressure you to make decisions, promise high investment returns, and lack the proper training and experience to help you.

✔ **Not doing your homework.** To get the best deal, you need to shop around, read reviews, and get advice from disinterested, objective third parties. You need to check references and track records so you don't hire incompetent, self-serving, or fraudulent financial advisors. But with all the different financial products available, making informed financial decisions has become an overwhelming task. I've done a lot of the homework for you with the recommendations in this book. I also explain what additional research you need to do and how to go about doing it.

✔ **Making decisions based on emotion.** You are most vulnerable to making the wrong moves financially after a major life change (a job loss or divorce, for example) or when you feel under pressure. Maybe your investments have plunged in value. Or perhaps a recent divorce has you fearing that you won't be able to afford to retire when you had planned, so you pour thousands of dollars into some newfangled financial product. Take your time and keep your emotions out of the picture. In Chapter 21, I discuss how to approach major life changes with an eye to determining what changes you may need to make to your financial picture.

✔ **Not separating the wheat from the chaff.** In any field in which you're not an expert, you run the danger of following the advice of someone who you think is an expert but really isn't. This book teaches you to separate the financial fluff from the financial facts. If you look in the mirror, you'll see the person who is best able to manage your personal finances. Educate and trust yourself!

- ✔ **Exposing yourself to catastrophic risk.** You're vulnerable if you or your family don't have insurance to pay for financially devastating losses. People without a savings reserve and support network can end up homeless. Many people lack sufficient insurance coverage to replace their income. Don't wait for a tragedy to strike to learn whether you have the right insurance coverages.

- ✔ **Focusing too much on money.** Too much emphasis on making and saving money can warp your perspective on what's important in life. Money is not the first or even second priority in happy people's lives. Your health, relationships with family and friends, career satisfaction, and fulfilling interests should be more important.

Most problems can be fixed over time and with changes in your behavior. That's what the rest of the book is all about.

The rest of this chapter puts you through a *financial physical* to help you detect problems with your current financial health. But don't get depressed and dwell on your "problems." View them for what they are — opportunities to improve your financial situation. In fact, the more areas for improvement that you can identify, the greater the potential you have to build real wealth and accomplish your financial and personal goals.

Bad Debt versus Good Debt

Why do you borrow money? Usually, it's because you don't have enough money to buy something you want or need — like a college education. If you want to buy a four-year college education, you could easily spend $50,000 to $100,000, perhaps even more. Not too many people have that kind of spare cash. So borrowing money to finance part of that cost enables you to buy the education.

How about a new car? A trip to your friendly local car dealer shows you that a new set of wheels will set you back around $15,000 or more. Although more people have the money to pay for that than, say, the college education, what if you don't? Should you finance the car the way you'd finance the education?

The auto dealers and bankers eager to make you an auto loan say you deserve to and can afford to drive a nice, new car, so borrow away.

I say, *NO! NO! NO!*

Why do I disagree with the auto dealers and lenders? For starters, I'm not trying to sell you a car or loan from which I derive a profit! More importantly, there's a *big* difference between borrowing for something that represents a long-term investment and borrowing for consumption.

If you spend, say, $1,500 on a vacation, the money is gone. Poof! You may have fond memories and even some Kodak moments, but you'll have no financial value to show for it. "But," you say, "vacations replenish my soul and make me more productive when I return. In fact, the vacation more than pays for itself!"

Great. I'm not saying don't take a vacation. By all means, take one, two, three, or as many as you can afford yearly. But that's the point — *what you can afford.* In order to take the vacation, if you had to borrow money in the form of an outstanding balance on your credit card for many months, then you *could not afford* the vacation you took.

I refer to debt incurred for consumption as *bad debt.* Don't get me wrong — you're not a bad person for having the debt, but the debt is harmful to your long-term financial health.

You'll be able to take many more vacations during your lifetime if you save the cash in advance to afford them. If you get into the habit of borrowing and paying all that interest for vacations, cars, clothing, and other consumer items, you'll spend more of your future income paying back the debt and interest. So you'll have *less* money available for vacations and all your other goals.

One of the reasons you'll have less money using bad debt is because of the relatively high interest rates banks and other lenders charge for such debt. Money borrowed through credit cards, auto loans, and other types of consumer loans not only carries a relatively high interest rate but is also not tax-deductible.

 I'm not saying never borrow money and that all debt is bad. Good debt, such as that used to buy real estate and small businesses, is generally available at lower interest rates than bad debt and is usually tax-deductible. If properly and smartly managed, these investments should also increase in value. Borrowing to pay for educational expenses can also make sense. Education is generally a good long-term investment. It should increase your earning potential.

How Much Bad Debt Is Too Much?

A useful way to size up your debt load is to calculate how much debt you have relative to your annual income. Ignore, for now, good debt — the loans you may owe on real estate, a business, an education, and so on. I'm focusing on bad debt, the higher-interest stuff used to buy items that depreciate in value.

For example, suppose that you earn $30,000 per year. Between your credit cards and an auto loan, you have $15,000 of debt. In this case, your bad debt represents 50 percent of your annual income.

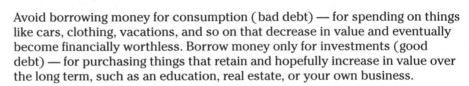

$$\frac{\text{bad debt}}{\text{annual income}} = \text{debt danger ratio}$$

The financially healthy amount of bad debt is zero. (Not everyone agrees with me. One major U.S. credit card company says in its "educational" materials, which it gives to schools to supposedly teach students about sound financial management, that it's just fine to carry consumer debt amounting to 10 to 20 percent of your annual income.)

When your *debt danger ratio* starts to push beyond 25 percent, that can spell real trouble. High-interest consumer debt on credit cards and auto loans is like cancer when it gets to those levels. As with cancer, the growth of the debt can snowball and get out of control unless something significant intervenes. If you have this much debt, see Chapter 5 to find out how to get out of debt.

How much good debt is acceptable? The answer varies. The key question is, are you able to save sufficiently to accomplish your goals? Later in this chapter, I help you figure how much you are actually saving, and in Chapter 3, I help you determine what you should be saving to accomplish your goals. Take a look at Chapter 14 to find out how much mortgage debt is appropriate to take on when buying a home.

Avoid borrowing money for consumption (bad debt) — for spending on things like cars, clothing, vacations, and so on that decrease in value and eventually become financially worthless. Borrow money only for investments (good debt) — for purchasing things that retain and hopefully increase in value over the long term, such as an education, real estate, or your own business.

Playing the credit card float

Given what I have to say about the vagaries of consumer debt, you might think that I am against using credit cards. Actually, I have credit cards and I use them — but I pay my balance in full each month. Besides the convenience credit cards offer me in not having to carry around extra cash and checks, I get another benefit. I have free use of the bank's money extended to me through my credit card charges. (Some cards offer other benefits such as frequent flyer miles. Also, purchases made on credit cards may be contested if the seller of the product or service doesn't stand behind what it sells.)

When you charge on a credit card that does not have an outstanding balance carried over from the prior month, you typically have several weeks, known as the *grace period,* from the date of the charge to when you must pay your bill. Financial types call this *playing the float.* Had you paid for this purchase by cash or check, you would have had to shell out the money sooner.

If you have difficulty saving money and plastic tends to burn holes through your budget, forget the float game. You'd be better off not using your credit cards. The same applies for those who pay their bills in full but who spend more because it's so easy to do so with a piece of plastic.

Your Financial Net Worth

Your financial net worth is an important barometer of your financial health. It indicates your capacity to accomplish major financial goals such as buying a home, retiring, and withstanding unexpected expenses or loss of income.

Before you crunch any numbers here and before you experience the thrill of bigness or the agony of nothingness or negativity, let's get one thing perfectly clear. Sit down. Take a deep breath. And repeat after me:

"My financial net worth has absolutely, positively, *no* relationship to my worth as a human being." This is not a test. You don't have to compare your number with your neighbor's. It's not the scorecard of life. So do we have an understanding? Good! I hate to see people get depressed about unimportant things that they have the power and ability to change.

Your *net worth* is your financial assets minus your financial liabilities.

```
Financial Assets - Financial Liabilities = Net Worth
```

Financial assets

A *financial asset* is worth real money or is something that you plan to convert to hard dollars that you can use to buy things now or in the future.

Financial assets generally include money in bank accounts, stocks, bonds, and mutual fund accounts (see Part III, which deals with investments). Also included is money that you have in retirement accounts, including those with your employer. You should also include the value of any businesses or real estate that you own.

I generally recommend that you exclude your personal residence. Include your home *only* if you expect to someday sell it or otherwise live off the money you now have tied up in it (perhaps by taking out a reverse mortgage, which I discuss in Chapter 14). If you plan on someday tapping into the equity (the difference between the market value and any debt owed on the property) in your home, add that portion of the equity that you expect to use to your list of assets.

Assets also include your future expected Social Security benefits and pension payments if your employer has such a plan. These are usually quoted in dollars per month rather than in a lump sum value. I show you in a moment how to account for these monthly benefits when tallying your financial assets.

Personal property such as your car, clothing, stereo, wine glasses, and straight teeth do *not* count as financial assets. I know adding these things to your assets makes your assets *look* larger (and some financial software packages and publications encourage you to list these items as assets), but you can't live off them unless you hock them at a pawn shop or otherwise sell them to meet your financial goals.

Financial liabilities

You must subtract your *financial liabilities* from your assets to arrive at your financial net worth.

Liabilities include loans and debts outstanding, like credit card and auto loan debts. Include money you've borrowed from family and friends (unless you're not gonna pay it back — I won't tell). Include mortgage debt on your home as a liability *only* if you include the value of your home in your asset list. Be sure to include debt owed on other real estate, no matter what.

Your net worth calculation

Ready? Table 1-1 provides a place for you to figure your financial assets. Go ahead and write in the spaces provided, unless you plan to lend this book to someone and you don't want to put your money situation on display.

Important note: See Table 3-1 in Chapter 3 to estimate your Social Security benefits.

Table 1-1	Your Financial Assets
Account	*Value*
Savings and investment accounts (including retirement accounts):	
Example: Bank savings account	$ 5,000
_____	$_____
_____	$_____
_____	$_____
_____	$_____
_____	$_____
_____	$_____

Account	Value
Total =	$_____

Benefits earned that pay a monthly retirement income:

Employer's pensions	$_____ / month
Social Security	$_____ / month
	x 240*
Total =	$_____
Total Financial Assets =	$_____

In Table 1-1, to convert benefits that will be paid to you monthly into a total dollar amount, I assume that you will live 20 years in retirement. (Ah, think of two decades of lollygagging around — vacationing, harassing the kids, spoiling the grandkids, starting another career, or maybe just living off the fat of the land.) As a shortcut, multiply the benefits that you'll collect monthly in retirement by 240 (12 months in a year times 20 years). Inflation may reduce the value of your employer's pension if it doesn't contain a cost-of-living increase each year in the same way that Social Security does. Don't sweat this now — you'll take care of it in the section on planning for retirement (see Chapter 3).

Now comes the potentially depressing part — your debts and loans in Table 1-2:

Table 1-2	Your Financial Liabilities
Loan	**Balance**
Example: Gouge 'Em Bank Credit Card	$ 4,000
_____	$_____
_____	$_____
_____	$_____
_____	$_____
_____	$_____
_____	$_____
_____	$_____
Total Financial Liabilities =	$_____

Now, you can subtract your liabilities from your assets to figure your net worth in Table 1-3:

Table 1-3	Your Net Worth
Find	Write It Here
Total Financial Assets (from Table 1-1)	$_____
Total Financial Liabilities (from Table 1-2)	−$_____
Net Worth =	$_____

Interpreting your net worth results

Your net worth is important and useful only to you and your unique situation and goals. What is a lot of money to a person with a simple lifestyle may seem like a pittance to another with desires for an opulent lifestyle and high expectations.

In Chapter 3, you need to crunch some more numbers to determine your financial status more precisely for such goals as retirement planning. I also discuss saving toward other important goals in that chapter. In the meantime, if your net worth (excluding expected monthly retirement benefits such as those from Social Security and pensions) is less than half your annual income or even negative, take notice. You have lots of company — in fact, you're in here with the majority of Americans. If you're in your 20s and just starting to work, this is less concerning. It's most important to get rid of your debts — and the highest-interest ones first. Then you need to build a safety reserve equal to three to six months of living expenses. You should definitely learn more about getting out of debt, reducing your spending, and developing tax-wise ways to save and invest your future earnings.

Savings Analysis

In the past year, how much money have you actually saved? By savings, I mean the amount of new money you have added to your nest egg, stash, or whatever you like to call it.

Most people don't know or have only a vague idea of the rate at which they are saving money. The answer may sober, terrify, or pleasantly surprise you. In order to calculate your savings over the past year, you need to calculate your net worth as of today *and* as of one year ago.

The amount you actually saved over the past year is equal to the change in your net worth over the past year — in other words, your net worth today minus your net worth from one year ago. I know it may be a pain to find statements showing what your savings and investments were worth a year ago, but bear with me; it's a useful exercise.

If you own your home, ignore this in the calculations. (You can consider as new savings extra payments you make to pay off your mortgage principal faster.) And don't include personal property such as your car, computer, clothing, and so on with your assets.

Okay, now you have your two figures. Go ahead and plug them into Step 1 of Table 1-4. You may be anticipating the exercise and are already subtracting your net worth of a year ago from what it is today in order to determine your rate of savings. Your instincts are correct, but the exercise is not quite that simple. You need to do a few more calculations in Step 2 of Table 1-4. Why? Well, counting the appreciation of investments you owned over the past year as savings wouldn't be fair. Suppose that you bought 100 shares of a stock a year ago at $17 per share, and now the value is at $34 per share. Your investment increased in value during the past year by $1,700. Although you would be the envy of your friends at the next party if you casually mentioned your investments, the $1,700 of increased value of your investment is not really savings. Instead, it represents appreciation on your investments, so you must remove this appreciation from the calculations.

Note: Just so you know, I'm not unfairly penalizing you for your shrewd investments — you also get to add back the decline in value of your less-successful investments.

Table 1-4	Your Savings Rate over the Past Year		
Step 1: Figuring your savings.			
Today		*One Year Ago*	
Savings & investments	$_____	Savings & investments	$_____
– Loans & debts	$_____	– Loans & debts	$_____
= Net worth today	$_____	= Net worth 1 year ago	$_____
Step 2: Correcting for changes in value of investments you owned during the year.			
Net worth today		$_____	
– Net worth 1 year ago		$_____	
– Appreciation of investments (over past year)		$_____	
+ Depreciation of investments (over past year)		$_____	
= Savings rate		$_____	

If all this gives you a headache or you get stuck or if you just hate crunching numbers, try the intuitive, seat-of-the-pants approach: Do you save a regular portion of your monthly income? You may save it in a separate savings account or retirement account.

How much do you save in a typical month? Get out your statements for accounts that you contribute to or save money in monthly. It doesn't matter if it's a retirement account that you can't access. Money is money. Savings is savings.

Note: If you're able to save, say, $200 per month for a few months but then spend it all on auto repairs, you're not saving. If you contributed $2,000 to an *individual retirement account* (IRA), for example, but depleted money that you had from long ago (in other words, it wasn't saved during the past year), you should not count the $2,000 as new savings.

As you'll see later, most people should be saving at least 5 to 10 percent of their annual income for longer-term financial goals such as retirement. If you're not, be sure to read Chapter 6 to find out how to reduce your spending so that you can increase your savings.

How Is Your Investing Knowledge?

Congratulations! You've completed the hardest part of your financial physical. The physical is a whole lot easier from here on in!

Regardless of how much or how little money you have invested in bank, mutual fund, or other types of accounts, you, of course, want your money invested in the wisest way possible.

Knowing the rights and wrongs of investing is vital to your long-term financial well-being. Few people have so much extra money that they can afford major or frequent investing mistakes. Answering "Yes" or "No" to the following questions can help you size up how much time you need to spend with my "Investing Crash Course" in Part III, which focuses on investing.

Note: The more *No* answers you reluctantly scribble, the more you need to learn about investing, and the faster you should turn to Part III.

_____ Do you understand the investments you currently hold?

_____ Is the money that you would need to tap in the event of a short-term emergency in an investment where the principal does not fluctuate in value?

_____ Do you know what marginal income-tax bracket (combined federal and state) you're in, and do you factor that into which investments you choose?

_____ For money outside of retirement accounts, do you understand how those investments produce income and gains and whether these types of investments make the most sense from the standpoint of taxes?

_____ Do you have your money in different, diversified investments that aren't dependent on one or a few securities or one type of investment (that is, bonds, stocks, U.S. investments, and so on)?

_____ Is the money that you will need for a major expenditure in the next few years invested conservatively rather than in riskier investments such as stocks, real estate, or pork bellies?

_____ Is the money that you have earmarked for longer-term purposes (more than five years) invested to produce returns well ahead of inflation?

_____ Is the bulk of your long-term money invested inside retirement accounts, and have you exhausted possibilities for directing more money into these tax-sheltered accounts?

_____ Is your longer-term money, particularly what is inside of retirement accounts, invested in quality, growth-oriented investments rather than preservation-of-principal-oriented investments?

_____ If you currently invest in or plan to invest in individual stocks, do you understand how to evaluate a stock, including reviewing the company's balance sheet, income statement, business strategy, competitive position, price-earnings ratio versus its peer group, and so on?

_____ If you work with a financial advisor, is that person compensated in a way that minimizes potential conflicts of interest in the strategies and investments he or she recommends?

Making and saving money is not a guarantee of financial success but rather a prerequisite. If you don't know how to choose quality investments that meet your needs, you will more than likely throw money away, which leads to the same end result as never having earned and saved it in the first place. Worse still, you won't have derived any enjoyment from spending the lost money on things that you perhaps needed or wanted. Turn to Part III to learn the best ways to invest; otherwise, you'll spin your wheels working and saving.

How Insurance Savvy Are You?

Now we're in the home stretch of your financial physical. In this section, you must deal with the prickly subject of protecting your assets and yourself with *insurance*. If you're like most people, reviewing your insurance policies and coverages is about as much fun as a root canal. Open wide!

_____ Do you understand the individual coverages and protection types and amounts of each insurance policy that you have?

_____ Does your *current* insurance protection make sense given your current financial situation (as opposed to your situation when you bought the policies)?

_____ If you couldn't make it financially without your income, do you have adequate long-term disability insurance coverage?

_____ If you have family members who are dependent on your continued income, do you have adequate life insurance coverage to replace that income should you die?

_____ Do you buy insurance through companies that sell directly to the public (bypassing agents) and through discount brokers and fee-for-service advisors?

_____ Do you carry enough liability insurance on your home, car (including umbrella/excess liability), and business to protect all your assets?

_____ Did you recently (in the last year or two) shop around for the best price on your insurance policies?

_____ Do you know whether your insurance companies have good track records regarding paying claims and keeping their customers satisfied?

That wasn't so bad, was it? If you answered "No" more than once or twice, don't feel dumb — more than nine out of ten people make major mistakes when buying insurance. Find your insurance salvation in Part IV. If you answered "Yes" to all the preceding questions, you can spare yourself from reading Part IV, but bear in mind that most people need help in this area as much as they do in other aspects of personal finance.

What is your relationship to money?

In this chapter, I help you analyze your current financial situation and knowledge. You crunch some numbers with me and take some quizzes to help determine your investment and insurance wisdom.

Over the years in my work as a financial counselor, I've learned that how a person relates to and feels about money has a great impact on how good he is at managing his money and making important financial decisions. For example, knowing that you have a net worth of negative $13,200 because of credit card debt is useful but probably not enough information for you to do something constructive about your problem. A logical next step for such a person would be for him to examine his current spending and take steps to reduce his debt load.

Although I cover practical solutions to common financial quandaries later in this book, I also discuss the more touchy-feely side of money. For example, some people who continually rack up consumer debt have a spending addiction. Other people who jump in and out of invest-ments and follow them like a hawk have psychological obstacles to getting on productive investment paths.

And then there are those somewhat philosophical and psychological issues relating to money and the meaning of life. Saving more money and increasing your net worth isn't always the best approach. In my work, I've come across numerous people who attach too much significance to personal wealth accumulation and neglect important human relationships in their pursuit of more money. Some retirees have a hard time loosening the purse springs and actually spending some of the money they worked so hard to save for their golden years.

Balancing your financial goals with other important life goals is key to your happiness. What's the point, for example, of staying in a well paying job and admired profession if you don't care for the work and you're mainly doing it for the financial rewards? Life is too short and precious to squander your days.

So, as you read through the various chapters and sections of this book, please consider your higher life goals and purposes. What are your non-financial priorities (family, friends, causes) and how can you best accomplish those with the financial resources you do have?

Chapter 2

Overcoming Obstacles to Personal Financial Success

● ●

In This Chapter

▶ Understanding financial illiteracy and its causes

▶ Believing what you read, see, and hear

▶ Identifying and overcoming what's holding you back

● ●

*W*e're barely acquainted, but I do know that you're not dumb. Real dummies don't read and educate themselves. And real dummies don't understand the value of investing in their education. Real dummies also can't deflate their egos enough to admit that they need help and guidance.

Here's what dumb is: Dumb is the man who walked into a convenience store, put a $20 bill on the counter, and asked for change. When the cashier opened the register, the man pulled a gun and demanded all the cash. The crook took the loot — $15 — and fled, leaving his $20 bill on the counter. Or how about the criminal who robbed a person who lacked cash? The victim offered the assailant a check, which the assailant later attempted to cash at the bank, where — surprise, surprise — he was arrested. These are both true stories!

So you are most definitely not dumb! But you may be financially illiterate.

Personal Financial Illiteracy

Sadly, most Americans don't know how to manage their personal finances because in most cases, they were never taught how to do so. Nearly all our high schools and colleges lack even one course to teach this vital, lifelong-needed skill.

For the handful of schools that do offer a course remotely related to a personal finance class, the class is typically an economics course and an elective at that. "Archaic theory is being taught and it doesn't do anything for the students as far as preparing them for the real world," says one high school principal that I know. Having taken more than my fair share of economics courses in college, I understand the principal's concerns.

Fortunate and lucky people learn the financial keys to success at home or from knowledgeable friends. Others never learn or learn the hard way: by making lots of costly mistakes. Lack of proficiency in personal financial management causes not only tremendous anxiety but also serious problems. Consider the following sobering statistics:

- ✔ More than one million personal bankruptcies are filed in the United States annually. That's about one in every one-hundred households. So in the next ten years, nearly one in every ten households in the United States — the most affluent country in the world — will file bankruptcy.

- ✔ Studies show that fewer than 20 percent of baby boomers are saving adequately for retirement, and one-quarter of adults between the ages of 35 and 54 have not even *begun* to save for retirement.

- ✔ One in two marriages ends in divorce. Studies show that financial disagreement is one of the leading causes of marital discord. In a survey conducted by *Worth* magazine and the market research firm of Roper/Starch, couples admitted fighting about money more than anything else and more than three times more often than they fight about their sex lives. And a staggering 57 percent of those surveyed agreed with the statement, "In every marriage, money eventually becomes the most important concern."

- ✔ Fewer than 10 percent of American adults understand a 401(k) well enough to explain it to someone else. Fewer than one in four can explain what a municipal bond is.

- ✔ In a Princeton Survey Research Associates investing basics test, approximately a third of those quizzed answered fewer than 50 percent of the questions correctly. These results are all the more stunning when you consider that all the questions only offered two or three multiple choice answers as options.

- ✔ Nearly 80 percent of consumers do not know how the grace period on a credit card works. An even greater percentage don't understand that interest starts accumulating *immediately* for new purchases on credit cards with outstanding debts.

- ✔ Fifty-three percent of people in an investing multiple choice quiz did not know that *total return* was the best overall measure of a mutual fund's performance.

The overall costs of personal financial illiteracy to our society are huge. The high rate of spending and low rate of saving in the United States lead to lower long-term economic growth and higher interest rates. Annually, billions of dollars are wasted through the purchase of inferior and inefficient financial products.

Teaching personal finance in schools

As part of her fifth-grade math class, Nancy Donovan teaches personal finance as a way to illustrate how math can be used in the real world. "Students choose a career, find jobs, and figure out what their taxes and take-home paychecks will be. They also have to rent apartments and figure out a monthly budget," says Donovan, adding, "Students like it and parents have commented to me how surprised they are with how much financial knowledge their kids can handle." Donovan also has her students invest $10,000 (play money) and track the performance of their investments.

To urge that our schools teach the basics of personal finance is just common sense. We should be teaching our children how to manage a household budget, about the importance of saving money for future goals, and about the consequences and dangers of overspending. Unfortunately, few schools offer classes like Nancy Donovan's. In most cases, the financial basics aren't taught at all.

Some people argue that it's the parents' job to teach their children the financial basics. However, this well-meant sentiment is what we rely on now, and for all too many, it isn't working. In some families, financial illiteracy is passed on from generation to generation.

We must recognize that education takes place in the home, on the streets, *and* in the schools. Therefore, schools must bear some responsibility for teaching this very important life skill. And with more students holding down after-school jobs, teaching money-management know-how through the schools makes even more sense.

Lobby your schools! Make sure that financial basics are taught in schools at all levels. If you think you're powerless to change the situation, you're mistaken. Many changes to our education system started at the grassroots level.

Talking money at home

I was fortunate that my parents taught and instilled in me the importance of personal financial management. Mom and Dad taught me a lot of things that have been invaluable throughout my life. Among the useful things my folks taught me were sound principles of earning, spending, and saving money. My parents had to know how to do these things because they were raising a family of three children on (usually) one modest income. They knew the importance of making the most of what you have and passing on that vital skill to your kids.

In many families, however, money is a taboo subject — parents don't level with their kids about the limitations, realities, and details of their budgets. Some parents I talk with believe that dealing with money is an adult issue that kids should be insulated from so that the kids can better enjoy being kids. In many families, kids may hear about money *only* when disagreements and financial crises bubble to the surface. Thus begins the harmful cycle of children having negative associations with money and financial management.

In other cases, some parents, with the best of intentions, do pass on their money-management habits. Unfortunately, some of those habits are *bad* habits. Now, I'm not saying that you shouldn't listen to your parents. But in personal finance, as in any other area, family advice can be problematic. Think about where your parents learned about money management and consider whether they had the time, energy, or inclination to research choices before making their decisions. For example, your parents may mistakenly think that banks are the best places to invest money (you can find where the better places are in Part III of this book).

In still other cases, the parents have the right approach, but the kids go to the other extreme out of rebellion. For example, if your parents spent money carefully and thoughtfully, you may tend to do the opposite, such as buying yourself gifts the moment any extra money comes your way.

Although you and I can't change what the educational system and your parents did or didn't teach you about personal finances, you have the ability to find out now what you need to know to manage your finances. And if you have children of your own, I'm sure you'll agree that kids really are amazing. Don't underestimate their potential or send them out into the world without the skills they need to be productive and happy adults. Buy them some good financial books when they head off to college or to their first jobs.

Illiteracy and conflicts in financial publishing and advising

Some people are smart enough to realize that they're probably not financial geniuses. So they set out to take control of their finances by reading or consulting a financial advisor. Because the pitfalls are so numerous and the challenges are so mighty in choosing an advisor, I devote Chapter 18 to the financial planning business and what you need to know to avoid being fooled.

Reading is good. Reading is fundamental. But reading to learn about managing your money can be dangerous if you're a novice. Surprisingly, written misinformation can come from popular and seemingly reliable information sources.

Won't gurus make me rich?

One formerly best-selling personal finance book (*Wealth Without Risk* by Charles Givens) advises you to "Buy disability insurance only if you are in poor health or accident prone." Putting aside the minor detail that *no* insurance company (that's interested in making a profit) would issue you a disability policy *after* you fall into poor health, how do you know when you'll be accident-prone? Because health problems and auto accidents cause many disabilities, you can't see disabilities coming unless your horoscope happens to warn you!

That same book also purports to describe how to send your kids to college "free." A few months before your child begins college, you're supposed to buy a four-bedroom property a few miles from campus. Then you're advised to rent out the house to students. The idea is that while your kid is completing a four-year degree, the value of your rental property will appreciate dramatically because of the shortage of off-campus housing in almost every college campus area.

You realize, I'm sure, that college students will give your property the same love and attention that people give to rental cars. And, on the financial side, a modestly priced property would need to roughly *double in value over a four-year period* for this college-financing scheme to work. This is about as common as triplets (yes, it happens, but rarely).

Furthermore, this risky strategy may cost more than junior's education. Some real estate markets *drop* in value over a four-year time period, and if that were to happen, your already substantial college costs would be added to, not paid off. Then you need to factor in the hassles and expenses of locating, buying, and selling the property. And another minor detail: How many parents paying tuition bills also have piles of extra cash lying around available for the down payment on a property?

Don't the media act as watchdogs?

You may be asking how Charles Givens became so popular despite the obvious flaws in his advice. He made the most of his talent for working the media and his great self-promotion through seminars. One of the problems of the mass media is that hucksters like Givens can get good coverage and publicity. Many members of the media are themselves financially illiterate. And they love a good story. So Givens got all sorts of free publicity, being quoted in the press and invited on a number of national programs such as *The Today Show, Oprah, Donahue,* and *Larry King Live.*

Thousands of people went to seminars conducted by Givens, partly because of the credibility Givens built through media appearances. As has now been well documented by some of those same media, many unsuspecting investors were sold commission-laden products, including risky limited partnerships, through his organization.

One example is the case of Helen Giszczak, a 69-year-old retired secretary. She invested nearly two-thirds of her modest life savings in limited partnerships, which she said were described to her as "probably the most conservative investments we know of." But some of her limited partnerships ended up in bankruptcy, and the others lost much of their value.

Helen Giszczak appeared on the *Donahue* show with John Allen, a former investment broker-turned-securities lawyer who helped her sue Givens's organization to get her money back. After a lengthy dialogue with Giszczak and Allen, Phil Donahue asked Helen how a smart person like her could get sucked in like that. She replied, "He was on your show and Oprah's. You gave him credibility. You gave him free advertising."

Just as at the circus, oddities sell with the media. Over recent years, I've done some work with different parts of the media and observed how and what the media follows and ignores. As anyone who followed the O.J. trial or the Jon Benet murder mystery knows, some members of the media love an unusual story. The financial media, when at its worst, is no different than the news media that fawned all over the O.J. trial and the Jon Benet story. The more bizarre and novel something is, the more attention it gets — never mind if it's good for the readers and viewers.

With financial "guru" Charles Givens, the appeal was that people believed they could get rich without taking risks. Recent years have seen a flood of "We Can Beat the Market" investing books written by a 17-year-old high school student, an investment club, and others. One such book was written by a couple of Generation Xers who, despite failing at publishing a print newsletter, soared to fame by claiming that, using the online world to research stocks, anybody can easily and with low risk make 25 to 35 percent or more in returns per year. As you see in Part III, such returns are unrealistic, but they play well with some of the media.

Don't assume that someone with something to sell who is getting good press will take care of you. That "guru" could just be good at press relations and self-promotion. Certainly, talk shows and the media at-large can and do provide useful information on a variety of topics, but be aware that sometimes bad eggs turn up on them. And the bad eggs don't always smell up front.

Don't financial media know what's going to happen next?

Scores of widely read financial publications offer predictive advice and commentary about investment markets. But such commentary can often be wrong or misguided.

For example, on October 16, 1987, just three days before the infamous (modern-day) U.S. stock market crash, a widely read daily business paper had this to say about the prior day's relatively minor stock market decline: "But it is not yet time to pry the rubber seals out of the office windows . . . On September 22nd, it should be remembered, the market had a record 75-point one-day rise. The underlying economic news is mostly good, not bad."

On the next trading day — Monday, October 19 — the stock market plunged 508 points — nearly 23 percent! Remember, that loss occurred in one trading day!

Although most financial publications shy away from making predictions, many love to quote predictions made by the "experts." The monthly, weekly, and daily barrage of conflicting crystal ball visions causes many investors — perhaps even you — to be paralyzed and fearful. As you can clearly see in Part III of this book, you don't need a working crystal ball or a guru telling you when to buy and sell. The best investments for growth are not difficult to identify, but, once bought, are generally best held for the long haul.

Don't writers know what they're writing about?

Writers are people, too — some good, some bad; some full of hot tips, some full of hot air. During the 1980s, one of the most widely read personal finance magazines ran a piece that purported to tell you where to get "safe, high yields." In addition to utility stocks and junk bonds, the article recommended real estate and oil and gas *limited partnerships* (LPs) sold through brokers. Such LPs are not safe investments. Over the past decade, most people who bought these problematic investment vehicles lost huge portions of their money.

Another popular business magazine ran an article that touted life insurance as one of the best investments. The piece advocated the purchase of *cash value insurance* — which contains an investment account as well as life insurance protection. The article went on to claim that life insurance should be the first consideration in most responsible investment programs. As you see in Parts III and IV of this book, this advice is *wrong* for the vast majority of working people who need life insurance. (They should buy *term insurance*, which is pure life insurance protection.) Any number of investment options would make a better first consideration than buying cash-value insurance, but you wouldn't have learned that from reading the article.

More than a few writers and talk-show hosts claim to be personal finance experts but hardly ever address spending and debt issues. Instead, they focus almost exclusively on investments. For example, they may make you feel like an undisciplined failure for not saving through your employer's retirement savings program to reduce your taxes when other considerations may also apply.

Don't book publishers exercise due diligence?

Book publishers are businesses first, and like most businesses, their business practices vary. Some have a reputation for care and quality; some just want to push a product out the door with maximum hype and minimum effort.

For instance, you may think that book publishers check out an author before they sign him or her to write an entire book. Well, you may be surprised to learn that some publishers don't do their homework.

What most publishers care about first is how marketable an author is. Some authors are marketable because of their well-earned reputation for sound advice. Others are marketable because of stellar promotional campaigns built on smoke and mirrors. Still others may have the potential for marketability if a publisher takes a chance on them, but most publishers like a sure thing.

Even more troubling, in the many advice guides on the market, few publishers require that the books be technically reviewed for accuracy by an expert in the field other than the author, who sometimes may not be an expert. You, the reader, are expected to be your own technical reviewer. But do you have the expertise to do that? (Don't worry; this book has been checked for accuracy.)

As an author and a financial counselor, I know that financial ideas and strategies can differ considerably. Different is not necessarily wrong. When a technical reviewer looks at my text and tells me that another, better way is out there, I take a second look. Maybe I even see things in a new way. That's not possible if I'm the only expert who sees my book before publication. How do you know whether a book's been technically reviewed? Check the credits page or the author's acknowledgments.

Authors write books for many reasons other than to teach and educate. The most common reason financial book authors write books is to further their own business interests. That may not always be a bad thing, but it's not the best thing for you when you're trying to educate yourself and better manage your own finances. For example, some investment books are written by investment newsletter sellers. Rather than teaching you how to make good investments, the authors make the investment world sound complicated so that you'll feel the need to subscribe to their ongoing newsletters.

Saving through your employer's retirement program is all well and good, but the truth is, many people live paycheck-to-paycheck. So unless you *first* learn how to reduce spending and get out from under high-cost consumer debt, the "experts" can talk until they're blue in the face about terrific investment strategies. If you don't have anything to invest in the first place, then they're not really helping you.

There are some good writers and smart writers at most financial publications. But there are also some people who would have been better off covering politics. Come to think of it, some of them *do* also cover politics, and therein lies the problem — you're getting financial advice from people who don't focus on the field, have little if any training in it, and have no experience as a practitioner working with people like you.

Pandering to advertisers

Newspapers, magazines, internet sites, radio, television — you name it — thousands of publications and media outlets dole out personal financial advice and perspectives. Although many of these "service providers" collect revenue from subscribers, virtually all are dependent — in some cases, fully dependent (especially on the internet, radio, and television) — on advertising dollars. Although advertising is a necessary part of capitalism, unfortunately and sadly, advertisers can taint and, in some cases, dictate the content of what you read, listen to, and view.

Consider this case from a nonfinancial publication — *Modern Bride* magazine. *Harper's* magazine got hold of an apologetic letter, which it humorously entitled "To Love, Honor And Obey Our Advertisers," that *Bride's* fashion advertising director sent to its advertisers. Here's an excerpt:

> *Bride's* recommends that its readers (your customers) negotiate price, borrow a slip or petticoat, and compare catalog shoe prices, and tells its readers that the groom's tuxedo may be free. It is difficult to understand why *Bride's* was compelled to publish this information. With 57 years of publishing experience and support to the bridal industry, *Bride's* could and should have been more sensitive to the retailers that it purports to serve. All of us in the bridal business must concentrate on projecting full-service bridal retailing in a positive light.

I don't find it difficult to understand why the writer of the criticized *Bride's* article revealed cost-saving strategies to its readers — she was trying to give them useful information and advice! Now, revealing letters like this one are hard to come by, so how can you, a consumer of financial information, separate the good from the advertiser-biased publications? I've developed some ideas on the subject from having written and worked for a number of publications and from observing the workings of even more.

First, consider how dependent a publication or media outlet is on advertising. I see the most conflicts of interest that involve pandering to advertisers done by "free" publications and radio and television, which derive all of their revenue from advertising. Much of what is on the internet is advertiser-driven as well. Many of the investing sites on the internet cater to offering advice about individual stocks. Interestingly, such sites derive much of their revenue from online brokerage firms seeking to recruit customers who are foolish enough to believe that selecting their own stocks is the best way for them to invest (see Part III for more information about your investment options).

Next, as you read various publications, watch TV, or listen to the radio, note how consumer-oriented these media are. Do you get the feeling that they're looking out for your interests? Or are they primarily creating an advertiser-friendly broadcast or publication? For example, if lots of auto manufacturers advertise, does the media outlet ever tell you how to save money when shopping for a car and the importance of buying a car within your means?

Real and Imaginary Hurdles

Perhaps you know that you should be living within your means, buying and holding sound investments for the long term, and securing proper insurance coverage. However, you can't bring yourself to do these things. Everywhere you turn lurks temptation to spend money. Ads show attractive and popular people enjoying the fruits of their labors — a new car, exotic vacation, and lavish home.

Maybe you felt deprived as a youngster by your tightwad parents or you're bored with life and like the adventure of buying new things. If only you could hit it big on one or two investments, you think, you could get rich quick and do what you really want with your life. As for disasters and catastrophes — well — those things happen to other people, don't they? Not to you. Besides, you'll probably have advance warning of pending problems and can prepare accordingly.

Your emotions and temptations can get the better of you. Certainly part of successfully managing your finances involves coming to terms with your shortcomings and the consequences of your behaviors. If you don't, you may end up enslaved to a dead-end job to keep feeding your spending addiction. Or you can spend more time with your investments than you do with your family and friends. Disasters and catastrophes can happen to anyone at any time.

Discovering the real hurdles holding you back

A variety of personal and emotional hurdles get in the way of people making the best financial moves. As I discuss earlier in this chapter, most people's lack of financial knowledge (which stems from a lack of personal financial education) stands in the way of making good decisions.

However, I have seen some people get caught in the psychological trap of blaming something else for their financial problems. For example, some people believe that all our adult problems can be traced back to our childhood and how we were raised. Behaviors ranging from substance abuse and credit card addiction to sexual infidelity are supposedly caused by our roots.

I don't want to diminish the negative impact particular backgrounds can have on some people's tendency to make the wrong choices during their lives. Exploring your personal history can certainly yield clues to what makes you tick. That said, we are adults making choices and engaging in behavior that affects ourselves as well as others. We shouldn't blame our parents for our own inability to plan for our financial futures, live within our means, and make sound investments.

Another common tendency is for some people to blame their financial short-comings on not earning more income. Such people believe that if they only earned more income, their financial (and personal) problems would melt away.

My experience working and speaking with people from diverse economic backgrounds has taught me that achieving financial success — and, more importantly, personal happiness — has virtually nothing to do with how much income a person makes but rather with what she makes of what she does have. I know financially wealthy people who have all the material goods they want yet are emotionally poor. Likewise, I know people who are struggling financially yet are quite happy, contented, and emotionally wealthy.

Americans — even those who have not had an "easy" life — should be able to come up with things to be happy about and grateful for: a family who loves them; friends who laugh at their stupid jokes; the freedom to catch a movie or play or read a good book; a great singing voice, sense of humor, or full head of hair; or the fact that they live in a country not at war with any other country.

Financially speaking, we Americans are pretty spoiled. Two-thirds of the people in the world have a standard of living that is a mere 20 percent of the U.S. average. Think about that. In other words, the average American is five times better off financially than two out of every three people in the world.

Practicing good habits

Once you learn the basic concepts and know where to buy the best financial products when you need to buy them, you'll soon see that managing your personal finances well is not much more difficult than other things you do regularly like tying your shoelaces and getting to and from work each day.

Regardless of your income, you can make your dollars stretch farther if you learn good financial habits and avoid mistakes. In fact, the lower your income, the more important it is that you make the most of your income and savings (because you don't have the luxury of falling back on your next fat paycheck to bail you out).

More and more industries are subject to global competition, and you need to be on your financial toes now more than ever. Job security is on the wane. Layoffs and retraining for new jobs are on the increase. Putting in 20 or 30 years for one company and retiring with the gold watch and lifetime pension are becoming as rare as never having computer problems.

Speaking of company pensions, odds are increasing that you work for an employer that has you save toward your own retirement rather than providing a pension for you. Not only do you need to save the money, you must also decide how to invest it.

Managing your personal finances involves much more than just managing and investing money. It also includes making all the pieces of your financial life fit together. It means lifting yourself out of financial illiteracy. Like planning a vacation, managing your personal finances means formulating a plan to make the best use of your limited time and dollars.

Here are a few areas you likely need to tackle:

- **Tracking and reducing spending.** If, like most people, you're not saving sufficiently to meet your future financial goals, then sound financial management also involves tracking and reducing your spending. See Part II.

- **Investing wisely.** Investing your savings is, of course, an important part of your financial puzzle. So, too, are understanding and making the best use of tax incentives, tax breaks, and your employer's benefits.

- **Making informed real estate and insurance purchases.** You need to ensure that you invest in real estate intelligently, that you have the right types of insurance coverage, and that you're not paying more than necessary.

Intelligent personal financial strategies have little to do with your gender, ethnicity, or marital status. We *all* need to manage our finances wisely. Some aspects of financial management become more or less important at different points in your life, but for the most part, the principles remain the same for all of us.

Knowing the right answers isn't enough. You have to practice good financial habits just as you practice other habits, such as brushing your teeth. Don't be overwhelmed. As you read this book, make a short list of your financial marching orders and then start working away. Throughout this book, I highlight ways you can overcome temptations and keep control of your money rather than letting your emotions and money rule you.

Chapter 3

Establishing and Accomplishing Goals

● ●

In This Chapter

▶ Defining your own happiness

▶ Establishing and prioritizing your financial goals

▶ Saving for a rainy day, a home purchase, a small business, or educational needs

▶ What you need to get through retirement and ways to make up for lost time

● ●

*I*n my work as a financial counselor, I always asked new clients what their short- and long-term personal and financial goals were. Quite a large portion of people reported that reflecting on this question was incredibly valuable because they hadn't considered it for a long time — if ever.

In this chapter, I help you dream about what you want to get out of life. Although my expertise is in personal finance, I wouldn't be doing my job if I didn't get you to consider your nonfinancial goals and how money fits into the rest of your life goals. So before I jump into how to establish and save toward common financial goals, I'd like to take a moment to discuss how you think about making and saving money and how to best fit your financial goals into the rest of your life.

Creating Your Own Definition of "Wealth"

Pick up just about any major financial magazine or newspaper or scan stories on the internet, and you will quickly see our culture's obsession with financial wealth. The more money financial executives, movie stars, or professional athletes make and have, the more publicity and attention they seem to get. In fact, many publications go so far as ranking those people who earn the most or have amassed the greatest wealth!

Bill Gates, founder and CEO of Microsoft, for example, has in recent years been in the #1 position among the world's wealthiest people. I applaud Mr. Gates for his success, but I have to shake my head as I watch reporters and others continually follow him around like he's some sort of hero or cult figure.

I'm frankly perplexed at why many of the most affluent and highest-income earners maintain workaholic schedules despite being married and having kids. From what I observe, our society seems to define "wealth" as the following:

- Fat paychecks

- Huge investment account balances

- The ability to hire full-time people to raise your children

- Being too busy at your career to maintain friendships or take an interest in your neighbors, community, or important social problems

- The freedom to be unfaithful to your spouse and to dump your mate when you're no longer pleased with him or her

What money can't buy

Recall the handful of moments in your life that you wouldn't trade for anything. Odds are, those moments don't include the time you bought a car or found a sweater that you liked for 50 percent off at your favorite retailer. The old saying is true: The most enjoyable and precious things of value in your life can't be bought.

What I am about to say should go without saying, but I must say it because too many people act as if it weren't so: Money can't buy happiness. It is tempting to think that if you could make only 10 or 20 percent more money, you'd be happier. You'd have more money to travel, eat out, and buy that new car you've been eyeing, right? Not so fast. A great deal of thoughtful research suggests that little relationship exists between money and happiness.

"Wealth is like health: Although its absence can breed misery, having it is no guarantee of happiness," summarizes Dr. David Myers, professor of psychology at Michigan's Hope College, in his book *The Pursuit of Happiness: Who Is Happy and Why.* (This guy has it good! Imagine studying happiness for a living.)

Despite cheap air travel, VCRs, compact discs, microwaves, computers, voice mail, and all the other stuff that's supposed to make our lives easier and more enjoyable, Americans aren't any happier than they were four decades ago. According to research conducted by the National Opinion Research Center, 35 percent of Americans in 1957 said that they were "very happy," whereas in the 1990s, fewer said the same. These unexpected results occurred even though incomes, after adjusting for inflation, more than doubled during that time.

As Dr. Myers observes in *The Pursuit of Happiness,* ". . . if anything, to judge by soaring rates of depression, the quintupling of the violent crime rate since 1960, the doubling of the divorce rate, and the tripling of the teen suicide rate, we're richer and less happy."

The balancing act

Believe it or not, some people save too much. In my financial counseling practice, I certainly saw plenty of people who fell into that category. If making and saving money is a good thing, then the more the merrier, right?

Well, take the admittedly extreme case of Anne Scheiber, who on a modest income started saving at a young age and allowed her money to compound in wealth-building investments such as stocks over many years. The result was that she was able to amass $20 million by the time that she passed away at the age of 101.

Scheiber lived in a cramped studio apartment and never used her investments. She didn't even use the interest or dividends — she lived solely on her Social Security benefits and the small pension from her employer. Scheiber was extreme in her frugality and obsessed with her savings. As reported by James Glassman in the *Washington Post,* "She had few friends . . . she was an unhappy person, totally consumed by her securities accounts and her money."

Most people, myself included, would not choose to live and save the way that Scheiber did. She saved for the sake of saving: no goal, no plan, no reward for herself. Saving should be a means to an end, not something that makes you mean to the end.

Even those who are saving for an ultimate goal can become consumed by their saving habits. I see some people pursuing higher-paying jobs and pinching pennies in order to retire early. But sometimes they make too many personal sacrifices today while chasing after some vision of their lives tomorrow. Others get consumed by work and then don't notice or understand why their family and friends feel neglected.

Another problem with seeking to amass wealth is that tomorrow might not come. Even if all goes according to plan, will you know how to be happy when you're not working if you spend your entire life making money? More importantly, who will be around to share your leisure time? One of the costs of an intense career is time spent away from friends and family. You may indeed realize your goal of retiring early, but you may be putting off too much living today in expectation of living tomorrow.

As Charles D'Orleans said in 1465, "It's very well to be thrifty, but don't amass a hoard of regrets."

Of course, at the other extreme are spendthrifts who live only for today. A friend of mine once said, "I'm not into delayed gratification." Shop 'til you drop seems to be the motto of this personality type. "Why bother saving when I might not be here tomorrow?" reasons this type of person.

The danger of this approach is that tomorrow may come after all, and most people don't want to spend all their tomorrows working for a living. The earlier neglect of saving, however, handicaps the possibility of not working when you are older. And if for some reason you can't work and have little money to live on, much less live enjoyably, the situation can be tragic. The only difference between a person without savings or access to credit and some homeless people is a few months of unemployment.

Making and saving money is like eating food. If you don't eat enough, you may suffer. If you eat too much, the overage may go to waste or make you overweight. The right amount, perhaps with some extra to spare, affords you a healthy, balanced, peaceful existence. Money should be treated with respect and acknowledged for what it is — a means to an end and a precious resource that shouldn't be thoughlessly squandered and wasted.

As Dr. David Myers, whom I discuss earlier in this chapter, says: "Satisfaction isn't so much getting what you want as wanting what you have. There are two ways to be rich: one is to have great wealth, the other is to have few wants." Find ways to make the most of the money that does pass through your hands, and never lose sight of all that is far more important than money.

Prioritizing Your Savings Goals

Most people that I know have financial goals. The rest of this chapter discusses the most common ones and how to work toward accomplishing them:

- ✔ **Become part of the landed gentry.** Renting and dealing with landlords can be a financial and emotional drag, so most folks want to buy into the American dream and own some real estate — the most basic of which is to own your own home.

- ✔ **Retire.** No, retiring does not imply sitting on a rocking chair watching the world go by while hoping that some long lost friend, your son's or daughter's family, or the neighborhood dog comes by to visit. *Retiring* is a catch-all term for discontinuing full-time work or perhaps not even working for pay at all.

- ✔ **Educate the kids.** No, all those diaper changes, late-night feedings, and trips to the zoo aren't enough to get junior out of your house and into the real world as a productive, self-sufficient adult. You may want to help your children get a college education, and, unfortunately, that can cost a truckload of dough.

✔ **Own your own business.** Many employees want to become employers so that they can face the challenges and rewards that come with being the boss. The primary reason that many people continue to dream without actually plunging into their own small businesses is that they lack the money to do so. Although many businesses don't require gobs of start-up cash, almost all require that you withstand a substantial reduction in your income in the early years.

Because each of us is unique, each of us can have goals other than those above and unique to our own situation. No matter — accomplishing such goals almost always requires saving money. As one of my favorite Chinese proverbs says, "Do not wait until you are thirsty to dig a well."

Know what's most important to you

Unless you earn really big bucks or have a large family inheritance to fall back on, your personal and financial desires will probably outstrip your resources. Thus, you must prioritize your goals if you want to accomplish them.

One of the biggest mistakes that I see people make is to rush into financial decisions without considering what is really important to them. Because many of us get caught up in the responsibilities of our daily lives, time for reflection often never happens.

From the experience I've had counseling and teaching many people about better personal financial management, I can tell you that the people who accomplish their goals aren't necessarily smarter or higher-income earners than those who don't. People who accomplish their goals identify their goals and work toward them.

The advantages of retirement accounts

Where possible, you should try to save and invest in accounts that offer you a tax advantage. That's precisely what retirement accounts do for you. These accounts — known by such enlightening acronyms and names as 401(k), 403(b), SEP-IRAs, Keoghs, and so on — offer tax breaks to people of all economic means (the different types of retirement accounts are detailed in Chapter 11):

✔ **Contributions are usually tax-deductible.** Retirement accounts should really be called *tax-reduction accounts*. If they were, people might be more excited about contributing to them. For many, avoiding higher taxes is the motivating force that opens the account and starts the contributions.

TIP

Avoiding retirement account early withdrawal penalties

There are times and ways to avoid the early withdrawal penalties that the tax gods normally apply.

Suppose that you read this book at a young age, develop sound financial habits early, and save enough to retire before age 59½. In that case, you can take money out of your retirement account without triggering penalties. The IRS allows you to withdraw money before 59½ if you do so in equal, annual installments based on your remaining life expectancy. The IRS (this is slightly chilling) even has a little table that allows you to look up your life expectancy.

You can now also make penalty-free withdrawals from Individual Retirement Accounts for either a first-time home purchase (limit of $10,000) or higher educational expenses for you, your spouse, your children, or your grandchildren.

The other conditions under which you can make penalty-free early withdrawals from retirement accounts are not as enjoyable: If you have major medical expenses or a disability, you may be exempt from the penalties under certain conditions.

If you get in a financial pinch while you're still employed, be aware that some company retirement plans allow you to borrow against your cash balance. This tactic is like loaning money to yourself — the interest payments go back into your account.

Another strategy to meet a short-term financial emergency is to withdraw money from your Individual Retirement Account (IRA) and return it within 60 days to avoid paying penalties. I don't generally recommend this because of the penalties invoked if you miss the 60-day deadline, even by just one crummy day.

If you lose your job and withdraw retirement account money simply because you need it to live on, the penalties do apply. However, if you're not working and earning so little income that you need to raid your retirement account, you are surely in a low tax bracket. The lower income taxes you pay as compared to the taxes you would have paid on that money had you not sheltered it in a retirement account in the first place should make up for most or all of the penalty.

By putting money in a retirement account, you not only plan wisely for your future, but you also get an immediate financial reward: lower taxes — and lower taxes mean more money available for saving and investing. Retirement account contributions are generally not taxed at either the federal or state income tax levels until withdrawal. If you're paying, say, 35 percent between federal and state taxes (refer to Chapter 7 to determine your tax bracket), a $5,000 contribution to a retirement account would lower your taxes by $1,750.

✔ **Returns on your investment compound over time without taxation.**
After money is in a retirement account, any interest, dividends, and
appreciation add to your account without being taxed. Of course, there's
no such thing as a free lunch — these accounts don't allow for complete
tax avoidance. Yet, you can get a really great lunch at a discount — you
get to defer taxes on all of the accumulating gains and profits until you
withdraw the money down the road. Thus, more money is working for
you over a longer period of time. (A new type of IRA that I discuss in
Chapter 11 offers no up-front tax breaks but does allow future tax-free
withdrawal of investment earnings.)

Dealing with competing goals

Unless you enjoy paying higher taxes, why would you save money outside of
retirement accounts? The reason is that accomplishing some financial goals
is not easily achieved through saving in these retirement accounts.

If you're accumulating down payment money for a home purchase or to start
or buy a business, for example, you'll probably need to save that money outside of a retirement account. Why? Because if you withdraw funds from retirement accounts before age 59½ and you are not retired, you not only have to
pay income taxes on the withdrawals, but you also must generally pay *early
withdrawal penalties* — 10 percent of the withdrawn amount in federal tax
and whatever your state charges. (See the sidebar "Avoiding retirement
account early withdrawal penalties," where I discuss exceptions to this rule.)

Because you're constrained by your financial resources, you must prioritize
your goals. Before funding your retirement accounts and racking up those tax
breaks, read on to consider your other goals.

Building Emergency Reserves

No one can predict the future. There is simply no reliable way to tell what
may happen with your job, health, or family. Because you don't know what
the future holds, preparing for the unexpected is financially wise. Even if
you're the lucky sort who sometimes finds $5 bills on street corners, you
can't control the sometimes chaotic world in which we live.

Conventional wisdom says that you should have approximately six months of
living expenses put away for an emergency. This particular amount may or
may not be right for you because it depends, of course, on how expensive the
emergency is. Why six months, anyway? And where should you put it?
Unfortunately, no hard and fast rules exist. How much of an emergency stash
you need depends on your situation.

I recommend saving the following emergency amounts under differing circumstances (in Chapter 12, I recommend good places to invest this money):

- **Three months' living expenses** if you have other accounts such as a 401(k) or family members and close friends that you could tap for a short-term loan. This minimalist approach makes sense when you're trying to maximize investments elsewhere (for example, in retirement accounts) or have stable sources of income (employment or otherwise).

- **Six months' living expenses** if you don't have other places to turn for a loan and/or have some instability in your employment situation or source of income.

- **Up to one year's living expenses** if your income fluctuates wildly from year to year or if your profession involves a high risk of job loss and it could take you a long time to find another job and you don't have other places to turn for a loan.

In the event that your only current source of emergency funds is a high-interest credit card, you should first save at least three months' worth of living expenses in an accessible account before funding a retirement account or saving for other goals.

Saving to Buy a Home or Business

When you're starting out financially, deciding whether to save money to buy a home or to put money into a retirement account presents a dilemma. In the long run, owning your own home is a wise financial move. On the other hand, saving sooner for retirement makes achieving your goal easier.

The bottom line is: Presuming both goals are important to you, you should be saving towards both buying a home *and* for retirement. If you're eager to own a home, then you can throw all of your savings toward achieving that goal and temporarily put retirement savings on hold. Save for both purposes simultaneously if you're not in a rush.

You may be able to have your cake and eat it too if you work for an employer that allows borrowing against retirement account balances. You can save money in the retirement account and then borrow against it for the down payment. Be careful, though. Retirement account loans typically must be paid back within a set number of years (check with your employer) or immediately if you quit or lose your job. As I mention earlier in this chapter, you are also allowed to make penalty-free withdrawals of up to $10,000 from Individual Retirement Accounts toward a first-time home purchase.

To save money for starting or buying a business, most people face the same dilemma as when deciding to save to buy a house: If you fund your retirement accounts to the exclusion of building money for your small-business dreams, your entrepreneurial aspirations may never become a reality. Generally, I advocate hedging your bets by saving some money in your tax-sheltered retirement accounts as well as some toward your business venture. As I discuss in Part III, an investment in your own small business can produce great rewards, so you may feel comfortable focusing your savings on your own business.

Saving for Kids' Educational Expenses

Wanting to provide for your children's future is perfectly natural. But doing so before you've saved adequately toward your own goals can be a major financial mistake. The college financial-aid system effectively penalizes you for saving money outside of retirement accounts and penalizes you even more if the money is invested in the child's name.

It may sound selfish, but you need to take care of *your* future first. You should first take advantage of saving through your tax-sheltered retirement accounts before you set aside money in custodial savings accounts for your kids. This practice isn't selfish — do you really want to have to leech off your kids when you're old and frail because you didn't save any money for yourself?

See Chapter 13 for a complete explanation for how to save for educational expenses.

Don't buy cash value life insurance plans

Life insurance salespeople are often eager to sell you cash value life insurance policies, which combine life insurance protection with a type of savings account. You may very well be suckered into buying a cash value life insurance policy as a savings vehicle for accomplishing goals such as retiring or paying for a child's educational costs. Don't fall for this sales trap.

Cash value life insurance policies give you no immediate tax deduction. By contrast, a retirement savings plan such as a 401(k), 403(b),

SEP-IRA, or Keogh allows you to deduct your contributions from your taxable income. Even if you don't have access to these plans, you're better off saving and investing through an IRA or annuity plan (these are detailed in Chapter 11).

Most people are far better off buying term life insurance (see Chapter 16 for more details). Because agents earn far larger commissions selling cash value policies, those policies generally get pitched.

Saving for Big Purchases

If you want to buy a car or a canoe or plane ticket to France, do not, I repeat, *do not* buy such things with consumer credit. As I explain in Chapter 5, cars, boats, vacations, and the like are consumer items, not investments that build wealth, such as real estate or a small business. A car begins to depreciate the moment you drive it off the sales lot. A plane ticket to France is worthless the moment you arrive back home. (I know your memories will be priceless, but they won't pay the bills.)

Paying for high-interest consumer debt can cripple your ability not only to save for long-term goals like retirement or a home but also to make major purchases in the future. Interest on consumer debt is exorbitantly expensive — up to 18 percent for most credit cards. When contemplating the purchase of a consumer item on credit, add up the total interest you end up paying on your debt and call it the price of instant gratification.

Don't deny yourself gratification; just learn how to delay it. Get into the habit of saving for your larger consumer purchases to avoid paying for them over time with high-interest consumer credit. When saving up for a consumer purchase like a car, a money market account (see Chapter 12) is a good place to store your short-term savings.

Preparing for Retirement

Many people toil away at work, dreaming about a future in which they can stop the daily commute grind; get out from under that daily deluge of faxes, voice mails, and e-mails; and do what they want when they want. People often assume that this magical day will arrive either on their next true day off or when they retire or win the lottery, whichever comes first.

I've never cared much for the term *retire.* It seems to imply idleness or the end of usefulness to society. But if retirement means not having to work at a job (especially one you don't enjoy) and having financial flexibility and independence, then I'm all for it.

Part of the American dream is to be able to retire sooner rather than later. But this idea has some obvious problems. First, you set yourself up for disappointment. If you want to retire by your mid-60s (when Social Security kicks in), you'll need enough money to live for an additional 20 years, maybe longer. Two decades is a long time to live off your savings. You're going to need a good-sized chunk — more than most people realize. The earlier you hope to retire, the more money you need to set aside and the earlier you have to start saving — unless you plan to work part-time in retirement to earn more income!

Most people I speak to say that they do want to retire, and most say the sooner, the better. Yet more than half of Americans between the ages of 18 and 34 and a quarter of those aged 35 to 54 have not begun to save for retirement. When I asked one of my middle-aged counseling clients, who had saved little for retirement, when he would like to retire, he deadpanned, "Sometime before I die." If you're in this group, and even if you're not, determine where you stand financially regarding retirement. If you're like most working people, you need to increase your savings rate for retirement.

What you need for retirement

If you hope to someday cease working or reduce the time you spend working for an income, you will need sufficient savings to support yourself. Many people — particularly young people and those who don't work well with numbers — underestimate the amount of money needed to retire. To figure out how much you should be saving per month given your retirement goals, you can't avoid crunching a few numbers (but don't worry, this number-crunching is easier than doing your taxes).

Luckily for you, you don't have to start cold. Studies have shown how people typically spend money before and during retirement. Most people need about 70 to 80 percent of their preretirement income throughout retirement to maintain their standard of living. For example, if your household earns $40,000 per year before retirement, you're likely to need $28,000–$32,000 (70–80 percent of $40,000) per year during retirement to live the way that you're accustomed to living. The 70–80 percent is an average. Some people may need more simply because they have more time on their hands to spend their money. Others adjust their standard of living and can live on less.

You, of course, are not average in any way — you're unique! So how do you estimate what *you* will need? The simplest method to estimate what you need is for me to tell you what percentage you need. (I know we've only known each other a short time, but let me offer some friendly counseling.) The following three profiles provide a rough estimate of the percentage of your preretirement income that you need during retirement. Pick the one that most accurately describes your situation. If you fall between two descriptions, pick a percentage in between.

To maintain your standard of living in retirement:

✔ You need **65 percent of your preretirement income** if you

- save a large amount (15 percent or more) of your annual earnings

- are a high-income earner

- will own your home free of debt by retirement, and

- do not anticipate leading a lifestyle in retirement that reflects your current high income.

If you're an especially high-income earner who lives well beneath his or her means, you may be able to do with even less than 65 percent. Try picking an annual dollar amount or percentage of your current income that should allow the kind of retirement lifestyle you desire.

✔ You need **75 percent of your preretirement income** if you

- save a reasonable amount (5 to 14 percent) of your annual earnings
- will still have some mortgage debt or a modest rent to pay by the time you retire, and
- anticipate having a standard of living in retirement that is comparable to what you have today.

✔ You need **85 percent of your preretirement income** if you

- save little or none of your annual earnings (less than 5 percent)
- will have a significant mortgage payment or sizeable rent to pay in retirement, and
- anticipate wanting or needing to maintain your current lifestyle throughout retirement.

Of course, you can use a more precise approach to figure out how much you need per year in retirement. Be forewarned, though, that this more personalized method is far more time-consuming, and because you're making projections into an uncertain future, it may not be any more accurate than the simple method I just explained. Those who are more data-oriented may feel comfortable tackling this method: You need to figure out where you're spending your money today (worksheets are located in Chapter 4) and then work up some projections for your expected spending needs in retirement (the information in Chapter 19 may help as well).

Retirement building blocks

Did you play with Lego blocks or Tinker Toys when you were a child? You start by building a foundation on the ground, and then you build up. Before you know it, you're creating bridges, castles, and panda bears. Although preparing financially for retirement isn't exactly like playing with blocks, the concept is the same: You need a basic foundation for your necessary retirement reserves to grow.

If you have been working steadily, you may already have a foundation, even when you haven't been actively saving toward retirement. In the pages ahead, I walk you through the probable components of your future retirement income and how to figure how much you should be saving to reach a particular retirement goal.

TIP

Don't neglect nonfinancial preparations for retirement

Investing your money is just one, and not even the most important, aspect of preparing for your retirement. In order to enjoy the lifestyle that your retirement savings will provide you, you need to invest energy into other areas of your life as well.

✔ Few things are more important than your health. Without your health, enjoying the good things in life is hard. Unfortunately, many people are not motivated to care about their health until after they discover problems. By then, it may be too late.

Although exercising regularly, eating a balanced and nutritional diet, and avoiding substance abuse cannot guarantee you a healthful future, they go a long way toward preventing many of the most common causes of death and debilitating disease. Regular medical exams also are important in detecting problems early.

✔ In addition to your physical health, invest in your psychological health. It is well documented that people live longer and are happier and healthier when they have a circle of family and friends around them for support.

Unfortunately, as they grow older, many people become more isolated as they lose regular contact with business associates, friends, and family members.

Happy retirees tend to be active and involved in volunteer organizations and in new social circles. They may travel to see old friends or to visit younger relatives who may be too busy to visit them.

Treat retirement life like a bubbly, inviting hot tub at 102 degrees. You want to ease yourself in, nice and slow; taking a hasty plunge can take most of the pleasantness out of the experience. Abruptly leaving your job without some sort of plan for spending all that free time is an invitation to boredom and depression. Everyone needs a sense of purpose, a sense of routine. Establishing hobbies, volunteer work, or a sideline business while gradually cutting back your regular work schedule can be a terrific way to ease the transition into retirement.

Lower yourself into the tub slowly. Take some time to get used to the temperature change. Ahhh . . . nice, isn't it?

Social Security

Social Security is the Rodney Dangerfield of U.S. government programs. According to a *Wall Street Journal*/NBC poll of American adults 18 and older, nearly half of those under the age of 35 and more than a third of those between the ages of 35 and 49 think that there will be *no* Social Security benefits by the time they retire.

Contrary to widespread cynicism, Social Security should be there for you when you retire, no matter how old you are today. In fact, it's one of the sacred cow political programs. Imagine what would happen to the group of politicians that voted not to pay any more benefits!

If you think you can never retire because you have no money saved, I'm happy to inform you that you're probably wrong. You've likely got some Social Security. But Social Security is generally not enough to live on comfortably.

Social Security is intended to provide you with a subsistence level of retirement income for the basic necessities: food, shelter, and clothing. It is *not* intended to be your sole source of income. Few people could maintain their current lifestyles without supplementing Social Security with personal savings and company retirement plans.

How much will I get from Social Security?

Table 3-1 shows the approximate size of your expected monthly allowance from Social Security. The first column gives your average *yearly employment earnings* (in today's dollars) on which you paid Social Security taxes. The second column contains your approximate *monthly benefit amount* (in today's dollars) that you'll receive when eligible for full benefits.

Note: The benefit amounts in Table 3-1 are for an individual income earner. If you're married, and one of you doesn't work for pay, the nonworking spouse collects 50 percent of what the working spouse collects. Working spouses are eligible for either individual benefits or half of their spouse's benefits, whichever amount is greater.

Table 3-1	Your Expected Social Security Benefits
Annual Earnings	*Approximate Monthly Benefit (Value in Today's Dollars)*
$10,000	$550
$20,000	$840
$30,000	$1,020
$40,000	$1,175
$50,000	$1,250
$60,000	$1,310
$70,000+	$1,360

More Social Security details

In the "good old days" (prior to changes made in Social Security regulations in 1983), if eligible, you could collect full Social Security payments at age 65. This rule no longer holds true. If you were born before 1938, you're still eligible to collect full Social Security benefits at age 65. If you were born in 1960 or after, you have to wait until age 67 for full benefits. If you were born between 1938 and 1959, full benefits are payable to you at age 66, plus or minus some number of months, depending on the year you were born.

The problem with Social Security is that when the system was created in the 1930s, its designers underestimated how long people would live in retirement (the Roosevelt administration must have included a lot of young people). Thanks to scientific advances and improved medical care, life expectancies have risen substantially since that time. As a result, many of today's retirees get back far more in benefits than they paid into the system.

For this reason, the age at which you can start collecting full benefits has been increased and may be increased again. It may seem unfair, but it's necessary to update the system for the realities of our increased longevity, large federal budget deficits, and aging baby boomers. Without changes, the Social Security system could collapse, because it will be fed by a relatively small number of workers while supporting large numbers of retirees.

In addition to paying for retirement-income checks for retirees, your Social Security taxes also provide for disability insurance for you, survivor income insurance for your financial dependents, and Medicare, the health-insurance program for retirees.

The amount of Social Security benefits that you receive in retirement depends on your average earnings during your working years. Don't worry about the fact that you probably earned a lot less many years ago. The Social Security benefits calculations increase your older earnings to account for the lower cost of living and wages in the good old days.

How much work makes me eligible?

To be eligible to collect Social Security benefits, you need to have worked a minimum number of quarters. If you will reach age 62 after 1990, you need 40 quarters of work credits to qualify for Social Security retirement benefits.

If for some reason you work only the first half of a year or only during summer months, don't despair. You don't need to work part of every quarter to get a quarter's credit. You get credits based on the income you earn during the year. As of this writing, you get the full four quarters credited to your account if you earn $2,960 or more in a year. (In earlier years, folks got one quarter's credit for each actual calendar quarter in which they earned $50.) To get 40 quarters of coverage, you basically need to work ten years.

To get credits, you must report the income and pay taxes on it, including Social Security tax. In other words, you and those you employ encounter problems when you neglect to declare income or if you pay people under the table — you may be cheating yourself or others out of valuable benefits.

In order to get a more precise handle on your Social Security benefits, call the Social Security Administration at 800-772-1213 and ask for Form 7004, which allows you to receive a record of your reported earnings and an estimate of your Social Security benefits (you may also visit the Social Security Administration Web site at www.ssa.gov). Alternatively, wait by your mailbox — the government now annually will send you a benefits statement. (Check your earnings record, because occasional errors do arise and — surprise — they are usually not in your favor.)

Personal savings/investments

Money that you are saving toward retirement can include money under the mattress as well as money in a retirement account such as an Individual Retirement Account (IRA), 401(k), or similar plan (see Chapter 11). You may have also earmarked investments in nonretirement accounts toward your retirement.

Equity in rental real estate can be counted as well. Deciding whether to include the equity in your primary residence (your home) is trickier. If you don't want to count on using this money in retirement, then don't include it when you tally your stash. You may want to count a portion of your home equity in your total assets for retirement. Many people do sell their homes when they retire to move to a cheaper region of the country, to move closer to family, or to downsize to a more manageable household. And increasing numbers of older retirees are tapping their homes' equity through reverse mortgages.

Pensions

Pension plans are a benefit offered by some employers — mostly larger organizations and government agencies. Even if your current employer does not offer a pension, you may have earned pension benefits through a previous job.

The plans I'm referring to are known as *defined-benefit plans*. You qualify for a monthly benefit amount to be paid to you in retirement based on your years of service.

Although each company's plan differs, all plans calculate and pay benefits based on a formula. A typical one might credit you with 1.5 percent of your salary for each year of service (full-time employment). For example, if you work ten years, you earn a monthly retirement benefit worth 15 percent of your monthly salary.

This type of benefit is quite valuable. In the better plans, an employer puts away the equivalent of 5–10 percent of your salary to pay your future pension. This money is not quoted as part of your salary — it's in addition to your salary. You never see it in your paycheck, and it is not taxed. What the employer is doing is putting money away in an account for your retirement.

To qualify for pension benefits, you don't have to stay with an employer long enough to receive the 25-year gold watch. Under current government regulations, an employee must be fully *vested* (entitled to receive full benefits based on years of service upon attaining retirement age) after five years of full-time service.

Defined-benefit pension plans are becoming rarer for two major reasons:

- First, they are costly for employers to maintain. Many employees don't understand how these plans work and why they're so valuable, so companies don't get mileage out of their pension expenditures — employees don't see the money, so they don't appreciate how generous the company is being.

- Second, most of the new jobs being generated in the U.S. economy are with small companies that typically don't offer these types of plans.

More employers are offering plans like 401(k)s, in which employees elect to save money out of their own paychecks. Known as *defined-contribution plans,* these plans allow you to save toward your retirement at your own expense rather than at your employer's expense. (To encourage participation in these plans, some employers "match" a portion of their employees' contributions.) More of the burden and responsibility for investing for retirement falls on your shoulders in 401(k) and similar plans. You must be educated about how these plans work. Most people are ill-equipped to know how much to save and how to invest the money. The retirement planning worksheet in the next section should help get you started with figuring the amount you should be saving. The "Investing Crash Course" in Part III can help you understand how to invest.

Retirement planning worksheet

Now that you've toured the components of your future retirement income, I'd like you to take a shot at tallying where you stand in terms of retirement preparations. Don't be afraid to do this exercise — it's not difficult, and you may find that you're not in such bad shape. I even explain how to catch up if you find that you are behind in saving for retirement.

Note: The following worksheet (Table 3-2 and the Growth Multiplier Minitable) assumes that you will retire at age 66 and that your investments will produce an annual rate of return 4 percent per year higher than the rate of inflation. (For example, if inflation averages 3 percent, this table assumes you will earn 7 percent per year on your investments.)

Table 3-2	Retirement Planning Worksheet
1. Annual retirement income needed in today's dollars (see earlier in this chapter).	$ _____ / year
2. Annual Social Security (see Table 3-1).	– $ _____ / year
3. Annual pension benefits (ask your benefits department). Multiply by 60% if your pension won't increase with inflation during retirement.	– $ _____ / year
4. Annual retirement income needed from personal savings (subtract lines 2 and 3 from line 1).	= $ _____ / year
5. Savings needed to retire at age 66 (multiply line 4 by 15).	$ _____
6. Value of current retirement savings.	$ _____
7. Value of current retirement savings at retirement (multiply line 6 by Growth Multiplier in following minitable).	$ _____
8. Amount you still need to save (line 5 minus line 7).	$ _____
9. Amount you need to save per month (multiply line 8 by Savings Factor in following minitable).	$ _____ / month

To get a more precise handle on where you stand in terms of retirement planning, especially if you'd like to retire earlier than your mid-60s, call T. Rowe Price (800-638-5660) and ask for the company's retirement planning booklets. You can also turn to Chapter 19, where I recommend retirement planning software and web sites that can save you a great deal of number crunching.

Growth Multiplier Minitable		
Your Current Age	*Growth Multiplier*	*Savings Factor*
26	4.8	.001
28	4.4	.001
30	4.1	.001
32	3.8	.001
34	3.5	.001
36	3.2	.001
38	3.0	.002
40	2.8	.002
42	2.6	.002
44	2.4	.002
46	2.2	.003
48	2.0	.003
50	1.9	.004
52	1.7	.005
54	1.6	.006
56	1.5	.007
58	1.4	.009
60	1.3	.013
62	1.2	.020
64	1.1	.041

How to make up for lost time

If the amount that you need to save per month to reach your retirement goals seems daunting, don't despair. All is not lost. In fact, here are my top recommendations to make up for lost time — none of which requires you to work for the rest of your life!

✔ **Question your spending.** There are only two ways to boost your savings: Earn more money or cut your spending (or do both). Most people don't spend their money nearly as thoughtfully as they earn it. Refer to Chapter 6 for spending reduction suggestions and strategies.

✔ **Be more realistic about your retirement age.** If you extend the age at which you plan to retire, you get a double financial benefit. You're earning and saving money for more years and spending your nest egg over fewer years. Of course, if your job is making you crazy, this option may not be too appealing. Try to find work that makes you happy and consider working, at least part-time, during the years typically considered the retirement years.

✔ **Use home equity.** Psychologically, the prospect of tapping the cash in your home can be troubling. After getting together the down payment, you probably worked for many years to pay off that sucker. You're delighted not to have to mail a mortgage payment to the bank anymore. But what's the use of owning a house free of mortgage debt when you lack sufficient retirement reserves? All that money tied up in the house can help to increase your standard of living in retirement.

There are a number of ways to tap your home's equity. You can sell your home and either move to a lower-cost property or rent. Tax laws allow you to realize up to $250,000 in tax-free profit from a house sale ($500,000 if you're married). Another option is a *reverse mortgage* — where you get a monthly income check as you build a loan balance against the value of your home. The loan is paid when your home is finally sold (see Chapter 14 for more information about reverse mortgages).

✔ **Get aggressive with your investments.** The faster the rate at which your money grows and compounds, the less you need to save each year to reach your goals. Earning just a few extra percentage points per year on your investments can dramatically slash the amount you need to save. The younger you are, the more powerful the effect. For example, if you're in your mid-30s and your investments appreciate 6 percent per year faster than the rate of inflation rather than 4 percent, the amount you need to save each month to reach your retirement goals drops by about 40 percent!

✔ **Turn a hobby into supplemental retirement income.** Even if you've earned a living in the same career over many decades, you have skills that are portable and can be put to profitable use. Pick something you enjoy and are good at, develop a business plan, and get smart about how to market your services and wares (check out *Small Business For Dummies,* which I co-wrote with veteran entrepreneur Jim Schell). Remember, as people get busier, more specialized services are being created to support their hectic lives. A demand for quality, homemade goods of all varieties also exists. Be creative! You never know — you may wind up profiled in a business publication!

✔ **Invest in a tax-wise way.** A free way to boost the effective rate of return on your investments without taking on additional risk is to insulate more of your money from taxation. Many people who are able to save money do not do so in a way that minimizes their taxes.

Direct your savings into tax-favored retirement accounts like a 401(k) plan. You get an immediate tax deduction for your contribution. For a typical person, a third or more of your contribution represents money you would have had to pay in federal and state income taxes. This money gets to work for you, rather than for the government, in the years ahead. Plus, the money compounds over the years without taxation.

As for money outside of tax-sheltered retirement accounts, if you're in a relatively high tax bracket, you may earn more by investing in tax-free investments and other vehicles that do not make a great amount of tax-able distributions. (I discuss tax-friendly investments and retirement accounts in detail in Chapter 11.)

✔ **Take a look at jobs that offer retirement plans.** When you're evaluating employers, cash is usually king. As long as the position includes health insurance, most people are concerned only about the salary. But having access to a retirement savings plan is a valuable benefit. Even more ben-eficial is a pension plan, which pays you a monthly retirement benefit based on your years of service (a completely pain-free way to build wealth for retirement). If you're lucky enough to have choices, check out these plans when considering a job offer.

What's a retirement savings plan such as a 401(k) worth in the long run? A lot. Suppose that a person who is 40 years old earns $35,000 per year and pays 35 percent in federal and state taxes on her last dollars of income. If she can contribute 10 percent of her salary, or $3,500, to a retirement savings plan, she reduces her current year's taxes by $1,225. Assume further that the money she contributes this year grows at the rate of 8 percent per year until she withdraws the money at age 65. If she pays taxes at the same rate she is paying today when she withdraws the money at age 65, she'll have about $15,580 left. If she hadn't saved this money through a retirement plan, she would have only $8,080 at 65. In other words, on *just one year's contribution* of $3,500, she nets $7,500 more in retirement because of the tax-deferred compounding allowed in the retirement account.

You tax gurus might feel that the previous comparison isn't completely fair. After all, when investing outside of a retirement account, not all of your investment return would likely be taxed annually since some of it would reflect not-yet-taxed appreciation on investments that you con-tinue to hold. And, as I discuss in Chapter 7, appreciation on assets held more than one year is taxed at a lower capital gains tax rate. Nonetheless, a retirement account investor still comes out substantially ahead even factoring these issues in. Also consider that if our mythical investor in the previous example is like most people, she probably would have been tempted to spend the money if she had access to it, so she might not have saved even the $8,080 if she hadn't used the retirement account!

✔ **Think about inheritances.** Although you should never count on an inheritance to support your retirement, in reality, you may someday inherit money. If you want to see what impact an inheritance has on your retirement calculations, simply add the amount (use a conservative estimate) that you expect to inherit to your current total savings in Table 3-2.

Overcoming objections to retirement accounts

Despite all the great tax benefits of investing through retirement accounts, many people aren't jumping at the opportunity to take advantage of them. Everyone has unique priorities. Maybe you're saving for a home purchase or paying off student loans. Some reasons, however, stem from a lack of knowledge and understanding. The following are the objections to contributing to tax-favored accounts that I hear most frequently. Some of these objections can be overcome, whereas others are legitimate reasons to not fund retirement accounts.

Retirement's a long way away

When you're in your 20s or 30s, age 65 seems like the distant future. For many people, it's not until middle age that some warning bells start to stimulate thoughts about one's golden years.

Delaying the age at which you start to sock away money is usually a financial mistake. The sooner you start to save, the less painful it is to save each year because your contributions have more years to compound. Each decade you procrastinate approximately doubles the percentage of your earnings you should save to meet your goals. For example, if saving 5 percent per year in your early 20s would get you to your retirement goal, waiting until your 30s may mean socking away 10 percent; your 40s, 20 percent; and so on.

When should you start saving toward retirement? Ideally, you should start saving a small portion of your employment earnings with your very first paycheck. Start your kids' saving habits while they're young!

Only losers who don't know how to have fun save for retirement

Some people really believe this statement. But I also know losers who don't save for retirement and still don't know how to have a good time (none of my counseling clients and friends, of course).

This attitude is just a rationalization. The reality is that if you manage your finances efficiently and start working toward your goals sooner, you can spend more *and* have more fun in the long run. Besides, who says spending all your money is the only way to have fun?

My taxes probably won't decrease in retirement

Some people feel that there's little point in contributing to retirement accounts if their tax rate will be the same or even higher in retirement. Although your taxes could increase when you retire, the following simple example shows you why your time is better spent worrying about more important issues.

Earlier in this chapter, I create the scenario of a woman earning $35,000 per year who pays 35 percent in federal and state taxes on her last dollars of income. She contributes 10 percent, or $3,500, per year to a retirement savings plan, thereby decreasing her current year's taxes by $1,225. Assume that the money she contributes grows at the rate of 8 percent per year until she withdraws the money at age 65. If she is still in the same tax bracket when she starts withdrawing money at age 65, her $3,500 contribution is worth $15,580. If she had saved this money through a nonretirement plan, she would have had only $8,080 at age 65.

Suppose that her career takes off and she earns more money (and pays more taxes) as she gets closer to retirement. How high would her retirement tax rate have to be before she should regret having saved in the retirement account? Answer: She would have to pay about 67 percent in taxes on the retirement account withdrawals to be worse off, a very unlikely occurrence. Remember, she was paying 35 percent in taxes during her working years. It's highly unlikely that your tax rate would increase this much.

You may actually be in a lower tax bracket in retirement, because most people have less income when they're not working. Thus, you get an added bonus from deferring taxes on your retirement account assets if you are in a lower tax bracket when you withdraw the money.

There are greener investment pastures elsewhere

Real estate is a good example. Some people find retirement accounts boring and believe that they can get a better return in the real estate market. Rental real estate can appreciate in value and produce increasing rental income over the years. Investing in real estate is a legitimate reason for not maximizing retirement plan contributions.

Although real estate provides some tax breaks, consider its drawbacks.

> ✔ First, while you accumulate the down payment, you may pay higher income taxes if you're sacrificing contributions to retirement accounts that are tax-deductible.

✓ Second, rental real estate produces income that is taxable and is added to all your other income during the year, which may push you into a higher tax bracket. Even if the extra real estate income doesn't push you into a higher tax bracket, this income is taxable at the ordinary income tax rates, which are higher than the tax rates on long-term capital gains (see Chapter 7).

In a retirement account, the earnings continue to compound without taxation, and you decide when you want to start drawing on the money.

There may be a way for you to invest in what you want and gain tax relief, too. Many types of investments — stocks, bonds, mutual funds, precious metals, and even real estate — can be held in retirement accounts. (See Chapter 11 for more details.)

I have no money left over to save

The more you spend, the less able you will be to fund retirement accounts. Thus, the extra taxes that you pay because you can't afford retirement account contributions are an additional cost of overspending today. So if you can reduce your expenditures (refer to Chapter 6), you can more easily meet your retirement goals. You'll have more money to contribute to retirement accounts, and you'll save on your taxes to boot!

In some cases, people have a pile of money not earmarked for specific future needs that's invested outside of tax-sheltered retirement accounts. They may use all of their monthly employment income to meet their ongoing living expenses. As a result, they believe they can't afford to save in a retirement account.

If you think this way, you're compartmentalizing your finances. Look at the big picture. For example, what if you save $300 per month through your tax-deductible retirement plan? Suppose that doing so reduces your taxes by $100 and thus really costs you only $200 a month? You then can take $200 from your savings outside the retirement account and put it toward living expenses.

What you're effectively doing is transferring your savings from outside retirement accounts to inside a retirement account. You're not really saving new money, but you're getting terrific tax savings by playing this perfectly legal investing shell game. Just be careful not to drain your emergency savings reserve down too far.

I love my job and will work forever

Are you one of those people who loves his or her work? You don't plan to retire and therefore don't need to amass a pile of money to live on for 20-plus years? If so, you can get away with saving a lot less than your eager-to-retire friends.

You may not, however, be *able* to work at your current job forever. What if you lose your job? What if something happens to your health? You can't assume that you will always be able to work — plan ahead for these what-ifs.

I've saved enough already

Congratulations! This is the single best excuse for not saving more for retirement. If you have a lot of money outside of tax-sheltered retirement accounts, you may still want to contribute to retirement accounts anyway for the tax deductions.

Part II
Saving More, Spending Less

The 5th Wave   By Rich Tennant

In this part . . .

1 show you how to identify where your hard-earned dollars are going. I detail numerous ways to make those dollars go toward helping you build up your savings rather than going to wasteful spending. What? You're buried in debt with little to show for it? Well, it's never too late to start digging out. Here you'll find out how to reduce your debt burden. I also devote an entire chapter to discussing taxes and legally minimizing them since too much of your money may be going to pay taxes.

Chapter 4

Where Did Your Money Go?

*I*n order for most people to accomplish their financial goals, they must live within their means. This means spending less than you earn and then taking that "savings" and hopefully investing it intelligently.

Many folks earn just enough to make ends meet. And some can't even do that; they simply spend more than they make. The result of such spending habits is, of course, accumulation of debt — witness the U.S. government and its five trillion dollars worth of debt accumulation.

Whatever your financial dreams, you need to save and invest (unless you plan on winning the lottery or gaining a large inheritance). To put yourself in a position that allows you to start saving, you need to take a close look at your spending habits.

Why You Overspend

Most of the influences on you in society are encouraging you to spend, and credit is so widely and easily available. Think about it. In the media and in the hallowed halls of our government, more often than not, you're referred to as a *consumer*. Not a person, not a citizen, not a human being — but a consumer.

In fact, some people I've worked with feel unpatriotic or inadequate if they don't spend enough. "Saving too much and not spending enough could hurt the economy," they say. "People could be thrown out of work, and it could be a friend or family member. My favorite politician might not get reelected if I don't do my part and spend."

Bunk! Ultimately, you are the one who suffers the consequences of spending more than you can afford.

Here are some of the adversaries you're up against as you attempt to control your spending. In Chapter 5, I explain detailed strategies for getting out of debt, and in Chapter 6, I share practical tactics for slimming your spending.

Access to credit

As you probably already know, spending your money is easy. Thanks to innovations like ATM machines and credit cards, your money is always available for spending, 24 hours a day, 365 days a year (except during leap years, when your money is available 366 days a year). Every little outlet in the mall is pitching its own credit card, including the gas station across the street and the convenience store down the road. It certainly won't surprise me when those two little kids on my block start taking credit cards at their lemonade stand. I can hear it now: "We take Visa, Mr. Tyson, but we don't take American Express."

Sometimes, it may seem as though lenders are trying to give away money by making credit so easily available. But this is a dangerous illusion. When it comes to consumer debt (credit cards, auto loans, and the like), lenders aren't giving away anything except the opportunity for you to get in over your head, rack up high interest charges, and delay your progress toward your financial and personal goals.

Credit is most dangerous when you make consumption purchases that you couldn't afford in the first place.

Using credit cards

The modern-day bank credit card was invented by Bank of America near the tail end of the baby boom. The credit industry has been booming along with the boomers ever since.

If you pay your bill in full every month, credit cards offer a convenient way to buy things with an interest-free, short-term loan. But if you carry your debt over month to month at high interest rates, credit cards encourage you to live beyond your means. Credit cards make spending money that you don't have easy and tempting.

If you have a knack for charging up a storm and spending more than you should with those little pieces of plastic, only one solution exists: Get rid of them. Put scissors to the plastic. Go cold turkey. You *can* function without them (see the next chapter for details if you think you can't live without credit cards).

Making minimum monthly payments

You'll *never* get your credit card debt paid off if you keep charging on your card and make only the minimum monthly payment. Interest continues to pile up on your outstanding debt. Paying only the minimum monthly payment is like using a Dixie cup to bail water from a sinking boat that has a basketball-sized hole in its bottom.

Taking out car loans

It's too easy to walk onto a car lot and go home with a new car that you could never afford if you had to pay cash. The dealer gets you thinking in terms of monthly payments that sound small compared to what that four-wheeler is *really* gonna cost you. Auto loans are easy for just about anyone to get (except maybe a recently paroled felon).

Suppose that you're tired of driving around in the old clunker. The car is battle-scarred and boring, and you don't like to be seen in it. Plus, the car is likely to need more repairs in the months ahead. So off you go to your friendly local car dealer.

You start looking around at all the shiny, new cars and then — like the feeling you experience when spotting a water fountain on a scorching hot day — there it is: the replacement for your old clunker. It's sleek and clean and — oooh, look! — it has A/C, stereo, and power everything.

Before you have an opportunity to read the fine print on the sticker page on the side window, the salesperson moseys on up next to you. He gets you talking about how nice the car is, the weather, anything but the price of that car.

"How," you begin to think to yourself, "can this guy afford to spend time with me without knowing if I can afford this thing?" After a test drive and more talk about the car, the weather, and your love life, or lack thereof, comes your moment of truth.

The salesperson, it seems, doesn't care about how much money you have. If, in fact, you have lots of money, that doesn't matter either. Either way, it's no problem!

The car is only $299 a month.

That's not bad, you think. Heck, you were expecting to hear that the car cost at least 20 grand. Before you know it, the dealer runs a credit report on you and has you sign a few papers, and minutes later you're driving home — the proud owner of a spanking new car.

See, the dealer wants you to think in terms of monthly payments because the cost *sounds* so cheap: $299 for a car. But, of course, that's $299 per month, every month, for many, many months. You're gonna be payin' forever — after all, you just bought a car that cost a huge chunk (perhaps 100 percent or more) of your yearly take-home income!

But it gets worse. What does the total sticker price come to when interest charges are added in? And how about insurance and registration and maintenance over the seven or so years that you'll own it? Now you're probably up to *more* than a year's worth of your income. Ouch! (See Chapter 6 for how to spend what you can afford on a car.)

Bending to peer pressure

You go out with some friends to dinner, a ballgame, or a show. Try to remember the last time one of you said, "Let's go someplace (do something) cheaper. I can't afford to spend this much."

On the one hand, you don't want to be a stick in the mud. But on the other hand, some of your friends have more money than you do — and the ones who don't may be running up debt fast.

Spending to feel good

Life is full of stress, obligations, and demands. "I work hard," you say. "And darn it, I deserve to indulge!" Especially after your boss took the credit for your last great idea or blamed you for his last major screwup. So you buy something expensive or go to a fancy restaurant. Feel better? You won't when the bill arrives. And the more you spend, the less you save, and the longer you'll be stuck working and working for jerks like that!

Becoming addicted to spending

Just as people can become addicted to alcohol, tobacco, television, and the internet, some become addicted to the high they get from spending. A number of psychological causes can be identified for spending addiction, some of which may date back to how your family handled money and spending. (And you thought you'd identified all the problems you can blame on Mom and Dad!)

If your spending and debt problems are chronic, Debtors Anonymous, a 12-step support group program patterned after Alcoholics Anonymous, can help. See Chapter 5 for more information.

Trying to keep current

You just have to see the latest hit movie or wear the latest designer clothes or get the new, superimproved, oversized tennis racquet with shock absorbers, double-wishbone suspension, and polyxylitol handgrips. All your friends are getting one, so you'd better get one, too. Right?

Wrong. Besides, many new technologies or products don't live up to their billing. Be smart and wait until a product is proven and you can afford it.

Ignoring your financial goals when buying

When was the last time you heard someone say that he decided to forego a purchase because he was saving toward retirement or a home purchase? Doesn't happen often, does it? Just dealing with the here-and-now and forgetting your long-term needs and goals are tempting. That's why people toil away for too many years in jobs they dislike.

Living for today has its virtues: Tomorrow *may* not come. But odds are good that it will. Will you still feel the same way tomorrow about today's spending decisions? Or will you feel guilty that you again failed to stick to your goals?

Of course, this assumes that you have financial goals to stick to. Most people haven't yet set goals and don't know how much they should be saving to accomplish them. Chapter 3 helps you to kick-start that process.

Wanting the "best" for your children

For children, many of the best things in life are free, just as they are for you. Junior *can* live without the latest $100 sneakers. Later on in life, your children will thank you: Better to pass on sound judgment and wise thriftiness than the worship of material goods.

Education can cost good money, I know. However, education experts — and my wife is one of them — are the first to dissuade you of the assumption that you're doing the best for your children if you spend lots of money to live in a town with a supposedly top-of-the-line school district or to fund the tuition of a private school education from pre school through high school if you can't be home enough to take care of your children's other wants and needs.

Education begins in and is best done in the home. I see some parents spend so much time running around working, working, working to afford all the supposedly best things for their kids that they neglect to spend *time* with their kids — the most important ingredient to their children's long-term happiness and success.

Analyzing Your Spending

Washing your face, brushing your teeth, and exercising regularly are good habits. The financial equivalents of these habits are spending less than you earn and saving enough to meet your future financial objectives.

Despite relatively high incomes compared with the rest of the world, most Americans have a hard time saving a good percentage of their incomes compared with the rest of the world. Why? We spend too much — often far more than is necessary.

The first step to saving more of the income that you work so hard for is to figure out where that income typically gets spent; that's what the spending analysis in the next section helps you determine.

You should do the spending analysis if any of the following apply to you:

- ✔ You aren't saving enough money to meet your financial goals (should you not know whether this is the case, please see Chapter 3).

- ✔ You feel as if your spending is out of control or you don't really know where all your income goes.

- ✔ You're anticipating a significant life change (for example, marriage, leaving your job to start a business, having children, retiring, and so on).

In the event that you're a good saver already, you may not need to complete the spending analysis. If you're saving enough to accomplish your goals, I don't see much value in continually tracking your spending. You've already established the good habit — saving. The good habit is *not* tracking exactly where you spend your money month after month. As long as you're saving enough and simply spending what's left over, I say, who cares where the money is being spent!

The immediate goal of a spending analysis is to figure out what you typically spend your money on. The long-range goal is to establish a good habit: to maintain a regular, automatic savings routine.

Notice the first four letters in the word *analysis*. (You may never have noticed, but I felt the need to bring it to your attention.) Knowing where your money is going each month is useful. It's terrific to make changes in your spending behavior and to cut out the fat so that you can save more money and meet your financial goals. But you'll perhaps make yourself and those around you unhappy campers if you try to be anal-retentive about documenting precisely where you're spending every single dollar and cent.

Remember: What matters is that you save what you want and need to achieve your goals.

Tracking your spending on paper

Doing your spending analysis is a little bit like being a detective. Your goal is to reconstruct the crime of *spending*. You probably have some major clues at your fingertips or piled somewhere on your desk or on the table where you plop yourself down to pay bills.

Unless you keep meticulous records that detail every dollar you spend, you won't have perfect information. Don't sweat it! A number of available sources should allow you to reconstruct where you have been spending the bulk of your money.

Get out your

- ✔ Recent pay stubs
- ✔ Tax returns
- ✔ Checkbook register or canceled checks
- ✔ Credit and charge card bills

Ideally, you should assemble the documents needed to track one year's (12 months') spending. But, if your spending patterns don't fluctuate greatly from month to month (or if your dog ate some of the old bills), you can reduce your data gathering to one six-month period or to every other or every third month for the past year. If you take a major vacation or spend a large amount on gifts during certain times of the year, make sure you include these months in your analysis.

The hardest transactions to track are cash transactions because they don't leave a paper trail. Over the course of a week or perhaps even a month, you *could* keep track of everything you buy with cash. Tracking cash can be an enlightening exercise — it can also be a hassle. If you're lazy like I sometimes am or lack the time and patience, try *estimating.* Think about a typical week or month — how often do you buy things with cash? For example, if you eat lunch out four days a week at work, paying around $5 a shot, that's about $80 a month. You might also add up all the cash withdrawals from your checking account statement and then work backwards to try to remember where you might have spent that cash.

Try to separate your expenditures into as many useful and detailed categories as possible. Table 4-1 gives you a suggested format — you can tailor it to fit your needs. Remember, if you lump too much of your spending into broad, meaningless categories like *Other,* you'll end up where you started: wondering where all the money went. (***Note:*** When completing the tax section in Table 4-1, you should report the total tax you paid for the year as tabulated on your annual income tax return rather than the tax withheld or paid during the year.)

Table 4-1	Detailing Your Spending	
Category	**Monthly Average ($)**	**Percent of Total Gross Income (%)**
Taxes, taxes, taxes (income)		_____
FICA (Social Security & Medicare)	_____	
Federal	_____	
State and local	_____	
The roof over your head		_____
Rent	_____	
Mortgage	_____	
Property taxes	_____	
Gas/electric/oil	_____	
Water/garbage	_____	
Phone	_____	
Cable TV	_____	
Furniture/appliances	_____	
Maintenance/repairs	_____	
Food, glorious food		_____
Supermarket	_____	
Restaurants and take-out	_____	
Getting around		_____
Gasoline	_____	
Maintenance/repairs	_____	
State registration fees	_____	
Tolls and parking	_____	
Bus or subway fares	_____	
Style		_____
Clothing	_____	
Shoes	_____	
Jewelry (watches, earrings)	_____	
Dry cleaning	_____	
Debt repayments (excluding mortgage)		_____
Credit/charge cards	_____	
Auto loans	_____	
Student loans	_____	
Other	_____	

Category	Monthly Average ($)	Percent of Total Gross Income (%)
Fun stuff		_____
Entertainment (movies, concerts)	_____	
Vacation and travel	_____	
Gifts	_____	
Hobbies	_____	
Pets	_____	
Other	_____	
Personal care		_____
Haircuts	_____	
Health club or gym	_____	
Makeup	_____	
Other	_____	
Personal business		_____
Accountant/attorney/financial advisor	_____	
Other	_____	
Health care		_____
Physicians and hospitals	_____	
Drugs	_____	
Dental and vision	_____	
Therapy	_____	
Insurance		_____
Homeowner's/renter's	_____	
Auto	_____	
Health	_____	
Life	_____	
Disability	_____	
Umbrella liability	_____	
Educational expenses		_____
Tuition	_____	
Books	_____	
Supplies	_____	

(continued)

Table 4-1 *(continued)*

Category	Monthly Average ($)	Percent of Total Gross Income (%)
Children		_____
Day care	_____	
Toys	_____	
Child support	_____	
Charitable donations	_____	_____
Other		_____
_____	_____	
_____	_____	
_____	_____	
_____	_____	
_____	_____	
_____	_____	

Tracking your spending on the computer

Plenty of software packages exist to assist you with paying bills and tracking your spending. The main advantage of these software packages is that they continually track your spending as long as you keep entering the information. And, after you learn how to use these packages (not always an easy thing to do), they can speed the process of writing checks.

But you don't need a computer and fancy software packages to figure where you're spending money and to pay your bills. Many software purchasers I know give up entering the data after a few months. If tracking your spending is what you're after, you're likely to have only the information in the software from bills you pay by check. Expenses you pay by credit card and cash need to be entered specially into the software if you want to capture that data, too.

Like home exercise equipment and exotic kitchen appliances, such software often ends up in the consumer graveyard.

Paper, pencil, and a calculator work just fine.

Don't waste time on financial administration

Tom is the model of financial organization. All his financial documents are neatly organized into color-coded folders. Every month, he enters all his spending information into his computer. He even carries a notebook to detail his cash spending so that every penny is accounted for.

Tom also balances his checkbook, "to make sure that everything is in order." He can't remember the last time his bank made a mistake, but he knows a friend who once found a $50 error.

If you spend seven hours per month as Tom does balancing your checkbook and detailing all your spending, you may be wasting nearly two weeks worth of time per year — the equivalent of two-thirds of your vacation time if you take three weeks annually.

Suppose that you're "lucky" enough, every other year, to find a $100 error the bank made in its favor. If you spend just three hours per month tracking your spending and balancing your checkbook to discover this glitch, you'll spend 72 hours over two years to find a $100 mistake. Your hourly pay: a wafer-thin $1.39 per hour. You could make more flipping burgers at a burger joint if you wanted to moonlight. (**Note:** If you make significant-sized deposits or withdrawals, be sure that those are captured on your statement.)

To add insult to injury, after working a full week and doing all your financial and other chores, you may not have the desire and energy left to do the more important stuff. Looking at your big personal financial picture — establishing goals, choosing wise investments, securing proper insurance coverage — may continue to be shoved to the back burner. As a result, you may lose thousands of dollars annually. Over the course of your adult life, this could translate into tens or even hundreds of thousands of lost dollars.

Tom, for example, didn't know how much he should be saving to meet his retirement goals. He hadn't reviewed his employer's benefit materials to understand his insurance and retirement plan options. He knows he pays a lot in taxes, but he hasn't educated himself about how to reduce his taxes.

You want to make the most of your money. Unless you truly enjoy dealing with money, you need to prioritize the money activities that you work on. Time is limited and life is short. Working harder on financial administration doesn't earn you bonus points. The more time you spend dealing with your personal finances, the less is available to gab with friends, watch a good movie, read a good novel, and do other things you really enjoy.

Don't get me wrong — nothing is inherently wrong with balancing your checkbook. In fact, if you regularly bounce checks because you don't know how low your balance is, the exercise might save you a lot in returned check fees. However, if you keep enough money in your checking account to rarely reach $0.00, balancing your checkbook is probably a waste of your valuable time, even if your hourly wages aren't lofty. I haven't balanced mine in years (but please don't tell my bank — it might start making some "mistakes" and siphon money out).

If you're busy, consider ways to reduce the amount of time spent on mundane financial tasks like bill paying. Increasing numbers of companies, for example, allow you to have your monthly bills paid to them electronically via your bank checking account or your credit card (only do this if you pay your credit card bill in full each month). The fewer bills you have to pay, the fewer separate checks and envelopes you must process each month. That translates into more free time for you and fewer paper cuts!

If you do want to try computerizing your bill payments and expense tracking, I recommend the best software packages currently available in Chapter 19.

The Secret to Growing Rich on Your Income

As a financial counselor, I work with people who bring in tiny incomes, incomes of hundreds of thousands of dollars or more, and everything in between. At every income level, people fall into one of the following three categories:

- ✔ People who spend more than they earn (accumulate debt)
- ✔ People who spend all that they earn (save nothing)
- ✔ People who save 2, 5, 10, even 20 percent (or more!)

I've seen $30,000 earners who save 20 percent of their income ($6,000), $60,000 earners who save just 5 percent ($3,000), and people earning well into six figures annually who save nothing or are accumulating debt.

Suppose that you currently earn $30,000 per year and spend all of it. You wonder: "How can I save money?"

Good question!

Rather than knocking yourself out at a second job or hustling for that next promotion, you could try living below your income — in other words, spend less than you earn. (I know spending less than you earn is hard to imagine, but you can do it.) Consider that for every discontented person earning and spending $30,000 per year, someone else is out there making do on $27,000.

A great many people live on less than you make. If you spent as they do, you could save and invest the difference.

Chapter 5

Solving Debt and Credit Problems

- -

In This Chapter

▶ Using your savings to reduce your debt

▶ Getting out of debt when you don't have savings

▶ The pros and cons of filing bankruptcy

▶ Dealing with credit problems

- -

As I discuss in Chapter 1, some debt is good, and some is bad. When debt is used for investing in your future, I call it *good debt*. Borrowing money to afford an education, buy real estate, or invest in a small business is like eating foods rich in calcium for strong bones or eating fruits and vegetables for their vitamins.

But accumulating *bad debt* (consumer debt) is like living on a diet of sugar and caffeine: a quick fix with no long-term nutritional value. Borrowing on your credit card to afford that vacation to Cabo is costly and detrimental to your long-term financial health.

In this chapter, I help you battle the increasing problem of consumer debt. Getting rid of your bad debts may be even more difficult than giving up the sugar-laden foods you love. But in the long run, you'll be glad you did; you'll be financially healthier and emotionally happier. And once you get rid of your high-cost consumer debts, practice the best way to deal with credit problems: *Don't borrow with bad debt.*

To decide which debt reduction strategies make sense for you, you first must consider your overall financial situation and assess your alternatives.

Using Savings to Reduce Your Debt

Many people have built up a psychological brick wall between their savings and investment accounts and their debt accounts. Failing to view their finances holistically, they have simply gotten into the habit of looking at these accounts individually. The thought of putting a door in that big brick wall hasn't occurred to them.

How you gain

Using savings to pay down debts may seem like you're losing money. You're *not* losing; you're gaining. Remember that the growth of your money is determined by your *net worth* — the difference between your assets and your liabilities (see Chapter 1). Hopefully, your savings and investments are earning decent returns, but if you have consumer debts, odds are that the interest on those debts is high.

Having consumer loans on a credit card at, say, 12 percent and paying them off is like finding an investment with a guaranteed return of 12 percent — *tax-free*. You would actually need an investment that yielded even more — around 18 percent — to net 12 percent after paying taxes in order to justify not paying off your 12 percent loans. The higher your tax bracket (see Chapter 7), the higher the return you need on your investments to justify keeping high-interest consumer debt.

If you have the savings to pay off high-interest credit card and auto loans, do so. You diminish your savings, true, but you also reduce your debts. You benefit financially because the interest on your savings is far less than the interest your debt accrues. Make sure to pay off the loans with the highest interest rates first.

Even if you think you're an investment genius and can earn more on your investments, swallow your ego and pay down the debts anyway. In order to chase that higher potential return from investments, you need to take substantial risk. You *may* earn more investing in that hot stock tip or that bargain real estate located on a toxic waste site, but more than likely, you won't.

If you use your accessible savings to pay down consumer debts, be careful to leave yourself enough of an emergency cushion. You want to be in a position to withstand an unexpected large expense or temporary loss of income. On the other hand, if you use savings to pay down credit card debt, unless your card gets canceled, you can run your credit card balances back up in a financial pinch (or turn to a family member or wealthy friend for a low-interest loan).

Money you may be overlooking

Have you ever reached into the pocket of an old winter parka and found a rolled-up $20 bill you forgot you had? Stumbling across some forgotten funds is always a pleasant experience. But before you root through all your closets in search of stray cash to help you pay down that nagging credit card or other costly consumer debt, check out some of these financial jacket pockets that you may have overlooked:

✔ **Borrow against your cash value life insurance policy.** If you were approached by a life insurance agent, odds are good that this is the type of policy you were sold because it pays high commissions to its agents. Or perhaps your parents bought one for you when you were a little gremlin. Borrow against the cash value to pay down your debts. *(Note:* Continuing with such a policy may not be the best thing to do — see Chapter 16 for more details.)

✔ **Borrow against your employer's retirement account.** Check with your employer's benefits department to see if you can borrow against your retirement account balance. The interest rate is usually reasonable, and as you repay the loan, the interest payments go back into your account. Be careful, though — if you choose to leave your job or are asked to leave, you will have to repay the loan within only 60 days.

✔ **Sell investments held outside of retirement accounts.** Maybe you have some shares of stock or a Treasury bond gathering dust in your safety deposit box. Consider cashing in these investments to pay down your loan balances. Just be sure to consider the tax consequences of selling, and if possible, only sell those investments that won't generate a big tax bill.

✔ **Borrow against the equity in your home.** If you're a homeowner, you may be able to tap into your home's *equity,* which is the difference between the property's market value and outstanding loan balance. You can generally borrow against real estate at a lower interest rate and get a tax deduction to boot.

✔ **Borrow from friends and family.** They know you, love you, realize your shortcomings, and — heck — probably won't be as cold-hearted as some bankers I know. Money borrowed from family members can have strings attached, of course. Treating the obligation seriously is important. It's also best to write up a simple agreement listing the terms and conditions of your loan to avoid misunderstandings. Unless your family members are like the worst bankers I know, you'll probably get a fair interest rate, and your family will have the satisfaction of helping you out — just don't forget to pay them back.

Decreasing Debt When You Lack Savings

"I don't have savings, you nincompoop," you exclaim. "That's why I have all this debt!"

If you read the preceding section, thank you for patiently waiting; I just wanted to make sure that you didn't have any money that you forgot about. (The number of people with consumer debt who can pay it down with savings but haven't done so always surprises me.)

But on to your quandary: You lack savings to pay off your high-interest consumer debt. Well, not surprisingly, you have some work to do. If you're currently spending all your income (and more!), you need to figure out how you can decrease your spending (see Chapter 6 for lots of great ideas) and/or increase your income. In the meantime, you need to slow the growth of your debt.

Transfer to lower-interest-rate credit cards

Different credit cards charge different interest rates. Why in the world should you pay 14, 16, 18 percent, or more when you can pay less? The credit card business has become quite competitive. Gone are the days when all banks charged 18 percent or more for VISA and MasterCard.

Here's one of the few times in your life when you should want to be below average! Until you get your debt paid off, make it more difficult for your debt to grow. You may be able to accomplish this slowing process by reducing the interest rate you're paying on your debt. Here are some ways to do that:

✔ **Apply for a lower-rate credit card.** If you are earning a decent income, are not *too* burdened with debt, and have a clean credit record, qualifying for lower-rate cards is relatively painless. Some persistence (and clean-up work) may be required if you have nicks in your credit report or have income and debt problems. Once you are approved for a new, lower-interest rate credit card, you can simply transfer your outstanding balance from your higher-rate card.

Among banks with consistently low-interest-rate credit cards, I like AFBA Industrial Bank (800-776-2265), which offers a no-annual-fee card with an 8.5 percent interest rate for the first 6 six months and 11.4 percent thereafter. *(Note:* After the introductory period, the future interest rate is set at a minimum of 11.4 percent but can be higher — it is determined by adding 2.9 percent to the so-called prime interest rate).

✔ **Call the bank(s) that issued your current high-interest-rate credit card(s) and say that you want to cancel your card(s) because you found a competitor that offers no annual fee and a lower interest rate.** Your bank may choose to match the terms of the "competitor" rather than lose you as a customer.

✔ **While you're paying down your credit card balance(s), stop making new charges on cards that have outstanding balances.** Many people don't realize that interest starts to accumulate *immediately* when they carry a balance. *You have no grace period* — the 20-odd days you normally have to pay your balance in full without incurring interest charges — if you carry a credit card balance month-to-month.

BEWARE

4.9-percent-interest-rate credit cards!

Buyer beware if you're lured into applying for a credit card that hypes its low interest rate — such as those offering a 4.9-percent rate. One such card advertises a 4.9-percent rate, but you have to dig into the fine print for the rest of the story.

First, any card that offers such a low interest rate inevitably will only honor that rate for a short period of time — in this case, six months. Then, the interest rate skyrockets to nearly 15 percent.

And, there's more. Make just one late payment or exceed your credit limit, and the company raises your interest rate to 19.8 percent in addition to whacking you $29 for each such infraction. Need a cash advance on your card? You'll get socked with a fee equal to 3 percent of the amount advanced.

Now, I'm not saying that everyone should avoid this type of card. Such a card could make sense for you if you want to transfer an outstanding balance and plan to pay off that balance within a matter of months, cancel the card, and avoid getting socked with the high fees on the card.

If you hunt around for a low-interest-rate credit card, be sure to check out all the terms and conditions. Start by reviewing the uniform rates and terms disclosure, which details the myriad fees and conditions. Also, be sure that you understand how the future interest rate is determined on cards that charge variable interest rates.

Cut 'em up, cut 'em all up

TIP

If you have a pattern of living beyond your means through buying on credit, get rid of the culprit — the credit card, that is. To kick the habit, a smoker needs to toss *all* the cigarettes, and an alcoholic needs to get rid of *all* the booze. Cut up *all* of your credit cards and call the issuers of the cards to cancel your accounts. And when you buy consumer items such as cars and furniture, do not apply for E-Z credit.

The world worked fine back in the years *B.C.* (Before Credit). Think about it: Just a couple of generations ago, credit cards didn't even exist. People paid with cash and checks — imagine that! You *can* function without buying anything on a credit card. In certain cases, you may need a card as collateral — like when you rent a car. When you bring back the rental car, however, you can pay with cash or check. Leave the card at home in the back of your sock drawer or freezer and pull (or thaw) it out only for the occasional car rental.

If you can trust yourself, keep a separate credit card *only* for new purchases that you know you can absolutely pay in full each month. No one needs three, five, or ten credit cards! You can live with one (and actually none), given the wide acceptance of most cards. Count 'em up, including retail store and gas cards, and get rid of 'em. Retailers such as department stores and gas stations just love to give you their cards. Not only do these cards charge outrageously high interest rates, they duplicate VISA and MasterCard. Virtually all retailers accept VISA and MasterCard. More credit lines mean more temptation to spend what you can't afford.

Should you decide to keep one widely accepted credit card instead of getting rid of them all, be careful. You may be tempted to let debt accumulate and roll over for a month or two, and you'll start the whole horrible process of running up your consumer debt again. Rather than keeping one credit card, consider getting a debit card.

Debit cards: The best of both worlds

Credit cards are the main reason that today's consumers are consuming more than they can afford. So logic would say that one way you can keep your spending in check is to not use your credit cards. But in a society used to flashing the widely accepted VISA and MasterCard plastic for purchases, changing habits is hard. And you may be legitimately concerned that carrying your checkbook or cash can be a hassle or costly if you're mugged.

Well, *debit cards* truly offer the best of both worlds. The beauty of the debit card is that it offers you the convenience of making purchases with a piece of plastic without the temptation and ability to run up credit card debt. Debit cards keep you from spending money you don't have and help you live within your means.

A debit card looks just like a credit card and has either the VISA or MasterCard logo. The big difference between debit cards and credit cards is that, as with checks you write, debit card purchase amounts are deducted electronically within days from your checking account. (Your bank ATM card is also a debit card, which most merchants don't accept for purchases.)

If you keep your checking account balance low and don't ordinarily balance your checkbook, you may need to start balancing your checkbook if you switch to a debit card. Otherwise, you could be facing unnecessary bounced check charges.

You should also know about other differences between debit and credit cards.

> ✓ If you pay your credit card bill in full and on time each month, charging on your credit card gives you free use of the money you owe until it's time to pay the bill; debit cards take the money out of your checking account almost immediately. (Note that some credit cards charge a fee even if you pay your balance in full each month. You didn't think the banks would let you use the float forever, did you?)

✔ Also, credit cards more easily allow you to dispute charges for problematic merchandise through the issuing bank. Most banks allow you to dispute charges for up to 60 days after purchase and will credit the disputed amount to your account pending resolution. Most debit cards offer a much shorter window, typically less than one week, to make disputes.

Should you decide to get a VISA or MasterCard debit card, finding one may take some time. Banks — the leading issuers of credit cards — have long been cool to promoting debit cards. In my previous work as a management consultant, I worked with some major credit card issuers that were contemplating these newer debit cards. Although technologically feasible, the card issuers feared debit cards because they thought the cards might cut into their highly profitable credit card business.

Because moving your checking account can be a hassle, first inquire of the bank where you currently have a checking account to see whether it offers VISA or MasterCard debit cards. If your bank does not offer one, shop among the larger banks in your area, which are more likely to offer the cards. Because such cards come with a checking account, please be sure to comparison shop account features and fees.

A number of investment firms offer VISA or MasterCard debit cards with their asset management accounts. These investment firm "checking accounts" not only can help you break the credit card overspending habit but may also get you thinking about saving and investing your money. One drawback is that most of these accounts require fairly hefty minimum initial investment amounts — typically $5,000 to $10,000. Among brokerages with competitive investment offerings and prices are Waterhouse (800-934-4443) and Muriel Siebert (800-872-0711). Charles Schwab & Co. (800-435-4000) and Fidelity Investments (800-544-7272) also offer such accounts but tend to charge more for their services due to their better name brand recognition with the public.

Filing Bankruptcy

For consumers in over their heads, the realization that their monthly income is increasingly exceeded by their bill payments is usually a painful one. In many cases, years can pass before drastic measures like bankruptcy are considered. Both financial and emotional issues come into play in one of the most difficult, painful, yet potentially beneficial decisions.

When Helen, a mother of two and a sales representative, contacted attorney Harry Orr, her total credit card debt of about $20,000 equaled her annual gross income of $20,000. Due to the crushing debt load, she could not meet her minimum monthly credit card payments. Rent and food gobbled up most of her earnings. What little was left over went to the squeakiest wheel.

Creditors were breathing down Helen's back. "I started getting calls from collection departments at home and work — it was embarrassing," relates Helen. Helen's case is typical in that credit card debt was the prime cause of her bankruptcy. "If credit card debt didn't exist, I wouldn't have a job," says bankruptcy attorney Harry Orr.

Helen's case is typical in other regards. Her debt accumulated over a number of years. A former homeowner with a Master's degree from a prestigious university, Helen had good credit until a couple of years before. After divorcing, Helen rented an apartment with her two children while holding down a job. Unfortunately, she was laid off when her employer encountered tough times.

At first, bills to her dentist and doctor went unpaid. Then when Helen went into business for herself, she used her credit cards to purchase office furniture and for other start-up expenses. "I would have done more corner cutting, but the credit cards were easily available cash and allowed me to think in terms of monthly payments," says Helen.

As the debt load grew, partly exacerbated by the double-digit interest rates on the cards, more and more purchases got charged — from the kids' clothing to repairs for the car. Finally, out of cash, she had to take a large cash advance on her credit cards to pay for rent and food.

Despite trying to work out lower monthly payments to keep everyone happy, most of the banks to which Helen owed money were inflexible. "When I asked one bank's VISA department if it preferred that I declare bankruptcy because it was unwilling to lower my monthly payment, the representative said yes," Helen says. Out of options, Helen filed personal bankruptcy.

Bankruptcy benefits

Every year now, more than one million American households (that's about 1 in every 100 households) file personal bankruptcy.

The value or benefit of bankruptcy is that certain types of debts can be completely eliminated or *discharged.* Debts that typically can be discharged include credit card, medical, auto, utilities, and rent. Debts that may not be canceled generally include child support, alimony, student loans, taxes, and court-ordered damages (for example, drunk driving settlements). Helen was an ideal candidate for bankruptcy because her debts (credit cards) were dischargeable.

Helen also met another important criterion — her level of high-interest consumer debt relative to her annual income was high. When this ratio (described fully in Chapter 1) exceeds more than 25 percent, filing bankruptcy may be your best option.

Eliminating your debt also allows you to start working toward your financial goals. Depending on the amount of debt you have outstanding relative to your income, you may need a decade or more to pay it all off. In Helen's case, at the age of 48, she had no money saved for retirement to supplement Social Security, and she was increasingly unable to spend money on her children.

In addition to the financial benefits are the emotional benefits of filing bankruptcy. "I was horrified at filing, but it is good to be rid of the debts and collection calls — I should have filed six months earlier. I was constantly worried. When I saw homeless families come to the soup kitchen where I sometimes volunteer, I thought that someday that could be me and my kids," she said.

Bankruptcy drawbacks

Filing bankruptcy, needless to say, has a number of drawbacks. First, bankruptcy appears on your credit report for ten years, so you will have difficulty obtaining credit, especially in the years immediately following your filing.

If you already have problems on your credit report, however, because of late payments or failure to pay previous debts, damage has already been done. And, without savings, you're probably not going to be making major purchases, such as a home, in the next several years anyway.

If you do file bankruptcy, getting credit in the future is not impossible. You'll probably be able to obtain a *secured credit card,* which requires you to deposit money in a bank account equal to the credit limit on your credit card. Of course, as I advocate earlier in this chapter, you would be better off without the temptation of any credit cards and better served with a debit card. Also know that if you can hold down a stable job, most creditors are willing to give you loans within a few years of your filing bankruptcy. Almost all lenders ignore bankruptcy after five to seven years.

Another bankruptcy drawback is that it costs money. I know this seems terribly unfair. You're already in financial trouble — that's why you're filing bankruptcy! Nevertheless, filing bankruptcy will probably set you back from several hundred dollars up to $1,000 in court filing and legal fees.

And, finally, most people find that filing bankruptcy causes emotional stress. Admitting that your personal income can't keep pace with your debt obligations is a painful thing to do. Although filing bankruptcy clears the decks of debt and gives you a fresh financial start, feeling a profound sense of failure (and sometimes shame) is normal. Despite the increasing incidence of bankruptcy, bankruptcy filers are reluctant to talk about it with others, including family and friends.

What you can keep if you file bankruptcy

In every state, you can retain certain property and assets, even though you're filing for bankruptcy. You may be surprised to learn that in some states (such as Florida, Iowa, Kansas, Minnesota, and Oklahoma), you can keep your home regardless of its value! Most states, though, allow you to protect a certain amount of home equity.

Additionally, you're allowed to retain some other types and amounts of personal property and assets. For example, most states allow you to retain household furnishings, clothing, pensions, and money in retirement accounts. So don't empty your retirement accounts or sell off personal possessions to pay debts unless you're absolutely sure that you won't be filing bankruptcy.

Another part of the emotional side of filing bankruptcy is that you must open your personal financial affairs to court scrutiny and court control during the several months it takes to administer a bankruptcy. A court-appointed bankruptcy trustee oversees your case and tries to recover as much of your property as possible to satisfy the *creditors* — those to whom you owe money.

Some people also feel that they're shirking responsibility by filing for bankruptcy. One client I worked with who should have filed couldn't bring herself to do it. She said, "I spent that money, and it's my responsibility to pay it back."

Most banks make gobs and gobs of money from their credit card businesses. As a former consultant who worked in the industry, I can tell you that credit cards are one of the most profitable lines of business for banks. If you don't believe me, consider that at a banking conference sponsored by the investment bank Salomon Brothers, CEO John Reed referred to the credit card business for banks as a "high-return, low-risk" business. Now you know why your mailbox is always filled with solicitations for more cards even though you're already up to your eyeballs in solicitations.

So if you file for bankruptcy, don't feel bad about not paying back the bank. The nice merchants where you bought the merchandise have already been paid. *Charge-offs* — the banker's term for taking the loss on debt that you discharge through bankruptcy — are part of their business. This is another reason why the interest rate is so high on credit cards and why you shouldn't borrow on credit cards.

Pick a number: 7 or 13

You can file one of two forms of personal bankruptcy:

- ✔ **Chapter 7** allows you to discharge or cancel certain debts. Chapter 7 bankruptcy makes the most sense when you have significant debts that you are legally allowed to cancel.

- ✔ **Chapter 13** comes up with a repayment schedule that requires you to pay your debts over several years. Besides being an unlucky number, Chapter 13 stays on your credit record just like Chapter 7 *but doesn't eliminate debt,* so its value is limited (usually to dealing with debts like taxes that can't be discharged through bankruptcy). Chapter 13 can keep creditors at bay, though, until a repayment schedule is worked out in the courts.

Bankruptcy advice

Be very careful where you get advice about whether to file for bankruptcy. Many people make the mistake of turning to and solely trusting bankruptcy attorneys or Consumer Credit Counseling Services (CCCS).

Attorneys who earn a legal fee from doing bankruptcy filings have a conflict of interest. All things being equal, their bias is to — you guessed it — *recommend bankruptcy,* which generates their fees.

In filing bankruptcy, hiring an attorney makes sense when you have major assets (such as a home) to protect. Attorney fees can easily exceed several hundred dollars to over $1,000 for complicated cases.

CCCS faces the opposite conflict. CCCS says that it is a nonprofit educational service to help consumers who are in debt. Although it's true that CCCS has some well-intentioned employees, it's also true that CCCS is funded by credit-card issuers. Thus, CCCS counselors are loathe to recommend bankruptcy. (See the sidebar "Conflicts of interest at CCCS" for more about how CCCS can skew your options in the wrong direction.)

If you want to learn more about the pros, cons, and details of filing for bankruptcy, pick up a copy of *How to File for Bankruptcy* by attorneys Elias, Renauer, and Leonard (Nolo Press). If you're comfortable with your decision to file and think you can complete the paperwork, you may be able to do it yourself. *How to File for Bankruptcy* comes with all the forms necessary to file. An intermediate approach is to hire a paralegal typing service to prepare the forms, which can be a cost-effective way to get help with the process if you don't need heavy-duty legal advice. Check your local yellow pages under "Paralegals."

Biased advice at CCCS

Every year, hundreds of thousands of debt-burdened consumers seek "counseling" from the more than 1,000 Consumer Credit Counseling Service (CCCS) offices. Unfortunately, people like Leona Davis find that the service may not always work the way it is pitched.

Davis, whose family racked up significant debt largely due to unexpected medical expenses and a reduction in her income, found herself in trouble with too much debt. So she turned to CCCS, which she had heard about through its advertising and marketing materials.

CCCS markets itself as a "nonprofit community service." Davis, like many others I know who have used CCCS, found that the "service" was not objective. After her experience with CCCS, Davis feels that a more appropriate name for this organization would be the Credit Card Collection Agency. I agree.

Unbeknownst to Davis and to most people who use CCCS is the fact that about 85 percent of CCCS's funding comes from fees that creditors pay to CCCS. CCCS collects fees on a commission basis — just as collection agencies do!

CCCS's strategy is to place those who come in for help on their "debt management program." Under this program, counselees like Davis agree to pay a certain amount per month to CCCS, which in turn parcels out the money to the various creditors. The debt management program usually ignores other non-credit-card debts that the counselees may have: in Davis's case, a mortgage and outstanding medical bills.

Because of Davis's tremendous outstanding consumer debt (it exceeded her annual income) and the fact that she didn't receive budgeting help from CCCS to plan her current expenses, her repayment plan was doomed to failure. Davis managed to make 10 months' worth of

payments, largely because she raided a retirement account for $28,000. Unfortunately, Davis did not know and was never told by CCCS that if she filed bankruptcy (which she ultimately needed to do), she could have kept her retirement money.

But Davis's CCCS counselor never discussed the bankruptcy option. "I received no counseling. Real counselors take the time to understand your situation and offer options. I was offered one solution, a forced payment plan," says Davis.

Others who have consulted CCCS, including one of my research assistants who, undercover, visited a CCCS office to seek advice, confirm that CCCS has a cookie-cutter approach to dealing with debt. CCCS typically recommends that debtors go on a repayment plan that has the consumer pay 3 percent of each outstanding loan balance to CCCS, which in turn pays the money to creditors.

Unable to keep up with the enormous monthly payments, Davis finally turned to an attorney and filed for bankruptcy — but not before she had unnecessarily lost thousands of dollars because of CCCS's one-sided approach to debt problems.

Although CCCS's promotional materials and counselors aren't shy about highlighting the drawbacks to bankruptcy, CCCS's counselors are reluctant to discuss the impact of signing up for a CCCS debt payment plan. Davis's CCCS counselor never told her that restructuring her credit card payments would tarnish her credit report. The counselor my researcher met with also neglected to mention this important fact. When asked, the counselor was evasive about the debt "management" program's impact on his credit report.

Ending the Spend-and-Debt Cycle

Regardless of how you deal with paying off your debt, you're in real danger of falling back into old habits. Backsliding happens not only to people who file bankruptcy but also to those who use savings or home equity to eliminate their debt. This section speaks to that risk and what to do about it.

Identifying and treating an addiction

As hard as they try to break the habit, some people become addicted to spending and debting. It becomes a chronic problem that starts to interfere with other aspects of their lives. Financial problems can lead to problems at work and with family and even friends.

Officially started in 1976, Debtors Anonymous (DA) is a nonprofit organization that provides support, primarily through group meetings, to people trying to break their debting and spending habits. DA is modeled after the 12-step Alcoholics Anonymous program.

Like AA, Debtors Anonymous works with people from all walks of life and socioeconomic backgrounds. It's typical to find people who are financially on the edge, $100,000-plus income earners, and everybody in between at a DA meeting. Even former millionaires join the program.

DA has a simple questionnaire that helps determine whether you are a problem debtor. If you answer *Yes* to at least 8 of the following 15 questions, you may be developing or already have a compulsive debting habit:

1. **Are your debts making your home life unhappy?**

2. **Does the pressure of your debts distract you from your daily work?**

3. **Are your debts affecting your reputation?**

4. **Do your debts cause you to think less of yourself?**

5. **Have you ever given false information in order to obtain credit?**

6. **Have you ever made unrealistic promises to your creditors?**

7. **Does the pressure of your debts make you careless of the welfare of your family?**

8. **Do you ever fear that your employer, family, or friends will learn the extent of your total indebtedness?**

9. **When faced with a difficult financial situation, does the prospect of borrowing give you an inordinate feeling of relief?**

10. **Does the pressure of your debts cause you to have difficulty sleeping?**

11. **Has the pressure of your debts ever caused you to consider getting drunk?**

12. **Have you ever borrowed money without giving adequate consideration to the rate of interest you are required to pay?**

13. **Do you usually expect a negative response when you are subject to a credit investigation?**

14. **Have you ever developed a strict regimen for paying off your debts, only to break it under pressure?**

15. **Do you justify your debts by telling yourself that you are superior to the "other" people, and when you get your "break," you'll be out of debt?**

To find a Debtors Anonymous support group in your area, check your local phone directory (in the "Business" section). Or write to DA's national head-quarters for meeting locations in your area and a literature order form at the following address: Debtors Anonymous, P.O. Box 400, Grand Central Station, New York, NY 10163-0400.

Resisting the credit temptation

Getting out of debt is usually challenging, but I have confidence that you can do it with this book by your side and me as your guide. In addition to the ideas discussed earlier in this chapter (eliminating all your credit cards, getting a debit card), the following are some additional tactics you can use to limit the influence credit cards hold over your life in the future:

- ✔ **Reduce your credit limit.** If you're not going to take my advice earlier in this chapter and get rid of all of your credit cards or secure a debit card, be sure to keep a lid on your credit card's credit limit (the maximum balance allowed on your card). Just because your bank keeps raising your credit limit to reward you for being such a profitable customer doesn't mean that you have to accept the increase. Call your credit-card service's 800 number and lower your credit limit to a level you're comfortable with.

- ✔ **Replace your credit card with a charge card.** A *charge card* (such as the American Express Card) requires you to pay your balance in full each billing period. You have no credit line or interest charges. Of course, spending more than you can afford to pay when the bill comes due is possible. But, you'll be much less likely to overspend if you know you have to pay in full monthly.

✔ **Never buy on credit anything that depreciates in value.** Meals out, cars, clothing, and shoes all depreciate in value. Never buy these things on credit. Borrow money only for sound investments — education, real estate, or your own business, for example.

✔ **Think in terms of total cost.** Everything sounds cheaper in terms of monthly payments — that's how salespeople lure you into buying things you don't have the money to afford. Take a calculator along if necessary to tally up the sticker price, interest charges, and upkeep. The total cost will scare you. *It should.*

✔ **Stop the junk mail avalanche.** Look at your daily mail — I bet half of it is solicitations and mail-order catalogs. Save some trees and your time sorting junk mail by removing yourself from most mailing lists. Write to the Direct Marketing Association, Mail Preference Service, P.O. Box 9008, Farmingdale, NY 11735-9008. To remove your name from the major credit reporting agency lists that are used by credit card solicitation companies, call 888-567-8688. Also, be sure to tell any credit card companies you keep cards with that you want your account marked to indicate that you do not wish to have any of your personal information shared with telemarketing firms.

✔ **Limit what you can spend.** Go shopping with a small amount of cash and no plastic or checks. That way you can only spend what little cash you have with you!

Dealing with Credit Mistakes

You may not know (or care), but you probably have a personal credit report. Creditors that are considering loaning you money generally examine your credit report before granting you a loan or credit line.

Many people don't realize that they have a blemish on their credit report until they are turned down for a loan or questioned by the creditor about the glitch. For example, when I applied for my first mortgage, I discovered a minor wart on my own credit report.

Although dealing with credit report problems takes up some of your time, it needn't be difficult if you know what and what not to do.

Obtain a copy of your credit report

If you're turned down for rental housing, employment, or a loan because of derogatory information on your credit report, most states require the prospective lender or the credit reporting bureaus to give you a copy of the report.

If you're applying for a mortgage or other major loan, most lenders will give you a copy of your credit report if you simply ask. And why shouldn't they if you're paying them to obtain the copy!

Reading a credit report is a challenge given all the abbreviations and jargon, so I recommend that, in addition to getting the report, you ask the lender what specific information on the report led to the denial of credit.

Get others to correct their mistakes

If you obtain your credit report and find a boo-boo on it that you do not recognize as being your mistake or fault, do *not* assume that the information is correct and is simply another indicator of your faulty memory. Credit reporting bureaus and the creditors who report credit information to these bureaus often make mistakes.

You would hope and expect that, if a credit bureau has negative and incorrect information in your credit report and you phone them to bring the error to their attention, they would graciously and expeditiously fix the mistake. If you believe that, then you're the world's greatest optimist; perhaps you also believe that you won't have to wait in line at the department of motor vehicles, post office, or your local bank around noon on paydays.

Odds are you're going to have to make more phone calls or write a letter or two to fix the problems. Here's how most errors that aren't your fault are corrected:

- ✔ **It's someone else's credit problem.** A surprising number of personal credit report glitches are the result of someone else's negative information getting on your credit report. If the bad information on your report is completely foreign-looking to you, tell the credit bureau and also explain that you need more information because you don't recognize the creditor.

- ✔ **It's the creditor's mistake.** Creditors make mistakes, too. You need to write or call the creditor to get them to correct the erroneous information that they sent to the credit bureau. Phoning first usually works best (the credit bureau should be able to tell you how to reach the creditor if you don't know how). If necessary, follow up with a letter.

Whether you're speaking with a credit bureau or an actual lender, make notes of your conversations. If representatives say they can fix the problem, get their names and extensions and follow up with them if they don't deliver as promised. If you're ensnared in bureaucratic red tape, escalate the situation by speaking with a department manager. By law, bureaus are required to respond to a request to fix a credit error within 30 days — hold the bureau accountable!

"Credit repair" firms

On late-night television and in the backs of newspapers and magazines, you may see ads for credit repair companies that claim to fix your credit report problems. In the worst cases I've seen, these firms charge outrageous amounts of money and don't come close to fulfilling their marketing hype.

If you have legitimate glitches on your credit report, credit repair firms *cannot* make the glitches disappear. Hope springs eternal, however — some people would like to believe that their credit problems can be fixed.

Remember — if your problems are fixable, you can fix them yourself, and you don't need to pay an outside firm big bucks to do it.

Tell your side of the story

With a minor credit infraction, some lenders may simply ask for an explanation. I had a credit report glitch that was the result of being away for several weeks and missing the payment-due date for a couple of small bills. When my proposed mortgage lender saw my late payments, all I had to do was provide a written explanation.

You and a creditor may not see eye-to-eye on a problem, and the creditor may refuse to budge. If that's the case, credit bureaus are required by law to allow you to add a 100-word explanation to your credit file.

Chapter 6

Reducing Your Spending

• •

In This Chapter

▶ The keys to successful spending

▶ Reducing your spending, category by category

• •

1 know a highly paid professional man, whom I'll call Bart, who lived in one of the most prestigious communities in America. He owned his own business, drove top-of-the-line cars outfitted with all the latest toys and gadgets, and belonged to the most expensive country club in the area.

Problem was, however, that he was a workaholic and seemed to be so in order to support his spending habits. Over time, his wife tired of the life they were leading and filed for divorce. Bart called me for a consultation soon after his divorce was finalized. He looked beaten and depressed. Although he said he needed help making some financial decisions, what he appeared to need more than anything else was a good, long vacation and some personal counseling.

At the other spending extreme, there was Justin, a young man in his mid-20s who, like Bart, was well-educated and intelligent. Justin lived a spartan lifestyle despite living in the same costly metropolitan area as Bart. Justin took a leave from his work to sail partway around the world with some friends. He was passionate about music and played in a band outside of work and found time to produce a CD. Justin was happy yet spent very little money.

Too often, especially in movies and in the media, people who make more money and have more toys are portrayed as being happier and more powerful. In my experience, I have come across far more Barts than Justins. In part because of his high income, Bart took no interest in learning how to spend smarter — as a result, he had little savings to show for all of his earnings. Justin, on the other hand, viewed living well beneath his means as both a welcome challenge and a means to an end. The better use he made of his money, the more freedom he felt he had.

No matter where you are or where you go today, you're bombarded with advertising and spending temptations. Thus, I'm not surprised to observe that the vast majority of us could spend our money more wisely.

Telling people how and where to spend their money is a risky undertaking because most people like to spend money, and most people hate to be told what to do. You'll be glad to hear that I'm *not* going to tell you exactly where you must cut spending. I'm simply going to give you strategies that have worked for other people. The final decision for what to cut rests solely with you. Only you can decide what's important to you and what's dispensable — should you cut out your weekly poker games or cut back on your shoe collection?

I assume throughout these recommendations that you value your time. Therefore, I'm not going to tell you to scrimp and save by doing things like cutting open a tube of toothpaste so that you can use every last bit of it. And I won't tell you to have your spouse do your ironing to reduce your dry-cleaning bills (no point in having money in the bank if you lose your significant other).

Probably, part of the reason you spend money the way you do is that you're busy. Therefore, the recommendations in this chapter focus on methods that don't involve a lot of time but produce significant savings. In other words, these strategies provide bang for the buck. I believe in saving wherever possible, but small change is awfully heavy to cart around — better to save the big bucks.

Four Keys to Successful Spending

For most people, spending money is a whole lot easier and more fun than earning it. Far be it for me to tell you to stop having fun and to turn into a penny-pinching, stay-at-home miser. Of course you can spend money. But there's a world of difference between spending money *carelessly* and spending money *wisely*.

Spending too much and not spending wisely puts pressure on your income and your future need to continue working. Savings dwindle, debts may accumulate, and you can't achieve your financial goals.

Sometimes, when you dive into details too quickly, you miss the big picture. So before I jump into the specific areas where you can trim your budget, here are the four overall keys to successful spending. These four principles run through most of the recommendations coming up in this chapter.

Live within your means

Spending too much is a *relative* problem. Two people can each spend $30,000 per year yet have drastically different financial circumstances. How? Suppose that one of them earns $40,000 annually, and the other makes just $25,000. The $40,000 income earner saves $10,000 each year. The $25,000 earner accumulates $5,000 of new debt (or spends that amount from prior savings). Spend within your means.

Don't let others and their spending habits dictate yours. Certain people — you know who they are — bring out the big spender in you. Do something else with them besides shopping. If you can't find any other activity to share with them, try shopping with limited cash and no credit cards. That way, you can't overspend on impulse.

How much you can safely spend while still working toward your financial goals depends on what your goals are and where you are financially. Chapter 3 assists you with figuring how much you should be saving and, therefore, what you can afford to spend to accomplish your financial goals.

Find the best values

You can find high quality and low cost in the same product. Conversely, paying a high price is no guarantee that you're getting high quality. Cars are a good example. Whether you're buying a subcompact, sports car, or luxury four-door sedan, some cars are more fuel-efficient and cost less to maintain than rivals that carry the same sticker price.

And when you evaluate the cost of a product or service, you need to think in terms of total, long-term costs. Suppose that you're comparing the purchase of two used cars: the Solid Sedan, which costs $10,000, and the Clunker Convertible, which weighs in at $8,000. On the surface, the Convertible appears cheaper. However, the price that you pay for a car is but a small portion of what a car ultimately costs you. If the Convertible is more costly to operate, maintain, and insure over the years, it could end up costing you much more. Sometimes paying more up front for a higher-quality product or service ends up saving you money in the long run.

Those who are selling particular products and services may initially appear to have your best interests at heart if they steer you toward buying something that isn't costly. However, you may be in for a rude awakening once you discover the ongoing service, maintenance, and other fees you'll face in the years ahead. Salespeople are generally trained to pitch you a lower-cost product if you indicate that's what you're after.

I urge you to be especially careful shopping via the internet for the supposed purpose of saving money. You won't have much difficulty finding relatively low advertised prices on the internet. However, many people overlook shipping costs and the cost of their computer equipment and monthly internet service fees when weighing how great a deal they're really getting shopping online. Also, what about the possibility that you're not going to be happy with the product once it's delivered? Then, you're probably stuck with paying the shipping costs back to the online retailer, which you hope is still in business, not to mention the hassle and inconvenience of returning the product.

Don't waste money on brand names

Don't compromise on quality, especially where the quality is important to you. But don't be snookered into believing that brand-name products are better or worth a substantially higher price. Be suspicious of companies that spend gobs on image-oriented advertising. Why? Heavy advertising costs many dollars, and, as a consumer of those companies' products and services, you're paying for all that advertising.

All successful companies do some advertising — advertising is cost-effective and good business if it brings in enough new business. But consider the products and services and the claims that companies make.

Does a cola beverage really taste better if "It's the real thing" or "The choice of a new generation?" Consider all the silly labels and fluffy marketing of beers. Blind taste testing demonstrates little if any difference between the expensive brand name products and the cheaper, less heavily advertised ones.

Now, if you can't live without your Coca-Cola, Pepsi, or Samuel Adams and think that these products are head and shoulders above the rest, drink them to your heart's content. But question the importance of the name and image in the products you buy. Companies spend a lot of money creating and cultivating an image, which has zero real impact on how their products taste or perform.

"Branding" is used in many fields to sell overpriced, mediocre products and services to consumers. Take the lowly can of paint. Tests show some differences among different brands of paint. However, when you can buy high-quality paints for about $20 a gallon, do you really think that spending $100 or more per gallon on a can of paint blessed with the name of Ralph Lauren or Martha Stewart makes it better?

D/L Laboratories, a testing firm, compared these $100-per-gallon snooty paints to $20-per-gallon high-quality alternatives and found little difference, at least no difference that was worth paying for. In fact, one of the "gourmet" paints splattered more, had a less uniform sheen, didn't cover the surface as well, was more prone to run when applied, and emitted a high level of volatile organic compounds! Some other snooty brands didn't fare much better. As people in the trade can tell you, thanks to computer-based matching, if you find a particular color of paint you like in a highbrow line, match it and buy it in a high-quality but far less costly line.

Get your money back

Take a look around your home for items you've never used. Odds are, you have some, perhaps many. Returning such items to their retail origin can be cathartic. Doing so reduces your home's clutter and puts more money in your pocket.

Also, consider the last several times that you bought a product or service and didn't get what was promised. What did you do about it? Most people do nothing and let the derelict company off the hook. Why? I think there are several common reasons:

- ✔ **Low standards.** We've come to expect shoddy service and merchandise due to the common lousy experiences we've had.

- ✔ **Conflict avoidance.** Most people shun confrontation. It makes us tense and anxious and churns our stomachs.

- ✔ **Most companies don't make it easy for complainers to get their money back or obtain other satisfaction.** To get restitution from some companies, you need the tenacity and determination of a pit bull.

I've lived in many parts of the country, and I've even discovered some regional difference on these points. For example, in the New York metropolitan area, I've found worse (on average) products and services and company follow-up with dissatisfied consumers than in the San Francisco Bay area. Now, I'm sure you're not going to choose a location to live in based on the service ethic in that area! No matter where you live, you can increase your odds of getting what you expect when you spend your money by doing business with companies that:

- ✔ **Have fair return policies.** Don't purchase any product or service until you understand the company's return policy. Be especially wary of buying from companies that charge hefty "restocking" fees for returned merchandise or that simply don't allow returns at all. Reputable companies will offer full refunds and won't make you take store credit (although taking credit is fine if you're sure you'll use it soon and the company will still be around).

- ✔ **Can provide good references.** Suppose you're going to install a fence on your property and will for the first time be speaking with fencing contractors. You can sift out many inferior firms by asking each contractor you interview for at least three references of people in your local area who have had a fence installed in the past year or two.

- ✔ **Are committed to the type of product or service.** Suppose your chosen fencing contractor does a great job, and now that you're in the market for new gutters on your home, that same contractor says no problem, he does gutters, too. Although the path of least resistance would be for you to simply hire the same contractor for your gutters, you should inquire about how many gutters the contractor has installed and also interview some other firms that specialize in such work. Your fencing contractor might have only done a handful of gutter jobs and may not know as much about such work.

The Better Business Bureau is not objective or independent

The Better Business Bureau (BBB) states that its mission is "to promote and foster the highest ethical relationship between businesses and the public." The reality of a typical consumer's experience dealing with the BBB doesn't live up to the BBB's marketing.

"They don't go after local established businesses — they are funded by these same businesses. The BBB certainly has a good public relations image, better than what is warranted. They don't do all that much for consumers," says consumer advocate Ralph Nader.

"It's a business trade organization and each local BBB is basically independent like a franchise. By and large, when somebody has a problem with a company and they fill out a complaint form with the BBB, if the company is a member of the BBB, there's ample evidence that consumers often end up not being satisfied. The BBB protects their members," says John Bear, an author of consumer advocacy books, including *Send This Jerk the Bedbug Letter: How Companies, Politicians, and the Mass Media Deal With Complaints and How to Be a More Effective Complainer* (Ten Speed Press).

Particularly problematic among the BBB's pro-business practices are the company reports the BBB keeps on file. Even when a legitimate complaint like yours comes in, the BBB will consider it satisfactorily resolved even though you're quite unhappy and the company is clearly not working to satisfy the problems for which it is responsible.

Bear also cites examples of some truly troubling BBB episodes. In one case, he says, a diploma mill (Columbia State University) was being run in Louisiana, and the company was a member of the local BBB. "When complaints started coming in, the BBB's response was always that the company met their standards and that the complaints were resolved. The reality was that the complaints weren't satisfactorily resolved and it took about two years until complaints reached into the hundreds for the BBB to finally cancel the diploma mill's membership and give out a bland statement about complaints. Two months later, the FBI raided the company. Millions of consumers' dollars were lost because the BBB didn't do its job," says Bear.

The President of a South Florida BBB, the fifth largest in the country, according to Bear, was ultimately imprisoned for taking bribes from companies in exchange for maintaining favorable reports on file.

The truth about the BBB is sad because as state consumer protection agencies are being cut back and dissatisfied consumers are being shunted to the BBB, more people are in for unsatisfactory experiences dealing with an organization that does not go to bat for them.

Following the guidelines should greatly diminish your chances of having unhappy outcomes with products or services you buy. And here's another important tip: Whenever possible, pay with a credit card. Doing so enables you to dispute a charge within the first 60 days and gives you more leverage for getting your money back.

Should you find yourself not making progress trying to get compensation for a lousy product or service, here's what I recommend that you do:

- **Document.** Taking notes whenever you talk to someone at a company makes good sense to validate your case down the road, should problems develop. However, how realistic is it for any of us to take notes every time we buy a product or service? Obviously, the bigger the purchase and the more you have at stake, the more carefully you should document what you've been told and promised. In many cases, though, you probably won't start carefully noting each conversation until a conflict develops. Keep copies of companies' marketing literature since such documents often make promises or claims that companies fail to live up to in practice.

- **Escalate.** Some front-line personnel either aren't capable of resolving disputes or lack the authority to do so. No matter the cause, speak with a department supervisor and continue escalating from there. If you're still not making progress, lodge a complaint to whatever state regulatory agency (if any) oversees such companies. Also, be sure to tell your friends and colleagues not to do business with the company (and let the company know that you're doing this until your complaint is resolved to your satisfaction).

- **Litigate.** Okay, I'm half joking here — after all, you're not a big corporation with deep pockets! However, if all else fails and it's worth your time, consider taking the matter to small claims court if the company continues to be unresponsive. The maximum dollar limit that you may recover varies by state but is usually a few thousand dollars. For larger amounts than are allowed in small claims court in your state, you could, of course, hire an attorney and pursue the traditional legal channels. You could end up throwing away more of your time and money. Mediation and arbitration are generally better for you than following through on a lawsuit.

Eliminate fat

If you want to reduce your overall spending by, say, 10 percent, you could just cut all of your current expenditures by 10 percent. Or you can reach your 10 percent goal by cutting some categories a lot and others not at all. You need to set priorities and make choices about what you can and can't live without.

What you spend your money on is sometimes a matter of habit rather than what you really want or value. For example, some people shop at whatever stores are closest because they know where the stores are; they never bother to look elsewhere.

Eliminating fat doesn't necessarily mean cutting back on your purchases. Buying in bulk is a good example. Some stores specialize in selling larger packages or quantities of a product at a lower price because they save money on the packaging and handling. You save money by buying in bulk. And even though that 20-pound bag of rice means more cash up front than the little box of Uncle Ben's, every meal from now on that you make from the 20-pound bag will be a great deal cheaper than the meal out of the box would have been. (If you're single, shop with a friend and split the bulk purchases.)

Avoid buying on credit

As I discuss in Chapters 4 and 5, buying items that depreciate — such as cars, clothing, and vacations — on credit is hazardous to your long-term financial health. Buy today only what you can afford today. If you'll be forced to carry a debt for months or years on end, then you can't really afford what you're buying on credit today.

Without a doubt, "renting-to-own" is the most expensive way to buy. Here's how it works. You see a huge ad blaring "$12.95 for a VCR!"

Well, there's a big hitch: That's $12.95 per week, for many weeks. When all is said and done and paid, buying a $200 VCR through a rent-to-own store costs a typical buyer more than $750!

Welcome to the world of rent-to-own stores, which offer cash-poor consumers the ability to lease consumer items and, at the end of the lease, an option to buy. Many items can be bought on this basis. Although this may be more of a troubling sign of the times, increasing numbers of stores are reported to offer rent-to-own engagement rings! One rent-to-own store manager said, "We do get some people with cold feet."

If you think paying an 18-percent interest rate on a credit card is expensive, imagine what you'll think of renting-to-own when I tell you that the effective interest rate charged on many purchases exceeds 100 percent and in some cases 200 percent or more! Renting-to-own makes buying on a credit card look like a deal.

I'm not sharing this information with you to encourage your buying on credit cards but to point out what a rip-off renting-to-own is. Such stores prey on cashless consumers who either can't get credit cards or don't understand how expensive renting-to-own really is.

Consumer credit is expensive and reinforces a bad habit: spending more than you can afford.

Strategies for Reducing Your Spending

Please keep in mind as you read through the following ideas that some of these strategies will make sense for you, and some of them won't. Start your spending reduction plan with the ones that come easily first. Work your way through them. Keep a list of the options that are more challenging for you — ones that require more of a sacrifice but that you can make work if necessary to achieve your spending and savings goals.

No matter which of the ideas in this chapter you choose for yourself, rest assured that keeping your budget lean and mean pays enormous dividends. After you implement a spending reduction strategy, you'll reap the benefits for years to come. Take a look at Figure 6-1: For every $1,000 that you can shave from your annual spending (that's just $83 per month), see how much more money you'll have down the road. (This chart assumes that you invest your new-found savings in a tax-favored retirement account and average 10 percent per year returns on your investments and that you're in a moderate combined federal and state tax bracket of 35 percent — see Chapter 7 for information on tax brackets.)

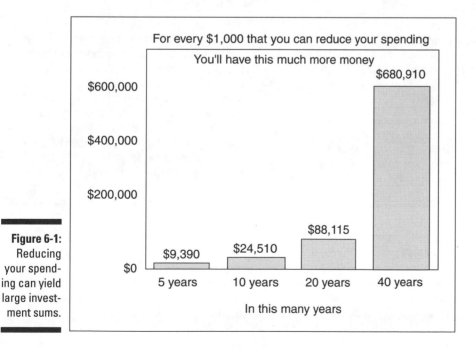

Figure 6-1:
Reducing your spending can yield large investment sums.

Budgeting to save more money

When most people hear the word *budgeting*, they usually think unpleasant thoughts — and, like dieting, rightfully so. But budgeting can help you move from knowing how much you spend on various things to successfully reducing your spending.

The first step in the process of budgeting, or planning your future spending, is to analyze where your current spending is going (refer to Chapter 4). After you do that, calculate how much more you'd like to save each month. Then comes the harder part: deciding where to make cuts in your spending.

Suppose that you're currently not saving any of your monthly income and that you want to save 10 percent. If you can save and invest money through a tax-sheltered retirement account such as an employer's 401(k) or 403(b), or a self-employed plan such as a SEP-IRA, Keogh, or your own IRA, you don't actually need to cut your spending by 10 percent to reach a savings goal of 10 percent (of your gross income).

When you contribute money to a tax-deductible retirement account, you reduce your federal and state taxes. If you're a moderate income earner paying, say, 35 percent in federal and state taxes on your marginal income, you actually only need to reduce your spending by 6.5 percent to save 10 percent. The "other" 3.5 percent of savings comes from the lowering of your taxes. (The higher your tax bracket, the less you need to cut your spending to reach a particular savings goal.)

So to boost your savings rate to 10 percent, go through your current spending, category by category, until you come up with enough proposed cuts to reduce your spending by 6.5 percent. Make your cuts in those areas that will be the least painful and where you're getting the least value from your current level of spending. Even if you don't have access to a tax-deductible retirement account, budgeting still involves the same process.

Rather than examining your current expenses and making cuts from that starting point, another method of budgeting involves starting completely from scratch. Ask yourself how much you'd like to be spending on different categories. The advantage of this approach is that it doesn't allow your current spending levels to constrain your thinking. You'll most likely be amazed at the discrepancies between what you think you should be spending and what you actually are spending in certain categories.

Food

One way to reduce your food expenditures is to stop eating. However, this tends to make you weak and dizzy, so it's probably not a viable long-term strategy. The following culinary strategies will keep you on your feet — and perhaps even improve your health — for less money.

Join a wholesale superstore

Superstores such as Costco and Sam's Club enable you to buy groceries in bulk at wholesale prices. And, contrary to popular perception, you *don't* have to buy 1,000 rolls of toilet paper at once — just 24.

I've done price comparisons between these kinds of stores and retail grocery stores and have found that wholesalers charge 30 to 40 percent less for the exact same stuff — all without the hassle of clipping coupons or hunting for which store has the best price on crackers this month!

In addition to saving you lots of money, buying in bulk means that you make fewer shopping trips. You'll have more supplies around your humble abode — so there is less need to eat out (which is costly) or make trips to the local grocer, who may be really nice but who charges you out the wazoo.

Perishables run the risk of living up to their name, so don't buy what you can't use. Repackage bulk packs into smaller quantities for the freezer if possible. If you're single, shop with a friend or two and split the order.

Be careful shopping at the warehouse clubs — you might be tempted to buy things you don't really need. These stores carry all sorts of items, including wide-screen TVs, computers, furniture, clothing, complete sets of baseball cards, and giant canisters of M&Ms and biscotti — beware! Try not to make impulse purchases, and be especially careful when you have kids in tow.

Check your local phone directory for superstores. Costco has a toll-free number to help you locate a store nearest you (800-774-2678).

Most of these stores charge a small membership fee and are, frankly, somewhat of a hassle to join. Costco, for example, charges $35 per year and asks for proof that you're a small-business owner or manager or that you work for a nonprofit health-care organization, utility, bank, savings and loan, airline, or the media. You can also join if you hold a professional license or are a member of a credit union.

The reason you need to jump through these hoops is that if *anyone* could join the warehouse stores, retailers who sell similar merchandise would be upset. Anyone could get the better deals that the warehouse clubs pass on from manufacturers. That's why people with a potential business reason can join.

The reality, though, is that if you really want to join, you can. Many community organizations that you may belong to, such as the YMCA/YWCA or Big Brothers/Big Sisters, can get you a membership. A small-business owner whom you know well can sponsor you. Or you can shop with a friend who's a member. Don't give up — the savings you can reap make joining a warehouse club well worth the hassle.

Eat out more frugally

Eating meals out or getting take-out can be a time-saver but can rack up big bills if done too often and lavishly. Eating out is a luxury — think of it as hiring someone to shop, cook, and clean up for you. Of course, some people hate to cook or don't have the time, space, or energy to do much in the kitchen. If this is you, choose restaurants carefully and order from the menu selectively. Here are a couple of tips:

- ✔ **Avoid beverages, especially alcohol.** Most restaurants make big profits on beverages. Drink water instead. (Water is also healthful and reduces the likelihood of your wanting a nap after a big meal.)

- ✔ **Order vegetarian.** Vegetarian dishes, including pasta and rice dishes, generally cost less than meat-based entrees (and are generally healthier for you).

I don't want to be a killjoy. I'm not saying that you should live on bread and water. You can have dessert — heck, have some wine, too! But perhaps not every time. Try eating appetizers and dessert at home, where they're a lot less expensive (especially if you follow my advice on shopping for food).

Mom was right about eating those vegetables

Not only is meat expensive, but it is coming under increasing scrutiny as being bad for your health. In a landmark report entitled "The Surgeon General's Report on Nutrition and Health" (produced under former U.S. Surgeon General C. Everett Koop, M.D.), reliance on a meat- and dairy-based diet — with its fat and cholesterol — was found to be the cause of the majority of premature deaths in the United States. In fact, five out of the top ten causes of death — heart disease, certain types of cancer, stroke, diabetes, and arteriosclerosis — are caused largely by Americans' poor diets.

In developing countries that are poorer economically than the U.S., people eat mainly grains, beans, and vegetables and have significantly lower rates of heart disease and diet-related cancers, such as cancer of the prostate and colon.

Meat is expensive, so the less meat you eat, the more money you save. Even if you choose to merely reduce your meat consumption rather than eliminate it, you can still save significant dough. Should you decide to eliminate meat from your diet, don't try to shift from burgers, pork chops, and meat loaf to tofu and sprouts overnight. Make changes in your diet gradually. For example, I first gave up beef, pork, and lamb, but I still eat some chicken, fish, and low-fat dairy products.

Besides saving you money and bolstering your health, a vegetarian diet is also friendlier to the environment. Raising cattle requires a great deal more land and water than growing vegetables does. Here's a tidbit sure to liven up a dull cocktail party conversation: Livestock also produce a great deal of flatulence, which adds more methane to the atmosphere. 100 million tons of the world's annual methane emissions — 20 percent of the total — are from cattle!

Shelter

Housing and all the costs associated with it (utilities, furniture, appliances, and, if you're a homeowner, maintenance and repairs) can gobble a large chunk of your monthly income. I'm not suggesting that you live in an igloo or teepee (even though they're probably less costly and more energy-efficient), but people often overlook common opportunities to save money in this category.

Don't take rent for granted

Rent can take up a sizable chunk of your monthly take-home pay. Many people consider rent to be a fixed and inflexible part of their expenses. It's not. Here are some things you can do to cut it down in size:

- ✔ **Move to a lower-cost rental.** Of course, a lower-cost rental may not be as nice — it may be smaller or lack a private parking spot or be in a less popular locale. Make the trade-off and shave $50 to $100 or more off your monthly rent. Don't forget: The less you spend renting, the more you can save toward buying your own place. Just be sure to factor in all the costs of a new location, including possibly higher commuting costs.

- ✔ **Share a rental.** Living alone has some benefits, but financially speaking, it's a luxury. Rent a larger place with roommates. Your rental costs should go way down, and you'll get more home for your rental dollars. You have to be in a sharing mood, though. Roommates can be a hassle at times but can also be a plus — you meet all sorts of new people and have someone else to blame if the kitchen's a mess.

- ✔ **Negotiate your rental increases.** Every year, like clockwork, your landlord bumps up your rent a certain percentage. If your local rental market is soft or your living quarters are deteriorating, stand up for yourself! You have more leverage and power than you probably realize. A smart landlord doesn't want to lose good tenants who pay rent on time. Filling vacancies takes time and money. State your case: You've been a responsible tenant, and your research shows comparable rentals going for less. Crying poor may help, too. At the very least, if you can't stave off the rent increase, maybe you can wrangle some improvements to the place.

- ✔ **Buy rather than rent.** Purchasing your own place can be costly, yes, but in the long run, owning should be cheaper than renting, and you'll have something to show for it in the end. If you purchase real estate with a 30-year fixed-rate mortgage, your mortgage payment (which is your biggest ownership expense) remains constant. Only your property taxes, maintenance, and insurance costs are exposed to the vagaries of inflation.

  As a renter, your entire monthly housing cost can rise with increases in the cost of living (unless you are the beneficiary of a rent-controlled apartment). See Chapter 14 to learn about buying real estate, even if you're short on cash.

Saving on your phone bill

Telephone expenses are a good example of not needing to reduce your usage to save money. Just adjust when you place your calls. In most areas, the most expensive time to place local toll or long-distance calls is weekdays between 8 a.m. and 5 p.m. From 5 p.m. to 11 p.m. is cheaper, and the cheapest time to call is late at night (usually 11 p.m. to 8 a.m.), which can save you 50-60 percent (and as a bonus, you may get the thrill of waking up the other party). This bargain rate is also available all weekend, usually beginning after 11 p.m. Friday night and ending Sunday at 5 p.m.

You may be able to save money on your toll calls by switching companies. Despite (or perhaps because of) the millions of dollars that AT&T pours into advertising to persuade you that its quality is better and prices are comparable, consider moving to MCI Worldcom (800-444-3333) or Sprint (800-877-4000). Quality is virtually the same from company to company, and AT&T is more expensive in most cases. Check with your long distance provider to be sure that you're on the lowest cost calling program given the patterns of your calls.

Sometimes sending a thoughtful letter is cheaper, more appreciated, and longer lasting than placing a phone call. Just block out an hour, grab a pen and paper, and rediscover the lost art form of letter writing. Formulating your thoughts on paper can be clarifying and therapeutic to boot. Computer users may find that they save money as well by sending e-mail.

Save on homeowner expenses

As every homeowner knows, houses suck money. You should be especially careful to watch your money in this area of your budget.

✔ **Know what you can afford.** Don't make the mistake of overstretching when buying a home. Whether you're on the verge of buying your first home or trading up to a more costly property, crunch some realistic numbers before you jump. When too little money is left over for your other needs and wants — such as taking trips, eating out, enjoying hobbies, or saving for retirement — your new dream house may become a financial prison.

Calculate how much you can afford to spend monthly on a home by figuring your other needs first. (Doing the exercises in Chapter 4 about where you're spending your money and in Chapter 3 about saving for retirement will help.)

Although real estate can be a good long-term investment, you can end up pouring a large portion of your discretionary dollars into your home. In addition to decorating and remodeling, some people feel the need to trade up to a bigger home every few years. Of course, after they're in their new home, the remodeling and renovation cycle simply begins again, which costs even more money. Appreciate what you have and remember that homes are to live in, not museums for display. If you have children, why waste a lot of money on expensive furnishings that take up valuable space and require you to constantly nag your kids to tread carefully? And don't covet — the world will always have people with bigger, nicer houses and toys than you have.

✔ **Rent out a room.** Since selling your home to buy a less expensive place can be a big hassle, consider taking in a tenant to reduce your housing expenses. Check out the renter thoroughly: Get references, run a credit report, and talk about ground rules and expectations before sharing your space. Don't forget to check with your insurance company to see whether your homeowner's policy needs adjustments to cover potential liability from renting.

✔ **Refinance your mortgage.** This step may seem like common sense, but surprisingly, many people don't keep up-to-date on mortgage rates. If interest rates are lower than when you obtained your current mortgage, you may be able to save money by refinancing (see Chapter 14 for more information).

✔ **Appeal your property-tax assessment.** You may be able to save money by appealing your assessment if you bought during a period when housing prices were higher in your area than they are now,. Also, if you live in a region of the country where your assessment is based upon how the local assessor valued the property (rather than what you paid for your home), your home may be over-assessed. Check with your local assessor's office for the appeals procedure to follow. You generally need to prove that your property is worth less today than when you bought it or that the assessor incorrectly valued your property. In the first case, an appraiser's recent evaluation of your property will do — you may already have one if you refinanced your mortgage recently. In the latter case, review how the assessor valued your property compared with similar ones nearby — mistakes happen.

✔ **Reduce utility costs.** Sometimes you have to spend money to save money. Old refrigerators, for example, can waste a lot of electricity. Insulate to save on heating and air-conditioning bills. Install water flow regulators in showerheads and toilet bowls. When planting your yard, don't select water-guzzling plants, and keep your lawn area reasonable. Even if you don't live in an area susceptible to droughts, why waste water unnecessarily (which isn't free)? Recycle — recycling means less garbage, which translates into lower trash bills and benefits the environment by reducing landfill.

Transportation

America is a car-driven society. In most other countries, cars are a luxury. More than 90 percent of the people in the rest of the world can't afford a new American car. If more people in the United States thought of cars as a luxury,

Americans might have far fewer financial problems (and accidents). Cars not only pollute the air and clog the highways but also cost you a bundle. Purchasing the best car you can and using it wisely can save you big dollars. So can using other transportation alternatives.

Contrary to advertising slogans, cars are not built to last — car manufacturers don't want you to stick with the same car year after year. New models are constantly introduced with new features and styling changes. Getting a new set of wheels every few years is an expensive luxury.

Don't try to keep up with the Joneses as they show off their new cars every year — for all you know, they're running themselves into financial ruin just trying to impress you. Let your neighbors admire you for your thriftiness and wisdom instead.

Research before you buy a car

When you buy a car, not only do you pay the initial sticker price, but you're also on the hook for gas, insurance, registration fees, maintenance, and repairs. Don't compare simple sticker prices; think about total, long-term costs of ownership.

Speaking of total costs, remember that you are also trusting your life to the car. With about 40,000 Americans killed in auto accidents annually (about half of which are caused by drunk drivers), safety should be an important consideration as well. Air bags, for example, may save your life.

The *Consumer Reports Buying Guide* summarizes all the latest information on cars and includes a list of the most reliable used cars in various price categories. For you data jocks, *The Complete Car Cost Guide* (published by Intellichoice) is packed with information about all categories of ownership costs, warranties, and dealer costs. The guide rates new cars based on total ownership costs. But can you *really* afford a new car?

Buy your car with cash

The main reason people end up spending more than they can afford on a car is that they finance it. As I discuss in Chapter 1 and elsewhere in this book, you should avoid borrowing money for consumption purchases, especially for items that depreciate in value like cars. A car is most definitely *not* an investment.

In most situations, leasing is even more expensive than borrowing money to buy a car. Leasing is like a long-term car rental. We all know how well rental cars get treated — well, leased cars are treated just as well, which is one of the reasons leasing is so costly.

Unfortunately, the practice of leasing cars or buying them on credit is increasingly becoming the norm in our society. This is certainly attributable to a lot of misinformation spread by car dealers and, in some cases, the media.

Consider the magazine article entitled "Rewards of Car Leasing." Compared to buying, the article claims, leasing is a great deal. Placed immediately next to the article were ads for auto dealers advertising auto leasing. The magazine, by the way, is *free* to subscribers — which means that 100 percent of its revenue comes from advertisers such as auto dealers. Also be aware that because of the influence of advertising (and ignorance), leasing is widely endorsed on internet sites that purport to provide information on cars.

Replace high-cost cars

Maybe you've realized by now that your car is too expensive to operate because of insurance, gas, and maintenance costs. Or maybe you bought too much car — people who lease or borrow money to buy a car frequently buy a far more expensive car than they can realistically afford.

Nothing says that you're stuck with it until the bitter end. *Dump* your expensive car and get something more financially manageable. The sooner you switch, the more money you'll save. Getting rid of a car on a lease is more of a challenge, but it can be done. I had one client who, when he lost his job and needed to slash expenses, convinced the dealer (by writing a letter to the owner) to take the leased car back.

But I can't buy a new car for cash!

"Come on, Eric," you may be thinking, "how can I and most wage earners today afford to buy a new car for cash — who has that kind of dough sitting around?!"

Some people feel that it's unreasonable of me to expect them to buy a new car using cash. After all, many publications, which not uncoincidentally derive great advertising revenue from auto dealers and lenders, effectively endorse and encourage loaning and leasing to buy a car.

If you knew me, you'd know that I'm a reasonable kinda guy. Believe me, I'm trying to look out for your best long-term financial interests. Please consider the following:

✔ If you lack sufficient cash to buy a new car, I say "DON'T BUY A NEW CAR!" Most of the world's population can't even afford a car, let alone a new one! Buy a car that you can afford — which for most people is not a new one.

✔ Don't fall for the new car buying rationalization that says that buying a used car means lots of maintenance, repair expenses, and problems. Do your homework and buy a good, used car and have the best of both worlds. A good used car costs less to buy and should cost you less to operate thanks to lower insurance costs.

✔ A fancy car is not needed to impress people for business purposes. Some people I know say that they absolutely must drive a brand spanking nice new car to set the right impression for business purposes. I'm not going to tell you how to manage your career, but I will ask you to consider that if clients and others see you driving an expensive new car, they may think that you spend money wastefully or that you're getting rich off of them!

Keep cars to a minimum

I've seen households that have one car per person — four people, four cars! Some people have a "weekend" car that they use only on days off! Maintaining two or more cars for most households is an expensive extravagance. Try to find ways to make do with fewer cars.

One of the ways to move beyond the confines of a car is to ride buses or trains or carpool to work. Some employers give incentives for taking public transit to work, and some cities and counties offer assistance in setting up vanpools or carpools along popular routes. By leaving the driving to someone else, you can catch up on reading or just relax on the way to and from work. And you're doing your share to cut down on pollution.

When you're considering where to live and the cost of living in different areas, don't forget to consider commuting costs. One advantage of living close to work, or at least close to public transit systems, is that you may be able to make do with fewer cars in your household or with no car at all.

Buy commuter passes

In many areas, you can purchase train, bus, or subway passes to reduce the cost of commuting. Many toll bridges also have booklets of tickets that you can buy at a discount. Some booths don't advertise that they offer these plans — maybe as a strategy to keep revenues up.

Buy regular unleaded gas

A number of studies have shown that "superduperultrapremium" gasoline is not worth the extra expense. Fill up your tank when you're on a shopping trip to the warehouse wholesalers (discussed earlier in this chapter). These superstores are usually located in lower-cost areas, so the gas is usually cheaper there, too. Also, don't use credit cards to buy your gas if you have to pay a higher price to do so.

Service your car regularly

Sure, servicing your car (for example, changing the oil every 5,000 miles) costs money, but it saves you dough in the long run by extending the operating life of the car. Servicing your car also reduces the chances that your car will crap out in the middle of nowhere, which requires a humongous towing charge to a service station. Even worse is stalling on the freeway during peak rush hour and having thousands of angry commuters stuck behind you.

Clothing and accessories

Given the amount of money that some people spend on clothing and related accessories, I've come to believe that people in nudist colonies must be great savers! But you probably live among the clothed mainstream of American society, so here's a short list of economizing ideas:

- ✔ **Avoid dry-cleanables.** When you buy clothing, try to stick with cottons and machine-washable synthetics rather than wools or silks that require dry cleaning. Check labels before you buy stuff. Despite his tremendous business success, Jack Bogle, founder of the thrifty Vanguard Group of mutual funds, wore wool ties to work. He proudly declared that his ties were more *efficient,* and he is right. They last longer and require less cleaning than silk ties!

- ✔ **Don't chase the latest fashions.** Fashion designers and retailers are constantly working to tempt you to buy more. Don't do it. Ignore publications that pronounce this season's look. In most cases, you simply don't need to buy racks of new clothes or an entire new wardrobe yearly. If your clothes are not lasting at least ten years, you're probably tossing them before their time or buying low durability clothing.

    Fashion, as defined by what people wear, changes quite slowly. In fact, the classics don't ever go out of style. If you want the effect of a new wardrobe every year, store last year's purchases away next year and then bring them out the year after! Or rotate your clothing inventory every third year. Set your own fashion standards. Buy basic, buy classic — don't let fashion gurus be your guide, or you'll have the biggest wardrobe in the poorhouse.

- ✔ **Minimize accessories.** Shoes, jewelry, handbags, and the like can gobble large amounts of money. Again, how many of these accessory items do you really need? The answer is probably very few, and each one should last many years.

Go to your closet or jewelry box and tally up the loot. What else could you have done with all that cash? See things you regret buying or forgot you even had? Don't make the same mistake again. Have a garage sale if you have a lot of stuff that you don't want.

Debt repayment

In Chapter 5, I discuss strategies to reduce the cost of carrying consumer debt. The *best* way to reduce the costs of such debt is to avoid it in the first place when you're making consumption purchases. You can avoid consumer debt by eliminating your access to credit or by limiting your purchase of consumer items that you can pay off each month. Remember, only borrow for long-term investments. (Refer to Chapter 1 for more information.)

Don't keep a credit card that charges you an annual fee, especially if you pay your balance in full each month. Many no-fee credit cards exist — and some even offer you a benefit for using them:

- ✔ Discover Card (800-347-2683) rebates up to 1 percent of purchases in cash.
- ✔ GM Card (800-846-2273) gives credits worth 5 percent of charges toward the purchase of a GM-manufactured vehicle (Saabs, Saturns, and EV1s are excluded).
- ✔ AFBA Industrial Bank (800-776-2265).
- ✔ USAA Federal Savings (800-922-9092).

Only consider the above cards if you pay your balance in full each month because these cards levy high interest rates for balances carried month-to-month. There's not much point in earning a small reward only to have it negated by greater interest charges.

If you have a credit card that charges an annual fee, try calling the company and saying that you want to cancel the card because you can get a competitor's card without an annual fee. Many banks will agree to waive the fee on the spot. Some require you to call back yearly to cancel the fee — a hassle that can be avoided by getting a true no-fee card.

Some cards that charge an annual fee and offer credits toward a purchase, such as a car or airline ticket, may be worth your while if you pay your credit card bill in full each month and charge $10,000 or more annually. *Note:* Be careful, however, because some people are tempted to charge more on a card that rewards them for more purchases. Spending more than you would otherwise to rack up bonuses defeats the purpose of getting the credits.

Indulgences

Having fun, taking time out for R & R, and lavishing gifts on those you love can be money well spent. But in these areas, financial extravagance can wreck an otherwise good budget.

Gifts

Think about how you approach buying gifts throughout the year — and especially during the holidays. I know people who spend so much money on credit cards during the winter holidays that it takes them until late spring or summer to pay their debts off!

Although I don't want to deny your loved ones gifts from the heart — or you the pleasure of giving them — spend wisely. Homemade gifts are less costly to the giver and may be dearer to recipients. Many children actually love durable, classic, basic toys that aren't necessarily advertised on Saturday morning TV. If the TV commercials dictate your kids' desires, maybe it's time to toss the TV or set better rules for what the kids are allowed to watch.

Perhaps because we don't like to feel cheap when buying a gift, some people forget their thrifty shopping habits when gift buying. As with other purchases you make, however, careful attention to where and what you buy can save you significant dollars. And don't make the mistake of equating the value of a gift with its dollar cost.

And, here's a good suggestion for getting rid of those old, unwanted gifts. One of the most entertaining and memorable holiday parties I've attended involved a "white elephant" gift exchange: Everyone brought a wrapped, unwanted gift from the past and exchanged it with someone else. Once the gifts were opened, trading was allowed.

Entertainment

Entertainment doesn't have to cost a great deal of money if you adjust your expectations. Especially in metropolitan areas, many movies, theaters, and museums offer discount prices on certain days and times. Same goes for restaurants.

Cultivate some interests and hobbies that are free or low-cost. Seeing friends, reading, hiking, and playing sports can be good for your finances as well as your health.

Vacations

For many people, vacations are a luxury. For others, regular vacations are essential parts of their routine. Regardless of how you recharge your batteries, remember that vacations are not investments, so you shouldn't borrow through credit cards to finance your travels. After all, how relaxed will you feel when you have to pay all those bills?

Try vacations that are shorter and closer to home. Have you been to a state or national park recently? Take a vacation at home and see the sights in your local area. Great places probably exist within 200 miles of you that you've always wanted to see but haven't visited for one reason or another. Or just block out some time and do what my cats do: Take lots of naps and just hang out around your home.

When you do travel far and are heading for a popular destination, travel during the off-season for the best deals on airfares and hotels. Keep an eye out for discounts and "bought-but-unable-to-use" tickets advertised in your local paper. A number of internet sites such as www.priceline.com can help you find low-cost travel options as well. Seniors generally qualify for special fares at most airlines — ask the airline what programs it offers.

Also, be sure to shop around even when working with a travel agent. Travel agents work on commission, so they may not work hard to find you the best deals. Tour packages, when they meet your interests and needs, can also save you money. If you have flexible travel plans, courier services can cut your travel costs significantly (but make sure that the company is reputable).

Personal care

You have to take care of yourself, but as with anything else, there are ways to do it that are expensive, and there are ways that can save you money.

- **Hair care.** One way to save money in this category is to go bald. I'm working on this one myself. In the meantime, if you have hair to be trimmed, a number of no-frills, low-cost hair-cutting joints can do the job. Supercuts is one of the larger chains. I know that some of you will insist that your stylist is the only one who can manage your hair the way you like it. At the prices charged by some of the trendy hair places, you have to really adore what they do to justify the cost. Consider going periodically to a no-frills stylist for maintenance after getting a fabulous cut at a more expensive place. If you're daring, you could try getting your hair cut at a local training school. For parents of young children, a great time and money saver is to buy a simple-to-use home hair electric shaving kit — no more agonizing trips with little ones to have their hair cut by a "stranger," and the kit pays for itself after just a couple of cuts!

- **Other personal-care services.** As long as we're on the subject of outward beauty, I have to say that in my personal opinion, the billions spent annually on cosmetics are a waste of money (not to mention all the time spent applying and removing it). Women look fine and in most cases better without makeup. And having regular facials, pedicures, and manicures can add up quickly.

- **Health club expenses.** Expenditure on exercise is almost always money well spent. But you don't have to belong to a trendy club to get benefits. If you belong to a gym or club for the social scene, whether it's for dating or business purposes, you have to judge whether it's worth the cost.

Low-cost exercise facilities are everywhere — look for them anywhere you see children and young adults. Local schools, colleges, and universities almost always have tennis courts, running tracks, swimming pools, basketball courts, and exercise rooms and often provide instruction. Community centers offer fitness programs and classes, too. Metropolitan areas that have lots of health clubs undoubtedly have the widest range of options and prices. *Note:* When figuring the cost of membership, be sure to factor in the cost of travel to and from these clubs and any parking costs (and the realistic likelihood of going there regularly to work out).

Don't forget that lots of healthy exercise can be done indoors or out, free of charge. Isn't biking in the park at sunset more fun than peddling away on a stationary bike, anyway? You may want to buy some basic gym equipment for use at home. Be careful though: Lots of rowing machines and free weights languish in a closet after their first week at home.

Look for value in the publications to which you subscribe

Everyone has a favorite and not-so-favorite publication. Some people don't realize how much they spend on publications, partly because they've never tallied up the cost.

Take *The New York Times.* Actually, consider not taking it. At $7.20 per week in the New York Metro area and $9.50 per week elsewhere, that's a whopping $374 and $494 per year! Most areas have decent newspapers that cost a fraction of these amounts. You can also keep up with news and events through weekly news magazines such as *Newsweek* — just $41 per year.

As I discuss elsewhere in this book, "free" publications are often driven by advertisers, so I don't encourage you to load up on them. But take a close look at the total amount you spend on publications and how much each one costs. Keep the ones that you're getting sufficient value from and cancel the rest. You can always read them at your local library.

If you took the money that you're spending on *The New York Times,* for example, and invested it in your retirement account and earned a mere 10 percent per year, in 25 years you'd have more than $55,000 (New York metro subscribers) or more than $74,000 (everyone else in the country)! And this assumes that they don't increase the price of their paper, which they always do. Knowing these figures, you'd really have to feel you're getting good value from *The New York Times* to keep subscribing!

Personal business

Accountants, lawyers, and financial advisors can be worth their expense if they're good. But be wary of professionals who create or perpetuate work and have conflicts of interest in their recommendations.

The best way to use professionals for tax, legal, or financial advice is to get organized before you meet with them. Do some background research to evaluate their strengths and biases. Make sure that you set goals and estimate fees in advance so that you know what you're getting yourself into.

Computer and printed resources (see Chapters 19 and 20) can be useful, low-cost alternatives to hiring professionals.

Medical care

Health care is a big topic nowadays, and the cost of it is going up fast. Your health insurance — if you have health insurance, that is — probably covers most of your health-care needs (Chapter 16 explains how to shop for health insurance). But many plans require you to pay for certain expenses out of your own pocket.

Medical care and supplies are like any other services and products — price and quality vary. And medicine in the United States, like any other profession, is a business, and a conflict of interest exists whenever the person recommending treatment benefits financially from providing that treatment. Many studies have documented unnecessary surgeries and other medical procedures.

When seeking health insurance, remember — as with any other service or product that you buy — shop around. And don't take any one physician's advice as gospel. Always get a second opinion for any major surgery. Most health insurance plans, out of economic self-interest, require one anyway.

Therapy can be useful and even lifesaving. Have a frank talk with your therapist about how much total time and money you can expect to spend and what kind of results you can expect. As with any professional service, a competent therapist should be able to give you a straight answer if he or she is looking out for your psychological *and* financial well being.

Alternative medicine (holistic, for example) is gaining attention because of its focus on preventive care and treatment of the whole body or person. Although alternative medicine can be dangerous to undertake if you are in critical condition, alternative treatment for many forms of chronic pain or disease may be worth your investigation. Alternative medicine may lead to better *and* lower-cost health care.

If you must take certain drugs on an ongoing basis and pay for them out-of-pocket, ordering through a mail-order company can bring down your costs and be more convenient for refilling prescriptions. Your health plan may be able to provide more information about this. The following mail order companies also offer generic drugs, which are medically equivalent to brand-name drugs but cost a lot less:

- ✔ Medi-Mail Pharmacy (800-922-3444)
- ✔ AARP Pharmacy Services (800-456-2277)

Examine your employer's benefit plans. Take advantage of being able to put away a portion of your income before taxes to pay for out-of-pocket health care expenses. Be careful, though, to understand "use it or lose it" provisions.

Insurance

Insurance is a vast mine field. Part IV explains the different coverages, suggests what to buy and avoid, and reveals how to save on policies. The following are the most common ways people waste money on insurance.

✔ **Keeping low deductibles.** The *deductible* is the amount of a loss that must come out of your pocket. On an auto insurance policy, for example, if your collision deductible is $100 and you get into an accident, you pay for the first $100 of damage, and your insurance company picks up the rest. Low deductibles, however, translate into much higher premiums for you. In the long run, you should save money with a higher deductible, even factoring in the potential for greater out-of-pocket costs to you when you do have a claim. Insurance should protect you from economic disaster. Don't get carried away with a really high deductible, though, which could cause financial hardship if you do have a claim and lack much savings.

If you have a lot of claims, your insurance premiums will escalate, so you still don't come out ahead with lower deductibles. Plus, low deductibles mean more claim forms to file for small losses (creating more hassle). Filing an insurance claim is usually not an enjoyable or quick experience.

✔ **Covering small potential losses or unnecessary needs.** You shouldn't buy insurance for anything that wouldn't be a financial catastrophe if you had to pay for it out of your own pocket. Although the postal service isn't perfect, insuring inexpensive gifts sent in the mail is not worth the price. Buying dental or home warranty plans also doesn't make financial sense for the same reason. And, if no one is dependent on your income, then you don't need to buy life insurance either (who will be around to collect when you're gone?).

✔ **Failing to shop around.** Rates vary *tremendously* from insurer to insurer. In Part IV, I recommend the best companies to call first for quotes and other cost saving strategies.

Taxes

Taxes probably represent one of the largest — if not *the* largest — of your expenditures. (So why is it last here? You will soon see.)

Retirement savings plans are one of the best and simplest ways to reduce your tax burden. I explain more about retirement savings plans in Chapter 11. Unfortunately, most people can't take full advantage of these plans because they spend everything they make. So not only do they have less savings, they also pay higher income taxes — a double whammy.

I've attended many presentations where a fast-talking investment guy in an expensive suit lectures about the importance of saving for retirement and explains how to invest your savings. Yet details and tips about finding the money to save (the hard part for most people) are left to the imagination.

In order to take advantage of the tax savings that come through retirement savings plans, you must first spend less than you earn. Only then can you afford to contribute to these plans. That's why the first part of this chapter is all about strategies to reduce your spending.

Another benefit of spending less and saving more is reduced sales tax. When you buy most consumer products, you pay sales tax. Therefore, the less money you spend and the more you save in retirement accounts, the more you reduce income *and* sales taxes. (See Chapter 7 for other tax-reduction strategies.)

Costly addictions

Human beings are creatures of habit. We all have habits that we wish we didn't have, and breaking those habits can be very difficult. Costly habits are the worst. The following tidbits may nudge you in the right direction toward breaking your own financially draining habits.

✔ **Kick the smoking habit.** Despite the decline in smoking over the past few decades, about 25 percent of all Americans still smoke. Using smokeless tobacco, which also causes long-term health problems, is on the increase. Americans spend more than $45 billion annually on tobacco products — that's a staggering $900 per year per tobacco user. The increased medical costs and lost work time costs are even greater, estimated at more than $50 billion every year. Of course, if you continue to smoke, you may eliminate the need to save for retirement.

Check with local hospitals for smoking-cessation programs. The American Lung Association (check your local phone directory) also offers Freedom from Smoking clinics around the country. The National Cancer Institute (800-4CANCER) and the Office on Smoking and Health at the Centers for Disease Control (1600 Clifton Road, Atlanta, GA 30333; phone 770-488-5703) offer free information guides containing effective methods to stop smoking.

✔ **Stop abusing alcohol and other drugs.** Nearly three-quarters of a million Americans seek treatment annually for alcoholism or drug abuse. These addictive behaviors, like spending, transcend all educational and socioeconomic lines in our society. Even so, studies have demonstrated that only one in seven alcoholic or drug abusers seek help. Three of the ten leading causes of death — cirrhosis of the liver, accidents, and suicides — are associated with excessive alcohol consumption.

The National Clearinghouse for Alcohol and Drug Information (800-729-6686) can refer you to local treatment programs such as Alcoholics Anonymous. It also provides pamphlets and other literature about various types of substance abuse. The National Substance Abuse Information and Treatment Hotline (800-662-HELP) can refer you to local drug treatment programs and provides literature as well.

✔ **Don't gamble.** The house *always* comes out ahead in the long run. Why do you think so many governments run lotteries? Because governments make money on people who gamble, that's why.

Casinos, horse and dog racetracks, and other gambling establishments are sure long-term losers for you. So, too, is the rapidly growing practice of daytrading stocks, which isn't investing but gambling. Getting hooked on the dream of winning is easy and tempting. And sure, occasionally you win a little bit (just enough to keep you coming back). Every now and then, a few folks win a lot. But it's built into the odds that your hard-earned capital mostly winds up in the pockets of the casino owners.

If you go just for the entertainment, take only what you can afford to lose. Gamblers Anonymous (213-386-8789; www.gamblersanonymous .org) can help those for whom gambling has become an addiction.

Chapter 7

Taming Taxes

● ●

In This Chapter

▶ Understanding the baffling tax system

▶ Figuring your marginal income tax rate

▶ Reducing the taxes on your employment and investment income

▶ Increasing your deductions

▶ Preparing your return with and without help

▶ What to do if you get an audit notice

● ●

*Y*ou pay a lot of money in taxes — probably more than you realize. Believe it or not, few people even know how much they pay in taxes each year. Most remember only whether they got a refund or owed money on their return. But when you file your tax return, all you're doing is settling up with tax authorities over the amount of taxes you paid during the year versus the total tax that you owe based on your income and deductions.

Understanding the Taxes You Pay

Some people feel lucky when they get a refund, but really, all a refund indicates is that you overpaid in taxes during the year. You should have had this money in your own account all along. If you're consistently getting big refunds, you should be paying less tax throughout the year. (Fill out a simple tax form, the W-4, to determine how much you should be paying in taxes throughout the year. You can obtain a W-4 through your employer's payroll department. Obtain Form 1040-ES by calling the IRS at 800-TAX-FORM if you're self employed.)

Instead of caring about whether you get a refund when you complete your annual tax return, you *should* care about the *total* taxes you pay. The only way to know the *total* taxes you pay is to get out your federal and state tax returns. On each of those returns is a line that shows the *total tax:* This is line 56 on the most recent federal 1040 returns. Add up the totals from your federal and state tax returns, and you'll probably see one of the single largest expenses of your financial life (unless you have an expensive home or a huge gambling habit).

The goal of this chapter is to help you legally and permanently reduce the total taxes you pay. The key to reducing your tax burden is to understand the tax system — if you don't, you will surely pay more in taxes than necessary. And your tax ignorance can lead to mistakes, which can be costly if the IRS and your state government catch errors in your favor. With the proliferation of computerized information and data tracking, discovering mistakes has never been easier.

The tax system, like other public policy, is built around incentives to encourage *desirable* behavior and activity. Home ownership, for example, is considered desirable because it encourages people to take more responsibility for maintaining buildings and neighborhoods. Clean, orderly neighborhoods are supposed to be the result of home ownership. Therefore, the government offers all sorts of tax perks, which I discuss later in this chapter, to encourage people to buy and own homes.

To understand the tax system is to understand what your government thinks you should be doing. Naturally, not all people follow the path the government encourages — after all, it's a free country. You've spent years rebelling against your parents. Why should the government get better treatment?

However, the difference between rebelling against your parents and being a rebellious taxpayer, of course, is that as a taxpayer, the cost of defiance comes out of your pocket (I haven't heard of many parents who penalize, in *cash,* their kids' unruliness). The *fewer* desirable activities that you engage in, the *more* you will pay in taxes. If you understand the options, you can choose those that meet your needs as you approach different stages of your financial life.

Many people resent the taxes they pay — they feel that they pay too much and get too little in return. Therefore, another potential benefit to understanding the tax system is that you can become a more informed voter and citizen in the democratic process.

The importance of your marginal tax rate

"What's marginal about my taxes?" I hear you asking. "They're huge! They're not marginal in my life at all!" *Marginal* is a term often applied to those things that are small or minimally acceptable — sort of like getting a C– on a school report card (or an A– if you're from an overachieving family).

Marginal tax rates are a powerful concept. Once you understand them, you can understand the implications of many financial strategies that affect the amount of taxes you pay. And because you pay taxes on your income from employment as well as on your investments held outside of retirement accounts, a lot of personal financial decisions are at stake.

First, you must understand that when it comes to taxes, *not all income is treated equally.* This fact is far from self-evident. If you work for an employer and have a constant salary during the course of a year, a steady and equal amount of federal and state taxes is deducted from each paycheck. Thus, it appears as though all that earned income is being taxed equally.

In reality, however, you pay less tax on your *first* dollars of earnings and more tax on your *last* dollars of earnings. For example, if you're single and your taxable income (a term I define in the next section) totaled $35,000 during 2000, you paid federal tax at the rate of 15 percent on the first $26,250 of taxable income and 28 percent on income from $26,250 up to $35,000.

Table 7-1 gives federal tax rates for singles and married households filing jointly.

Table 7-1	2000 Federal Income Tax Brackets and Rates	
Singles Taxable Income	**Married-Filing-Jointly Taxable Income**	**Federal Tax Rate (Bracket)**
Not over $26,250	Not over $43,850	15%
Over $26,250 – $63,550	Over $43,850 – $105,950	28%
Over $63,550 – $132,600	Over $105,950 – $161,450	31%
Over $132,600 – $288,350	Over $161,450 – $288,350	36%
Over $288,350	Over $288,350	39.6%

Your *marginal tax rate* is the rate of tax that you pay on your *last* or so-called *highest* dollars of income. In the example of a single person with taxable income of $35,000, that person's federal marginal tax rate is 28 percent. In other words, she effectively pays 28 percent federal tax on her last dollars of income — those dollars in excess of $26,250.

Your marginal tax rate allows you to quickly calculate additional taxes that you would pay on additional income. Conversely, you can delight in quantifying the amount of taxes that you save by reducing your taxable income, either by decreasing your income or by increasing your deductions.

As you are probably painfully aware, you pay not only federal income taxes but also state income taxes — that is, unless you live in one of the handful of states (Alaska, Florida, Nevada, South Dakota, Texas, Washington, or Wyoming) that have no state income tax. *Note:* Some states such as New Hampshire do not tax employment but do tax other income such as that from investments.

Your *total marginal rate* includes your federal *and* state tax rates.

You can look up your state tax rate by getting out your most recent year's state income tax-preparation booklet.

Taxable income defined

Taxable income is the amount of income on which you actually pay taxes. In the sections that follow, I explain strategies for reducing your taxable income. First, I'll define what I mean. You don't pay taxes on your total income for the following two reasons:

- **Not all income is taxable.** For example, you pay federal tax on the interest you earn on a bank savings account but not on the interest from municipal bonds.

- **You get to subtract deductions from your income.** Some deductions are available just for being a living, breathing human being. In 2000, single people get an automatic $4,400 standard deduction, and married couples filing jointly get $7,350. (People over age 65 and those who are blind get a slightly higher deduction.) Other expenses, such as mortgage interest and property taxes, are deductible to the extent that your total deductions exceed the standard deductions. When you contribute to qualified retirement plans, you also effectively get a deduction.

Alternative minimum tax (say what?)

You may find this hard to believe, but (as if the tax system weren't already complicated enough) there is actually a second tax system. This second system may raise your taxes even higher than they would have been normally. Let me explain while you reach for some aspirin.

Over the years, as the government has grown hungrier for revenue, taxpayers who slash their taxes by claiming lots of deductions have come under greater scrutiny. So the government created a second tax system — the alternative minimum tax (AMT) — to ensure that those with high deductions pay at least a certain percentage of taxes on their incomes.

If you have a lot of deductions from state income taxes, real estate taxes, certain types of mortgage interest, and passive investments (for example, rental real estate), you may fall prey to AMT. You may also get tripped up by AMT if you have exercised certain types of stock options.

At the federal level are two AMT tax brackets: 26 percent for AMT income up to $175,000 and 28 percent for everything over that amount. AMT restricts you from claiming certain deductions and requires that you add back in normally tax-free income (like certain municipal-bond interest). So you have to figure your tax under the AMT system and under the other system and pay whichever amount is higher. Hope that aspirin is starting to kick in.

Trimming Employment Income Taxes

You are supposed to pay taxes on income you earn from work. Countless illegal ways are available to reduce your employment income — for example, not reporting it — but you could very well end up with a heap of penalties and extra interest charges on top of the taxes you owe. And you might even get tossed in jail. Because I don't want you to lose even more money by paying unnecessary penalties and serving jail time to boot, this section focuses on the many *legal* ways to reduce your taxes.

Retirement plan contributions

A retirement plan is one of the few painless and completely legal ways to reduce your taxable employment income. Besides reducing your taxes, you build up a nest egg so that you don't have to work for the rest of your life.

From your taxable income you can deduct money that you tuck away into employer-based retirement plans, such as 401(k) or 403(b) accounts, or into self-employed plans like SEP-IRAs or Keoghs. Therefore, if you contribute $1,000 to one of these plans and your combined federal and state marginal tax rate is 35 percent, you reduce your federal and state taxes by $350. Like the sound of that? How about this: Contribute another $1,000, and your taxes drop *another* $350 (as long as you're still in the same marginal tax rate). And, once inside a retirement account, your money can compound and grow without taxation.

This process is a great tax-reducing device. You benefit both in the short-term and the long-term. So why don't more people take advantage of this tax break?

Many people miss this opportunity to reduce their taxes because they *spend* all (or too much) of their current employment income and, therefore, have nothing (or little) left to put into a retirement account. Should you be in this predicament, you need to reduce your spending first in order to be able to contribute money to a retirement plan. Take an immediate tour through Chapter 6, which explains how to decrease your spending.

Should your employer not offer the option of saving money through a retirement plan, see whether you can drum up support for it. Lobby the benefits and human resources departments. If they resist, you might add this to your list of reasons to consider other employment. Many employers offer this valuable benefit, but others don't. Some company decision-makers themselves don't understand the value of these accounts or feel that these accounts are too costly to set up and administer.

If your employer does not offer a retirement savings plan, individual retirement account (IRA) contributions may or may not be tax-deductible, based on your circumstances. You should first exhaust contributions to the previously mentioned accounts that are tax-deductible. Chapter 11 can help you determine whether you should contribute to an IRA and if so, what type and whether your IRA contributions are tax-deductible.

Income shifting

Income shifting, which has nothing to do with money laundering, is a more esoteric tax-reduction technique and is an option only to those who can control *when* they receive their income.

For example, suppose that your employer tells you in late December that you're eligible for a bonus. You are offered the option to receive your bonus in either December or January. Looking ahead, if you're pretty certain that you will be in a higher tax bracket next year, you should choose to receive your bonus in December.

Or suppose that you run your own business and think that you'll be in a lower tax bracket next year. Perhaps you plan to take time off to be with a newborn or take an extended trip. You can send out some invoices later in the year so that your customers won't pay you until January, which falls in the next tax year.

Reducing Investment Income Taxes

For investments that you hold in *tax-sheltered* retirement accounts — IRAs and 401(k) plans, for example — you don't need to worry about taxes. This money is generally not taxed until you actually withdraw funds from the retirement account.

For investments that you hold outside of tax-sheltered retirement accounts, the distributions and profits on those investments are exposed to taxation when you receive them. Interest, dividends, and profits (called *capital gains*) from the sale of an investment at a price higher than the purchase price are all taxed.

Taxes on investment income should definitely concern you if you are in a relatively high tax bracket. If you're in the 31 percent or higher federal bracket (see Table 7-1), you should pay attention to the rest of this section.

If you're in the 28 percent federal tax bracket, these strategies may or may not help. Pay close attention to the issues that increase or decrease the benefits of following each of the strategies.

If you're in the 15 percent federal bracket, you can probably skip this section. Or you may sit quietly at your desk and amuse yourself until the rest of the class is finished.

Although this section explains some of the best methods to reduce the taxes on investments exposed to taxation, Chapter 12 discusses in detail how and where to invest money held outside of tax-sheltered retirement accounts.

Fill up those retirement accounts

The distributions and profits from investments outside retirement accounts are exposed to taxation. Unless you have earmarked that money for some specific nonretirement account purpose such as buying a home, and as long as hefty taxes aren't involved from selling those investments at a great profit, the money will probably serve you better in a tax-sheltered retirement account.

Taking advantage of opportunities to direct money into retirement accounts gives you two possible tax bonuses. First, your contributions to the retirement account may be immediately tax-deductible (see Chapter 11 for details). Second, the distributions and growth of the investments in the retirement accounts aren't generally taxed until withdrawal.

Invest in tax-free money market funds and bonds

When you're in a high enough tax bracket, you may find that you come out ahead with tax-free investments. Tax-free investments pay investment income, which is exempt from federal tax, state tax, or both.

Such investments yield less than comparable investments that produce taxable income. But because of the difference in taxes, the earnings from tax-free investments *can* end up being greater than what you're left with from taxable investments.

Tax-free money market funds can be a better alternative to bank savings accounts, the interest from which is subject to taxation. Likewise, tax-free bonds are longer-term investments that pay tax-free interest and may be a better investment option for you than bank certificates of deposit, Treasury bills and bonds, and other investments that produce taxable income. (See Chapter 12 for specifics on which tax-free investments may be right for your situation.)

Select other tax-friendly investments

Too often, when selecting investments, people mistakenly focus on past rates of return. We all know that the past is no guarantee of the future. But an even worse mistake is choosing an investment with a reportedly high rate of return without considering tax consequences. What you get to keep — after taxes — is what matters in the long run.

Mutual funds are a good example. When comparing two similar funds, most people prefer a fund that averages returns of 14 percent per year to a fund earning 12 percent. But what if the 14-percent-per-year fund causes you to pay a lot more in taxes? What if, after factoring in taxes, the 14-percent-per-year fund nets just 9 percent, while the 12-percent-per-year fund nets an effective 10-percent return? In such a case, you'd be unwise to choose a fund solely on the basis of the higher (pre-tax) reported rate of return.

I call investments that appreciate in value and don't distribute much in the way of taxable income *tax friendly* (some in the investment business use the term "tax efficient"). Examples include growth stocks, which pay low taxable dividends, and mutual funds that invest in such stocks. See Chapter 10 for more information.

Real estate is one of the few areas with privileged status in the tax code. In addition to deductions allowed for mortgage interest and property taxes, you can depreciate rental property to reduce your taxable income. *Depreciation* is a special tax deduction allowed for the gradual wear and tear on rental real estate. When you want to sell investment real estate, you may be eligible to conduct a tax-free exchange when buying a so-called replacement rental property. See Chapter 14 for a crash course in real estate.

Make your profits long-term

As I discuss in Part III, when you buy growth investments such as stocks and real estate, you should do so for the long-term — ideally 10 or more years. The tax system rewards your patience with lower tax rates on your profits.

When you are able to hold onto an investment (outside of a retirement account) such as a stock, bond, or mutual fund for more than one year, you get a tax break when you sell that investment at a profit. Specifically, your profit is taxed under the lower capital gains tax rate schedule.

For those normally in the 28 percent or higher federal income tax bracket, you pay just 20 percent of your profit in federal taxes. For investments bought after the year 2000 and held for more than five years, the long-term capital gains tax rate drops to 18 percent. If you're normally in the 15 percent federal income tax bracket, the long-term capital gains tax rate is just 10 percent and drops to 8 percent for investments bought after the year 2000 and held for more than five years.

Strategies to Increase Your Deductions

Deductions are just that: You subtract them from your income after totaling your income and before calculating the tax you owe. To make things more complicated, the IRS gives you two methods for determining your total deductions. The good news is that you get to pick the method that leads to greater deductions — and, hence, lower taxes.

Selecting standard versus itemized deductions

The first method for deductions requires no thinking or calculating. If you have a relatively uncomplicated financial life, taking the so-called standard deduction is generally the better option. Symptoms of a simple tax life are not earning a high income, renting your house or apartment, and lacking unusually large expenses from medical bills, moving expenses, charitable contributions, or loss due to theft or catastrophe.

As I mention earlier in this chapter, single folks qualify for a $4,400 standard deduction, and married couples filing jointly get a $7,350 standard deduction in 2000. If you're 65 or older or blind, you get a slightly higher standard deduction.

The other method of determining your allowable deductions is itemizing them on your tax return. This method is definitely more of a hassle, but if you can tally up more than the standard amounts noted in the preceding section, itemizing saves you money. Use Schedule A of IRS Form 1040 for summing up your itemized deductions.

Many of the categories on Schedule A, such as line 10, "Home mortgage interest and points reported to you on Form 1098," are reasonably self-evident. (If you own your home and have a mortgage, early in the new year your bank should send you Form 1098, which tells you how much deductible mortgage interest you paid.)

Organizing your deductions

The hard part for most people is locating Form 1098 and all the other scraps of paper you need when you're completing your tax return. Setting up a filing system can be a big time-saver:

✔ **One receptacle.** If you have limited patience for setting up neat file folders and you lead an uncomplicated financial life (that is, you haven't saved receipts throughout the year that you need for tax purposes), you can confine your filing to January and February. During those months, you should receive tax summary statements on wages paid by your employer (Form W-2), investment income (Form 1099), and home mortgage interest (Form 1098) in the mail. Set up a folder that's labeled with something easy to remember ("2000 Taxes" is a brilliant choice) and dump these papers as well as your tax booklet into it. When you're ready to crunch numbers, you should have everything you need to complete the form.

✔ **Many receptacles.** A more thorough approach is to organize the bills you pay into individual folders during the entire year. This method is essential if you own your own business and need to tabulate your expenditures for office supplies each year. No one is going to send you a form totaling your office expenditures for the year — you're on your own.

✔ **Software as receptacle.** Software programs can help organize your tax information during the year and can save you time and accounting fees come tax-preparation time. See Chapter 19 for more information about tax and financial software.

The following sections explain the most *overlooked* deductions and deduction strategies. Some are listed on Schedule A, and others appear on Form 1040 itself.

Shifting or bunching deductions

When you total your itemized deductions on Schedule A and the total is lower than the standard deduction, then you should take the standard deduction. This total is worth checking each year, because you may have more deductions in some years than others, and itemizing may make sense.

Because you can control when you pay particular expenses that are eligible for itemizing, you can *shift* or *bunch* more of them into the select years when you have enough deductions to take advantage of itemizing. Suppose, for example, that you are using the standard deduction this year because you don't have many itemized deductions. Late in the year, though, you become certain that you'll be buying a home next year. With mortgage interest and property taxes to write off, you also know that you can itemize next year. It makes sense, then, to shift and collect as many deductible expenses as possible into next year. For example, if you typically make more charitable contributions in December because of the barrage of solicitations you receive when you're in the giving mood, you may want to write the checks in January rather than in December.

When you're sure that you won't have enough deductions in the current year to itemize, try to shift as many expenses as you can into the next tax year.

Purchasing real estate

When you buy a home, two big ongoing expenses of home ownership — the interest on your mortgage and your property taxes — are deductions you can claim on Schedule A. You are allowed to claim mortgage interest deductions for a primary residence (where you actually live) and on a second home for mortgage debt totaling $1,000,000 (and a home equity loan of up to $100,000).

You can also deduct the full amount of your property taxes, even if you live in a multimillion-dollar mansion. Such a deal!

In order to buy real estate, most people need to first accumulate a down payment, which requires maintaining a lid on your spending. See the earlier chapters in this book for help with prioritizing and achieving important financial goals.

Trading consumer debt for mortgage debt

When you own real estate and haven't borrowed the maximum that you can and you've run up high-interest consumer debt, you may be able to trade one debt for another. You may be able to save on interest charges by refinancing your mortgage or taking out a home equity loan and pulling out extra cash to pay off your credit card, auto loan, or other costly credit lines. You can usually borrow at a lower interest rate for a mortgage and get a tax deduction as a bonus, which lowers the effective borrowing cost further. Consumer debt, such as that on auto loans and credit cards, is not tax-deductible.

This strategy involves some danger. Borrowing against the equity in your home can be an addictive habit. I've seen cases in which people run up significant consumer debt three or four times and then refinance their home the same number of times over the years to bail themselves out.

An appreciating home creates the illusion that excess spending isn't really costing you. But debt is debt, and all borrowed money has to be repaid. In the long run, you wind up with greater mortgage debt, and paying it off takes a bigger bite out of your monthly income. Refinancing and establishing home equity lines cost you more in terms of loan application fees and other charges (points, appraisals, credit reports, and so on).

At a minimum, continued expansion of your mortgage debt handicaps your ability to work toward other financial goals. In the worst case, easy access to borrowing encourages bad spending habits that can lead to bankruptcy or foreclosure on your debt-ridden home.

Charitable contributions and expenses

You can deduct contributions made to charities if you itemize your deductions. For example, most people know that when they write a check for $50 to their favorite church or college, they can deduct it. *Note:* Make sure to get a receipt for contributions of $250 or more because a canceled check is no longer sufficient documentation for the IRS.

Many taxpayers overlook the fact that you can also deduct expenses for work you do with charitable organizations. For example, when you go to a soup kitchen to help prepare and serve meals, you can deduct your transportation costs to get there. You just need to keep track of your bus fares or driving mileage.

You also can deduct the fair market value (which could be determined from thrift stores selling similar merchandise) of donations of clothing, household appliances, furniture, and other goods to charities, many of which will even drive to your home to pick up the stuff. See whether organizations such as the Salvation Army, Goodwill, or others are interested in your donation. Just make sure that you keep some documentation — write up an itemized list and get it signed by the charity. Consider taking pictures of more valuable donations. You can even donate securities and other investments to charity. In fact, donating an appreciated investment gives you a tax deduction for the full market value of the investment and eliminates your someday needing to pay tax on the (unrealized) profit.

Auto registration fees and state insurance

If you don't currently itemize, you may be surprised to learn that your state income taxes are itemizable. When you pay a fee to the state to register and license your car, you can itemize the expenditure as a deduction (on line 7, "Personal Property Taxes"). The IRS allows you to deduct that part of the fee that relates to the value of your car. The state organization that collects the fee should be able to tell you what portion of the fee is deductible (some states detail on the invoice what portion of the fee is tax-deductible).

Several states — California, New Jersey, New York, Rhode Island, Washington, and West Virginia — have state disability insurance funds. If you pay into these funds (check your W-2), you can deduct this fee as state and local income taxes on line 5 of Schedule A. You may also claim a deduction on this line for payments that you make into your state's unemployment compensation fund.

Bad news — limitations on deductions

If you are a high income earner, tax laws limit how much in itemized deductions you may subtract when calculating your taxable income. You have to reduce your total itemized deductions by 3 percent of your income above $126,600.

Here's how it works. Say that your income is $146,600 and your total itemized deductions come to $30,000. Because your income exceeds $126,600 by $20,000, you have to reduce your itemized deductions by $600 ($20,000 × 3 percent). Although you started with itemized deductions of $30,000, you can deduct only $29,400.

Of course, given a large enough income and low enough total deductions, the 3 percent rule threatens to wipe out any deductions at all. Don't worry. The IRS has benevolently set a limit on the amount that your deductions can be reduced — no more than 80 percent. So if we take the preceding example but boost your income to $1 million, you would still get to deduct $6,000 because your $30,000 in deductions cannot be reduced by more than $24,000 ($30,000 × 80 percent).

If you are in this high income category and your spirits are down, here's a little consolation (and something to make it all a little more complicated). Not all of your deductions are subject to the 3 percent rule: Medical and dental expenses, investment interest, casualty and theft losses, and gambling losses are all exempt.

If you are a high income earner, knowing this 3 percent rule and all of its nuances is important because it can affect some of your financial decisions. The 3 percent rule raises your effective tax rate and may encourage you, for example, to spend less on a home or to pay off your mortgage faster because you don't merit a full deduction.

Deducting miscellaneous expenses

A number of so-called *miscellaneous expenses* are deductible on Schedule A. Most of these relate to your job or career and management of your finances:

- ✔ **Educational expenses.** You may be able to deduct the cost of tuition, books, and travel to and from classes if your education is related to your career. Specifically, you can deduct these expenses if your course work improves your work skills. Continuing education classes for professionals may be deductible. If the law or your employer requires you to take courses to maintain your position, they are deductible. *Note:* Educational expenses that allow you to change or move into a new field or career are not deductible.

- ✔ **Job search and career counseling.** After you obtain your first job, you may deduct legitimate costs related to finding another job within your field. For example, suppose that you're a chef in a steak house in Chicago and decide that you want to do stir fry in Los Angeles. You take a crash course in vegetarian cooking and then fly to L.A. a couple of times for interviews. You can deduct the cost of the course and your trips — *even if you don't change jobs.* And if you hire a career counselor to help you figure everything out, you can deduct that cost as well. On the other hand, if you're burned out on cooking and decide that you want to become a professional volleyball player in L.A., that's a new career. You may get a better tan, but you won't generate deductions from changing jobs.

✔ **Unreimbursed expenses related to your job.** When you pay for your own subscriptions to trade journals to keep updated in your field or buy a new desk and chair to ease back pain, you can deduct these costs. If your job requires you to wear special clothes or a uniform, you can write off the cost of purchasing and cleaning them, as long as the clothes aren't suitable for wearing outside of work. When you buy a computer for use outside the office at your own expense, you may be able to deduct the cost if it's for the convenience of your employer, is a condition of your employment, and is used more than half the time for business. Union dues and membership fees for professional organizations are also deductible.

✔ **Investment and tax-related expenses.** Investment and tax-advisor fees are deductible, as are subscription costs for investment-related publications. Accounting fees for preparing your tax return or conducting tax planning during the year are deductible, as are legal fees related to your taxes. If you purchase a home computer to track your investments or prepare your taxes, you can deduct that expense, too.

When you deduct miscellaneous expenses, you get to deduct only the amount of these costs that exceeds 2 percent of your AGI (adjusted gross income). AGI is your total wage, interest, dividend, and all other income minus retirement account contributions, self-employed health insurance, alimony paid, and losses from investments.

Self-employment expenses

When you are self-employed, you can deduct a multitude of expenses from your income before calculating the tax that you owe. If you buy a computer or office furniture, you can deduct those expenses (sometimes they need to be gradually deducted or *depreciated* over time). Salaries for your employees, office supplies, rent or mortgage interest for your office space, and phone expenses are also generally deductible.

Some self-employed folks don't take all the deductions they should. In some cases, people simply aren't aware of the wonderful world of deductions. Others are worried that large deductions will raise the risk of an audit. Spend some time learning more about tax deductions; you will be convinced that taking full advantage of your eligible deductions makes sense and saves you money.

The following are common mistakes made by people who are their own bosses:

✔ **Being an island unto yourself.** When you're self-employed, going it alone is usually a mistake when it comes to taxes. You must educate yourself to make the tax laws work for you rather than against you. It's worth the money to hire tax help — either in the form of a tax advisor and/or other resources I recommend later in this chapter.

✔ **Making administrative tax screwups.** When you are self-employed, you are responsible for the correct and timely filing of all taxes owed on your income or on that of your employees. You need to make estimated tax payments on a quarterly basis. And if you have employees, you also need to withhold taxes on their income from each paycheck they receive and make timely payments to the IRS and to the appropriate state authorities. In addition to federal and state income tax, you also need to withhold and send in Social Security and any other state or locally mandated payroll taxes.

For paying taxes on your income, you can obtain Form 1040-ES with instructions from the IRS (call 800-TAX-FORM). This form comes complete with an estimated tax worksheet and the four payment coupons to send in with your quarterly tax payments. If you want to learn the rules regarding withholding and submitting taxes from employees' paychecks, ask the IRS for Form 941 as well as Form 940, which is for unemployment insurance. And unless you're lucky enough to live in a state with no income taxes, remember to call for your state's estimated income tax package. Another alternative is to hire a payroll firm, such as Paychex, to do all this drudgery for you.

✔ **Not documenting expenses.** When you pay with cash, following the paper trail for all the money you spent is hard for you (and the IRS, in the event you're ever audited). At the end of the year, how are you going to remember how much you spent for parking or client meals if you keep no record? How would you survive an IRS audit without proper documentation? For purchases under $75, you don't need a receipt as proof, but you do need a system or written record of your daily petty cash purchases. Most pocket calendars or daily organizers include ledgers that allow you to track these small purchases. If you can't be that organized, at least get a receipt for cash transactions and stash them in a file folder in your desk. Or keep receipts in envelopes labeled with the month and year.

✔ **Choosing the wrong entity or form of organization.** When you set up your own business, you can structure its legal and tax organization in a variety of ways. A *corporation* is a separate legal entity from you, the individual. For example, if a customer slips on a stray banana peel at your office and decides to sue, if you're incorporated, the customer can sue your company but can't go after your personal assets. Incorporating makes more sense if you have employees or customers who visit the office, or if you do business with many vendors.

Incorporating is not always the right answer. For professional service providers such as self-employed attorneys, physicians, or tax advisors, incorporating may not necessarily be useful as protection against professional negligence suits related to their work. In such cases, the law treats the business and the professional as one and the same. The answer for these folks is *professional liability insurance.* Check with the professional associations in your field for information on insurers who offer such policies.

✔ **Not funding a retirement plan.** I am amazed by the number of tax preparers who do not encourage their clients to contribute to retirement plans to reduce taxes. You should be saving money toward retirement anyway, and you can't beat the tax break. People who are self-employed are allowed to save up to about 20 percent of their net income on an annual basis. To learn more about SEP-IRAs, Keoghs, and other retirement plans, see Chapter 11.

✔ **Not using numbers to help manage business.** If you are a small-business owner who doesn't track his income, expenses, staff performance, and customer data on a regular basis, your tax return may be the one and only time during the year when you take a financial snapshot of your business. After you go to all the time, trouble, and expense to file your tax return, make sure that you reap the rewards of all your work: Use those numbers to help analyze and manage your business.

Some bookkeepers and tax preparers can provide you with management information reports on your business from the tax data they compile for you. Just ask! Likewise, software packages can help. See my recommendations later in this chapter.

✔ **Not paying family help.** If your children, spouse, or other relatives help with some aspect of your business, consider paying them for the work. Besides showing them that you value their work, this practice may reduce your family's tax liability. For example, a child is usually in a lower tax bracket than you are. So by shifting income to the child, you cut your tax bill.

Tax Resources

All sorts of ways to prepare your tax return exist. Which approach makes sense for you depends on the complexity of your situation and your level of interest and knowledge in taxes.

Regardless of which approach you take, you should be taking financial moves during the year to reduce your taxes. By the time you actually file your return in the following year, it's usually too late for you to take advantage of many tax-reduction strategies.

IRS assistance

If you have a simple, straightforward tax return, filing it on your own using only the IRS instructions is fine. This approach is as cheap as you can get. The main costs are time, patience, photocopying expenses (you should always keep a copy for your files), and postage to mail the completed tax return.

IRS publications don't, in general, have Tip or Warning icons like this book has. Another danger of relying on the IRS is that it has been known to give wrong information on a more-than-infrequent basis. When you call the IRS with a question, be sure to take notes about your conversation to protect yourself in the event of an audit. Date your notes and include the name of the tax employee you talked to, what you asked, and the employee's responses. File your notes in a folder with a copy of your completed return.

In addition to the standard instructions that come with your tax return, the IRS offers some free (actually paid for with your tax dollars) and sometimes useful booklets. Publication 17, *Your Federal Income Tax,* is designed for individual tax-return preparation. Publication 334, *Tax Guide for Small Businesses,* is for (you guessed it) small-business tax-return preparation. These publications are more comprehensive than the basic IRS instructions. Call 800-TAX-FORM to request these booklets or visit the IRS web site at www.irs.gov.

Preparation and advice guides

Books about tax preparation and tax planning that are written in clear, simple English and that highlight common problem areas are invaluable. They supplement the official instructions not only by helping you to complete your return correctly but also by showing you how to save as much money as possible. Consider picking up a copy of *Taxes For Dummies,* which I co-author.

Software

If you have access to a computer, good tax-preparation software can be helpful. For recommendations on using tax software and a current review of the best programs on the market, please pick up a copy of the latest edition of *Taxes For Dummies.*

Hiring help

Competent tax preparers and advisors can save you money — sometimes more than enough to pay their fees — by identifying tax-reduction strategies you may overlook. They can also reduce the likelihood of an audit, which can be triggered by blunders you might make. Mediocre and lousy tax preparers, on the other hand, may make mistakes and not be aware of sound ways to reduce your tax bite.

Tax practitioners come with varying backgrounds, training, and credentials. One credential is not necessarily better than another. The four main types are preparers, enrolled agents (EAs), Certified Public Accountants (CPAs), and tax attorneys. The more training and specialization a tax practitioner has (and the more affluent his clients), the higher his hourly fee usually is. Fees and competence at all levels of the profession vary significantly. If you do hire a tax advisor and you're not sure of the quality of work performed and the soundness of the advice, try getting a second opinion.

Preparers

Among all the tax practitioners, preparers generally have the least amount of training, and a greater proportion of them work part-time. As with financial planners, no national regulations apply to preparers, and no licensing is required.

The appeal of preparers is that they are relatively inexpensive — they can do most basic returns for around $100 or so. The drawback, of course, is that you may hire a preparer who doesn't know much more than you do.

Preparers make the most sense for folks who have relatively simple financial lives, who are budget minded, and who hate doing their own taxes. If you're not good about hanging onto receipts or don't want to keep your own files with background details about your taxes, you should definitely shop around for a tax preparer who's going to be around for a few years. You may need all that stuff someday for an audit, and many tax preparers keep and organize their clients' documentation rather than returning everything each year. Also, going with a firm that is open year-round may be safer (some small shops are open only during tax season) in case tax questions or problems arise.

Enrolled agents (EAs)

A person must pass IRS scrutiny in order to be called an *enrolled agent*. This license allows the agent to represent you before the IRS in the event of an audit. Continuing education is also required. Training to become an EA is generally longer and more sophisticated than that for a typical preparer.

Enrolled agents' prices tend to fall between those of a preparer and a CPA. Returns with a few of the more common schedules (such as Schedule A for deductions and Schedule B for interest and dividends) shouldn't cost more than a couple hundred dollars to prepare.

EAs are best for people with moderately complex returns who don't necessarily need complicated tax-planning advice throughout the year (although some EAs provide this service as well as prepare returns). You can get names and telephone numbers of EAs in your area by contacting the National Association of Enrolled Agents (800-424-4339).

Certified public accountants (CPAs)

Certified public accountants go through significant training and examination to receive the CPA credential. In order to maintain this designation, a CPA must also complete a fair number of continuing education classes every year.

CPA fees vary tremendously. Most charge around $100 per hour, but CPAs at large companies and in high-cost-of-living areas tend to charge somewhat more.

CPAs are of greatest value to people completing some of the more unusual and less user-friendly schedules, such as K-1 for partnerships, Schedule C for self-employed folks, or Form 8829 for home office deductions. Paying for the additional cost of a CPA on an ongoing basis makes sense if you can afford it and if your situation is reasonably complex or dynamic. When you are self-employed and/or file lots of other schedules, it may be worth hiring a CPA. But you needn't do so year after year. If your situation grows complex one year and then stabilizes, consider getting help for the perplexing year and then using preparation guides, software, or a lower-cost preparer or enrolled agent in the future.

Tax attorneys

Tax attorneys deal with more complicated tax problems and issues, which usually have some legal angle. Unless you're a superhigh-income earner with a complex financial life, hiring a tax attorney to prepare your annual return is prohibitively expensive. In fact, many tax attorneys don't prepare returns as a normal practice.

Because of their level of specialization and training, tax attorneys tend to have the highest hourly billing rates — $200 to $300 per hour is not unusual.

Dealing with an Audit

On a list of real-life nightmares, most people would rank tax audits right up there with rectal exams and court appearances. The primary trauma of an audit is that many people feel like they're on trial and are being accused of a crime. Take a deep breath and don't panic.

You might be getting audited simply because a business that reports tax information on you, or someone at the IRS, made an error regarding the data on your return. In the vast majority of cases, the IRS conducts its "audit" by corresponding with you through the mail.

The most feared type of audit is when you have to schlep to the local IRS office. In those cases, about 20 percent of such audited returns are left unchanged by the audit — that is, you don't end up owing more money. In fact, if you're the lucky sort, you may be one of the 5 percent of folks who actually gets a refund because the audit finds a mistake in your favor!

Unfortunately, you'll most likely be one of the roughly 75 percent of audit survivors who end up owing more tax money. The amount of additional tax that you owe in interest and penalties hinges on how your audit goes.

Audit preparation

Preparing for an audit is sort of like preparing for a test in school. The IRS informs you of which sections of your tax return the agency wants to examine.

The first decision you face when you get an audit notice is whether to handle it yourself or turn to a tax advisor to represent you. Hiring representation costs money out-of-pocket but may save you time, stress, and money.

 If you normally prepare your own return and are comfortable with your understanding of the areas being audited, then do it yourself. When the amount of tax money in question is small in comparison to the fee you'd pay the tax advisor to represent you, self-representation is probably the answer. However, if you're likely to turn into a babbling, intimidated fool and are unsure of how to present your situation, hire a tax advisor to represent you (see the "Hiring help" section earlier in this chapter for information about whom to hire).

If you decide to handle the audit yourself, get your act together sooner rather than later. Don't wait until the night before to start gathering receipts and other documentation. You may find, for example, that you can't find certain documents and need to contact others to get copies.

You need to document and be ready to speak with the auditor only about the areas the audit notice says are being investigated. Organize the various documents and receipts into folders. You want to make it as easy as possible for the auditor to review your materials. *Don't* show up, dump shopping bags full of receipts and paperwork on the auditor's desk, and say, "Here it is — *you* figure it out."

Whatever you do, *don't ignore your audit request letter.* The IRS is the ultimate bill-collection agency. And if you end up owing more money (the unhappy result of most audits), the sooner you pay, the less interest and penalties you'll owe.

The day of reckoning

Two people with identical situations can walk into an audit and come out with very different results. The loser can end up owing much more in taxes and have the audit expanded to include other parts of the return. The winner can end up owing less tax money than he or she really should pay under the tax laws.

Here's how to be a winner:

- ✔ **Treat the auditor as a human being.** Obvious advice, yes, but very often not practiced by taxpayers. You may be resentful or angry about being audited. You may be tempted to gnash your teeth and tell the auditor how unfair it is that an honest taxpayer like you had to spend hours getting ready for this. You might feel like ranting and raving about how the government wastes too much of your tax money or that the party in power is out to get you. Bite your tongue.

  Believe it or not, most auditors are decent people just trying to do their job. They are well aware that taxpayers don't like seeing them. Don't suck up, either — just relax and be yourself. Behave as you would around a boss whom you like — with respect and congeniality.

- ✔ **Stick to the knitting.** Your audit is to discuss *only* the sections of your tax return that are in question. The more you talk about other areas or things that you're doing, the more likely the auditor will probe into other items. Don't bring documentation for parts of your return not being audited. Besides creating more work for yourself, you might be opening a can of worms that needn't be opened. Should the auditor inquire about areas not covered by the audit notice, politely say that you're not prepared to discuss those other issues and that another meeting should be scheduled.

- ✔ **Don't argue when you disagree.** State your case. When the auditor wants to disallow a deduction or otherwise increase the taxes you owe and you don't agree, state once why you don't. If the auditor won't budge, don't get into a knock-down, drag-out confrontation. He or she may not want to lose face and is inclined to find additional tax money — that's the auditor's job. *Remember:* When necessary, you can plead your case with several layers of people above your auditor. If that fails and you still feel wronged, you can take your case to tax court.

✔ **Don't be intimidated.** Most auditors are not tax geniuses. The work is stressful — being in a job in which people dislike seeing you is not easy. Turnover is quite high. Thus, many auditors are fairly young, just-out-of-school types who majored in something like English, history, or sociology. They may know less about tax and financial matters than you do. The basic IRS tax boot camp that auditors go through doesn't come close to covering all the technical details and nuances in the tax code. So you may not be at such a disadvantage in your tax knowledge after all, especially if you work with a tax advisor (most of whom know more about the tax system than the average IRS auditor).

Part III
Investing Crash Course

The 5th Wave   By Rich Tennant

"Hey, Luke, I was just thinking—why don't we try investing some of the stolen loot in some mutual funds, bonds, maybe check out some international funds, or real estate ...shoot, what am I talking about? Let's just stash it in the old mine shaft like before."

In this part . . .

1 lay out the basics of investing and show you how to choose your investments wisely. Earning and saving are hard work, so you should be careful where you invest the fruits of your labor. This part is where you find out the real story on such things as stocks, bonds, mutual funds, the differences between investing in retirement and non-retirement accounts, how to invest for college, and how to buy a home.

Chapter 8

Important Investment Concepts

*M*aking wise investments need not be complicated. However, many investors get bogged down in the morass of the thousands of investment choices out there. This chapter helps you grasp the important, "bigger picture" issues that will ensure that your investment plan meshes with your needs and the realities of the investment marketplace.

First, Establish Your Goals

Before you select a specific investment, you should first determine your investment needs and goals. Why are you saving this pile of money? What are you going to use it for? You can't and don't need to earmark *every* dollar, but you should set some major objectives. Doing so is important because the expected use of the money determines how much time it's going to be invested. And that, in turn, helps determine which investment you choose.

Suppose the money you plan on using for Uncle Louie's sure-win deal is all the liquid cash you have available. What if Louie's deal goes bust? What are you going to tap in the event of an emergency? Bad things don't just happen to "other" people. You need a safety net in case you lose your job or are hit with unexpected expenses.

The risk level of your investments should factor in your time frame *and your comfort level*. There's no sense investing in high-risk vehicles if you're going to spend all your profits on ulcer-induced medical bills. For example, suppose you've been accumulating money for a down payment on a home that you'd like to buy in a few years. You can't afford much investment risk with that money. You're going to need that money sooner rather than later. Putting that money in the stock market, then, is probably not a wise move. As you see later in this chapter, the stock market can drop a lot in a year or over several consecutive years. So stocks are probably too risky a place to invest home down payment money you plan on using soon.

Perhaps you're saving toward a longer-term goal, such as retirement, that is 20 or 30 years away. In this case, you're in a position to make riskier investments because your holdings have more time to bounce back from temporary losses or setbacks. A retirement account that you leave alone for 20 years or longer may be where you should consider investing in growth investments like stocks. You can tolerate year-to-year volatility in the market — you have time on your side. If you haven't yet done so, take a tour through Chapter 3, which helps you contemplate and establish your financial goals.

The Major Investment Flavors

Jumping right into picking a particular investment is the fun and exciting part for most people. Or, perhaps you're tired of thinking about where to invest and watching others make profits while you sit on the sidelines. You may have an idea from some reading you've done or from some entertaining-investment-type touting investments on television or online. Or maybe Uncle Louie is whispering in your ear that he's gonna get you in on the ground floor of a great new opportunity — a real sure thing.

Lending investments

For a moment, forget all the buzzwords and jargon and product names you've heard tossed around in the investment world — in many cases, they're only meant to obscure what an investment really is and to hide the hefty fees and commissions it charges. Imagine a world with only two investment flavors — chocolate and vanilla ice cream (or low-fat, nondairy frozen dessert for you health-minded folks). Just two choices. Might make the ice cream shop a lot less interesting, but it would sure simplify your decision.

The investment world is really just as simple. You have only two major investment choices: You can be either a lender or an owner.

You're a *lender* when you invest your money in a bank certificate of deposit, a Treasury bill, or a bond issued by a company like General Motors, for example. In each case, you lend your money to an organization — a bank, the federal government, or GM. You are paid an agreed-upon rate of interest for lending your money. You are also promised to have your original investment (the *principal*) returned to you on a specific date.

The best that can happen with a lending investment is that you are paid all of the interest in addition to your original investment — the *principal* — as promised. Given that the investment landscape is littered with carcasses of failed investments, this is not a result to take for granted.

The worst that can happen is that you don't get everything you were promised. Promises can be broken under extenuating circumstances. When a company goes bankrupt, for example, you can lose all or part of your original investment.

Another risk is that you get what you were promised, but because of the ravages of inflation, your money is worth less — it has less purchasing power than you thought it would. Back in the 1960s, for example, high-quality companies issued long-term bonds that paid approximately 4 percent interest. At the time, buying a long-term bond seemed like a good deal because the cost of living was increasing only 2 percent per year.

When inflation rocketed to 6, 8, 10 percent and higher, those 4 percent bonds didn't seem so attractive any longer. The interest and principal didn't buy nearly the amount they did years earlier when inflation was lower. Table 8-1 shows the reduction in the purchasing power of your money at varying rates of inflation after just ten years.

Table 8-1	Reduction in Purchasing Power Due to Inflation
Inflation Rate	*Reduction in Purchasing Power after 10 Years*
6 percent	− 44 percent
8 percent	− 54 percent
10 percent	− 61 percent

A common mistake that some conservative-minded investors make is that they think they are diversifying their long-term investment money by buying several bonds, some CDs, Treasuries, and an annuity. The problem, however, is that all these investments pay a relatively low fixed rate of return that is exposed to the vagaries of inflation.

A final drawback to lending investments is that you do not share in the success of the organization to which you lend your money. If the organization doubles or triples in size and profits, neither your principal nor your interest rate doubles or triples in size along with it; they stay the same. Of course, such success should ensure that you will get your promised interest and principal back.

Ownership investments

You're an *owner* when you invest your money in an asset, such as a company or real estate, which has the ability to generate earnings or profits. In the first case, suppose that you own 100 shares of Gap stock. With hundreds of millions of shares of stock outstanding, Gap is a mighty big company — your 100 shares represent a tiny piece of it.

What do you get for your small slice of Gap? As a stockholder, you share in the profits of a company in the form of annual dividends as well as an increase (you hope) in the stock price if the company grows and becomes more profitable. That's when things are going well. The downside is that if Gap's business declines, your stock can become worth less (or even worthless!).

Although much of this part of the book is devoted to stocks, I am surprised by how many investors I talk with these days haven't considered other financially rewarding ownership investments such as real estate. Real estate can produce profits by being rented out for income (profits come when rental income exceeds the expense of owning the property) or by being sold at a higher price than what you paid to buy it. I know numerous successful real estate investors who have earned excellent long-term profits.

As with other ownership investments, the value of real estate depends not only on the particulars of the individual property but also on the health and performance of the local economy. When the local economy is growing and more jobs are being produced at higher wages, real estate should do well. When companies in the community are laying people off left and right and excess housing is sitting vacant because of previous overbuilding, then rents and property values are likely to fall.

A third way many Americans have built substantial wealth is through small business. According to *Forbes* magazine, more of the U.S. and world's wealthiest individuals have built their wealth through their stake in small businesses than through any other vehicle. Small business is the engine that drives much of our economic growth. Although firms with fewer than 20 employees account for about one-quarter of all employees, such small firms in the past two decades were responsible for nearly half of all new jobs created.

You can participate in small business in a variety of ways. You can start your own business, buy and operate an existing business, or simply invest in promising small businesses.

In the chapters ahead, I explain each of these major investment types in detail.

Shun gambling instruments and behaviors

Although investing is often risky, it's not gambling — at least not the way that I advocate that you invest. *Gambling* is putting your money into schemes that are sure to lose you money over time. That's not to say that everyone loses or that you lose every time you play. However, the deck is stacked against you. The house wins most of the time.

In some cases, as with horse racing, gambling casinos, and lotteries, the system is set up to pay out 50 to 60 cents on the dollar. The rest goes to administration of the system and — don't forget that these are businesses — profits. Sure, your chosen horse may win a race or two, but in the long run, you're almost guaranteed to lose about 40 to 50 percent of what you bet. Would you put your money in an "investment" where your expected return was negative 40 percent?

Gambling in the investment world is *speculation* — these opportunities are found in sales and trading of futures, options, and commodities. Futures, options, and commodities are *derivatives*, financial investments with value derived from the performance of another security such as a stock or bond.

You may have heard the radio ad by the firm of Fleecem, Cheatem, and Leavem, advocating that you buy heating oil futures because the cold weather months lead to the use of more heating oil. You call and are impressed by the smooth-talking vice president who spends so much time with little ol' you. His logic makes sense, and he's spent a lot of time with you, so you send him a check for $10,000.

State governments pushing gambling

More and more states are getting into the gambling business as a way to bring in tax revenue. This is wrong for many reasons. First, it's been well documented that lotteries and casinos obtain most of their business from those least able to afford them — primarily middle- and low-income earners. They end up creating an additional tax on the less economically well off and operate on the basis of false hopes.

Second, government endorsement of gambling promotes the get-rich-quick mentality. Why get an education and work hard over the years when you can solve all your financial concerns with the next ticket you buy or slot you pull?

Gambling also contributes to our nationally low personal savings rate.

Finally, gambling, like alcohol and tobacco, can be addictive and destructive. In the worst cases, gambling and gambling debts can split up families and lead to divorce or even suicides and murders.

It's bad enough that legalized gambling exists. It's even worse that, in the pursuit of short-term profits and a quick fix, local governments are piling into this business. Government is fostering an irresponsible attitude toward money.

Doing so isn't much different from blowing $10,000 at the craps tables in Las Vegas. Futures prices depend on short-term, highly volatile price movements. As with gambling, you occasionally win when the market moves the right way at the right time. But in the long run, you're gonna lose. In fact, you can lose it all.

Options are the same — you're betting on short-term movements of a specific security. If you have inside information, as Ivan Boesky did, such that you know in advance when a major corporate development is going to occur, you can get rich. But don't forget one minor detail — insider trading is illegal. You may end up in the slammer like Boesky.

Honest brokers who help their clients invest in stocks, bonds, and mutual funds tell you the truth about commodities, futures, and options. A former broker I know who used to work for Merrill Lynch and Shearson Lehman over a period of 12 years told me, "I had one client who made money in options, futures, or commodities, but the only reason he came out ahead was because he was forced to pull money out to close on a home purchase just when he happened to be ahead. The commissions were great for me, but there's no way a customer will make money in them." Remember these words if you're tempted to gamble with futures, options, and the like.

Daytrading — which is the rapid buying and selling of securities online — is a newer and equally foolish vehicle for individual investors to pursue. While placing trades via the internet is far cheaper than the older methods of trading (such as telephoning a broker), the more you trade, the more trading costs will eat into your investment capital. Frequent trading also increases an investor's tax bill as profits realized over short periods of time are taxed at the investor's highest possible tax rate (see Chapter 7). During a rising stock market, daytraders can certainly make some profits. However, over an extended period of time, daytraders inevitably underperform the broad market averages. In those rare instances where a daytrader does a little better, it's rarely worth the time and personal sacrifices that the daytrader and his family and friends endure.

Investment Returns

You know the difference between ownership and lending investments. Hopefully, you can also distinguish gambling and speculation from true investments.

"That's all well and good," you say, "but how do I choose which type of investments to put my money into? How much can I make, and what are the risks?"

Good questions. I'll start with the returns you *might* make. I say "might" because I'm looking at history, and history is a record of the past. Using history to predict the future, especially the near future, is dangerous. History may repeat itself, but not always in exactly the same fashion and not necessarily when you expect it to.

This century, ownership investments like stocks and real estate have returned around 10 percent per year, handily beating lending investments such as bonds (around 5 percent) and savings accounts (roughly 4 percent) in the investment performance race. Inflation has averaged 3 percent per year.

If you already know that the stock market can be risky, perhaps you're wondering why it's worth the anxiety and potential losses to invest in stocks. Why bother for a few extra percent per year? Well, over many years, a few extra percent per year can really magnify the growth of your money (see Table 8-2). The more years you have to invest, the greater the difference a few percent makes in your returns.

If you invest $10,000 for 25 years or 40 years:

Table 8-2	The Difference a Few Percent Makes	
At This Rate of Investment Return on $10,000	*You'll Have This Much in 25 Years*	*You'll Have This Much in 40 Years*
4% (savings account)	$26,658	$48,010
5% (bond)	$33,863	$70,399
10% (stocks and real estate)	$108,347	$452,592

Investing is not a spectator sport. You can't earn good returns in stocks and real estate if you keep your money in cash and sit on the sidelines. When you do invest in growth investments such as stocks and real estate, don't chase one new investment after another trying to beat the market average returns. *The biggest value is to be in the market, not to beat it.*

Investment Risks

Many investors have a simplistic understanding of what risk means and how to apply it to their investment decisions. For example, when compared to the yo-yo motions of the stock market, a bank savings account may seem like a less risky place to put your money. Over the long term, however, the stock market usually beats the rate of inflation; money in a savings account does not. Thus, if you are saving your money for a long-term goal like retirement, a savings account can be a "riskier" place to put your money.

Before you invest, ask yourself these three questions:

- ✔ What am I saving and investing this money for? In other words, what's my goal?
- ✔ What is my timeline for this investment?
- ✔ What is the historical volatility of the investment I'm considering, and does that suit my comfort level and timeline for this investment?

With answers to these questions, you will have a better understanding of *risk,* and you will be able to match your savings goals to their most appropriate investment vehicles. In Chapter 3, I help you to consider your savings goals and timeline. I address investment risk and returns in the sections that follow.

Stock and bond risks

Given the relatively higher historic returns I mention for ownership investments in the last section, some people think they should put all of their money in stocks and real estate. So what's the catch?

Investments with a potential for higher returns carry greater risks. Risk and return go hand-in-hand. If you're not willing to accept more risk, you're not going to be able to achieve higher rates of return.

The risk with ownership investments is the short-term fluctuations in their value. On average, during this century for example, stocks have declined by more than 10 percent in a year every five years. Drops in stock prices of more than 20 percent occurred, on average, once every ten years. Real estate prices suffer similar periodic setbacks.

Thus, in order to earn those generous long-term returns from ownership investments like stocks and real estate, you must be willing to tolerate volatility. That's why you absolutely should not put all your money in the stock or real estate market. At a minimum, you should not invest your emergency money or money you expect to use within the next five years in such volatile investments.

The shorter the time period that you have, the less likely that growth-oriented investments like stocks will beat out lending-type investments like bonds. Table 8-3 illustrates the historical relationship between stock and bond returns based on number of years held.

Table 8-3	Stocks versus Bonds
Number of Years Investment Held	*Likelihood of Stocks Beating Bonds*
1	60%
5	70%
10	80%
20	91%
30	99%

Some types of bonds have higher yields than others, but the risk-reward relationship remains intact. A bond generally pays you a higher rate of interest as compared to other bonds when it is:

- ✔ Lower credit — to compensate for the higher risk of default and higher likelihood of losing your investment
- ✔ Longer-term maturity — to compensate for the risk that you'll be unhappy with the bond's interest rate if interest rates move up

Focus on the risks that you can control

I always ask students in my personal finance class to write down what they would like to learn. Here's what one student had to say: "I want to learn what to invest my money in now as the stock market is overvalued and interest rates are about to go up, so bonds are dicey and banks give lousy interest — HELP!"

This student recognizes the risk of price fluctuations in her investments, but she also seems to believe, like too many people, that there's a way to expect or predict what's going to happen. How does *she* know that the stock market is overvalued, and why hasn't the rest of the world figured it out? How does *she* know that interest rates are about to go up, and why hasn't the rest of the world figured that out, either?

When you invest in stocks and other growth-oriented investments, you must accept the volatility of these investments. Invest the money that you have earmarked for the longer-term in these vehicles. Minimize the risk of these investments through diversification. Don't buy just one or a two stocks; buy a number of stocks. Later in this chapter, I discuss what you need to know about diversification.

Investing lump sums via dollar cost averaging

Whether through accumulation of funds over the years, an inheritance, or a recent windfall from work that you've done, you have a problem when you have a large chunk of cash to invest. Many people, of course, would like to have your problem. (You're not complaining, right?) You want to invest your money, but you're a bit skittish, if not outright terrified, at the prospect of investing the lump of money all at once.

If the money is residing in a savings or money market account, you may feel like it's wasting away. You want to put it to work!

My first words of advice: Don't rush. Nothing is wrong with earning only a few percentage points on your money in a money market account (see Chapter 12 for recommendations of the best money funds). Remember that a money market fund beats the heck out of rushing into an investment in which you might lose 20 percent or more. I sometimes get calls from people in a state of near panic. Typically, these folks have CDs coming due and feel that they must decide exactly where they want to invest the money in the 48 hours before the CD matures.

Take a deeeep breath. You have absolutely no reason to rush into an important decision. Instruct your friendly banker that when the CD matures, you'd like the proceeds to be put in the bank's highest-yielding savings or money market account. That way, your money still earns interest while you buy yourself some breathing room.

One approach to investing is called dollar-cost averaging (DCA). DCA is a process in which you invest your money in equal chunks on a regular basis, such as once a month.

For example, if you have $60,000 to invest, you can invest $2,500 per month until it's all invested, which takes a couple of years. The money that's awaiting future investment isn't lying fallow. You keep it in a money market-type account earning a bit of interest while it's waiting its turn.

The attraction of DCA is that it allows you to ease into riskier investments instead of jumping in all at once. The benefit may be that if the price of the investment drops after some of your initial purchases, you can buy some later at a lower price. Had you instead dumped all your money into the "sure win" investment at once and then it dropped like a stone, you'd kick yourself for not waiting.

The flip side of DCA is that when your investment of choice appreciates in value, you may wish that you had invested your money faster. Another possible drawback of DCA is that you may get cold feet continuing to pour money into an investment that's dropping in value. Many people who are attracted to DCA out of fear of buying before a price drop end up bailing out of what feels like a sinking ship.

DCA can also cause headaches with your taxes when the time comes to sell investments held outside retirement accounts. When you buy an investment at many different times and prices, accounting is muddied as you sell blocks of the investment.

DCA is most valuable when the money you want to invest represents a large portion of your total assets and you can stick to a schedule. Make DCA automatic so that you're less likely to chicken out should the investment fall after your initial purchases. Most investment firms recommended in the next few chapters provide automatic exchange services.

Low-risk, high-return investments

Despite what professors teach in the nation's leading business and finance graduate school programs, low-risk investments that almost certainly will lead to high returns *are* available.

I can think of at least four such investments:

- ✔ **Pay off consumer debt.** If you're paying 10, 14, or 18 percent interest on an outstanding credit card or other consumer loan, pay it off before investing. To get a comparable return through other investment vehicles (after the government takes its share of your profits), you would have to start a new career as a loan shark. If between federal and state taxes you're in a 33-percent tax bracket, and you're paying 12 percent interest on a consumer loan, you'd need to annually earn a whopping 18 percent on your investments pre-tax to justify not paying off the debt. Good luck!

  When your only source of funds to pay off debt is a small emergency reserve equal in size to a few months' living expenses, paying off debt may involve some risk. Only tap into your emergency reserves if you have a backup source — for example, the ability to borrow from a willing family member or to borrow against a retirement account balance.

- ✔ **Invest in your health.** Eat healthy, exercise, and relax.

- ✔ **Invest in friends and family.** Improve your relationships with loved ones. Invest the time and effort in making them better.

- ✔ **Invest in personal and career development.** Learn a new hobby, improve your communication skills, or read widely. Take an adult education course or go back to school for a degree. Your investment will surely pay off in higher paychecks and greater happiness.

Diversification

Diversification is one of the most powerful investment concepts. All it really means is that you save and place your eggs (or investments) in different baskets.

Diversification requires you to place your money in different investments with returns that are not completely correlated. This is a fancy way of saying that with your money in different places, when some of your investments are down in value, odds are that others are up.

To decrease the odds of all of your investments getting clobbered at the same time, you must put your money in different types or classes of investments such as bonds, stocks, real estate, and small business (I cover all these investments and more in Chapter 9). You can further diversify your investments by investing in domestic as well as international markets.

Within a given class of investments such as stocks, to diversify by investing in different types of stocks that perform well under various economic conditions is important. For this reason, mutual funds, which are diversified portfolios of securities such as stocks or bonds, are a highly useful investment vehicle. You buy into the mutual fund, which in turn pools your money with that of many others to invest in a vast array of stocks or bonds.

You can look at the benefits of diversification in two ways:

- Diversification reduces or dampens the volatility in the value of your whole portfolio. In other words, you can achieve the same rate of return that a single investment can provide with reduced fluctuations in value.

- Diversification allows you to obtain a higher rate of return for a given level of risk.

Keep in mind that no one, no matter whom he works for or what credentials he has, can guarantee returns on an investment. You can do good research and you can be lucky, but no one is free from the risk of losing money. Diversification allows you to hedge the risk of your investments. See Figures 8-1, 8-2, and 8-3 to get an idea of how diversifying can reduce your risk (figures in these charts are adjusted for inflation). Notice that different investments did better during various time periods. Because the future can't be predicted, you are safer diversifying your money into different investments. (In case you're wondering what the 1990s looked like, stocks appreciated greatly and bonds did pretty well, too, while gold and silver did poorly.)

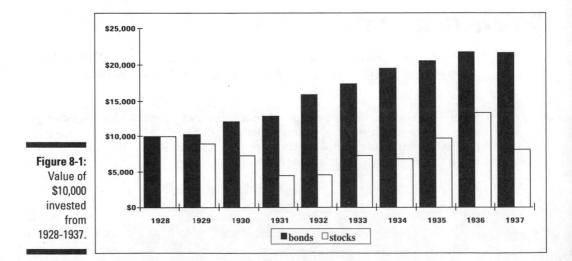

Figure 8-1:
Value of
$10,000
invested
from
1928-1937.

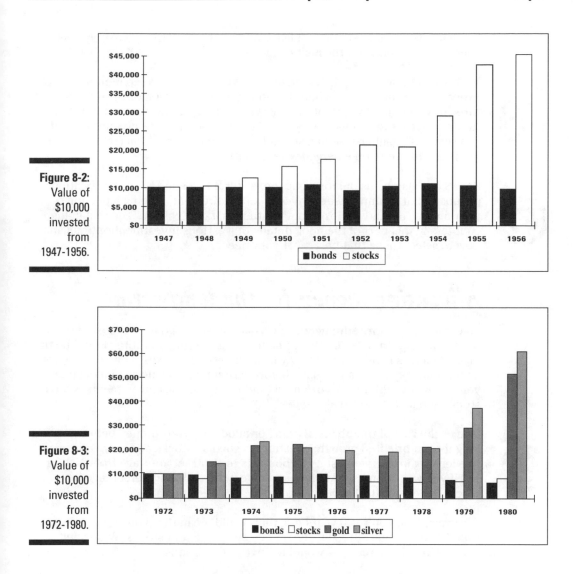

Figure 8-2:
Value of
$10,000
invested
from
1947-1956.

Figure 8-3:
Value of
$10,000
invested
from
1972-1980.

Asset allocation: Spreading it around

How you spread your investing dollars among different investment options
(stocks, bonds, money market accounts, and so on) is known as *asset allocation.* Before you can intelligently decide how to allocate your assets, you
should consider a number of issues, including your present financial situation,
your goals and priorities, as well as the pros and cons of various investment
options.

Although stocks and real estate offer investors attractive long-term returns,
they can and do suffer significant declines in value from time to time. Thus,

these investments are not suitable for money that you think you may want or need to use within, say, the next five years.

Money market and bond investments are good places to keep money that you expect to use sooner. Everyone should have a reserve of money — about three to six months' worth of living expenses in a money market fund — that they can access in an emergency. Shorter-term bonds or bond mutual funds can serve as a higher-yielding, secondary emergency cushion (refer to Chapter 3 for more on emergency reserves).

Bonds can also be useful for some longer-term investing for diversification purposes. For example, when investing for retirement, placing a portion of your money in bonds helps to buffer stock market declines. The remaining chapters in this part of the book detail your various investment options and how to select those that best meet your needs.

Allocating money for the long-term

Investing money for retirement is a classic long-term goal that most of us have. Your current age and the number of years until you retire should be the biggest factors in allocating money for long-term purposes. The younger you are and the more years you have before retirement, the more comfortable you should be with growth-oriented (and more volatile) investments, such as stocks and investment real estate.

One useful rule of thumb for dividing or allocating your money between longer-term-oriented growth investments such as stocks and more conservative lending investments such as bonds is to subtract your age from 100 (or 120 if you want to be aggressive) and invest the resulting percentage in stocks. Invest what's left over in bonds.

For example, if you're 30 years old, that would mean that you could invest from 70 (100 minus 30) to 90 (120 minus 30) percent in stocks. What's left over — 10 to 30 percent — would be invested in bonds.

Table 8-4 lists some guidelines for allocating long-term money. All you need to figure out is how old you are and the level of risk you're comfortable with.

Table 8-4	Allocating Long-Term Money	
Your Investment Attitude	*Bond Allocation (%)*	*Stock Allocation (%)*
"Play it safe"	= Age	= 100–age
"Middle of the road"	= Age–10	= 110–age
"Aggressive"	= Age–20	= 120–age

For example, if you're the conservative sort who doesn't like a lot of risk but recognizes the value of striving for some growth and making your money work harder, you're a *middle-of-the-road* type. Using Table 8-4, if you're 40 years old, you might consider putting 30 percent (40–10) in bonds and 70 percent (110–40) in stocks.

In most employer retirement plans, mutual funds are the typical investment vehicle. If your employer's retirement plan includes more than one stock mutual fund as an option, you may want to try discerning which options are best by using the criteria outlined in Chapter 10. In the event that all your retirement plan's stock fund options are good, you can simply divide your stock allocation equally among the choices.

When one or more of the choices is an international stock fund, consider allocating a percentage of your stock fund money to overseas investments: at least 20 percent for *play-it-safe* investors, 25 to 35 percent for *middle-of-the-road* investors, or as much as 40 to 50 percent for *aggressive* investors.

If the 40-year-old middle-of-the-roader from the previous example is investing 70 percent in stocks, then about 25 to 35 percent of the stock fund investments (which works out to be about 18 to 24 percent of the total) could be invested in international stock funds.

Historically, most employees haven't had to make their own investing decisions with retirement money. Pension plans, in which the company directs the investments, were more common in previous years. It's interesting to note that in a typical pension plan, companies choose to allocate the majority of money to stocks (about 60 percent), with a bit less in bonds (about 35 percent) and other investments. For more information on investing in retirement accounts, please see Chapter 11.

Stick with your allocations: Don't trade

Your allocation of your investment dollars should be driven by your goals and desire to take risk. As you get older, for most investors, it makes sense to gradually scale back on the riskiness (and therefore growth potential) of your portfolio.

Don't tinker with your portfolio daily, weekly, monthly, or even annually. (Every five years or so, you may want to "rebalance" your holdings to get your mix to a desired asset allocation as discussed in the previous section.) You should not engage in trading in the hopes of buying into a hot investment and selling your losers. Although hopping onto a "winner" and dumping a "loser" may provide some short-term psychological comfort, in the long-term, such an investment strategy can produce below-average returns.

By the time an investment gets front-page coverage and everyone is talking about its stunning rise, it's definitely time to take a reality check. The higher the value of an investment rises, the greater the danger that it's overpriced. Its next move may be downward. Don't follow the herd.

In recent years, some technology (especially internet) stocks have had spectacular rises, thus attracting a lot of attention. Although the U.S. economy is increasingly becoming technologically based, that doesn't mean that any price you pay for a technology stock is fine. Some investors who neglected to do basic research and who bought into attention-grabbing, high-flying technology stocks recently have lost 50 percent or more of their investments — and this during a time period when the overall stock market was moving higher. Ouch!

Conversely, when things look bleak, giving up hope is easy — who wants to be associated with a loser? However, investors who panicked and sold *after* the October 1987 U.S. stock market crash missed out on a tremendous buying opportunity. Ditto for those who dumped stocks after the smaller declines in the U.S. stock market in 1990, 1994, and 1998.

Most people like buying everything from clothing to cars to ketchup on sale — yet whenever the stock market has a clearance sale, most investors stampede for the exits instead of snatching up great buys. Demonstrate your courage; don't follow the herd. After all, lemmings die that way. (By the way, how is it that lemmings aren't extinct?)

Investment Firms Are Not Created Equal

Thousands of firms sell investments and manage money. Banks, mutual fund companies, securities brokerage firms, and even insurance companies all vie for your hard-earned dough.

Just to make matters more complicated, each industry plays in the others' backyards. You can find mutual fund companies that offer securities brokerage, insurance firms that are in the mutual fund business, and mutual fund companies that offer banking-like accounts and services. You benefit somewhat from all this competition and one-stop shopping convenience. On the other hand, some firms are novices at particular businesses and count on the fact that some people shop by brand-name recognition.

Where to focus

The firms with whom you should do business are those that do the following:

✔ **Offer the best value investments in comparison to their competitors.**
Value combines performance and cost. Given the level of risk that you're
comfortable with, you'd like investments that offer higher rates of
return, but you don't want to have to pay a small fortune for them.
Commissions, management fees, maintenance fees, and other charges
can turn a high-performance investment into a mediocre or poor one.

✔ **Employ representatives who do not have an inherent self-interest in
steering you into a particular type of investment.** This criterion has
nothing to do with whether an investment firm hires polite, well-educated,
or well-dressed people. The most important factor is the way the company compensates its employees. If the investment firm's personnel are
paid on commission, pass on that firm. Give preference to investing
through firms that do not tempt their employees to push one investment
over another in order to generate more fees.

No-load (commission-free) mutual fund companies

Mutual funds are an ideal investment vehicle for most investors. *No-load
mutual fund companies* are firms through which you can invest in mutual funds
without paying sales commissions. In other words, every dollar you invest
goes to work in the mutual funds you choose — nothing is siphoned off to pay
sales commissions. See Chapter 10 for details on investing in mutual funds.

Discount brokers

Just over a generation ago, when investors bought or sold stocks, bonds, and
other securities, they were charged fixed commissions. In other words, no
matter which brokerage firm an investor did business with, the cost of the
firm's services was set. And the level of commissions was high.

In one of the most beneficial changes for investors in this century, the
Securities and Exchange Commission (SEC), effective May 1, 1975, deregu-
lated the retail brokerage industry. Brokerage firms could then charge people
whatever their little hearts desired. You may think that this change opened
the door to exorbitantly high rates. In fact, it did the opposite. A fair and
open free market is good for consumers. Competition inevitably resulted in
more and better choices.

Most firms that were in business before that time, such as Merrill Lynch,
Prudential, and E. F. Hutton, continued doing business as usual: That is, they
continued to pay their brokers based on the amount of trading their customers did and which investments they sold.

Fortunately, many new brokerage firms opened that did not do business the
old way. They were dubbed *discount brokers* because the fees they charged
customers were substantially lower than what brokers charged under the old
fixed-fee system.

Even more important than saving the customer money, discount brokers established a vastly improved compensation system that greatly reduced conflicts of interest. Discount brokers generally pay their brokers salaries. The term *discount broker* is actually not an enlightening one. It is certainly true that this new breed of brokerage firm saves you lots of money when you invest. You can easily save 50 to 80 percent through the major discount brokers. But these firms' investments are not "on sale" or second-rate. Discount brokers are simply brokers without major conflicts of interest. Of course, like any other for-profit enterprise, they want your business and they are in business to make money, but they're much less likely to steer you wrong for their own benefit.

Note: Be careful of discount brokers selling load mutual funds.

Places to consider avoiding

The worst places to invest are those that charge you a lot, have mediocre or poorly performing investments, and have major conflicts of interest. The prime conflict of interest comes with investment firms that pay their brokers commissions on the basis of how much and what they sell. The result: The investment firms sell lots of stuff that pays fat commissions, and they churn your account (because each transaction has a fee, the more you buy and sell, the more money they make).

The major firms that historically have compensated their brokers mostly on commissions include Prudential Securities, Smith Barney Shearson, PaineWebber, Dean Witter, Merrill Lynch, and Kidder Peabody. You probably recognize the names of many of these firms. Think about that. Do you know many people who have made lots of money and beaten the securities market averages by investing with them? Or do you know of them because of all the advertising they do and the negative publicity so many of these firms have received over the years? Going by a catchy slogan or by brand-name recognition is *not* smart shopping. These firms sold billions of dollars of the dreaded limited partnerships, which I briefly discuss in the next chapter.

Many folks who call themselves *financial planners* or *financial consultants* work on commission. In addition to working at the bigger brokerage firms, many of them belong to so-called *broker-dealer networks,* which provide back-office support and investment products to sell. When a person claiming to be a financial planner or advisor is part of a broker-dealer network, odds are quite high you're dealing with an investment salesperson. See Chapter 18 for more background on the financial planning industry and questions to ask an advisor you might hire.

Commissions and their impact on human behavior

Investment products bring in widely varying commissions. The products that bring in the highest commissions tend to be the ones that money-hungry brokers push the hardest.

Table 8-5 lists the commissions that you pay and that come out of your investment dollars when you work with brokers, financial consultants, and financial planners working on commission.

Table 8-5	Investment Sales Commissions	
Investment Type	*Average Commission on $20,000 Investment*	*Average Commission on $100,000 Investment*
Annuities	$1,400	$7,000
Initial public offerings (new stock issue)	$1,000	$5,000
Limited partnerships	$1,800	$9,000
Load mutual funds	$1,200	$6,000
Options and futures	$2,000+	$10,000+

Besides the fact that you can never be sure that you're getting an unbiased recommendation from a salesperson working on commission, you're wasting unnecessary money. All good investments can be bought on a no-load (commission-free) basis. No-load mutual funds are a good example.

When you're unsure about an investment product that's being pitched to you (and even when you *are* sure), ask for a copy of the prospectus. In the first few pages, check out whether the investment includes a commission (also known as a load). While salespeople can hide behind obfuscating titles such as vice president or financial consultant, a prospectus must detail whether the investment carries a commission.

Investment salespeople's conflicts of interest

Financial consultants (also known as stockbrokers), financial planners, and others who sell investment products can have enormous conflicts of interest in the strategies and specific investment products that they recommend. Commissions and other financial incentives can't help but skew the advice of even the most earnest and otherwise well-intentioned salespeople.

What to do if you've been fleeced by a broker

You can't sue a broker just because you lose money on that person's investment recommendations. That's life in the big city. However, if you have been the victim of one of the following cardinal financial sins, you may have some legal recourse:

- **Misrepresentation and omission.** If you were told, for example, that a particular investment guaranteed returns of 15 percent per year and the investment ends up plunging in value by 50 percent, you were misled. Misrepresentation can also be charged if you are sold an investment with hefty commissions but were originally told that it was commission-free.

- **Unsuitable investments.** Retirees who need access to their capital are often advised to invest in limited partnerships (discussed in Chapter 9) for safe, high yields. The yields on most LPs end up being anything but safe. LP investors have also discovered how illiquid their investments are — some can't be liquidated for up to ten years or more.

- **Churning.** If your broker or financial planner is constantly trading your investments, odds are that his or her weekly commission check benefits at your expense.

- **Rogue elephant salespeople.** When your planner or broker buys or sells without your approval or ignores your request to make a change, you may be able to collect for losses caused by these actions.

Two major types of practitioners — securities lawyers and arbitration consultants — stand ready to help you recover your lost money. You can find securities lawyers by looking under "Attorneys — Securities" in the Yellow Pages or by calling your local bar association for referrals. Arbitration consultants can be found under "Arbitrators." If you come up dry, try contacting business writers at a major newspaper in your area or at your favorite personal finance magazine. These sources may be able to give you names and numbers of folks they know.

Most lawyers and consultants work on a contingency-fee basis — they get a percentage of damages (about 20 to 40 percent of the amount collected). They also usually ask for an up-front fee ranging from several hundred to several thousand dollars to help them cover their expenses and time. If they take your case and lose, they generally get to keep the up-front money. Securities lawyers are usually a more expensive option.

You generally don't end up in a courtroom *L.A. Law*-style. You'll probably go to arbitration — an agreement you made (probably not realizing it) when you set up an account to work with the broker or planner. Arbitration is usually much quicker, cheaper, and easier for you. You can even choose to represent yourself. Both sides present their case to a panel of three arbitrators who make a decision that both sides can't squabble over or appeal.

If you decide to prepare for arbitration yourself, the nonprofit American Arbitration Association can send you a background package of materials to help with your case. Check your local phone directory or contact the association's headquarters (140 West 51st Street, New York, NY 10020; phone 212-484-4000; www.adr.org).

Numerous conflicts of interest can damage your investment portfolio. The following are the most common conflicts to watch out for:

- **Pushing higher-commission products.** As I discuss earlier in this chapter, commissions vary tremendously on investment products. At the worst end of the spectrum for you (and the best for a salesperson) are products like limited partnerships, commodities, options, and futures. At the best end of the spectrum for you (and therefore, the worst for a salesperson) are investments such as no-load mutual funds and Treasury bills that are 100 percent commission-free.

  Surprisingly, commission-based brokers and financial planners need not give you the prospectus (where commissions are detailed) before you buy a financial product that carries commissions (as with a load mutual fund). In contrast, commission-free investment companies, such as no-load mutual fund companies, must send a prospectus in advance of taking a mutual fund order. Commission-based investment salespeople should also have to provide prospectuses in advance of a sale, and they should be required to disclose any commissions up front and in writing. I suppose if that happened, more people would choose to buy investments elsewhere, and politicians might start telling the truth!

- **Recommending active trading.** Investment salespeople often advise you to trade frequently into and out of different securities. They usually base their advice on current news events or an analyst's comments on the security. Sometimes, these moves are valid; more often, they are not. In extreme cases, brokers trade on a monthly basis. By the end of the year, they've churned through your entire portfolio. Needless to say, all these transactions cost you big money in trading fees.

  Diversified mutual funds (discussed in Chapter 10) make more sense for most people. You can invest in mutual funds free of sales commissions. Besides saving money on commissions, you earn better long-term returns by having an expert money manager work for you.

- **Failing to recommend investing through retirement plans.** If you're not taking full advantage of retirement savings plans (see Chapter 11), you may be missing out on valuable tax benefits. Your initial contributions to most retirement plans are tax-deductible, and your money compounds without taxation over the years. An investment salesperson is not likely to recommend that you contribute to your employer's retirement plan — a 401(k) for example. Such contributions cut into the money you have available to invest with your friendly salesperson.

  If you're self-employed, salespeople are somewhat more likely to recommend that you fund a retirement plan because they can set up such plans for you. You're better off doing so yourself through a no-load mutual fund company (see Chapters 10 and 11).

✔ **Pushing high-fee products.** Many of the brokerage firms that used to sell investment products only on commission (for example, Prudential, Merrill Lynch, Smith Barney Shearson, Paine Webber, and Dean Witter) are moving into fee-based investment management. This change is an improvement for investors because it reduces some of the conflicts of interest caused by commissions.

On the other hand, these brokers charge extraordinarily high fees (which are usually quoted as a percentage of assets under management) on their managed investment (wrap) accounts (see the sidebar on wrap accounts).

BEWARE

Wrap or managed accounts

Wrap, or managed, accounts are all the rage among commission-based brokerage firms. These accounts go under a variety of names but are similar in that they charge a fixed percentage of the assets under management to invest your money through money managers.

Wrap accounts are poor investments because their management expenses are extraordinarily high — often up to 3 percent per year (some even higher) of assets under management. Remember that in the long haul, stocks can return about 10 percent per year before taxes. So, if you're paying 3 percent per year to have the money managed in stocks, 30 percent of your return (before taxes) is siphoned off. But don't forget — because the government sure won't — that you pay a good chunk of money in taxes on your 10-percent return as well. So the 3-percent wrap actually ends up depleting 40 to 50 percent of your after-tax profits!

Forbes magazine said it best in an article on wrap accounts: "Brokerage firms love wrap accounts because they're so lucrative — for them."

No-load (commission-free) mutual funds offer investors access to the nation's best investment managers for a fraction of the cost of wrap accounts. You can invest in dozens of top-performing funds for an annual expense of 1 percent per year or less. Some of the best fund companies offer excellent funds for a cost as low as 0.2 to 0.5 percent (see Chapter 10).

So how do brokerage firms trick investors into paying 3 to 15 times as much for access to investment managers? Marketing. Slick, seductive, deceptive, misleading pitches that include some outright lies.

You may be told that you're getting access to investment managers who don't normally take money from small-fry investors like you. Not a single study shows that the performance of money managers has anything to do with the minimum account they handle. Besides, no-load mutual funds hire many of the same managers who work at other money management firms.

You also may be told that you'll earn a higher rate of return, so the extra cost is worth it. You could have earned 18 to 25 percent per year, they say, had you invested with the "Star of Yesterday" investment management company. The key word here is "had." History is history. Many of yesterday's winners become tomorrow's losers or mediocre performers.

You also must remember that, unlike mutual funds, whose performance records are audited by the SEC, wrap account performance records may include marketing hype. The most common ploy is showing only the performance of selected accounts — those that performed the best!

The value of brokerage research

One of the arguments frequently advanced by brokerage firms and the brokers who work for them is that their research is better. With their insights and recommendations, they say, you'll do better and "beat the market averages."

Don't believe them. A number of studies clearly demonstrate that their research is barely worth the cost of your morning paper (sometimes not even that)! If the brokerage firms' research were superior, then their mutual fund returns should be exceptional, right? They're not. Not a single brokerage firm mutual fund family produces above-average returns when considering all their funds!

Wall Street analysts are often overly optimistic when it comes to predicting corporate profits. If analysts were simply inaccurate or bad estimators, you would expect that they would sometimes underestimate and other times overestimate companies' earnings. The discrepancy identifies yet another conflict of interest among many of the brokerage firms.

Brokerage firm analysts are loath to write a negative report about a company because the firms these analysts work for also solicit companies to issue new stock to the public. What better way to show your potential for selling shares at a high price to the public than by showing how much you believe in certain companies and writing glowing reports about their future prospects?

Brokerage analysts have great difficulty being objective. Investment banking (the business of helping companies sell new securities) cannot objectively be done by companies supposedly evaluating and rating the same securities for the investing public.

Experts Who Predict the Future

A common mistake that some investors make is believing that they can increase their investment returns when they follow the prognostications of certain gurus. Many of us may want to believe that some experts can divine the future of the investment world. Believing in gurus makes it easier to accept the risk that you know you're taking to make your money grow. The sage predictions in an investment newsletter or by an "expert" who is repeatedly quoted in financial publications make you feel protected. It's sort of like Linus and his security blanket.

Investment newsletter subscribers and guru followers would be better off instead buying a warm blanket — it has a lot more value and costs a whole lot less! No one can predict the future. If they could, they would be so busy investing their own money and getting rich that they wouldn't have the time and desire to share their secrets with you.

Investment newsletters

Many investment newsletters purport to time the markets, telling you exactly the right time to get into and out of certain stocks or mutual funds (or the financial markets in general). Such an approach is doomed to failure in the long run. By failure, I mean that this approach is not going to beat the tried-and-true strategy of buy and hold.

I see people paying hundreds of dollars annually to subscribe to all sorts of market-timing and stock-picking newsletters. One client, an attorney, had subscribed to several newsletters. When I asked him why, he said that their marketing materials claimed that if you followed their advice, you would make a 20 percent per year return on your money. But in the four years that Ken had followed their advice, he had actually *lost* money, despite appreciating financial markets overall.

Before you ever consider subscribing to any investment newsletter, you should examine its historic track record. The newsletter's marketing materials typically hype the supposed returns that the publication's recommendations have produced. Sadly, newsletters seem to be able to make lots of bogus claims without suffering the timely wrath of securities regulators.

Mark Hulbert tracks the performance of the recommendations made by newsletter writers. Hulbert's organization looks at the cold, hard facts of actual returns and shows how your portfolio would have done if you had followed the recommendations of given newsletters.

If you had been so omniscient as to know in advance which five newsletters would give the best advice during the past 15 years (see Table 8-6), after adjusting for the level of risk that each had taken, you would have done worse in four of the five cases than the overall rate of return of the Wilshire 5000 index, the broadest measure of the overall performance of small, medium, and large companies' U.S. stocks.

Table 8-6	The "Best" Newsletters
Newsletter	*Risk-Adjusted Performance Ranking*
Systems & Forecast	108.4
The Chartist	89.1
No-Load Fund X	86.7
Investor's World	82.2
Value Line Investment Survey	80.2
Wilshire 5000 Index	100.0

Source: Hulbert's Financial Digest

Hulbert uses *risk-adjusted returns,* which are corrected for the differences in the amount of risk different newsletters took in their recommendations. For comparative purposes, the risk-adjusted return of the Wilshire 5000 index is set at 100. The best newsletter in Table 8-6, which has a rating of 108.4, has produced an 8.4 percent higher return than expected given the level of risk it takes. Note that four of the five "best" newsletters over the past 15 years have a rating less than 100, implying that their recommendations, given the risk entailed, performed worse than the Wilshire 5000 index.

Because you can actually invest in the Wilshire 5000 index via an index mutual fund (see Chapter 10), don't waste your money subscribing to investment newsletters in the hopes of beating the stock market's overall returns!

If, by bad luck, you had been suckered into following the advice of some of the worst newsletters, your investment results would have been disastrous, especially in comparison to what you could have earned in Treasury bills or the Wilshire 5000 stock index. Check out Table 8-7.

Table 8-7	The Worst Newsletters Compared to the Market
Newsletter Portfolio	**Past Five-Year Return**
Futures Hotline	−99 %
Overpriced Stock Price	−96 %
Elliott Wave Theorist	−95 %
Short on Value	−86 %
Option Advisor	−64 %
Granville Market Letter	−62 %
Wilshire 5000 Index	+149 %

Source: Hulbert's Financial Digest

Don't use newsletters for predictive advice. If newsletter writers were that smart about the future of financial markets, they would be money managers making lots more money. The only types of investment newsletters and periodicals that you should consider subscribing to are those that offer research and information rather than predictions. I discuss those that fit the bill in the subsequent investment chapters.

Investment gurus

Investment gurus come and go. Some of them get their 15 minutes of fame on the basis of one or two successful predictions that someone in the press remembers (and makes famous). A classic example is a former market analyst at Shearson named Elaine Garzarelli.

Ms. Garzarelli became famous for predicting the stock market's plummet in the fall of 1987. Garzarelli's fund, Smith Barney Shearson Sector Analysis, was established just before the crash. Supposedly, Garzarelli's indicators warned her to stay out of stocks, which she did, and in doing so, she saved her fund from the plunge.

Shearson, being a money-minded brokerage, quickly motivated its brokers to sell shares in Garzarelli's fund. In addition to her having avoided the crash, it didn't hurt that Shearson brokers were being rewarded with a hefty 5 percent sales commission for selling her fund. By the end of 1987, investors had poured nearly $700 million into this fund.

In 1988, Garzarelli's fund was the worst-performing fund among funds investing in growth stocks. From 1988 to 1990, Garzarelli's fund underperformed the Standard & Poor 500 average by about 43 percent! In 1987 — the year of the crash — Garzarelli outperformed the S&P 500 by about 26 percent. So what she saved her investors by avoiding the crash she lost back — and more — in the years that followed. In fact, Garzarelli's performance was so dismal in the years following the crash that Shearson eventually fired her.

Despite her subpar long-term track record, Garzarelli is still widely quoted as a market soothsayer. She now manages money privately and is hawking investment newsletters. This marketing hype promoting her newsletter recently appeared in a mailed brochure entitled "The Garzarelli Edge":

> "The proven, scientific system that has produced compounded yearly gains of 20.2% since 1982!"

> "Elaine Garzarelli has called every major turn in the Dow since 1982."

Now, if the above were true, why did Garzarelli's investment fund perform so poorly, and why did Shearson fire her in the mid-1990s following numerous years of wrong predictions and dismal performance of her mutual fund? It's also humorous to note that the 20.2-percent return was reportedly "audited by a Big-6 accounting firm." Down in the fine print, however, it says, "Audit Pending." I bet it's still pending.

Every year, new gurus emerge. All it seems to take to leap to guru status these days is one right call or one good stock pick. Recently, for example, prognosticators who recommended one of the high-flying technology stocks were nearly vaulted to instant guru status as the stocks continued climbing.

Pundits who pitched investing in Presstek and Iomega attracted fairly large followings as these stocks seemed to defy gravity and rationale valuations as they rocketed ever skyward. Like Ms. Garzarelli, however, these stocks and their promoters were brought back to reality during the late 1990s when the stocks plummeted by more than 65 percent.

And like other high-flying stocks and the pundits made famous by them, many investors weren't attracted to invest in Presstek and Iomega until nearly everybody was talking about them. By then, those stocks were peaking, and those who bought got clobbered.

Herb Greenberg, a former business writer for the *San Francisco Chronicle,* held a stock market contest that a group of 13-year-olds won. The reason: They put most of their money into Iomega while it was still heading up. Does this make these 13-year-olds investing geniuses to whom we should look for guidance on the next hot stock? Of course not. Treat other pundits who happened to guess right the same way.

Commentators and experts who publish predictive newsletters and who are interviewed in the media can't predict the future. Ignore the predictions and speculations of self-proclaimed gurus and investment soothsayers. The few people who have a slight leg up on everyone else aren't going to share their investment secrets — they're too busy investing their own money! If you have to believe in something to offset your fears, believe in good information and proven investment managers. And don't forget the value of optimism, faith, and hope — regardless of What or Whom you believe in!

Final Thoughts

I cover a lot of ground in this chapter. In the remaining chapters in this section, I detail different investment choices and accounts and how to build a champion portfolio! Before you move on, here are several other issues to keep in mind as you make important investing choices:

- ✔ **Don't invest based on sales solicitations.** Companies that advertise and solicit prospective customers aggressively using tactics such as telemarketing offer some of the worst financial products with the highest fees. Companies with great products don't have to reach their potential customers this way. Of course, all companies have to do some promotion. But the companies with the best investment offerings don't have to use the hard sell approach and get plenty of new business through word-of-mouth recommendations of satisfied customers.

- ✔ **Don't invest in what you don't understand.** The mistake of not understanding the investments you purchase usually follows from the preceding no-no — buying into a sales pitch. When you don't understand an investment, odds are good that it won't be right for you. Slick-tongued brokers (who may call themselves financial consultants, advisors, or planners) who earn commissions based on what they sell often talk you into inappropriate investments. Before you invest in anything, you should know its track record, its true costs, and how liquid it is.

✔ **Minimize fees.** Avoid investments that carry high sales commissions and management expenses (usually disclosed in a prospectus). Virtually all investments today can be purchased without a salesperson. Besides paying unnecessary commissions, the bigger danger in investing through a salesperson is that you may be directed to a path that's not in your best interests. Management fees create a real drag on investment returns. Not surprisingly, higher-fee investments, on average, perform worse than alternatives with lower fees. High ongoing management fees often go toward lavish offices, glossy brochures, and skyscraper salaries or toward propping up small, inefficient operations. Do you want your hard-earned dollars to support either of these types of businesses?

✔ **Pay attention to tax consequences.** Even if you never become an investment expert, you're smart enough to know that the more money you pay in taxes, the less you have to invest and play with. Channeling investment money into retirement accounts allows your money to grow without taxation, and therefore faster, over time (see Chapter 11). For investments outside retirement accounts, you need to match the types of investments to your tax situation (see Chapter 12).

Chapter 9

Investment Vehicles

● ●

In This Chapter

▶ Safe and boring investments: bank and money market accounts and bonds

▶ Investments to grow on: stocks, real estate, and small business

▶ Oddball investments: precious metals, annuities, collectibles, and life insurance

● ●

*I*n the investment world, you can place your money in many different types of investment vehicles. Decent investment vehicles work their way methodically around the racetrack, rarely deterred but also never at a fast rate. The best ones make their way through the course at a faster clip, only occasionally slowed by a bump or detour. The worst ones sputter in fits and starts and sometimes crash and burn in a flaming heap.

Which vehicle you choose for your trip depends on where you're going, how fast you want to get there, and what risks you're willing to take along the way. If you haven't yet read Chapter 8, please do so now. In it, I cover a number of investment concepts, such as the difference between lending and ownership investments, that will enhance your ability to choose among the common investment vehicles I discuss in this chapter.

Lending Vehicles for Slow-Trip Money

Everyone should have some money riding in stable, safe investment vehicles. For example, as I discuss in Chapter 3, money that you have earmarked for your short-term bills, both expected and unexpected, should have a seat belt on in the back seat of a Volvo. Likewise, if you're saving money for a home purchase within the next few years, you certainly don't want to risk that money on the roller coaster of the stock market.

The vehicles that follow are appropriate for money that you don't want to put at great risk.

Transaction/checking accounts

These accounts are best used for depositing your monthly income and paying for your expenditures. When you want to have unlimited check-writing privileges and access to your money with an ATM card, checking accounts at local banks are your best bet. Make sure that you shop around for accounts that don't ding you $1 here for use of an ATM machine and $10 there for a low balance.

With interest rates as low as they are now, focus on avoiding monthly service charges rather than chasing after a checking account with a slightly higher interest rate. Some banks, for example, do not require you to maintain a minimum balance to avoid a monthly service charge when you direct deposit your paychecks.

If you don't need access to ATM machines on every other street corner — an option usually available through larger banks — you can generally get a better checking account deal at a credit union or a smaller bank. Because you can easily obtain cash through ATM outlets in supermarkets and other retail stores, you may not need to do business with Big City Bank with branch offices at every intersection.

In any event, you should only keep enough money in the account to service your monthly bill payment needs. If you consistently keep more than a few thousand dollars in a checking account, get the excess out. You can earn more in a savings or money market account, which I describe in the next section.

Some folks I know have no bank checking account at all. How do they do that? They have discount brokerage accounts — see Chapter 10 for recommended firms — that allow unlimited check writing. Also see my discussion in Chapter 19 about paying your bills via your computer.

Savings and money market accounts

Savings accounts are available at banks; money market funds are available through mutual fund companies. Savings accounts and money market funds are nearly identical except that money market funds generally pay a better rate of interest. The interest rate paid to you, also known as the *yield,* fluctuates over time, depending on the level of interest rates in the overall economy. (Note that some banks offer money market *accounts* which are basically like savings accounts and should not be confused with money market mutual *funds*.)

Bank savings accounts are backed by the federal government through Federal Deposit Insurance Corporation (FDIC) insurance. Money market funds are not. I wouldn't give preference to a bank account just because your investment (principal) is insured. In fact, you should prefer money market funds because the better ones are higher yielding than the better bank savings accounts. And money market funds offer check writing and other easy ways to access your money.

Money market funds are closely regulated by the U.S. Securities and Exchange Commission. Hundreds of money market funds invest hundreds of billions of dollars of individuals' and institutions' money. Never has the industry caused an individual to lose even a penny of principal.

Money market securities are extremely safe; many are guaranteed or backed by a federal government agency. The risk difference versus a bank account is nil. General-purpose money market funds invest in safe, short-term bank certificates of deposit, U.S. Treasuries, and corporate commercial paper (short-term debt), which is issued by the largest and most credit-worthy companies.

Money market fund investments can exist only in the most credit-worthy securities and must have an average maturity of less than 120 days. In the unlikely event that an investment in a money market fund's portfolio goes sour, the mutual fund company that stands behind the money market fund would almost certainly cover the loss.

If the lack of insurance on money market funds still spooks you, here's a way to get the best of both worlds: Select a money market fund that invests exclusively in U.S. government securities, which are virtually risk-free because they are backed by the full strength and credit of the federal government (as is the FDIC insurance system). These types of accounts typically pay less interest, usually ¼ percent less (although the interest is free of state income tax).

Bonds

When you invest in a bond, you effectively lend your money to an organization. When a bond is issued, it includes a specified maturity date at which time the principal will be repaid. Bonds are also issued at a particular interest rate or what's known as a "coupon." That rate is fixed on most bonds. So, for example, if you buy a five-year, 7 percent bond issued by IBM, you're lending your money to IBM for five years at an interest rate of 7 percent per year. Bond interest is usually paid in two equal semi-annual installments.

The value of a bond generally fluctuates with changes in interest rates. For example, if you're holding a bond issued at 8 percent and rates increase to 10 percent on comparable, newly issued bonds, your bond decreases in value. (Why would anyone want to buy your bond at the price you paid if it yields just 8 percent and she can get 10 percent elsewhere?)

The overused CD

Another type of bond is a certificate of deposit (CD), which is issued by a bank. With a CD, as with a real bond, you agree to lend your money to an organization (in this case, a bank) for a predetermined number of months or years. Generally, the longer you agree to lock up your money, the higher the interest rate you receive.

With CDs, you pay a penalty for early withdrawal. If you want your money back before the end of the CD's term, you'll get whacked with the loss of a number of months' worth of interest. CDs also don't tend to pay very competitive interest rates. You can usually beat the interest rate on shorter-term CDs (those that mature within a year or so) with the best money market mutual funds, which offer complete liquidity without any penalty.

Some bonds are tied to variable interest rates. For example, you can buy bonds that are adjustable-rate mortgages, on which the interest rate can fluctuate. As an investor, you're actually lending your money to a mortgage borrower — indirectly, you are the banker making a loan to someone buying a home.

Bonds differ from one another in the following major ways:

- ✔ The type of institution to which you are lending your money — state government (municipal bonds), federal government (treasuries), mortgage holder (GNMA), or corporation (corporate bonds).

- ✔ The credit quality of the borrower to whom you lend your money (in other words, the probability that the borrower will pay you the interest and return your principal as agreed).

- ✔ The length of maturity of the bond. Bonds generally mature within 30 years. Short-term bonds mature within a few years, intermediate bonds within 7 to 10 years, and long-term bonds within 30 years. Longer-term bonds generally pay higher yields but fluctuate more with changes in interest rates.

Bonds are rated by major credit-rating agencies for their safety, usually on a scale on which AAA is the highest possible rating. For example, high-grade corporate bonds (AAA or AA) are considered the safest (that is, most likely to pay you back). Next in safety are general bonds (A or BBB), which are still safe but just a little less so. Junk bonds (rated BB or lower), popularized by Michael Milken, are actually not all that junky; they're just lower in quality and have a slight (1 or 2 percent) probability of default.

Some bonds are *callable,* which means that the lender can decide to pay you back earlier than the previously agreed-upon date. This event usually occurs when interest rates fall and the lender wants to issue new, lower-interest rate bonds to replace the higher-rate bonds outstanding. To compensate you for early repayment, the lender typically gives you a small premium or bonus over what the bond is really worth.

Ownership Vehicles to Build Wealth

The three best legal ways to build wealth are to invest in stocks, real estate, and small business.

Stocks

Stocks are the most common ownership investment vehicle and represent shares of ownership in a company. When companies go "public," they issue shares of stock that people like you and I can purchase on the major stock exchanges, such as the New York Stock Exchange, American Stock Exchange, and NASDAQ (National Association of Securities Dealers Automated Quotation system) or the over-the-counter market.

As the economy grows and companies grow with it and earn greater profits, stock prices generally follow suit. Stock prices don't move in lockstep with earnings, but over the years, the relationship is pretty close. In fact, the *price-earnings ratio* — which measures the level of stock prices relative to (or divided by) company earnings — of U.S. stocks has averaged approximately 15 during this century (although it's tended to be higher during periods of low inflation). A price-earnings ratio of 15 simply means that stock prices per share on average are selling at about 15 times those companies' earnings per share.

Companies that issue stock (called *publicly held* companies) include automobile manufacturers, computer software producers, fast food restaurants, hotels, magazine and newspaper publishers, supermarkets, wineries, zipper manufacturers, and everything in between! By contrast, some companies are "privately held," which means they have elected to have their stock owned by senior management and a small number of affluent outside investors. Privately held companies' stocks do not trade on a stock exchange; that means that folks like you and me can't buy stock in such firms.

International stocks

Not only can you invest in company stocks that trade on the U.S. stock exchanges, but you can also invest in stocks overseas. Aside from folks with business connections abroad, why would the average citizen want to do so?

Several reasons. First, many investing opportunities exist overseas. If you look at the total value of all stocks outstanding worldwide, the value of U.S. stocks is now less than half the total.

Another reason for investing in international stocks is that when you confine your investing to U.S. securities, you miss a world of opportunities, not only because of business growth available in other countries but also because you get the opportunity to diversify your portfolio further. International securities markets don't move in tandem with U.S. markets. During various U.S. stock market drops, some international stock markets dropped less while others actually rose in value.

Some people hesitate to invest in overseas securities for silly reasons. In some cases, people read idiotic columns like one I came across in a big city paper. It was entitled "Plenty of Pitfalls in Foreign Investing: Timing is all in earning a decent return." The piece went on to say, "But as with sex, commuting and baseball, timing is everything in the stock market." Smart stock market investors know better than to try to time their investments. The piece also ominously warned, "Foreign stock markets have been known to evaporate overnight." I wish I could say the same for the jobs of some bone-headed financial journalists!

Others are concerned that overseas investing hurts the U.S. economy and contributes to a loss of American jobs. I have some counter-arguments. First, if you don't profit from the growth of economies overseas, someone else will. If there is money to be made, Americans may as well be there to participate. Profits from a foreign company are distributed to all stockholders, no matter where they live. Dividends and stock price appreciation know no national boundaries.

Also, you must recognize that you already live in a global economy — making a distinction between U.S. and non-U.S. companies is no longer appropriate. Many companies that are headquartered in the U.S. also have overseas operations. Some U.S. firms derive a large portion of their revenue from their international divisions. Conversely, many firms based overseas also have operations here. Increasing numbers of companies are worldwide operations. You don't get the full benefit of international investing through buying just large multinational companies headquartered in the U.S. The overseas diversification advantage is obtained by investing in companies that trade on foreign exchanges.

Companies differ in what industry or line of business they're in and also vary in size. In the financial press, you often hear companies referred to by their *market capitalization,* which is the value of their outstanding stock (the number of total shares multiplied by the market price per share). When describing the sizes of companies, Wall Street has done away with such practical adjectives as "big" and "small" and replaced them with babbling expressions like "large cap" and "small cap" (where *cap* stands for *capitalization*). Such is the language of financial geekiness.

As with raising children or going mountain climbing, investing in the stock market involves occasional setbacks and difficult moments, but the overall journey should be worth the effort. Over the past two centuries, the U.S. stock market has produced an annual average rate of return of about 10 percent. However, the market, as measured by the Dow Jones Industrial Average, has fallen more than 20 percent during 16 different periods in the 20th century. On average, these periods of decline lasted less than two years. So if you can withstand a temporary setback over a few years, the stock market is a proven place to invest for long-term growth.

You can invest in stocks by making your own selection of individual stocks or by letting a mutual fund manager (discussed in Chapter 10) do it for you.

The relative advantages of mutual funds

Efficiently managed mutual funds offer investors of both modest and substantial means low-cost access to high-quality money managers. Mutual funds span the spectrum of risk and potential returns from nonfluctuating money market funds (which are similar to savings accounts) to bond funds (which generally pay higher yields than money market funds but fluctuate with changes in interest rates) to stock funds (which offer the greatest potential for appreciation but also the greatest short-term volatility).

Mutual funds make better sense than individual securities for investors. To illustrate, imagine the following scenario. You just bought your first home. It's an older, lived-in property with barf-brown carpets that have accumulated 20-plus years of food spills and pet accidents. You want to tear out the yucky old carpet and install hardwood floors.

Imagine that you can either redo your flooring work yourself or pay a contractor just $200 to do it for you. You would hire the contractor if you could hire him this cheaply. The only type of person who would choose to go it alone is someone who really enjoys this type of work. You're not going to be able to do a faster, better job than a full-time contractor if you do a decent job searching for a good one.

The same thinking process should go into your decision making when you consider how to invest in stocks and bonds. Investing in individual securities should be done only by those who really enjoy doing it. Mutual funds, if properly selected, are a low-cost, quality way to hire professional money managers.

In the long haul, you're not going to beat full-time professional managers who are investing in the securities of the same type and risk level that you are. As with hiring a contractor, you need to do your homework to find a good money manager. Even if you think that you can do as well as the best, remember that most "superstar" money managers have only beaten the market averages by a few percent per year. Chapter 10 is devoted to mutual funds.

Isn't the stock market just legalized gambling?

A student in a personal finance class I used to teach at the University of California at Berkeley brought in a copy of a *New York Times* article entitled "Gaming on Wall Street." In the piece, the writer said, "Increasingly, the stock market itself has become just another commodity — as its recent volatility has shown."

After having read this, the student put her comment/question to me in writing: "Unless you're a superstar in your field, have stock options in a high tech company, or inherited wealth, it's increasingly difficult for a working person to provide for the future merely with hard work and savings. One is forced to invest in a stock market that is acting more like a commodity and has little to do with economic rules or real value. It is more and more like gambling. I resent turning over my hard-earned money to something that resembles a casino, but there's really no other game in town. Your thoughts?"

First, I suggested to the student that she might choose better reading material. The writer of this piece had not bothered to do his homework.

If he had, he would know that, in the years before this piece was published, by historic standards, the U.S. stock market was actually less volatile than normal. He also implied that the increasing stock prices were inflated and unjustified by the economy. In fact, corporate profits have been booming in recent years, and that inevitably drives stock prices higher.

Second, I told my student that, although the stock market can sometimes be temperamental, in the long run the market is driven by the performance of our economy. That's not gambling — that's investing.

Third, as I discuss later in this chapter, the stock market is hardly the only game in town. To build wealth, in addition to the U.S. stock market, you can invest in stocks outside the U.S. as well as in real estate, small business, or your own career.

A capitalistic economy isn't always fair. But it rarely rewards pessimists, spectators, and those unwilling to take some risks.

Investing in individual stocks

My experience is that more than a few otherwise smart, fun-loving people choose to invest in individual securities because they think that they're smarter or luckier than the rest. I don't know you personally, but it's safe to say that in the long run, your investment choices are not going to outperform those of a full-time investment professional.

I've noticed a distinct difference between the sexes on this issue. Perhaps because of differences in how people are raised, testosterone levels, or whatever, men tend to have more of a problem swallowing their egos and admitting that they're better off not going with individual securities. Maybe men's desires to be stock pickers are genetically linked to not wanting to ask for directions!

Investing in individual stocks should generally be avoided. Success is difficult to attain; the drawbacks and pitfalls are numerous:

✔ **Significant research time and cost are required.** You should know a lot about the company you're investing in when you are considering the purchase of an individual security. Relevant questions to ask about the company are: What products does it sell? What are its prospects for future growth and profitability? How much debt does the company have? You need to do your homework not only before you make your initial investment but also on an ongoing basis as long as you hold the investment.

Don't fool yourself or let others with a vested interest fool you into believing that picking and following individual companies and their stocks is simple, requires little time, and is far more profitable than investing in mutual funds.

✔ **Your emotions will probably get in your way.** Analyzing financial statements and corporate strategy and competitive position requires great intellect and insight. However, those skills aren't nearly enough. Will you have the stomach to hold on after what you thought was a sure-win stock plunges 50 percent while the overall stock market holds steady or even climbs? Will you have the courage to dump such a stock if your new research suggests that the plummet is the beginning of the end rather than just a big bump in the road? When your money is on the line, emotions often kick in which will undermine your ability to make sound long-term decisions. Few people have the psychological constitution to outfox the financial markets.

✔ **You're less likely to diversify.** Unless you have tens of thousands of dollars to invest in different stocks, you probably can't cost-effectively afford to develop a diversified portfolio. For example, when you're investing in stocks, you should hold companies in different industries, different companies within an industry, and so on. Not diversifying unnecessarily adds to your risk.

✔ **You'll face accounting and bookkeeping hassles.** When you invest in individual securities outside retirement accounts, every time you sell a specific security, you must report that transaction on your tax return. Even if you pay someone else to complete your tax return, you still have the hassle of keeping track of statements and receipts.

Of course, you can find some people (with a vested interest) who will try to convince you that picking your own stocks and managing your own portfolio of stocks is easy and more profitable than investing in, say, a mutual fund. In my experience, such stock-picking cheerleaders fall into at least one of the following categories:

- ✔ **Newsletter writers.** Whether in print or on an internet site, you can find plenty of pundits who pitch the notion that professional money managers are just overpaid buffoons and that you can handily trounce the pros with little investment of your time by simply putting your money into the pundits' stock picks. Of course, what these self-anointed gurus are really selling is either an ongoing print newsletter (which can run upwards of several hundred dollars per year) or your required daily visitation of their advertising-stuffed internet sites. How else will you be able to keep with their announced buy and sell recommendations? These supposed experts want you to be dependent upon continually following their advice. Of course, you may be wondering, "Hey, if these pundits were such geniuses at picking the best stocks, why aren't they making piles of money just investing rather than selling their supposed brilliant insights on the cheap?" Go to the head of the class and don't waste your time and money following such pundits' picks! (I discuss investment newsletters in Chapter 8 and internet sites in Chapter 19.)

- ✔ **Book authors.** Go into any bookstore with a decent size investing section and you'll find plenty of books claiming that they can teach you a stock picking system to beat the system. Never mind the fact that the author has no independently audited track demonstrating his success! In Chapter 20, I present examples of such hucksters, including one investment group whose book publisher is now being sued over hyping and distorting the group's actual investment success.

- ✔ **Stockbrokers.** Although a true broker will sell you whatever he thinks you'll buy in order to produce commissions, some brokers will steer you toward individual stocks for several reasons that benefit the broker and not you. First, as I discuss in Chapter 8, the high commission brokerage firms can make handsome profits for themselves by getting you to buy stocks. Secondly, brokers can use changes in the company's situation to encourage you to then sell and buy different stock, generating even more commissions. Lastly, as with newsletter writers, this whole process creates your dependency upon the broker, leaving you broker!

Researching individual stocks can be more than a full-time job, and if you choose to take this path, remember that you'll be competing against the professionals who do so on a full-time basis. If you derive sheer ecstasy from picking and following your own stocks or want an independent opinion of some stocks you happen to own now, probably the best research reports available are from the *Value Line Investment Survey.* This superb publication provides concise, user-friendly, single-page summaries of thousands of stocks. Libraries with good business sections usually carry this publication. You can order a 10-week trial by calling Value Line at 800-833-0046. I would also recommend that you limit your individual stock picking to no more than 20 percent of your overall investments.

Dividend reinvestment plans for individual stock purchases

Increasing numbers of corporations allow existing shareholders to reinvest their dividends in more shares of stock without paying brokerage commissions. In some cases, companies allow you to make additional cash purchases of more shares of stock, also commission-free.

In order to qualify, you must first generally buy some shares of stock through a broker (although some companies allow the initial purchases to be made directly from them). Ideally, you should purchase these initial shares through a discount broker to keep your commission burden as low as possible. Some investment associations also have plans that allow you to buy one or just a few shares to get started.

I am not enamored of these plans because investing this way is generally available and cost-effective for investments held outside retirement accounts. Doing so increases your tax bill, especially with stocks that pay dividends.

Also, you typically need to complete a lot of paperwork to invest in a number of different companies' stock. Life is too short to bother with these plans for this reason alone.

Finally, even with those companies that do sell stock directly without charging an explicit commission as a brokerage firm would, you'll pay plenty of other fees. Many plans charge an up-front enrollment fee as well as fees for reinvesting dividends as well as another fee when you want to sell.

Real estate

Over the generations, real estate owners and investors have enjoyed rates of return comparable to those produced by the stock market, thus making real estate another time-tested method for building wealth. However, real estate is not a gravy train or a simple way to get wealthy. Like stocks, real estate goes through good and bad performance periods. Most people who make money investing in real estate do so because they invest over many years.

The best place to start investing in real estate is to buy your own home. The *equity* (the difference between the market value of the home and the loan owed on it) in your home that builds over the years can become a significant part of your net worth. Among other things, this equity can be tapped to help finance other important money and personal goals such as retirement, college, and starting or buying a business.

Over your adult life, owning a home should be less expensive than renting a comparable home. The reason: As a renter, your housing costs are fully exposed to inflation (unless you're the beneficiary of a rent-controlled apartment). As a homeowner, the bulk of your housing costs — your monthly mortgage — is not exposed to inflation if you finance your home purchase with a fixed-rate mortgage. And your mortgage interest and property tax costs are generally deductible expenses for tax purposes. You can also make substantial tax-free profits when you sell your home.

See Chapter 14 to learn the best ways to buy and finance real estate.

Real estate: not your ordinary investment

Besides providing solid rates of return, real estate differs from most other investments in several other respects. Here's what makes real estate unique as an investment.

- ✔ **Usability.** You can't live in a stock, bond, or mutual fund (although I suppose you could glue together a substantial fortress with all the paper these companies fill your mailbox with each year). Real estate is the only investment that you can use (live in or rent out) to produce income.

- ✔ **Land is in limited supply.** Last time I checked, the percentage of the Earth occupied by land wasn't increasing. And because humans like to reproduce, the demand for land and housing continues to grow. Consider the areas that have the most expensive real estate prices in the world — Hong Kong, Tokyo, Hawaii, San Francisco, and Manhattan. In these densely populated areas, there is virtually no new land upon which to build.

- ✔ **Zoning shapes potential value.** Local government regulates the zoning of property, and zoning determines what a property can be used for. In most communities these days, local zoning boards are against big growth. This bodes well for future real estate values. Also know that in some cases, a particular property may not have been developed to its full potential. If you can see how to develop the property, you can reap large profits.

- ✔ **Leverage.** Real estate is also different from other investments because to buy it, you can borrow a lot of money — up to 80 to 90 percent or more of the value of the property. This is known as exercising *leverage*: With only a small investment of 10 to 20 percent down, you are able to purchase and own a much larger investment. When the value of your real estate goes up, you make money on your investment and on all the money that you borrowed. (In case you're curious, you can leverage non-retirement-account stock and bond investments through margin borrowing. However, you will have to make a much larger "down payment" — about double to triple compared with buying real estate.)

  For example, suppose that you plunk down $20,000 to purchase a property for $100,000. If the property appreciates to $120,000, on paper you've made a profit of $20,000 on your investment of just $20,000. In other words, you've made a 100 percent return on your investment. But leverage cuts both ways. If your $100,000 property decreases in value to $80,000, even though it's only dropped 20 percent in value, you've actually lost (on paper) 100 percent of your original $20,000 investment.

✔ **Hidden values.** In an *efficient market*, the price of an investment accurately reflects its true worth. Some investment markets are more efficient than others because of the large number of transactions and easily accessible information. Real estate markets can be *in*efficient at times. Information is not always easy to come by, and you may find an ultramotivated or uninformed seller. If you are willing to do some homework, you may be able to purchase a property below, perhaps by as much as 10 to 20 percent, its fair market value.

Just as with any other investment, real estate has its drawbacks. For starters, it generally takes time and significant cost to buy or sell a property. Also, holding a property typically costs a good deal of ongoing money. When you're renting property, you will discover firsthand the occasional headaches of being a landlord. And, especially in the early years of rental property ownership, the property's expenses may exceed the rental income, producing a net cash drain.

The best real estate investment options

Although it is in some ways unique, real estate is like other types of investments in that prices are driven by supply and demand. You can invest in homes or small apartment buildings and rent them out. In the long run, investment-property buyers hope that their rents and the value of their properties will increase faster than their expenses.

When selecting real estate for investment purposes, remember that local economic growth is the fuel for housing demand. In addition to a vibrant and diverse job base, limited supplies of both existing housing and land on which to build are things to look for. When you identify potential properties in which you might invest, run the numbers to understand the cash demands of owning the property and the likely profitability. See Chapter 14 for help determining the costs of real estate ownership.

When you want to invest directly in real estate, residential housing — such as single-family homes or small multi-unit buildings — is a straightforward and attractive investment for most people. Buying properties close to "home" offers the advantage of allowing you to more easily monitor and manage what's going on. The downside is that you'll be less diversified — more of your investments will be dependent upon your local economy.

Real estate versus stocks

Real estate and stocks have historically produced comparable returns. Deciding between the two depends less on the performance of the markets than it does on you and your situation. Consider the following major issues when deciding which investment may be better for you.

The first and most important question to ask yourself is whether you're cut out to handle the responsibilities that come with being a landlord. Real estate is a time-intensive investment. Investing in stocks can be time-intensive as well, but it doesn't have to be if you use professionally managed mutual funds.

An often-overlooked drawback to investing in real estate is that you earn no tax benefits while you're accumulating your down payment. Retirement accounts such as 401(k)s, SEP-IRAs, Keoghs, and so on (discussed in Chapter 11) give you an immediate tax deduction as you contribute money to them. If you haven't exhausted your contributions to these accounts, consider doing so before chasing after investment real estate.

Also ask yourself which investments you know more about. Some folks feel uncomfortable with stocks and mutual funds because they don't understand them. If you have a better handle on what makes real estate tick, you have a good reason to consider investing in it.

Finally, what will make you happy? Some people enjoy the challenge that comes with managing and improving rental property. It's a bit like running a small business. If you're good at it and have some good fortune, you can make money and derive endless hours of enjoyment.

Although few will admit it, some real estate investors get an ego rush from a tangible display of their wealth. Sufferers of this "edifice complex" can't obtain similar pleasure from a stock portfolio that is detailed on a piece of paper (although others have been known to boast of their stock-picking prowess).

If you don't want to be a landlord — one of the biggest drawbacks of investment real estate — consider investing in real estate through real estate investment trusts (REITs). *REITs* are diversified real estate investment companies that purchase and manage rental real estate for investors. A typical REIT invests in different types of property, such as shopping centers, apartments, and other rental buildings. You can invest in REITs either by purchasing them directly on the major stock exchanges or by investing in a real estate mutual fund (see Chapter 10) that invests in numerous REITs.

The worst real estate investments

Not all real estate investments are good; some are not even real investments. The bad ones are characterized by burdensome costs and problematic economic fundamentals:

✔ **Limited partnerships.** Limited partnerships (LPs) sold through brokers and financial consultants should be avoided. LPs are inferior investment vehicles. They are so burdened with high sales commissions and ongoing management fees that deplete your investment that you can do better elsewhere. The investment salesperson who sells you such an investment stands to earn a commission of up to 10 percent or more — so only 90 cents of each dollar gets invested. Each year, LPs typically siphon off another several percent for management and other expenses. Most partnerships have little or no incentive to control costs. In fact, they have a conflict of interest to charge more to enrich the managing partners.

Unlike a mutual fund, you can't vote with your dollars. If the partnership is poorly run and expensive, you're stuck. LPs are *illiquid.* You can't get out your money until the partnership is liquidated, typically seven to ten years after you buy in.

Brokers who sell LPs often tell you that while your investment is growing at 20 percent or more per year, you get handsome dividends of 8 percent or so per year. Many of the yields on LPs have turned out to be bogus. In some cases, partnerships propped up their yields by paying back investors' principals (without telling them, of course). As for returns — well — most LP investors of a decade ago are lucky to have half their original investment left. The only thing limited about a limited partnership is its ability to make you money.

✔ **Time shares.** Time shares are another nearly certain money loser. With a time share, what you buy is a week or two per year of ownership, or usage, of a particular unit, usually a condominium in a resort location. If you pay $8,000 for a week (in addition to ongoing maintenance fees), you're paying the equivalent of more than $400,000 for the whole unit, but a comparable unit nearby may sell for only $150,000. All the extra mark-up pays the salespeople's commissions, administrative expenses, and profits for the time share development company.

People usually get lured into buying a time share when they're enjoying a vacation someplace. They're easy prey for salespeople who want to sell them a souvenir of the trip. The cheese in the mousetrap is an offer of something free (for example, a free night's stay in a unit) for going through the sales presentation.

If you can't live without a time share, consider buying a used one. Many previous buyers, who almost always have lost a good hunk of money, are trying to dump their shares (which should tell you something). You may be able to buy a time share at a fair price. But why commit yourself to taking a vacation in the same location and building at the same time each year? Many time shares let you trade your weeks for other times and other places; however, doing so is a hassle, you will be charged an extra fee, and your choices are usually limited to time slots that other people don't want — that's why they're trading them!

✔ **Second homes.** A sometimes romantic notion and extended part of the so-called American dream is the weekend getaway — a place you can escape to a couple of times a month. When it's not in use, you may be able to rent it out and earn some income to help defray the expense of keeping it up.

When you can realistically afford the additional costs of a second, or vacation, home, I'm not going to tell you how to spend your extra cash. But please don't make the all-too-common mistake of viewing a second home as an investment. The way most people use them, they're not. Most second home owners seldom rent out their property — they typically do so 10 percent or less of the time. As a result, second homes are usually money drains.

Part of the allure of a second home is the supposed tax benefits. Even when you qualify for some or all of them, tax benefits only partially reduce the cost of owning a property. I've seen more than a few cases in which the second home is such a cash drain that it prevents its owners from contributing to and taking advantage of tax-deductible retirement savings plans.

If you don't rent out a second home property most of the time, ask yourself whether you can afford such a luxury. Can you accomplish your other financial goals — saving for retirement, paying for the home in which you live, and so on — with this added expense? Keeping a second home is more of a consumption than an investment decision. Few people can afford more than one home.

Investing in small business

With what type of investment have more people built great wealth? If you said the stock market or real estate, you're wrong. The answer is small business. You can invest in small business by starting one yourself (and thus finding yourself the best boss you've probably ever had), buying an existing business, or investing in someone else's small business.

Launching your own enterprise

When you have self-discipline and a product or service you can sell, starting your own business can be both profitable and fulfilling. Consider first what skills and expertise you possess that you can use in your business. You don't need a "eureka"-type idea or an Eli Whitney–type invention to justify going into small business. Millions of people operate successful businesses such as dry cleaners, restaurants, tax preparation firms, and so on that are hardly unique.

Start exploring your idea first by developing a written business plan. Such a plan should detail what your product or service will be, how you will market it, who your customers and competitors are, and what the economics of the business are, including the start-up costs.

Of all your small-business options, starting your own business involves the greatest amount of work. Although you can do this work on a part-time basis in the beginning, most people end up in their business full-time — it's your new job, career, or whatever you want to call it.

I've run my own business for most of my working years and wouldn't trade that experience for the corporate life. That's not to say that running my own business doesn't have its drawbacks and down moments. But in my experience counseling small-business owners, I've seen many people of varied backgrounds, interests, and skills succeed and be happy with running their own businesses.

In the eyes of most people, starting their own business is the riskiest of all small-business investment options. But if you're going into a business that utilizes your skills and expertise, the risk is not nearly as great as you may think. Many businesses can be started with little cash by leveraging your existing skills and expertise. You can build a valuable company and job if you have the time to devote to building "sweat equity." As long as you check out the competition and offer a valued service at a reasonable cost, the principal risk with your business is that you won't do a good job marketing what you have to offer. If you can market your skills, you're home free.

As long as you're thinking about the risks of starting a business, consider the risks of staying in a job you don't enjoy or that isn't challenging or fulfilling you. If you never take the plunge, you may regret that you didn't pursue your dreams.

Buying someone else's business

If you don't have a specific product or service you want to sell but are skilled at managing and improving the operations of a company, buying a small business might be for you. Finding and buying a good small business takes much time and patience, so be willing to devote at least several months to the search. You will probably also need to enlist the help of financial and legal advisors to help inspect the company, look over its financial statements, and hammer out a contract.

Although you don't have to go through the riskier start-up period if you take this route, you will likely need more capital to buy a going enterprise. You also need to be able to deal with stickier personnel and management issues. The history of the organization and the way things work will predate your ownership of the business. If you don't like making hard decisions, firing people who don't fit with your plans, and coercing people into changing the way they did things before you arrived on the scene, buying an existing business likely isn't for you.

Some people perceive buying an existing business as safer than starting one. Buying someone else's business can actually be riskier. You're likely to shell out far more money up front, in the form of a down payment to buy a business. If you don't have the ability to run the business and it does poorly, you have a lot more to lose financially. Another risk is that the business is for sale for a reason — it's not very profitable, it's in decline, or it's generally a pain in the neck to operate.

Good businesses don't come cheaply. If the business is a success, the current owner has removed the start-up risk from the business, so the price of the business should be at a premium to reflect this lack of risk. When you have the capital to buy an established business and you have the skills to run it, consider going this route.

Investing in someone else's small business

Do you like the idea of profiting from successful small businesses but don't want the day-to-day headaches of being responsible for managing the enterprise? Investing in someone else's small business may be for you. Although this route may seem easier, fewer people are actually cut out to be investors in other people's businesses. The reason: Finding and analyzing opportunities isn't easy.

Are you astute at evaluating corporate financial statements and business strategies? Investing in a small, privately held company has much in common with investing in a publicly traded firm (as is the case when you buy stock). One difference is that private firms aren't required to produce comprehensive, audited financial statements that adhere to certain accounting principles the way that public companies are. Thus, you have a greater risk of not having sufficient or accurate information when evaluating a small private firm.

Another difference is that it's harder to unearth private small-business investing opportunities. The best private companies seeking investors don't generally advertise but instead find prospective investors through networking with people such as business advisors. Increase your chances of finding private companies to invest in by speaking with tax, legal, and financial advisors who work with small businesses. You can also find interesting investing opportunities through your own contacts or experience within a given industry.

You should consider investing in someone else's business only if you can afford to lose all of what you're investing — you can lose all your investment when investing in a small, privately held company. Also, you should have sufficient assets so that what you are investing in small, privately held companies is only a small portion (20 percent or less) of your total financial assets.

Investment Odds and Ends

In Chapter 8, I tell you that the investment world offers you only two flavors: lending investments and ownership investments. Well, I sort of oversimplified.

The investments that I discuss in this section sometimes belong on their own planet. Here are the basics on these other common, but odd, investments.

Precious metals

Gold and silver have been used by many civilizations as currency or as a medium of exchange. One advantage of precious metals as a currency is that they can't be debased by the government. With a paper-based currency, such as U.S. dollars, the government can print more to pay off debts. This process can lead to the devaluation of a currency and inflation. It takes a whole lot more work to make more gold. Just ask Rumplestiltskin.

Holdings of gold and silver can provide a so-called *hedge* against inflation. In the U.S. in the late 1970s and early 1980s, inflation rose dramatically. This largely unexpected rise in inflation depressed stocks and bonds. Gold and silver, however, rose tremendously in value — in fact, more than 500 percent (even after adjusting for inflation) from 1972 to 1980 (refer to Figure 8-3 in Chapter 8). Such periods are unusual. Over many decades, precious metals tend to be lousy investments. Their rate of return tends to keep up with the rate of inflation, but not surpass it.

When you want to invest in precious metals as an inflation hedge, your best option is to do so through mutual funds (see Chapter 10). Don't purchase precious metals futures. They are not investments; they are short-term gambles on which way gold or silver prices might head over a short period of time. You should also stay away from firms and shops that sell coins and *bullion* (not the soup, but bars of gold or silver). Even if you can find a legitimate firm (not an easy task), the cost of storing and insuring gold and silver is quite costly. You won't get good value for your money. I hate to tell you, but the Gold Rush is over.

Annuities

Annuities are a peculiar type of insurance and investment product. They are a sort of savings-type account with slightly higher yields that are backed by insurance companies.

As in other types of retirement accounts, money placed in an annuity compounds without taxation until withdrawal. However, unlike most other types of retirement accounts such as 401(k)s, SEP-IRAs, and Keoghs, your contributions to an annuity give no up-front tax breaks. Thus, consider an annuity only after you fully fund tax-deductible retirement accounts.

The best annuities available today are distributed by no-load (commission-free) mutual fund companies. For more help on deciding whether to invest in an annuity, be sure to read Chapter 11.

Collectibles

Collectibles are a catchall category for antiques, art, autographs, baseball cards, clocks, coins, comic books, diamonds, dolls, gems, photographs, rare books, rugs, stamps, vintage wine, and writing utensils — in other words, any material object that through some kind of human manipulation has become more valuable to certain humans.

Notwithstanding the few people who discover on *The Antiques Road Show* that they own an antique of significant value, as an investment vehicle, collectibles are generally lousy. Dealer markups are enormous, maintenance and protection costs are draining, research is time-consuming, and people's tastes are quite fickle. All this for returns that, after you factor in the huge markups, rarely keep up with inflation.

Buy collectibles for your love of the object, not for financial gain. Treat collecting as a hobby, not as an investment. When buying a collectible, try to avoid the big markups by cutting out the middlemen. Buy directly from the artist or producer if you can.

Life insurance with a cash value

Life insurance should not be used as an investment, especially if you haven't exhausted your contributions to retirement accounts. Life insurance that combines life insurance protection with an account that has a cash value is usually known as *universal, whole,* or *variable life.* Agents love to sell it for the high commissions.

The only reason to consider buying cash value life insurance is if the proceeds paid to your beneficiaries can be free of estate taxes. You need to have a fairly substantial estate at your death to benefit from this feature. (See Chapter 16 for more on life insurance and why term life insurance is best for the vast majority of people.)

Chapter 10

Mutual Funds: Investments for All of Us

● ●

In This Chapter

▶ Why funds?

▶ The different types of funds

▶ Choosing the best mutual funds

▶ Good and bad information sources

▶ Evaluating your fund's performance

● ●

Mutual funds are managed by investment companies that pool your money with that of thousands of other like-minded individuals and invest it in stocks, bonds, and other securities. Think of it as a big investment club without the meetings! When you invest through a typical mutual fund, several hundred million to a billion dollars or more is invested along with your money.

Mutual Fund Benefits

Mutual funds rank right up there with microwave ovens, videocassette recorders, sticky notes, and plastic wrap as the best inventions of modern times. To understand their success is to grasp how and why funds can work for you. Read on to discover their benefits:

✔ **Professional management.** Mutual funds are managed by a portfolio manager and research team whose full-time jobs are to screen the universe of investments for those that best meet the stated objectives of the fund. These professionals call and visit companies, analyze companies' financial statements, and speak with companies' suppliers and customers. In short, the team does more due diligence and research than you could ever hope to do in your free time.

Fund managers are typically graduates of the top business and finance schools in the country, where they learn the principles of portfolio management and securities valuation and selection. (Despite their time in the groves of academe, most of them do a good job of investing money.) The best fund managers typically have five or more years of experience in analyzing and selecting investments, and many measure their experience in decades rather than years.

✔ **Low cost.** The most efficiently managed stock mutual funds cost less than 1 percent per year in fees (bonds and money market funds cost much less). Because mutual funds typically buy or sell tens of thousands of shares of a security at a time, the commissions they pay are generally far less than what you pay to buy or sell a few hundred shares on your own. In addition, when you buy a *no-load fund,* you avoid paying sales commissions (known as loads) on your transactions. I say more about these types of funds later in this chapter.

✔ **Diversification.** Mutual fund investing enables you to achieve a level of diversification that is difficult without several hundred thousand dollars and a lot of time to invest. To go it alone, you should invest money in at least 8 to 12 different securities in different industries to ensure that your portfolio can withstand a downturn in one or more of the investments. Proper diversification allows a mutual fund to receive the highest possible return at the lowest possible risk given its objectives. I'm not suggesting that mutual funds are able to escape share price declines during major market downturns. For example, over the past two decades, when the U.S. stock market has suffered occasional corrections ranging from 10 percent to 35 percent in value, mutual funds that invested in U.S. stocks certainly declined by similar magnitudes. However, the most unlucky investors during these episodes were individuals who had all of their money riding on only a few stocks. Some shares plunged in price by as much as 80 to 90 percent.

✔ **You don't need big bucks.** Most mutual funds have low minimum-investment requirements, especially for retirement account investors. And when you invest in a mutual fund, you get the same attention given to the rich and famous: full-time, professional money management. Even if you have a lot of money to invest, you should also consider mutual funds. Join the increasing numbers of companies and institutions (who have the biggest bucks of all) who are turning to the low-cost, high-quality money-management services that a mutual fund provides.

✔ **Audited performance records and expenses.** In their prospectuses, all mutual funds are required to disclose historical data on returns, operating expenses, and other fees. The Securities and Exchange Commission (SEC) and accounting firms oversee these disclosures for accuracy.

✔ **Flexibility in risk level.** Among the different mutual funds, you can choose a level of risk that you're comfortable with and that meets your personal and financial goals. If you want your money to grow over a long period of time, you may want to select funds that invest more heavily in stocks. If you need current income and don't want investments that fluctuate in value as widely as stocks, you may choose more conservative bond funds. If you want to be sure that your invested principal does not drop in value because you may need your money in the short term, you can select a money market fund.

✔ **Freedom from salespeople.** Stockbrokers (a.k.a. financial consultants) and commission-based financial planners make more money by encouraging trading activity and by selling you investments that provide them with high commissions — limited partnerships and mutual funds with high load fees, for example. No-load (commission-free) mutual fund companies do not push products. Their toll-free telephone lines are staffed with knowledgeable people who earn salaries, not commissions. Their recommendations don't carry inherent conflicts of interest.

The rise of the mutual fund industry

Just as computers have replaced typewriters because they allow for more efficient word processing, mutual funds are replacing less-efficient institutions that manage money. That's not to say that banks and commission-based brokerage firms are going to disappear — but you'll probably see fewer of them in the coming years.

As for safety, mutual funds have a virtually zero risk of bankruptcy. Unlike banks and insurance companies, which have failed and will continue to fail, mutual funds have never failed and probably won't in the future. The situation in which the demand for money back (*liabilities*) exceeds the value of a fund's investments (*assets*) cannot occur with a mutual fund.

Of course, the value of a fund fluctuates with the value of the securities in which it is invested. But this variation doesn't lead to the failure or bankruptcy of a mutual fund company. In fact, because the Investment Company Act of 1940 was passed to regulate the mutual fund industry, no fund has ever gone under.

In contrast, hundreds of banks and dozens of insurance companies have failed in recent decades. Banks and insurers can fail because their liabilities can exceed their assets. When a bank makes too many loans that go sour at the same time depositors want their money back, the bank fails. Likewise, if an insurance company makes several poor investments or underestimates the number of claims that will be made by insurance policy holders, it, too, can fail.

And you don't have to worry about fund companies stealing your money. The specific securities in which a mutual fund is invested are held at a *custodian* — a separate organization independent of the mutual fund company. The employment of a custodian ensures that the fund management company can't embezzle your funds and use assets from a better-performing fund to subsidize a poor performer.

Fund Types

One of the major misconceptions about mutual funds is that they are all invested in stocks. They're not. Figure 10-1 shows how the money currently invested in mutual funds breaks down:

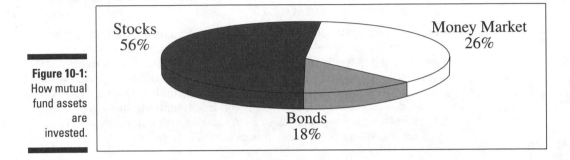

Stocks
56%

Money Market
26%

Bonds
18%

Figure 10-1:
How mutual
fund assets
are
invested.

As you can see, significant mutual fund money (more than four out of every ten dollars) is *not* invested in stocks. When you hear folks talk about the "riskiness" of mutual funds, even in the media, you'll know that they're over-looking this fact: All mutual funds are not created equal. Some funds, such as money market funds, carry virtually *no* risk that your investment will decline in value.

Throughout this discussion, remember that when mutual fund companies package and market their funds, the names they give their funds aren't always completely accurate or comprehensive. For example, a stock fund may not be *totally* invested in stocks. Twenty percent of it may be invested in bonds. Don't assume that a fund invests exclusively in U.S. companies, either — it may invest in international firms as well.

Note: If you haven't yet read Chapters 8 and 9, which provide an overview of investment concepts and vehicles, doing so will enhance your understanding of rest of this chapter.

Money market funds

Money market funds are the safest type of mutual funds for those concerned about losing their invested dollars. Money market funds are like bank savings accounts in that the value of your original investment does not fluctuate.

Money market funds have several advantages over bank savings accounts.

✔ The best money market funds have higher yields.

✔ If you're in a higher tax bracket, you have the option of using tax-free money market funds. No savings account pays tax-free interest.

✔ Most money market funds come with free check-writing privileges. (The only stipulation is that each check must be written for a minimum amount — $250 is common.)

As with money you'd put into bank savings accounts, money market funds are suitable for money that you can't afford to see dwindle in value.

Bond funds

Bonds are IOUs. When you buy a newly issued bond, you lend your money, typically to a corporation or government agency. A bond mutual fund is nothing more than a large group (pack, herd, gaggle, whatever) of bonds.

Bond funds typically invest in bonds of similar *maturity* (the number of years that elapse before the borrower must pay back the money you lend). The names of most bond funds include a word or two to provide clues about the average length of maturity of their bonds. For example, a short-term bond fund concentrates its investments in bonds maturing in the next 2 to 3 years. An intermediate-term fund generally holds bonds that come due within 7 to 10 years. The bonds in a long-term fund usually mature in 20 years or so.

In contrast to an individual bond that you buy and hold until it matures, a bond fund is always replacing bonds in its portfolio to maintain its average maturity objective. Therefore, if you know that you absolutely, positively must have a certain principal amount back on a particular date, individual bonds may be more appropriate than a bond fund.

Like money market funds, bond funds can invest in tax-free bonds, which may be appropriate for investing money you hold outside retirement accounts if you're in a reasonably high tax bracket.

Bond funds are useful when you want to live off dividend income or when you don't want to put all your money in riskier investments such as stocks and real estate (perhaps because you plan to use the money soon).

Hybrid funds

Hybrid funds invest in a mixture of different types of securities. Most commonly, they invest in bonds and stocks. These funds are usually less risky and volatile than funds investing exclusively in stocks. In an economic downturn, bonds usually hold up in value better than stocks do. However, during good economic times when the stock market is booming, the bond portions of these funds tend to drag down their performance a bit.

Hybrid mutual funds are typically known as balanced or asset allocation funds. *Balanced funds* generally try to maintain a fairly constant percentage of investment in stocks and bonds. *Asset allocation funds* tend to adjust the mix of different investments according to the portfolio manager's expectations of the market. Of course, there are exceptions — some balanced funds make major shifts in their allocations whereas some asset allocation funds maintain a relatively fixed mix. You should note that most funds that shift money around instead of staying put in good investments rarely beat the market averages over a number of years.

Hybrid funds are a way to make fund investing simple. They give you instant diversification across a variety of investing options. They also make it easier for stock-skittish investors to invest in stocks while avoiding the high volatility of pure stock funds.

Stock funds

Stock mutual funds, as their name implies, invest in stocks. These funds are often referred to as *equity* funds. Equity — not to be confused with equity in real estate — is another word for stocks. Stock mutual funds are usually categorized by the type of stocks they invest in.

Stock types are first defined by size of company (small, medium, and large). The total market value (capitalization) of a company's outstanding stock determines its size. Small-company stocks, for example, are usually defined as companies with total market capitalization of less than $1 billion.

Stocks are further categorized as growth or value. *Growth stocks* are companies that are experiencing rapidly expanding revenues and profits, and typically have high stock prices relative to their current earnings or asset (book) values. These companies tend to reinvest most of their earnings back into their infrastructure to fuel future expansion. Thus, growth stocks pay low dividends.

At the other end of the spectrum are *value stocks.* Value stock investors look for good buys. They want to invest in stocks that are cheaply priced in relation to the assets and profits of the company.

These categories are combined in various ways to describe how a mutual fund invests its money. One fund may focus on large-company growth stocks; another fund may limit itself to small-company value stocks. Funds are further qualified by the geographical focus of their investments: U.S., international, worldwide, and so on (see the following section).

Funds of funds

Increasing numbers of fund providers are responding to overwhelmed investors by offering a simplified way to construct a portfolio: a mutual fund that diversifies across numerous other mutual funds. When a fund of funds is done right, it helps focus fund investors on the important big picture issue of asset allocation — how much of your investment money you put into bonds versus stocks.

Although the best of such funds of funds appear to deliver a high-quality, diversified portfolio of funds in one fell swoop, funds of funds are not all created equal and are not all worthy of your investment dollars.

The funds of funds concept is not new. In fact, it's been around many years. High fees gave the earlier funds of funds, run in the 1950s by the late Bernie Cornfeld, a bad name. He established a fund of funds outside the U.S. and tacked on many layers of fees. While the funds were profitable for his enterprise, duped investors suffered a continual drain of high fees. The Cornfeld episode is an important reason why the Securities and Exchange Commission has been careful in approving new funds of funds.

The newer funds of funds being developed by the larger fund companies are investor-friendly. Both Vanguard's LifeStrategy and T. Rowe Price's Spectrum funds of funds add no extra fees for packaging together the individual funds. Annual operating fees on the underlying funds at Vanguard are a razor-thin one-third of one percent.

Other funds of funds, which layer on high fees, merit a much more skeptical look. Some funds of funds charge annual operating expenses of 1.5 to 3 percent on top of the fees of the underlying mutual funds that they invest in. When you add it all up, investing in mutual funds through these funds can siphon off a whopping 3 to 4 percent annually of your investment balances.

Remember that stocks' historic annual returns average just 10 percent. So paying 3 to 4 percent in fees gives away about 30 to 40 percent of your expected returns. Not surprisingly, in terms of performance, the high-fee funds of funds have badly lagged behind the stock market indexes.

U.S., international, and global funds

Most funds focus their investments in the U.S. unless they have words like *international, global, worldwide,* or *world* in their names. But even funds without one of these terms attached often invest money internationally.

The only way to know for sure where a fund is currently invested (or where the fund may invest in the future) is to ask. You can start by calling the 800 number of the mutual fund company that you're interested in. A fund's annual report also details where the fund is investing.

The term *international* typically means that a fund can invest anywhere in the world except the U.S. The term *worldwide* or *global* generally implies that a fund can invest anywhere in the world, including the U.S. I generally recommend avoiding worldwide or global funds for two reasons. First, thoroughly following the financial markets and companies in so many parts of the world is difficult for a fund manager. Following financial markets and companies is hard enough to do so solely in the U.S. or in a specific international market. Second, most of these funds charge high operating expenses — often well in excess of 1 percent per year — which puts a drag on returns.

Exceptions to this rule are the funds of funds — T. Rowe Price's Spectrum funds and Vanguard's Star and Life Strategy funds — that I discuss in the sidebar, "Funds of funds." With these funds, multiple managers are at work.

Index funds

Index funds are funds that can be (and are, for the most part) managed by a computer. An index fund's assets are invested to replicate an existing market index such as Standard & Poor's 500, an index of 500 large U.S. company stocks.

Over long periods (ten years or more), index funds outperform about three quarters of their peers! How is that possible? How can a computer making mindless, predictable decisions beat an intelligent, creative, MBA-endowed portfolio manager with a crack team of research analysts scouring the market for the best securities? The answer is largely cost. The computer does not demand a high salary or need a big corner office. And index funds don't need a team of research analysts.

Most active fund managers cannot overcome the handicap of high operating expenses that pull down their funds' rates of return. As I discuss later in this chapter, operating expenses include all the fees and profit that a mutual fund extracts from a fund's returns before the returns are paid to you. For example, the average U.S. stock fund has an operating expense ratio of 1.2 percent per year. So a U.S. stock index fund with an expense ratio of just 0.2 percent per year has an advantage of 1 percent per year.

Another not-so-inconsequential advantage of index funds is that you can't underperform the market. Some funds do just that due to the burden of high fees and poor management. If you were unfortunate enough to have been involved in the following loser mutual funds in the past ten years, you fared about 25 percent worse per year in your rate of return than if you had invested in a boring old index fund (Vanguard S&P's 500 Index over the same time period provided an average annual rate of return of 17.0 percent or more). See Table 10-1.

Table 10-1	Mutual Funds (Diversified) that Will Fetch a Stick
Fund	*Average Annual Rate of Return (10 years)*
American Heritage	–10.5%
Ameritor Industry	–10.4%
Comstock Partners Capital Value	–7.3%

For money invested outside retirement accounts, index funds have an added advantage: Fewer taxable distributions (discussed later in this chapter) are made to shareholders because less trading of securities is conducted and a more stable portfolio is maintained.

Yes, index funds may seem downright boring. When you invest in them, you give up the opportunity to brag to others about your shrewd investments that beat the market averages. On the other hand, you have no chance of doing much worse than the market, which more than a few mutual fund managers do.

Index funds make sense for a portion of your investments because it's very difficult for portfolio managers to beat the market. The Vanguard Group (800-662-7447, www.vanguard.com), headquartered in Valley Forge, Pennsylvania, is the largest and lowest-cost mutual-fund provider of index funds.

Specialty (sector) funds

Specialty funds don't fit neatly into the previously discussed categories. These funds are often known as *sector* funds because they tend to invest in securities in specific industries.

In most cases, you should avoid investing in specialty or sector funds. Investing in stocks of a single industry defeats a major purpose of investing in mutual funds — diversification. Another good reason to avoid sector funds is that they tend to carry much higher expenses than other mutual funds.

The nation's largest mutual fund company — Fidelity — offers many sector funds. The company's Fidelity Select funds are the result of slicing and dicing the universe of companies into various portfolios such as Banking, Biotechnology, Computers, Electronics, Retailing, Technology, Transportation, and so on. All told, 29 out of 35 (a whopping 83 percent) Fidelity Select funds with a five-year track record have underperformed the Standard & Poor's 500 Index over that time period. Why the poor performance? These funds carry high costs — in addition to a 3-percent sales load, the Select funds often carry hefty operating expense ratios well in excess of 1 percent.

Socially responsible funds

Increasing numbers of mutual funds that are popping up are labeling themselves *socially responsible*. This term means different things to different people. In most cases, though, it implies that the fund avoids investing in companies — tobacco manufacturers, for example — whose products or services harm people or the world at large. Because cigarettes and other tobacco products kill hundreds of thousands of people and add billions of dollars to health-care costs, most socially responsible funds shun tobacco companies.

Socially responsible investing presents a couple of problems. For example, your definition of social responsibility may not match the definition of the investment manager who's running a fund. Another problem is that even if you can agree on what's socially irresponsible (such as selling tobacco products), funds aren't always as clean as you would think or hope. Although a fund may avoid tobacco manufacturers, it may well invest in retailers that sell tobacco products.

If you want to consider a socially responsible fund, call the investment company and ask it to send you a recent annual report that lists the specific investments that the fund owns. Also consider giving directly to charities and get a tax deduction as well.

Specialty funds that invest in real estate or precious metals may make sense for a small portion (10 percent or less) of your investment portfolio. These types of funds can help diversify your portfolio because they can do better during times of higher inflation. Be careful with technology funds, which were hot during the late 1990s. Many of these stocks are selling at premium valuations. When you invest in diversified stock funds, you get plenty of exposure to the technology sector.

Selecting the Best Mutual Funds

When you go camping in the wilderness, you can do a number of things to maximize your chances for happiness and success. You can take maps to keep you on course, food to keep you from getting hungry, proper clothing to stay dry and warm, and some first-aid gear to treat minor injuries. But regardless of how much advance preparation you do, you may have a problematic experience. You may take the wrong trail, trip on a rock and break your ankle, or lose your food to a tenacious bear that comes romping through camp one night.

And so it is with mutual funds. Although most mutual fund investors are rewarded for their efforts, there are no guarantees. You can, however, follow some simple, common sense guidelines that will keep you on the trail and increase your odds of investment success and happiness. The issues in this section are the main ones you should consider.

Cost

The charges you pay to buy or sell a fund, as well as the ongoing fund operating expenses, can have a big impact on the rate of return you earn on your investments. Many novice investors pay too much attention to a mutual fund's prior performance (in the case of stock funds) or to the fund's current yield (in the case of bond funds). Doing so is dangerous because a fund can inflate its return or yield in many (risky) ways. And what worked yesterday may flop tomorrow.

A study conducted by the Investment Company Institute confirmed what I've long observed among fund buyers. Only 43 percent of recent fund buyers who were surveyed bothered to examine the fees and expenses of the fund they ended up buying. The majority of fund buyers — 57 percent, to be exact — don't know what the funds are charging them to manage their money!

Fund costs are an important factor in the return that you earn from a mutual fund. Fees are deducted from your investment. All other things being equal, high fees and other charges depress your returns. What are a fund's fees, you ask? Good question — read on to find the answers.

Loads

Loads are up-front commissions paid to brokers who sell mutual funds. Loads typically range from 4 percent to as high as 8.5 percent of your investment. Sales loads have two problems:

> ✔ **First, sales loads are a needless cost that drags down your investment returns.**

Because commissions are paid to the salesperson and not to the fund manager, the manager of a load fund does not work any harder and is not any more qualified than a manager of a no-load fund. Common sense suggests and studies confirm that load funds perform *worse,* on average, than no-loads when the load is factored in.

And don't think that spotting a load fund is easy. Just as some jewelers flog fake diamonds on late-night TV commercials, increasing numbers of brokers and financial planners sell bogus funds that they *call* no-loads, but these funds are *not* no-loads — they just hide the sales commission.

"Stay in this fund for five to seven years," the broker will tell you, "and you don't have to pay the back-end sales charge that would normally apply upon sale of the investment." Although this claim may be true, it is also true that the fund is probably charging you very high ongoing operating expenses (usually 1 percent more per year than true no-load funds) that the fund uses to pay the salesperson a hefty commission. So one way or another, the broker gets his pound of flesh (that is, his commission) from your investment dollars.

✔ **The second problem with sales loads is the power of self-interest.**

Although this issue is rarely discussed, it is even more problematic than the issue of extra sales costs. Brokers who work for a commission are interested in selling you commission-based investment products; therefore, their best interests often conflict with your best interests.

Although you may be mired in high-interest debt or underfunding your retirement plan, salespeople almost never advise you to pay off your credit cards or put more money into your 401(k). To get you to buy, they tend to exaggerate the potential benefits and obscure the risks and drawbacks of what they sell. They don't take the time to educate investors. I've seen too many people purchase investment products through brokers without understanding what they're buying, how much risk they are taking, and how these investments will affect their overall financial lives.

Invest in no-load (commission-free) funds. The only way to be sure that a fund is truly no-load is to look at the prospectus for the fund. Only there, in black and white and without marketing hype, must the truth be told about sales charges and other fund fees. (An astonishing 73 percent of fund buyers surveyed by the Investment Company Institute didn't know whether the fund they bought charged a sales load!) When you want investing advice, hire a financial advisor on a fee-for-service basis (see Chapter 18), which should cost you less and minimize potential conflicts of interest.

Operating expenses

All mutual funds charge ongoing fees. The fees pay for the operational costs of running a fund — employees' salaries, marketing, servicing the toll-free phone lines, printing and mailing published materials, computers for tracking investments and account balances, accounting fees, and so on. Despite being labeled "expenses," whatever profit a fund company extracts for running a fund is added to the tab as well.

A fund's operating expenses are quoted as an annual percentage of your investment and are essentially invisible to you. That's because they're deducted before you're paid any return. The expenses are charged on a daily basis, so you don't need to worry about trying to get out of a fund before these fees are deducted.

You can find a fund's operating expenses in the fund's prospectus. Look in the expenses section and find a line that says something like "Total Fund Operating Expenses." You can also call the fund's 800 number and ask a representative.

Within a given sector of mutual funds (for example, money market, short-term bonds, or international stock), funds with low annual operating fees can more easily produce higher total returns for you. Although expenses matter on all funds, some types of funds are more sensitive to high expenses than others. Expenses are critical on money market mutual funds and greatly important on bond funds. Fund managers already have a hard time beating the averages in these markets; with higher expenses added on, it's nearly impossible.

With stock funds, expenses are a less important (but still significant) factor in a fund's performance. Don't forget that over time, stocks have averaged returns of about 10 percent per year. So if one stock fund charges 1 percent more in operating expenses than another fund, you're already giving up an extra 10 percent of your expected returns.

Some people argue that stock funds that charge high expenses may be justified in doing so if they generate higher rates of return. Evidence doesn't show that they do generate higher returns. In fact, funds with higher operating expenses tend to produce *lower* rates of return. This trend makes sense because operating expenses are deducted from the returns that a fund generates.

Stick with funds that maintain low total operating expenses and don't charge loads (commissions). Both types of fees come out of your pocket and reduce your rate of return.

You have no reason to pay a lot for the best funds, as Table 10-2 shows. (In Chapters 11 and 12, I provide some specific fund recommendations as well as sample portfolios for investors in different situations.)

Table 10-2	Mutual Fund Operating Expense Ratios	
Fund Type	*Expense Ratio Range*	*Who Has Good Ones*
Money market funds	0.2% to 0.5%	Vanguard, Fidelity (Spartan), USAA
Bond funds	0.2% to 0.5%	Vanguard, Fidelity (Spartan), PIMCO, USAA
Hybrid	0.2% to 1%	Vanguard, Dodge & Cox, Fidelity, T. Rowe Price

(continued)

Table 10-2 (continued)

Fund Type	Expense Ratio Range	Who Has Good Ones
U.S. stock	0.2% to 1%	Fidelity, Vanguard, T. Rowe Price, others
International stock	0.4% to 1.3%	Vanguard, T. Rowe Price, others
Index	0.2% to 0.5%	Vanguard
Specialty	0.4% to 1.0%	Fidelity, Vanguard

Historic performance

A fund's *performance,* or historic rate of return, is another factor to weigh when selecting a mutual fund. As all mutual funds are required to tell you, past performance is no guarantee of future results. Analysis of historic mutual fund performance proves that some of yesterday's stars turn into tomorrow's skid-row bums.

Many former high-return funds achieved their results by taking on high risk. Funds that assume higher risk should produce higher rates of return. But high-risk funds usually decline in price faster during major market declines. Thus, in order for a fund to be considered a *best* fund, it must consistently deliver a favorable rate of return given the degree of risk it has taken.

When assessing an individual fund, compare its performance and volatility over an extended period of time (five or ten years will do) to a *relevant* market index. For example, compare funds that focus on investing in large U.S. companies to the Standard & Poor's 500 Index. Compare funds that invest in U.S. stocks of all sizes to the Wilshire 5000 Index. Indexes also exist for bonds, foreign stock markets, and almost any other type of security you can imagine.

Fund manager and fund family reputation

Much is made of who manages a specific mutual fund. As Peter Lynch, retired and famous former manager of the Fidelity Magellan fund, said, "The financial press made us Wall Street types into celebrities, a notoriety that was largely undeserved. Stock stars were treated as rock stars. . . ."

Although the individual fund manager is important, no fund manager is an island. The resources and capabilities of the parent company are equally important. Different companies have different capabilities and levels of expertise in relation to different types of funds. When you're considering a particular fund — for example, the Barnum & Barney High-Flying Foreign Stock fund — examine the performance history and fees not only of that fund but also of similar foreign stock funds at the Barnum & Barney company. If Barnum's other foreign stock funds have done poorly or Barnum & Barney offers no other such funds because it's focused on its circus business, those are strikes against its High-Flying fund. Also be aware that "star" fund managers also tend to be associated with higher-expense funds to pay their rock star salaries.

Tax-friendliness

Investors often overlook tax implications when selecting mutual funds for nonretirement accounts. Numerous mutual funds effectively reduce their shareholders' returns because of their tendency to produce more taxable distributions — that is, capital gains and dividends — which I discuss later in this chapter.

"Ranking Mutual Funds on an After-Tax Basis," a pioneering study conducted by John B. Shoven and Joel M. Dickson at Stanford University, demonstrated that mutual fund capital gains distributions have a significant impact on an investor's after-tax rate of return. The Shoven and Dickson study found large differences between the before-tax and after-tax rates of return generated by stock mutual funds.

The following example highlights the dangers of picking a stock mutual fund for a nonretirement account simply on the basis of its reported rate of return. Over a five-year period, the Founders Special fund averaged a 20.6 percent annual rate of return, outpacing the 20th Century Heritage fund, which averaged 17.6 percent per year. On the surface, it would seem that Founders, beating its rival by 3 percent per year, is the better of the two funds.

But that's only part of the story. All mutual fund managers buy and sell stocks during the course of a year. Whenever a mutual fund manager sells securities, any gain or loss from those securities must be distributed to fund shareholders. Securities sold at a loss can offset those sold at a profit.

When a fund manager has a tendency to cash in more winners than losers, investors in the fund receive a high amount of taxable gains. Over the past five years, the Founders Special fund has made capital gains distributions averaging a whopping 9.5 percent of shareholder principal per year. The 20th

Century Heritage fund, on the other hand, has averaged just 3.3 percent in annual capital gains distributions. So, even though the Founder's fund says it produces higher total returns, *after* factoring in taxes, it doesn't.

Choosing mutual funds that minimize capital gains distributions helps you to defer taxes on your profits. By allowing your capital to continue compounding as it would in an IRA or other retirement account, you receive a higher total return. When you're a long-term investor, you benefit most from choosing mutual funds that minimize capital gains distributions. The more years that appreciation can compound without being taxed, the greater the value to you as the investor.

In addition to capital gains distributions, mutual funds also produce dividends that may be subject to higher income tax rates for some investors, both for high-income earners and Social Security recipients (refer to Chapter 7 for details).

Investors who purchase mutual funds outside tax-sheltered retirement accounts should also consider the time of year they purchase shares in funds. December is the most common month in which mutual funds make capital gains distributions. When making purchases late in the year, ask if and when the fund may make a significant capital gains distribution. Consider delaying purchases in such funds until after the distribution date.

Your needs and goals

Selecting the best funds for you requires an understanding of your investment goals and risk tolerance. A good fund for your next-door neighbor is not necessarily a good fund for you. You have a unique financial profile.

Reading prospectuses and annual reports

Mutual fund companies produce information that can help you make decisions about mutual fund investments. Every fund is required to issue a *prospectus.* This legal document is reviewed and audited by the U.S. Securities and Exchange Commission. Most of what's written isn't worth the time it takes to slog through it.

The most valuable information — the fund's investment objectives, costs, and performance history — is summarized in the first few pages of the prospectus. This part you should read. Skip the rest, comprised mostly of tedious legal details.

Funds also produce annual reports that discuss how the fund has been doing and provide details on the specific investments that a fund holds. If, for example, you want to know which countries an international fund invests in, you can find this information in the fund's annual report.

If you've determined your needs and goals already, terrific! If you haven't, refer to Chapter 3. Understanding yourself is a good part of the battle. But don't shortchange yourself by not being educated about the investment you're considering. If you do not understand what you are investing in and how much risk you are taking, then you should stay out of the game.

Fund Rankings and Performance

Whether you're a novice or an experienced mutual fund investor, trying to get a handle on which funds are the best in various categories (such as international stocks or mortgage bonds) through mutual fund information and rating services can be overwhelming.

Beware the worst sources

With the popularity of mutual funds, more and more business, personal finance, and news magazines publish mutual fund articles and rankings. For a variety of reasons, much of this information isn't useful to folks trying to make informed decisions. In fact, making decisions based on some of these so-called mutual fund studies is downright dangerous.

One of the nation's largest business magazines committed a number of major errors in its recent "Top Funds" analysis. First of all, the article awarded high returns without paying any attention to risk or volatility. Funds that took more risk and were able to generate higher rates of return were awarded higher rankings.

The most egregious error was the ranking of funds solely on the basis of rate of return over a three-year period. Three years is a short time to look at fund performance. This particular three-year period witnessed a nearly uninterrupted upward march in stock and bond prices. Imagine betting on an athlete to win the Olympic decathlon after the shot-put competition. Sure, a stocky, muscular type can shot-put farther than his competitors, but he may be huffing and puffing his way around the track in the mile run.

Another example of the "garbage in, garbage out" phenomenon is the rankings done by Lipper Analytic Services, which are often published in newspapers and magazines. This organization assigns letter grades to funds just like your junior high school teacher did, except that your teacher's system was probably more sound. Lipper grades funds within broad categories based solely on total return, completely ignoring risk. The performance rankings that wind up in some newspapers can be for periods as short as *one year*.

Another mistake that some publications make in published mutual fund rankings is dumping a truckload of data on you. They then order the mutual funds alphabetically so that you sift through page after page of rows and columns of numbers. You have better things to do with your time.

Sadly, one of the reasons some publications confuse more than they convey is *advertising*. I once got a call from a financial reporter. Mr. Reporter had an outline for an article he wanted to write about mutual fund investing in which he would profile mutual fund investors that had specific fund companies' investments. The list included a number of load funds, all of which were heavy advertisers in the magazine.

As best I could tell, the reporter, who came from a political background, had little — if any — experience with the financial services industry. A few minutes into our conversation, he asked me to explain a couple of terms I had used. He didn't know the difference between a stock fund and a bond fund! To this day, I marvel about this experience. I hope you enjoy the fact that, having read this chapter, you know a lot more about mutual funds than this reporter did.

Consider fund directories

Both Value Line and Morningstar put out behemoth mutual fund directories, which can be found in most public libraries, that track thousands of mutual funds. They're reference publications, not newsletters or magazines. Given their substantial subscription costs (their three-month trials being an exception), you won't find buying your own copies worthwhile unless you already have a large portfolio of funds that you've invested in or want to check out a large number of other funds because you have a significant amount to invest.

The services are more similar than they are different. Value Line is the newer kid on the block. Both use a similar format, devoting a single page packed with all sorts of details, numbers, and a bit of commentary about each fund. Funds are ranked on a scale of one to five (Morningstar uses stars; Value Line uses numbers).

The most common mistake investors make in using these publications is focusing too much on the ranking of specific funds. Both publications' lengthy guidebooks (which most people don't read) warn against doing so, although they don't say it strongly enough for my taste.

Their ratings are somewhat useful in that they look at *risk-adjusted performance* — the performance of a fund in relation to the risk (or volatility) that it took to achieve it. The rankings have a number of limitations, however. One fatal flaw with both services is that they lump funds into broad categories, when in fact, many funds within the category invest in different types of securities.

For example, in the various stock fund categories, you find funds that invest exclusively in stocks and others that invest some of their money in bonds or other high-dividend-paying securities, such as preferred stocks. These types of securities tend to reduce the volatility of a portfolio and do well in times of declining interest rates, whereas they underperform when stocks are beating bonds.

The rankings also ignore fund operating expenses. Because the past is at best a weak predictor of things to come, you're more likely to succeed with funds that keep expenses down. As I explain earlier in this chapter, high expenses are a handicap to generating good future returns.

Brokers and financial planners love the rating system because they can sell you funds with commissions (load funds) easier. They push those with high ratings, saying, "Here's an independent rating service's assessment of the fund we talked about."

Lipper (which I discuss in the previous section) is now peddling fund reports for brokers to use. As *The Wall Street Journal* reported, these slick reports are ". . . designed as a tool to help brokers sell mutual-fund shares."

Few publications in this world should be called *independent.* Morningstar, Value Line, and Lipper are not among them. Many of those who subscribe to these publications are investment salespeople who sell load (commission-able) mutual funds. A contributing editor at Morningstar, who has since left, once told me, "We could never say to avoid load funds — otherwise we'd lose a large number of subscribers."

Understanding your fund's performance

When you look at a statement for your mutual fund holdings, odds are that you're not going to understand it. It's not you — it's the statement.

The hardest part is getting a handle on how you're doing. Most people want to know, and have a hard time figuring out, how much they've made or lost on their investment.

You cannot deduce your return by comparing the share price of the fund today to the share price that you originally paid for the fund. Why not? Because mutual funds make distributions, both of dividends and capital gains, which lead to your getting more shares of the fund.

Distributions create an accounting problem because they reduce the share price of a fund. (Otherwise, you could buy into a fund just before it made a distribution and make a profit from the distribution.) Therefore, over time, following just the share price of your fund doesn't tell you how much money you've made or lost.

Imagine that the share price of your mutual fund is like a balloon with a small rock tied to the end of a string attached to it. The balloon (representing fund share price) struggles to rise, but the rock (representing fund distributions) keeps pulling down on the balloon.

The only way to figure out exactly how much you've made or lost on your investment is to compare the total value of your holdings in a fund today versus the total dollar amount you originally invested. When you've invested chunks of money at various points in time, this exercise becomes more complicated, if you want to factor in the timing of your various investments. (Check out my investment software recommendations in Chapter 19 if you want your computer to help you crunch the numbers.)

The *total return* of a fund is the percentage change of your investment over a specified period. For example, a fund may tell you that in 1999, its total return was 15 percent. Therefore, if you had invested $10,000 in the fund on the last day of 1998, your investment would be worth $11,500 at the end of 1999. To find out a fund's total return, you can call the fund company's 800 number or read the fund's annual report.

The following three components make up your total return on a fund:

- Dividends
- Capital gains distributions
- Share price changes

Dividends

Dividends are income paid by investments. Both bonds and stocks can pay dividends. Bond fund dividends tend to be higher (as a percentage of the amount you have invested in a fund). When a dividend distribution is made, you can receive it as cash (which is good if you need money to live on) or as more shares in the fund. In either case, the share price of the fund drops by an amount to offset the payout. So if you are hoping to strike it rich by buying into a bunch of funds just before their dividends are paid, don't bother. You'll just end up paying more in income taxes.

If you hold your mutual fund outside a retirement account, the dividend distributions are taxable income (unless they come from a tax-free municipal bond fund). Dividends are taxable whether or not you reinvest them as additional shares in the fund.

Capital gains

When a mutual fund manager sells a security in the fund, net gains realized from that sale (the difference from the purchase price) must be distributed to you as a *capital gain*. Typically, funds make one annual capital gains distribution in December, but distributions can be paid multiple times per year.

As with a dividend distribution, you can receive your capital gains distribution as cash or as more shares in the fund. In either case, the share price of the fund drops by an amount to offset the distribution.

For funds held outside retirement accounts, your capital gains distribution is taxable. As with dividends, capital gains are taxable whether or not you reinvest them in additional shares in the fund. Capital gains distributions can be partly of short-term and long-term gains. As I discuss in Chapter 7, profits realized on securities sold after more than a one year holding period are taxed at the lower long-term capital gains rate. Short-term gains are taxed at the ordinary income tax rate.

As I discuss in more detail in the next chapter, you may want to check with a fund to determine when capital gains are distributed if you want to avoid making an investment in a fund that is about to make a capital gains distribution. This increases your current-year tax liability for investments made outside of retirement accounts.

Share price changes

You also make money with a mutual fund when the share price increases. This occurrence is just like investing in a stock or piece of real estate. If it's worth more today than when you bought it, you have made a profit (on paper, at least). In order to realize or lock in this profit, you need to sell your shares in the fund.

There you have it — the components of a mutual fund's total return are the following:

```
Dividends + Capital Gains Distributions + Share Price Changes
          = Total Return
```

Following and selling your funds

How closely you follow your funds is up to you, depending on what makes you happy and comfortable. I do not recommend tracking the share prices of your funds (or other investments, for that matter) on a daily basis. It is time-consuming and nerve-racking and will make you lose sight of the long term. You are more likely to panic when times get tough if you track your investments too closely. And for investments held outside of retirement accounts, every time you sell an investment at a profit, you get hit with taxes.

A monthly or quarterly check-in is more than frequent enough to follow your funds. Many publications carry total return numbers over varying periods so that you can determine the exact rate of return that you've been earning.

Trying to time and trade the markets to buy at lows and sell at highs rarely works. Yet an entire industry of investment newsletters, hotlines, online services, and the like have sprung up purporting to be able to tell you when to buy and sell. Don't waste your time and money on such nonsense (see Chapter 8 to read about gurus and newsletters).

You should consider selling a fund when it no longer meets the criteria mentioned in the section "Selecting the Best Mutual Funds," earlier in this chapter. If a fund has underperformed its peers for at least a two-year period or if a fund jacks up its management fees, it may be a good time to sell. But if you do your homework and buy good funds from good fund companies, you should need to do little trading.

Finding and investing in good funds isn't rocket science. Chapters 11 and 12 recommend some specific mutual funds using criteria discussed earlier in the chapter. If you're still not satiated, pick up a copy of the latest edition of *Mutual Funds For Dummies,* another book I've written in this infamous series.

Chapter 11

Investing in Retirement Accounts

• •

In This Chapter

▶ Types of retirement accounts

▶ Investments to avoid in retirement accounts

▶ How to allocate money in employer-sponsored plans

▶ How to allocate in plans that you design

▶ How to transfer retirement accounts

• •

*T*his chapter explains how to make decisions about investing money you currently hold inside retirement accounts or money you plan to contribute to a retirement account.

Compared to the often overwhelming world of investing outside retirement accounts, investing inside tax-sheltered retirement accounts — IRAs, 401(k)s, SEP-IRAs, and Keoghs — is far less complicated. There are two reasons for this:

✔ **The range of possible retirement account investments is more limited.** Direct investments, such as real estate and investments in small, privately owned companies, are not generally available or accessible in most retirement accounts.

✔ **When investing in a retirement account, your returns aren't taxed as you earn them.** Money inside retirement accounts compounds and grows without taxation. You generally only pay taxes on these funds when you withdraw money from the account (direct transfers to another investment firm are not withdrawals, so they are not taxed). So when you are choosing an investment for your retirement account, don't rack your brain over dividends and capital gains; save all that worry for your money in nonretirement accounts.

Types of Retirement Accounts

Retirement accounts offer numerous benefits. In most cases, your contributions are tax-deductible. And once inside the retirement account, your money compounds without taxation until you withdraw it. The rest of this section describes the major types of accounts and explains how to determine whether you are eligible for them.

Employer-sponsored plans

Your employer sets up these retirement plans. No muss, no fuss for you — the employer does all the work, including the selection of investment options. All you have to do is contribute away!

401(k) plans

For-profit companies offer 401(k) plans. The silly name comes from the section of the tax code that establishes and regulates these plans. A 401(k) generally allows you to save up to approximately $10,500 per year (for 2000), usually through payroll deduction. Your employer's plan may have lower limits, though, because not enough employees save enough. Your contributions to a 401(k) are excluded from your reported income and thus are generally free from federal and state income taxes.

Some employers don't allow you to contribute to a 401(k) plan until you've worked for them for a full year. Others allow you to start contributing right away. Some employers also match a portion of your contributions. They may, for example, match half of your first 6 percent of contributions, so in addition to saving a lot of taxes, you get a bonus from the company.

High-income earners may lose out on some of that matching money if they don't spread their contributions over the full calendar year. This may happen when you contribute such a significant percentage of each paycheck that you hit the plan maximum before the end of year. Check with your company's benefits department for your plan's specifics.

Thanks to technological innovations and the growth of the mutual fund industry, smaller companies (those with fewer than 100 employees) can consider offering 401(k) plans, too. In the past, it was prohibitively expensive for smaller companies to administer 401(k)s. If your company is interested in this option, contact some of the leading mutual fund organizations and discount brokerage firms I discuss later in this chapter and the next.

Can your employer steal your retirement plan money?

The short answer, unfortunately, is yes. However, the vast majority of employees, particularly those who work for larger and more established companies, need not worry.

Some companies that administer 401(k) plans have been cited by the U.S. Labor Department for being too slow in putting money that employees had deferred from their paychecks into employee 401(k) investment accounts. In the worst cases, companies diverted employees' 401(k) money to pay for corporate bills. Many business owners who engaged in such practices, rather than intent on fraud, used 401(k) money as a short-term emergency fund.

In cases where companies failed and funds were diverted from employee 401(k) accounts, the funds were lost. In situations where the money was delayed in being put into the employees' 401(k) accounts, employees simply lost out on earning return on their investments during the period. Once your contributions are in your 401(k) account, they are financially and legally separate from your employer. Thus, your funds will still be protected even if your employer goes bankrupt.

After conducting hundreds of investigations, the Labor Department issued rulings requiring employers to contribute employee retirement contributions to their proper accounts within 90 days. In addition to keeping tabs on your employer to ensure that money withheld from your paycheck is contributed into your account within this time frame, you should also periodically check your 401(k) statement to make sure that your contributions are being invested as you have instructed.

403(b) plans

Nonprofit organizations offer 403(b) plans to their employees. As with 401(k)s, your contributions to these plans are excluded from federal and state tax income taxes. The 403(b) plans are more often known as *tax-sheltered annuities,* the name for insurance company investments that satisfy the requirements for 403(b) plans. For the benefit of 403(b) retirement-plan participants, *no-load* (commission-free) mutual funds can be used in 403(b) plans.

Nonprofit employees are allowed to annually contribute up to 20 percent or $10,500 of their salary, whichever is less. Employees who have 15 or more years of service may be allowed to contribute a few thousand dollars beyond the $10,500 limit. Ask your employee benefits department or the investment provider for the 403(b) plan about eligibility requirements and details about your personal contribution limit.

If you work for a nonprofit or public-sector organization that doesn't offer this benefit, make a fuss and insist on it. Nonprofit organizations have no excuse not to offer a 403(b) plan to their employees. Unlike a 401(k), this type of plan includes virtually no out-of-pocket expenses to the employer. The only requirement is that the organization must deduct the appropriate contribution from employees' paychecks and send the money to the invest-ment company handling the 403(b) plan.

Some nonprofits don't offer 403(b)s, or in addition to 403(b)s offer insurance company tax-sheltered annuities. No-load (no sales charges) mutual funds are superior investment vehicles compared to insurance company annuities on several fronts:

- ✔ Mutual fund companies have a longer and more successful investment track record than do insurance companies, many of which have only recently entered the mutual fund arena.

- ✔ Insurance annuities charge higher annual operating expenses, often two to three times those of efficiently managed no-load mutual funds. These high expenses reduce your returns.

- ✔ Insurance company insolvency can risk the safety of your investment in an annuity, whereas the value of a mutual fund depends only on the value of the securities in the fund.

- ✔ Insurance annuities come with severe charges and fees for early surrender; 403(b) plans with mutual funds do not.

With some 403(b) plans, you may borrow against your fund balance without penalty. If this capability is important to you, check with your employer to see whether the company plan allows you to borrow without penalty. Although many insurance annuities advertise borrowing as an advantage, it is also a drawback because it may encourage you to raid your retirement savings.

As long as your employer allows it, you may open a 403(b) account at my suggested investment companies later in this chapter.

What's a 457 retirement plan?

Some nonprofit organizations offer what are called 457 plans. Like 403(b) or 401(k) plans, 457 plans offer participants the ability to contribute money from their paychecks on a pre-tax basis and thus save on federal and state taxes.

457 plans, however, differ in the following impor-tant ways. First, money that you contribute into a 457 plan is not separate from the organization's finances. Thus, if the nonprofit goes belly up — a rare but not impossible occurrence in the nonprofit world — your retire-ment funds could be in jeopardy. Second, 457 plan contributions are limited to $8,000 per year.

Don't consider contributing to a 457 plan until you've exhausted contributions to your 403(b).

Self-employment plans

When you work for yourself, you don't have an employer to do the legwork to set up a retirement plan. You need to take the initiative. Although there's more work for you, the good news is that you can select and design a plan that meets your needs. Self-employment retirement savings plans often allow you to put *more* money away on a tax-deductible basis than employers' plans do.

When you have employees, you are required to provide coverage for them under these plans with contributions comparable to the company owners' (as a percentage of salary). Some part-time (fewer than 1,000 hours per year) and newer employees (less than a few years of service) may be excluded. Many small-business owners don't know about this requirement or choose to ignore it; they set up plans for themselves but fail to cover their employees. The danger is that the IRS and state tax authorities may discover small-business owners' negligence, sock them with big penalties, and disqualify their prior contributions. Because self-employed people and small businesses get their tax returns audited at a relatively high rate, don't muck up this area.

Don't avoid setting up a retirement savings plan for your business just because you have employees and you don't want to make contributions on their behalf. Making retirement contributions need not increase your personnel costs. In the long run, you build the contributions you make for your employees into their total compensation package — which includes salary and other benefits like health insurance.

To get the most from contributions as an employer, consider the following:

- ✔ Educate your employees about the value of retirement savings plans. You want them to understand, but more importantly, you want them to appreciate your investment.

- ✔ Select a Keogh plan that requires employees to stay a certain number of years to vest fully in their contributions. Reward long-term contributors to your company's success.

- ✔ Consider offering a 401(k) plan if you have more than 20 employees.

SEP-IRAs

Simplified employee pension individual retirement account (SEP-IRA) plans require little paperwork to set up. SEP-IRAs allow you to sock away 13 percent (13.04 percent, to be exact) of your self-employment income (business revenue minus deductions), up to a maximum of $25,500 per year (for 2000). Each year, you decide the amount you want to contribute — there are no minimums. Your contributions to a SEP-IRA are deducted from your taxable income, saving you big-time on federal and state taxes. As with other retirement plans, your money compounds without taxation until you withdraw it.

BEWARE

Don't be hoodwinked into a "private pension plan"

Employers who don't want to make retirement plan contributions on behalf of their employees are bait for insurance salespeople selling so-called private pension plans. Basically, these plans are cash value life insurance policies, which combine life insurance protection with a savings-type account (see Chapter 16 for more details).

The selling hook of these plans is that you can save money for yourself but need not contribute money on your employees' behalf. And your contributions compound without taxation over the years.

Sound good? Well, life insurance salespeople who earn hefty commissions from selling cash value life policies won't tell you about the big negatives of these plans. Unlike contributions to true retirement savings plans such as SEP-IRAs and Keoghs, you derive *no* up-front tax deduction.

Also, if you don't need life insurance protection, the cost of such coverage is wasted if you save through these plans.

If you're wondering what's with the oddball percentage — 13.04 percent — a somewhat reasonable explanation exists. SEPs actually allow you to contribute 15 percent of your *net* self-employment income. However, you need to subtract your SEP contribution and half of your self-employment (Social Security) taxes to arrive at your net self-employment income. Multiplying by 13.04 percent is simpler; it factors in the necessary subtractions for you.

Keoghs

Keogh plans require a bit more paperwork to set up and administer than SEP-IRAs. The appeal of certain types of Keoghs is that they allow you to put away a greater percentage (20 percent) of your self-employment income (revenue less your deductions), up to a maximum of $30,000 per year.

All types of Keogh plans allow *vesting schedules,* which require employees to remain with the company a number of years before they earn the right to their full retirement account balances.

Keogh plans also allow for *Social Security integration*. Without going into all the gory tax details, *integration* effectively allows those in the company who are high-income earners (usually the owners) to receive larger-percentage contributions for their accounts than the less highly compensated employees. The logic behind this idea is that Social Security benefits top out once you earn more than $72,600 (for 1999). Social Security integration allows you to make up for this ceiling.

Just to make life complicated, Keoghs come in four main flavors:

✔ **Profit-sharing plans.** These plans have the same contribution limits as SEP-IRAs. So why would you want the headaches of a more complicated plan when you can't contribute more to it? These plans appeal to owners of small companies who want to minimize the contributions to which employees are entitled, which is done through use of vesting schedules and Social Security integration.

✔ **Money-purchase pension plans.** You can contribute more to these plans than you can to a profit-sharing plan or SEP-IRA: 20 percent of your self-employment income up to a maximum of $30,000 per year. While allowing for a larger contribution, there is *no* flexibility allowed on the percentage contribution you make each year — it's fixed. Thus, these plans make the most sense for employers who are comfortable enough financially to continue making contributions that are a high percentage of their salary.

If the simplicity of the money-purchase pension plan appeals to you, don't be too concerned about not being able to make the required contribution. You can amend your plan and change the contribution percentage starting the next year. As long as you have a reason, the IRS generally allows you to discontinue the plan altogether. Prior contributions can remain in the Keogh account — you can even transfer them to other investment providers if you like. Discontinuing the plan simply means that you won't be making further contributions. You don't lose the money. Usually, people reduce contributions because their business income drops off. The silver lining to your shrinking income is that Keogh plan contributions are set as a percentage of your earnings. So less income means proportionately smaller contributions.

✔ **Paired plans.** These plans combine the preceding profit-sharing and money-purchase plans. Although they require a little more paperwork to set up and administer, paired plans take the best of both individual plans.

You can attain the maximum contribution possible (20 percent of your self-employment income) that you get with the money-purchase pension plan but have some of the flexibility that comes with a profit-sharing plan. You can fix your money-purchase pension plan contribution at 8 percent and contribute anywhere from 0 to 12 percent of your net income to your profit-sharing plan.

✔ **Defined-benefit plans.** These plans are for people who are willing and able to put away more than $30,000 per year — which, as you can imagine, few people can do. Consistently high-income earners older than 45 or 50 who want to save more than $30,000 per year in a retirement account should consider these plans. If you are interested in defined-benefit plans, hire an actuary to crunch the numbers to calculate how much you can contribute to such a plan.

Individual retirement accounts (IRAs)

Anyone with employment income can contribute to IRA accounts. You may contribute up to $2,000 each year. If you don't earn $2,000 a year, you can contribute as much as you'd like (and can afford) up to that amount. One exception to the above rule is if you are a nonworking spouse, in which case you're eligible to put up to $2,000 per year into a so-called *spousal IRA* and up to $2,000 into the working spouse's IRA, as long as the working spouse had at least $4,000 in earned income.

Another exception to earning employment income makes you eligible to contribute to an IRA: Receiving alimony also qualifies you for an IRA contribution.

Your contributions to an IRA may or may not be tax-deductible. For tax year 1999, if you're single and your adjusted gross income is $31,000 or less for the year, you can deduct your full IRA contribution. If you're married and file your taxes jointly, you're entitled to a full IRA deduction if your AGI (adjusted gross income) is $51,000 per year or less. (For 2000, these thresholds bump up to $32,000 and $52,000, respectively.)

If you make more than these amounts, you can take a full IRA deduction if and only if you are *not* an active participant in any retirement plan. The only way to know for certain whether you're an active participant is to look at your W-2 Form: that smallish (4 by 8½-inch) document your employer sends you early in the year to file with your tax returns. Little boxes in box 15 on that form indicate whether you are an active participant in a pension or deferred-compensation plan. When either of these boxes is checked, you're an active participant.

If you are a single-income earner with an adjusted gross income above $31,000 but below $41,000, or part of a couple with an AGI above $51,000 but below $61,000, you're eligible for a partial IRA deduction, even if you're an active participant in another plan. The size of the IRA deduction that you may claim depends on where you fall in the income range.

✔ For example, a single-income earner at $36,000 is entitled to half ($1,000) of the full IRA deduction because his or her income falls halfway between $31,000 and $41,000.

✔ A couple earning $53,500 loses just a quarter of the full IRA amount because their incomes are a quarter of the way from $51,000 to $61,000. Thus they can take a $1,500 IRA deduction.

The IRS 1040 instruction booklet comes with a worksheet that allows you to do the calculations for your situation.

Retirement account inequities

To put everyone on more equal footing, those who don't work for employers with retirement savings plans should be allowed to contribute more to their IRAs. It's not fair that people who work for companies that have no retirement savings plans can deduct only $2,000 per year from their taxable income for an IRA.

Take an example of two households that each have annual employment income of $50,000. One household has access to a 401(k) plan, while the other household has no access to retirement plans other than an IRA. The household with the 401(k) can put away and deduct from their taxable income thousands of dollars more per year than the household with just the IRA.

This inequity has persisted because of the federal government's debt. Allowing more people to make larger tax-deductible contributions to retirement accounts would reduce government revenues in the short-term. Tax deductions for retirement savings are included in the tax system to encourage people to provide for their own retirement. But telling people the importance of saving for retirement and not giving them more equal access to do so is hypocritical.

If you can't deduct your contribution to a standard IRA account, consider making a contribution to a newer type of IRA account called the Roth IRA. Single taxpayers with an AGI less than $95,000 and joint filers with an AGI less than $150,000 can contribute up to $2,000 per year to a Roth IRA, provided they have at least $2,000 in earned income. Although the contribution is not deductible, earnings inside the account are shielded from tax, and unlike a standard IRA, "qualified withdrawals" from the account, including investment earnings, are free from income tax.

To make a qualified withdrawal, you must be at least 59½ and have held the account for at least 5 years. An exception to the age rule is made for first-time home buyers, who are allowed to withdraw up to $10,000 toward the down payment on a principal residence.

Before you consider a Roth IRA, make sure that you've exhausted deductible contributions to the retirement accounts available to you — 401(k), Keogh, standard IRA, and so on. If your AGI prevents you from contributing to a Roth IRA, consider making a nondeductible contribution to a regular IRA for the tax-deferred compounding of your investment earnings.

Another type of IRA account called the Education IRA is discussed in Chapter 13.

Annuities: An odd investment

Annuities are peculiar investment products. They are contracts that are backed by an insurance company. If you, the annuity holder (investor), die during the so-called *accumulation phase* (that is, prior to receiving payments from the annuity), your designated beneficiary is guaranteed to receive the amount of your contribution. In this sense, annuities look a bit like life insurance.

Annuities, like IRAs, allow your capital to grow and compound without taxation. You defer taxes until withdrawal. Annuities carry the same penalties for withdrawal prior to age 59½ as do other retirement accounts.

Unlike an IRA that has a $2,000 annual contribution limit, you can deposit as much as you want in any year into an annuity — even a million dollars plus if you have it! As with a so-called nondeductible IRA, you get no up-front tax deduction for your contributions.

Because the contribution to an annuity is not tax-deductible, contributing to an annuity makes sense if:

- ✔ **You have exhausted contributions to employer-sponsored and self-employed plans.** Your contributions to these plans are tax-deductible; annuity contributions are not.

- ✔ **You have also made the maximum contribution that you can to an IRA account, even if it's not tax-deductible.** Annuities carry higher fees (which reduce your investment returns) because of the insurance that comes with them; IRA investments offer you better returns.

- ✔ **You expect to leave the money compounding in the annuity for at least 15 years.** It typically takes this long for the benefits of tax-deferred compounding to outweigh the higher annuity fees. If you're close to or actually in retirement, tax-friendly investments made outside of retirement accounts (discussed in Chapter 12) are preferable.

For more details about other investment options and the best places to purchase annuities, see Chapter 12, where I discuss investing money outside of retirement accounts.

Inappropriate Retirement Account Investments

Some investments for retirement accounts are simply inappropriate. The basic problem stems from otherwise intelligent folks forgetting, ignoring, or simply not knowing that retirement accounts are sheltered from taxation so you want to maximize that benefit by selecting investment vehicles that would otherwise be taxed. This section discusses investments that you should *not* make in retirement accounts.

Tax-free bonds

Investments that produce income that is tax-free either at the federal or state level don't make much sense inside retirement accounts. Tax-free securities always yield less than their taxable counterparts, so you are essentially giving away free yield when you invest in such securities inside retirement accounts.

A big no-no is investing in municipal bonds inside a retirement account. Municipals are free from federal taxation (and state tax, too, if you buy such a bond issued in your state). As such, they yield significantly less than an equivalent bond that pays fully taxable dividends. Municipal bonds definitely don't belong in a retirement account. The better investment firms don't let you make this mistake.

"Okay," you may be saying, "I'm smart enough to know not to invest in municipal bonds inside a retirement account." Terrific, I say. But lots of people make the mistake, albeit a smaller one, of investing in Treasuries — that is, U.S. Treasury bills, notes, or bonds — inside retirement accounts.

When you buy Treasuries, although you get the safety net of a government guarantee, you also get a bond that produces interest free of state tax. (By the way, I've never understood why some investors think that lending their money to the U.S. government, an organization with more than $5 trillion in debt outstanding, is 100-percent safe.) Fully taxable bonds yield more than state-tax-free Treasuries. And, the safety of Treasuries can easily be replicated in other bonds.

Some diversified mutual funds invest a portion of their funds in Treasuries. Holding such a fund is not a mistake as long as the portion invested in these tax-free holdings is less than about 20 to 30 percent of the portfolio. Avoid funds that invest the majority or all of their assets in Treasuries. A surprising number of company retirement plans offer treasury mutual funds (which are nearly all Treasuries) as an investment option. Should your plan, send a copy of this book to your company's benefits department!

Annuities

Annuities, although retirement vehicles, as noted earlier in this chapter, have no place inside retirement accounts. Annuities allow your investment dollars to compound without taxation. In comparison to other investments that don't allow such tax deferral, annuities carry much higher annual operating expenses, which depress your returns.

Purchasing an annuity inside an IRA, 401(k), or other type of retirement account is like wearing a belt and suspenders together. Either you have a peculiar sense of style, or you are spending too much time worrying about your pants falling down. In my experience, many people who mistakenly invest in annuities inside retirement accounts have been misled into the investment by investment salespeople.

Annuities pay hefty commissions, sometimes as high as 10 percent or more of the amount invested. In some cases, I don't think the salespeople are being conniving and unethical — they just don't know any better. The insurance companies behind these products, in their enthusiasm to pump up sales-people to peddle them, conveniently skip over the details about when it's inappropriate to invest in annuities and when it's not.

When you work for a nonprofit organization, your employer may allow you to contribute some of your paycheck into *tax-sheltered annuities* (TSAs). If you have other options, don't. TSAs are also inferior investment choices. The tax laws allow nonprofit employees to invest their retirement money in mutual funds. Well-managed no-load (commission-free) funds have lower operating expenses and other advantages over TSAs (see my discussion of nonprofit 403(b) retirement plans earlier in the chapter).

Limited partnerships

Limited partnerships are treacherous, high-commission, high-cost, and hence low-return investments sold through investment salespeople. Part of their supposed allure, however, is the tax benefits that they generate. But when you buy and hold a limited partnership in a retirement account, you lose the ability to take advantage of many of the tax deductions. The illiquidity of LPs may also mean that you can't make required retirement account withdrawals when needed. These are just some of the many reasons to avoid investing in limited partnerships. For more reasons, see Chapter 9.

Allocating Your Money in Retirement Plans

With good reason, people are concerned about placing their retirement account money in investments that can decline in value. You may feel that you're gambling with dollars intended for the security of your golden years.

But in order to attain that security, most working folks need to make their money work hard in order for it to grow fast enough. That involves taking some risk; you have no way around it. Luckily, if you have 15 to 20 years or more before you need to draw on the bulk of your retirement account assets, time is on your side. If some of your investments drop a bit over a year or two, what's the big deal as long as the value of your investments has time to recover? The more years until you are going to retire, the greater your ability to take risk.

If you haven't yet done so, read the section on asset allocation in Chapter 8. That section helps you decide how to divide your money among different investment options based upon your time frame and risk tolerance.

Prioritizing retirement contributions

When you have access to more than one type of retirement account, prioritize which accounts to use first by what they give you in return. Your first contributions should be to employer-based plans that match your contributions. After that, contribute to any other employer or self-employed plans that allow tax-deductible contributions. When you've contributed as much as possible to tax-deductible plans or do not have access to such plans, contribute to an IRA. If you've maxed out on contributions to an IRA or don't have this choice because you lack employment income, consider an annuity (discussed earlier in this chapter).

Setting up a retirement account

No-load, or commission-free, mutual fund and discount brokerage firms are your best bet for establishing a retirement account. (See my recommendations later in this chapter for more specifics.)

Investments and account types are different issues. People sometimes get confused when discussing the investments they make in retirement accounts, especially people who have a retirement account, such as an IRA, at a bank. They don't realize that you can have your IRA at a variety of financial institutions (for example, a mutual fund company or brokerage firm). At each financial institution, you can choose among the firm's investment options for putting your IRA money to work.

Allocating money when your employer selects the investment options

In some company-sponsored plans, such as 401(k)s, you are limited to the predetermined investment options your employer offers. Plans differ in the specific options they offer, but they usually offer similar basic choices. In what follows, I discuss a 401(k) plan's typical investment options, in order of increasing risk and hence, likely return. Then, I follow with examples for how to allocate your money across the different types of common employer retirement plan options.

Money market/savings accounts

For regular contributions coming out your paycheck, the money market or savings account option makes little sense. Some people who are skittish about the stock and bond markets are attracted to money market and savings accounts because those accounts cannot drop in value. However, the returns are low . . . so low that you are at great risk that your investment will not stay ahead of, or even keep up with, inflation and taxes (which are due upon withdrawal of your money from the retirement account).

For those of you who may be tempted to use a money market fund as a parking place until the time that you think stocks and bonds are cheap, don't. In the long run, you won't be doing yourself any favors if you do so. As I discuss in Chapter 8, timing your investments to attempt to catch the lows and avoid investing at the peaks is impossible. If you can figure out how to do that, you're wasting your time in whatever occupation you're now employed. You could make a fortune as a professional money manager.

 You may need to keep money in the money market investment option if you utilize the borrowing feature that some retirement plans allow. Check with your employee benefits department for more details. You might also use a money market after you retire to hold money you expect to withdraw and spend within the next year or so.

Bond mutual funds

Bond mutual funds (which I describe in Chapter 10) invest in a mixture of typically high-quality bonds. Bonds pay a higher rate of interest or dividends than money funds. Depending on whether your plan's option is a short-term, intermediate-term, or long-term fund (maybe you have more than one type), the bond fund's current yield is probably a percent or two higher than the money market fund's yield.

Bond funds carry higher yields than money market funds, but they also carry greater risk because their value can fall if interest rates increase. However, bonds tend to be more stable in value than stocks.

Aggressive, younger investors should keep a minimum amount of money in bond funds. Older folks who want to invest more conservatively can place more money in bonds (see the asset allocation discussion in Chapter 8).

Guaranteed-investment contracts (GICs)

GICs are backed by an insurance company and typically quote you a rate of return projected one or a few years forward. The return is always positive and certain — thus you don't have the uncertainty that you would normally face with bond or stock investments (unless, of course, the insurance company fails).

The attraction of these investments is that your account value does not fluctuate (at least, not that you can see). Insurers normally invest your money mostly in bonds and maybe a bit in stocks. The difference between what these investments generate for the insurer and what they pay in interest is profit to the insurer. A GIC's yield is usually comparable to that of a bond fund.

For people who would hit the eject button the moment that a bond fund slides a bit in value, GICs are soothing to the nerves. And they're certainly higher yielding than a money market or savings account.

Like bonds, however, GICs don't give you the opportunity for long-term growth of your money. Over the long haul, you should earn a better return in a mixture of bond and stock investments. In GICs, you pay for the peace of mind of a guaranteed return in the form of lower long-term returns.

GICs also have another minor drawback: Insurance companies, unlike mutual funds, can and do fail, putting GIC investment dollars at risk. Some employers' retirement plans have been burned by insurance company failures.

Balanced mutual funds

Balanced mutual funds invest in a mixture primarily of stocks and bonds. This one-stop-shopping concept makes investing easier and smoothes out fluctuations in the value of your investments — funds investing exclusively in stocks or in bonds make for a rougher ride. These funds are solid options and, in fact, can be used for a significant portion of your retirement plan contributions. Refer to Chapter 10 to learn more about balanced funds.

Stock mutual funds

Stock mutual funds invest in stocks, which usually provide greater long-term growth potential but also wider fluctuations in value from year to year. Some companies offer a number of different stock funds, including funds that invest overseas. Unless you plan to borrow against your funds for a home purchase (if your plan allows), you should have a healthy helping of stock funds. Please see Chapter 10 for an explanation of the different types of stock funds as well as details on how to evaluate a stock fund.

Stock in the company you work for

Some companies offer employees the option of investing in the company's stock. I generally advocate avoiding this option for the simple reason that your future income and other employee benefits are already riding on the success of the company. If the company hits the skids, you may lose your job and your benefits. You certainly don't want the value of your retirement account to depend on the same factors.

If your employer does not offer you any retirement account investing options other than putting money in company stock, complain. Start with your benefits department. Benefits folks should know that 401(k) plans are supposed to offer several diversified investment options — offering your employer's stock as the one and only option doesn't pass muster.

If you think that your company has its act together and the stock is a good buy, investing a portion of your retirement account is fine — but no more than 25 percent. Now, if your company is on the verge of hitting it big and the stock is soon to soar, you'll of course be kicking yourself for not putting more of your money into the company's stock. But when you place a big bet on your company's stock, be prepared to suffer the consequences if the stock tanks. Don't forget that lots of smart investors track companies' prospects, so odds are that the current value of your company's stock is fair.

Some employers offer employees the ability to buy company stock at a discount, sometimes as much as 15 percent, compared to its current market value. If you can do this, so much the better. When you sell the stock as your employer's plan allows, usually after a certain length holding period, you should be able to lock in a decent profit.

Some asset allocation examples

Using the methodology that I outline in Chapter 8 for allocating money, Table 11-1 shows a couple of examples of how people in different employer plans might choose to allocate their 401(k) investments among the plan's investment options.

Please note that making allocation decisions is not a science. Use the formulas in Chapter 8 as a guideline.

Table 11-1	Allocating 401(k) Investments		
	25-Year-Old, Aggressive Risk	45-Year-Old, Moderate Risk	60-Year-Old, Moderate Risk
Bond Fund	0%	35%	50%
Balanced Fund (50% stock/50% bond)	10%	0%	0%
Blue Chip/Larger Company Stock Fund(s)	30–40%	20–25%	25%
Aggressive/Smaller Company Stock Fund(s)	25%	20%	10%
International Stock Fund(s)	25-35%	20–25%	15%

Allocating money in plans that you design

With self-employed plans (SEP-IRAs and Keoghs), certain 403(b) plans for nonprofit employees, and IRAs, you get to select the investment options as well as the allocation of money among them. In the sections that follow, I give some specific recipes that you may find useful for investing at some of the premier investment companies.

To establish your retirement account at one of these firms, simply pick up your telephone and dial the company's 800 number and ask it to mail you an account application for the type of account (for example, SEP-IRA, 403(b), and so on) you desire. At the time you call, you can also have the company mail you background on specific mutual funds that you may be interested in. (For those who are less patient and who are enamored of the internet, some investment firms provide account applications online that you may download. However, this can be a tedious process, especially if you also need other information such as investment prospectuses and annual reports.)

Note: For each firm, I recommend a conservative and an aggressive portfolio. These terms are used in a relative sense. Because some of the recommended funds do not maintain fixed percentages of their different types of investments, the actual percentage of stocks and bonds that you end up with may vary slightly from the targeted percentages. Don't sweat it.

Where you have more than one fund choice, you can pick one or split the suggested percentage among them. If you don't have enough money today to divide it up as I suggest, you can achieve the desired split over time as you add more money to your retirement accounts.

Vanguard

Vanguard (800-662-7447; `www.vanguard.com`) is a mutual fund powerhouse. It's the largest no-load fund company around and consistently has the lowest operating expenses in the business. Historically, Vanguard's funds have excellent performance versus those of its peers, especially among conservatively managed bond and stock funds.

A conservative portfolio with 50 percent stocks, 50 percent bonds

Vanguard Total Bond Market Index — 25 percent

Vanguard Star (fund of funds) — 55 percent

Vanguard International Growth **and/or** Vanguard Total International Stock Index — 20 percent

An aggressive portfolio with 80 percent stocks, 20 percent bonds

Vanguard Star (fund of funds) — 50 percent

Vanguard Total Stock Market Index — 10 to 20 percent

Vanguard International Growth — 30 to 40 percent

or

Vanguard LifeStrategy Growth (fund of funds) — 100 percent (note that this portfolio places less money overseas than the previous one).

Should I use one investment firm or more than one?

The recommended firms listed in this chapter offer a large enough variety of investment options, managed by different fund managers, that you can feel comfortable concentrating your money at one firm. The advantages of a focused approach are learning the nuances and choices of just one firm rather than several, and having fewer administrative hassles.

If you like the idea of spreading your money around, you may want to invest through a number of the different firms. With a discount brokerage account (refer to Chapter 8), you can have your cake and eat it, too. You can diversify across different mutual fund companies through one brokerage firm. However, you will pay small transaction fees on some of your purchases and sales of funds.

Fidelity

Fidelity Investments (800-544-8888; www.fidelity.com) is the largest provider of mutual funds in terms of total assets. However, a number of Fidelity's funds assess sales charges (no such funds are recommended in what follows), so Vanguard is still the largest pure no-load fund company. My recommendations are for a conservative mix and an aggressive mix. Fidelity's strength historically has been with investing in domestic stocks. The company's bond funds have slightly high management fees, and its foreign funds have traditionally lagged, although they have perked up versus their peers in recent years.

ERIC'S PICKS

A conservative portfolio with 50 percent stocks, 50 percent bonds

Fidelity Asset Manager — 33⅓ percent

Fidelity Puritan — 33⅓ percent

Dodge & Cox Balanced — 33⅓ percent

An aggressive portfolio with 80 percent stocks, 20 percent bonds

Fidelity Puritan — 35 percent

Fidelity Equity-Income — 25 percent

Fidelity Low Priced Stock — 20 percent

T. Rowe Price International Stock
and/or Vanguard Total International
and/or Vanguard International Growth — 20 percent

Discount brokers

As I discuss in Chapter 8, a discount brokerage account can allow you centralized, one-stop shopping and holding of mutual funds from a variety of the leading fund companies. Although some funds are available without transaction fees, with most of the better funds, you will pay a small transaction fee to buy funds through a discount broker. The reason: The discounter is a middleman between you and the fund companies. You have to weigh the convenience of being able to buy and hold funds from multiple fund companies in a single account versus the lower cost of buying funds directly from their providers. Especially if you're investing smaller amounts, a $25 to $30 transaction fee can gobble a sizeable chunk of what you have to invest.

Among brokerage firms or brokerage divisions of mutual fund companies, for breadth of fund offerings and competitive pricing, I like Waterhouse

(800-934-4410 ; www.waterhouse.com), T. Rowe Price (800-225-5132; www.troweprice.com), and Vanguard (800-992-8327; www.vanguard.com).

A conservative portfolio with 50 percent stocks, 50 percent bonds

Vanguard Fixed-Income Short-Term Corporate — 20 percent

PIMCO Total Return or Dodge & Cox Income — 20 percent

Dodge & Cox Balanced — 20 percent

T. Rowe Price Spectrum Growth (fund of funds) — 30 percent

Artisan International
and/or Vanguard International Growth — 10 percent

An aggressive portfolio with 80 percent stocks, 20 percent bonds

PIMCO Total Return
and/or Vanguard Total Bond Market Index — 20 percent

Vanguard Total Stock Market Index
and/or Dodge & Cox Stock
and/or Neuberger & Berman Focus — 40 to 50 percent

T. Rowe Price International Stock
and/or Artisan International
and/or Vanguard International Growth — 30 to 40 percent

Transferring Retirement Accounts

With the exception of plans maintained by your employer that limit your investment options, such as most 401(k)s, you can move your money held in SEP-IRAs, Keoghs, IRAs, and many 403(b) plans (also known as *tax-sheltered annuities*) to almost any major investment firm you please. Moving the money is pretty simple. If you can dial an 800 number, fill out a couple of short forms, and send them back in a postage-paid envelope, you can transfer an account. The investment firm to which you are transferring your account does the rest.

Transferring accounts you control

Here's a step-by-step list of what you need to do to transfer a retirement account to another investment firm. Even if you're working with a financial advisor, you should be aware of this process (called a *direct trustee to trustee transfer*) to ensure that no hanky-panky takes place on the advisor's part:

1. **Decide where you want to move the account.** I recommend several investment companies in this chapter, along with some sample portfolios within those firms.

2. **Obtain an account application and asset transfer form.** Call the 800 number of the firm you are transferring the money to and ask for an *account application and asset transfer form* for the type of account you are transferring — for example, SEP-IRA, Keogh, IRA, or 403(b). You can also visit web sites, but for this type of request, I think most people find it easier to speak with a live person.

   Important note: Ask for the form for the *same* type of account you currently have at the company from which you are transferring the money. You can determine the account type by looking at a recent account statement — the account type should appear near the top of the form or in the section with your name and address. If you can't figure it out on a cryptic statement, call the firm where the account is currently held and ask a representative to tell you what kind of account you have.

   Never, ever sign over assets such as checks and security certificates to a financial advisor, no matter how trustworthy and honest he or she may seem. The advisor could abscond with them quicker than you can say "Bonnie and Clyde." Transfers should not be completed this way. Besides, you'll find it easier to handle the transfer the way I describe in this
   section.

3. **Complete and mail the account application and asset transfer form.** Completing these for your new investment firm opens your new account and authorizes the transfer.

   You shouldn't take possession of the money in your retirement account yourself to get it over to the new firm. The tax authorities impose huge penalties if you do a transfer incorrectly. Let the company to which you're transferring the money do the transfer for you. If you have questions or problems, the firm(s) to which you are transferring your account have armies of capable employees waiting to help you. Remember, these firms know that you are transferring your money to them, so they should roll out the red carpet.

4. **Figure out which securities you want to transfer and which need to be liquidated.** Transferring existing investments in your account to a new investment firm can sometimes be a little sticky. If you're transferring cash (money market funds) or securities that trade on any of the major stock exchanges, transferring such assets is not a problem.

If you own publicly traded securities, transferring them *as is* (known as "in kind") to your new investment firm is better, especially if the firm offers discount brokerage services. You can then sell your securities through that firm more cheaply.

If you own mutual funds unique to the institution you're leaving, check with your new firm to see if it can accept them. If not, you need to contact the firm that currently holds them to sell them.

CDs are tricky to transfer. Ideally, you should send in the transfer forms several weeks or so before the CDs mature — few people do this. If the CD matures soon, call the bank and instruct it that when the CD matures, you would like the funds to be invested in a savings or money market account that you can access without penalty when your transfer request lands in the bank's mailbox.

5. **(Optional) Let the firm from which you're transferring the money know that you are doing so.** If the place you're transferring from doesn't assign a specific person to your account, definitely skip this step. When you're moving your investments from a brokerage firm where you've dealt with a particular broker, the decision is more difficult.

Most people feel obligated to let their representative know that they are moving their money. In my experience, calling the person with the "bad news" is usually a mistake. Brokers or others who have a direct financial stake in your decision to move your money will try to sell you on staying. Some may try to make you feel guilty for leaving, and some may even try to bully you.

Writing a letter may seem like the coward's way out, but writing usually makes leaving your broker easier for both of you. You can polish what you have to say, and you don't put the broker on the defensive. Or (although I don't want to encourage lying) not telling the *whole* truth may be better. Excuses, such as you have a family member in the investment business who will manage your money for free, may help you to avoid an uncomfortable confrontation.

Then again, telling an investment firm that its charges are too high or that it misrepresented and sold you a bunch of lousy investments may help the firm to improve in the future. Don't fret too much — do what's best for you and what you're comfortable with. Brokers are not your friends. Even though the broker may know your kids' names, your favorite hobbies, and your birthday, you have a *business* relationship.

Transferring your existing assets typically takes a month to complete. Should the transfer not be completed within one month, get in touch with your new investment firm to determine what the problem is. If your old company is not cooperating, call a manager there to help get the ball rolling.

The unfortunate reality is that an investment firm will cheerfully set up a new account to *accept* your money on a moment's notice, but it will drag its feet, sometimes for months, when the time comes to relinquish your money. To light a fire under the behinds of the folks at the investment firm, tell a manager at the old firm that you're sending letters to the National Association of Securities Dealers (NASD) and the Securities and Exchange Commission (SEC) if it doesn't complete your transfer within the next week.

Moving money from an employer's plan

When you leave a job, particularly if you are retiring or being laid off after many years of service, money-hungry brokers and financial planners probably will be on you like a pack of bears on a tree leaking sweet honey. Tread carefully and slowly if you seek financial help — be sure to read Chapter 18 to avoid the pitfalls in hiring such assistance.

When you leave a job, you are confronted with a slightly different transfer challenge: moving money from an employer plan into one of your own retirement accounts. (As long as your employer allows it, you may be able to leave your money in your old employer's plan. Evaluate the quality of the investment choices using the information I provide in this part of the book.) Typically, employer retirement plan money can be rolled over into your own IRA. Check with your employer's benefits department or a tax advisor for details.

Federal tax law requires employers to withhold as a tax 20 percent of any retirement account disbursements to plan participants. So if you are personally taking possession of your retirement account money in order to transfer it to an IRA, you must wait to be reimbursed by the government for this 20 percent withholding until you file your annual tax return. This withholding creates a problem because if you don't replace the 20 percent withholding into the rollover IRA, the IRS treats the shortfall as an early distribution subject to income tax as well as penalties.

My advice is: Never take personal possession of money from your employer's retirement plan. To avoid the 20 percent tax withholding and a lot of other hassles, simply inform your employer where you want your money to be sent. Prior to doing so, you should establish an appropriate account (an IRA, for example) at the investment firm you intend to use. Then tell your employer's benefits department to what investment firm you would like your retirement money transferred. Ideally, you can send your employer a copy of your account statement, which contains the investment firm's mailing address and your account number.

Chapter 12

Investing Outside Retirement Accounts

*I*n this chapter, I discuss investment options for money held *outside* retirement accounts, and I include some sample portfolio recommendations. Chapter 11 reviews investments for money *inside* retirement accounts. This distinction may seem somewhat odd — this distinction is not one that is made in most financial books and articles — but I have my reasons.

Thinking of the two pots of money differently is useful.

✔ **Investments held outside retirement accounts are subject to taxation.** You have a whole range of different investment options to consider when taxes come into play.

✔ **Money held outside retirement accounts is also more likely to be used sooner than funds held inside retirement accounts.** Why? Because you'll generally have to pay far more in income taxes to access money inside rather than outside retirement accounts.

✔ **Funds inside retirement accounts have their own nuances.** For example, when you invest through your employer's retirement plan, your investment options are usually limited to a handful of choices. And special rules govern transfer of your retirement account balances.

Getting Started

Suppose that you have some money sitting around in a bank savings account or money market mutual fund. Your money is earning several percent in interest, but you want to invest it more profitably. Never forget two things about investing this type of money:

✔ **Earning a few percent is better than losing 20 to 50 percent or more.** Just talk to anyone who's bought a lousy investment. So be patient. Educate yourself first *before* you invest.

✔ **To earn a higher rate of return, you must be willing to take more risk.** (This is true unless you jump into a higher-yielding money market fund, discussed later in this chapter.) Earning a better rate of return means considering investments that can fluctuate in value — and, of course, the value can drop as much as it can rise.

You approach the vast sea of investment options and start stringing up your rod to go fishing. You hear stories of people catching big ones — cashing in big on stocks or real estate that they bought years ago. Even if you don't have delusions of grandeur, you'd at least like your money to grow faster than the cost of living.

But before you cast your investment line, consider the following frequently overlooked ways to put your money to work and earn higher returns without as much risk. These options may not be as exciting as hunting the big fish out there, but they should easily improve your financial health.

Pay off high-interest debt

Many folks have credit card or other consumer debt that costs more than 10 percent per year in interest. Paying off this debt with savings is like putting your money in an investment with a guaranteed return equal to the rate you are paying on the debt.

For example, if you have credit card debt outstanding at 14-percent interest, paying off that loan is the same as putting your money to work in an investment with a sure 14-percent annual return. Remember that the interest on consumer debt is not tax-deductible, so you actually need to earn *more* than 14 percent investing your money elsewhere in order to net 14 percent after paying taxes. Refer to Chapter 5 for more details if you're still not convinced.

Paying off some or all of your mortgage may make sense, too. This financial move isn't as clear because the interest rate is lower than on consumer debt and is usually tax-deductible. (See Chapter 14 for more details on this decision.)

Contribute to retirement accounts

When you have a chunk of money, make sure that you take advantage of the *terrific* tax benefits offered by a retirement account. If you work for a company that offers a retirement savings plan such as a 401(k), try to fund it at the highest level you can manage. When you earn self-employment income, look into SEP-IRAs and Keoghs. (Retirement-plan options are discussed in Chapter 11.)

If you need to save money outside retirement accounts for short-term purposes (for example, to buy a car or a home), then by all means, save money outside retirement accounts. But remember that investing money outside retirement accounts does not provide you tax deductions and requires greater thought and consideration because your investments can produce taxable distributions.

Taxes on Your Investments

When you invest money outside of a retirement account, *investment distributions* — such as interest, dividends, and capital gains — are all exposed to taxation. Too many folks (and too many of their financial advisors) ignore the tax impact of their investment strategies. You need to pay attention to the tax implications of your investment decisions *before* you invest your money.

Consider a person in the combined 40 percent tax bracket (federal plus state taxes) who keeps extra cash in a taxable savings account paying 3 percent interest. If she pays 40 percent of her interest earnings in taxes, she ends up keeping just 1.8 percent. With a tax-free money market fund from the major mutual fund providers (stay tuned to this chapter for more on these), she could easily earn more than this amount, completely free of federal and/or state taxes. See Chapter 7 for help determining your tax bracket.

Another mistake some people make is investing in securities that produce tax-free income when they are not in a high enough tax bracket to benefit. Consider a person in a combined 20 percent tax bracket who is investing in securities that produce tax-free income. Suppose that he invests in a tax-free investment that yields 4.5 percent. A comparable taxable investment is yielding 7 percent. If he had instead invested in the taxable investment at a 7 percent yield, the after-tax yield would be 5.6 percent. Thus, he is losing out on yield by being in the tax-free investment, even though he may feel happy in it because the yield isn't taxed.

To decide between comparable taxable and tax-free investments, you need to know your tax bracket and the rates of interest or yield on each investment. Here are some general guidelines based upon your federal income tax bracket:

✔ **31 percent or higher federal tax bracket.** If you're in this bracket, you should generally avoid investments that produce taxable income. (Check out Table 7-1 in Chapter 7 to see what tax bracket you're in.)

✔ **28 percent federal bracket.** In most cases, you should be as well or better off in investments that do not produce taxable income when investing outside retirement accounts. This may not be the case, however, if you're in tax-free money market and bond funds whose yields are depressed due to high operating expenses (you won't find them recommended in this chapter!).

✔ **15 percent federal bracket.** Investments that produce taxable income are just fine for you. You may end up with *less* if you purchase investments that produce tax-free income.

In the sections that follow, I give specific advice about investing your money while keeping an eye on taxes.

Savings/Emergency Reserve Investments

In Chapter 3, I explain the importance of keeping sufficient money in an emergency reserve account. From such an account, you need two things:

✔ **Accessibility.** When you need to get your hands on the money for an emergency, you want to be able to do so quickly and without penalty.

✔ **Highest possible return.** You want to get the highest rate of return possible without risking your principal. This doesn't mean that you should simply pick the money market or savings option with the highest yield, because other issues such as taxes are a consideration. What good is earning a slightly higher yield if you pay a lot more in taxes?

Bank and credit union accounts

When you have a few thousand dollars or less, your best and easiest path is to keep this excess savings in a local bank or credit union. Look first to the institution where you keep your checking account.

Keeping this stash of money in your checking account, rather than in a separate savings account, makes financial sense if the extra money helps you avoid monthly service charges because your balance occasionally dips below the minimum. Compare the service charges on your checking account with the interest earnings from a savings account.

For example, suppose that you're keeping $2,000 in a savings account to earn 4-percent interest versus earning no interest on your checking account money. Over the course of a year, you earn $80 interest on that savings account. If you incur a $9 per month service charge on your checking account, that's $108 per year. So, keeping your extra $2,000 in a checking account may be better if that keeps you above a minimum balance and erases that monthly service charge. (However, if you're more likely to spend the extra money if it's in your checking account, keeping it in a separate savings account where you won't be tempted to spend it might be better.)

Money market mutual funds

Money market funds, a type of mutual fund (see Chapter 11), are just like bank savings accounts — but better, in most cases. The best money market funds pay higher yields than bank savings accounts and offer you check-writing privileges. And if you're in a high tax bracket, you can select a tax-free money market fund, which pays interest that is free from federal and/or state tax — a feature you can't get with a bank savings account.

The yield on a money market is an important consideration. The operating expenses deducted before payment of dividends is the single biggest determinant of yield. All other things being equal (which they usually are with different money market funds), lower operating expenses translate into higher yields for you.

Another factor that may be important in your choice of a money market fund is what other types of fund investing you can do at the fund company where you establish a money market fund. Doing most or all of your fund shopping, money-market and otherwise, at one good fund company can reduce the clutter in your investing life; chasing after a slightly higher yield offered by another company is sometimes not worth the extra paperwork and administrative hassle. On the other hand, there's no reason why you can't invest in funds at multiple firms (as long as you don't mind the extra paperwork), using each for its relative strengths.

Most mutual fund companies don't have many local branch offices, so you'll probably open and maintain your money market mutual fund through the fund's toll-free 800 phone line and the mail. Distance has its advantages. Because you can conduct business by mail, internet, and phone, you don't need to go schlepping into a local branch office to make deposits and withdrawals. I'm *happy* to report that I haven't visited a bank office in years.

Despite the distance, your money is still accessible via check-writing, and you can also have money wired to your local bank on any business day. Don't fret about a deposit being lost in the mail. It rarely happens, and no one can legally cash a check made payable to you anyway. Just be sure to endorse the check with the notation "for deposit only" under your signature.

(For that matter, driving or walking to your local bank isn't 100-percent safe. Imagine all the things that could happen to you or your money en route to the bank. You could slip on a banana peel, drop your deposit down a sewer grate, or get mugged, kidnapped, or run over by a bakery truck. Who knows — you could walk into a bank holdup and end up being taken hostage.)

Watch out for "sales"

Beware of money market mutual funds running specials. Some mutual funds aren't above resorting to some of the same marketing gimmicks that make retailers so endearing. The most common ploy is for funds to have a "sale." They do so by temporarily waiving (sometimes called *absorbing*) operating expenses, which results in a fund being able to boost its yield. But these sales never last long; the operating expenses come back and deflate that too-good-to-be-true yield like a nail in a bike tire. Some fund companies run sales because they know that a good percentage of the fund buyers lured in won't bother leaving when they jack up the prices (operating expenses).

You're better off sticking with funds that maintain "everyday low prices" (for operating expenses) to get the highest long-term yield. I recommend such funds later in this chapter. However, if you want to move your money to companies having specials and then move it back out when the special's over, be my guest. If you have lots of money and don't mind paperwork, it may be worth the bother.

Recommended money market mutual funds

In the sections that follow, I recommend good money market mutual funds. As you peruse these lists, remember that the money market fund that works best for you depends upon your tax situation. Throughout the list, I try to guide you to funds that generally make sense for people in particular tax brackets.

Money market funds that pay taxable dividends are appropriate when you're not in a high tax bracket (less than or equal to 28 percent federal). See Table 12-1 for my recommendations.

Fidelity: 800-544-8888. T. Rowe Price: 800-638-5660. Vanguard: 800-662-7447. USAA: 800-382-8722.

Table 12-1	Recommended Taxable Money Market Funds	
Fund	*Operating Expenses*	*Minimum to Open*
Fidelity Spartan Money Market	0.5%	$20,000
T. Rowe Price Summit Cash Reserves	0.5%	$25,000

Fund	Operating Expenses	Minimum to Open
USAA Mutual Money Market	0.5%	$3,000
Vanguard Money Market Reserves Prime Portfolio	0.3%	$3,000

U.S. Treasury money market funds are appropriate if you prefer a money fund that invests in U.S. Treasuries, which have the safety of government backing, or if you're not in a high federal tax bracket (less than or equal to 28 percent) but *are* in a high state tax bracket (5 percent or higher). Table 12-2 lists a few that I recommend.

Table 12-2   Recommended U.S. Treasury Money Market Funds

Fund	Operating Expenses	Minimum to Open
Vanguard Money Market Reserves U.S. Treasury	0.3%	$3,000
Vanguard Admiral U.S. Treasury Money Market	0.15%	$50,000
Fidelity Spartan U.S. Treasury Money Market	0.5%	$20,000

The tax-free money market funds such as those in Table 12-3 are appropriate when you're in a high federal (31 percent) *and* state tax bracket (5 percent or higher).

Fidelity: 800-544-8888. Vanguard: 800-662-7447. USAA: 800-382-8722.

Table 12-3   Recommended State-and-Federal-Tax-Free Money Market Funds

Fund	Operating Expenses	Minimum to Open
Fidelity Spartan AZ Muni Money Market	0.4%	$25,000
Vanguard CA Tax-Free Money Market	0.2%	$3,000
USAA Tax-Exempt CA Money Market	0.4%	$3,000
Fidelity Spartan FL Muni Money Market	0.5%	$25,000

(continued)

Table 12-3 *(continued)*

Fund	Operating Expenses	Minimum to Open
USAA Tax-Exempt FL Money Market	0.5%	$3,000
Fidelity Spartan MA Muni Money Market	0.5%	$25,000
Vanguard NJ Tax-Free Money Market	0.2%	$3,000
USAA Tax-Exempt NY Money Market	0.5%	$3,000
Vanguard OH Tax-Free Money Market	0.2%	$3,000
Vanguard PA Tax-Free Money Market	0.2%	$3,000
USAA Tax-Exempt TX Money Market	0.5%	$3,000
USAA Tax-Exempt VA Money Market	0.5%	$3,000

A number of states do not have money market fund options listed in Table 12-3 (and some that do may have minimums that are too high for you). In some cases, none exists. In other cases, the funds available (and not on the recommended list) for that state have such high annual operating expenses, and therefore such low yields, that you are better off in a more competitively run federal-tax-free-only fund listed in Table 12-4.

Federally tax-free only money market funds (the dividends on these are state taxable) are appropriate when you're in a high federal (31 percent and up) but *not* state (less than 5 percent) bracket or if you live in a state that doesn't have competitive state and federally tax-free funds available (refer to Table 12-3 to make sure).

Table 12-4   Federally Tax-Free Only Money Market Funds

Fund	Operating Expenses	Minimum to Open
Vanguard Municipal Money Market	0.2%	$3,000
Fidelity Spartan Municipal Money Market	0.4%	$25,000
USAA Tax-Exempt Money Market	0.5%	$3,000

Investing Money for the Longer Term

Important note: This section (together with its recommended investments) assumes that you have a sufficient emergency reserve stashed away and are taking advantage of tax-deductible retirement account contributions already. Refer to Chapter 3 for more on these goals.

Which investments you should consider depends on your comfort level with risk. But your choice of investments should also be suited to how much *time* you have until you plan to use the money. I'm not talking about investments that you won't be able to sell on short notice if need be (most of them you can). Investing money in a more volatile investment is riskier if you need to liquidate it in the short term.

For example, suppose that you're saving money for a down payment on a house and are about one year away from having enough to make your foray into the real estate market. If you had put this "home" money into the U.S. stock market near the beginning of one of the stock market's 20- to 50-percent corrections, a year later, you'd have been a mighty unhappy camper. You could have seen a substantial portion of your money *vanish* in short order and your home dreams put on hold.

Most of the following recommended investments are different types of *no-load* (commission-free) mutual funds. Mutual funds can be sold on any business day, usually with a simple phone call. Funds come with all different levels of risk, so you can choose funds that match your time frame and desire to take risk. (Chapter 10 discusses all the basics of mutual funds.)

The different investment options in the remainder of this chapter are organized by time frame. All the recommended investment funds that follow assume that you have *at least* a several-year time frame. The recommended investments are also organized by your tax situation. (If you don't know your current tax bracket, be sure to review Chapter 7.) The following are summaries of the different time frames:

✔ **Short-term investments.** These investments are suitable for a period of a few years — perhaps you're saving money toward a home or some other major purchase in the near future. When investing for the short-term, look for liquidity and stability — features that rule out real estate on one hand and stocks on the other. Recommended investments include shorter-term bond funds, which are higher-yielding alternatives to money market funds. If interest rates increase, these funds drop slightly in value — a couple of percent or so (unless rates rise tremendously). I also discuss Treasuries and certificates of deposit later in this chapter.

✓ **Intermediate-term investments.** These investments are appropriate for more than a few but less than ten years. Investments that fit the bill are intermediate-term bonds and well-diversified hybrid funds (which include some stocks as well as bonds).

✓ **Long-term investments.** If you have a decade or more, then you can consider potentially higher-return (and therefore riskier) investments. Stocks, real estate, and other growth-oriented investments can earn the most money if you're comfortable with the risk involved.

Bond funds

Bond funds that pay taxable dividends are appropriate when you're not in a high tax bracket (less than or equal to 28 percent federal). Table 12-5 lists some bond funds that I recommend.

Table 12-5	Recommended Taxable Bond Funds		
Fund	Investments	Operating Expenses	Minimum to Open
Short-term			
Vanguard Short-Term Corporate	Mostly corporate; some treasuries	0.3%	$3,000
Intermediate-term			
Dodge & Cox Income	Mostly corporate	0.5%	$1,000
Vanguard Total Bond Market Index	Corporate and mortgages; some treasuries	0.2%	$3,000
Long-term			
Vanguard Long-Term Corporate	Corporate bonds; some treasuries	0.3%	$3,000
Vanguard High-Yield Corporate	Lower-quality corporate bonds	0.3%	$3,000

U.S. Treasury bond funds

U.S. Treasury bond funds are appropriate if you prefer a bond fund that invests in U.S. Treasuries (which have the safety of government backing) or when you're not in a high federal tax bracket (less than or equal to 28 percent) but *are* in a high state tax bracket (5 percent or higher). For good Treasury bond funds, look no further than the Vanguard Group, which offers short-, intermediate-, and long-term U.S. Treasury funds with a $3,000

Asset allocation

Asset allocation is the process of figuring out what portion of your wealth you should invest in different types of investments. You frequently (and most appropriately) practice asset allocation with retirement accounts. Ideally, more of your saving and investing should be conducted through tax-sheltered retirement accounts. That's generally the best way to lower your long-term tax burden (see Chapter 11 for details).

If you have sufficient assets that you plan to invest outside retirement accounts, for that portion of your investments that you intend to hold for the long term (ten or more years), see the asset allocation section in Chapter 8.

minimum investment and a low 0.3-percent operating expense ratio. With a $50,000 minimum, Vanguard's Admiral series of U.S. Treasury funds offers even higher yields thanks to an even lower expense ratio of .15 percent.

Buying Treasuries direct

There's an even cheaper method of investing in Treasury bonds than through the thrifty Vanguard Treasury funds: You can purchase Treasuries directly from the Federal Reserve Bank. To open an account through the Treasury Direct program, look in your local phone book under "Federal Government" for the nearest Federal Reserve Bank.

The Federal Reserve Bank charges $25 annually for accounts with more than $100,000 in Treasury bonds. Smaller accounts are free of any maintenance or management fees or charge. The operating expenses of even the leanest mutual funds cannot compete with these rates!

You do sacrifice a bit of liquidity, however, when purchasing Treasury bonds directly from the government. While you can sell your bonds through the Treasury, it takes some time and hassle. If you would like daily access to your money, buy a recommended Vanguard fund and pay the company's low management fee.

State-and-federal-tax-free bond funds

The state-and-federal-tax-free bond funds listed in Table 12-6 are appropriate when you're in high federal (31 percent and up) *and* state (5 percent or higher) tax brackets.

Inflation-indexed Treasury bonds

Like a handful of other nations, the U.S. Treasury now offers *inflation-indexed* government bonds. Because a portion of these Treasury bonds' return is pegged to the rate of inflation, these bonds offer investors a safer type of Treasury bond investment option.

To understand the relative advantages of an inflation-indexed bond, take a brief look at the relationship between inflation and a normal bond. When an investor purchases a normal bond, he is committing himself to a fixed yield over a set period of time — for example, a bond that matures in 10 years and pays 7 percent interest. However, changes in the cost of living (inflation) are not fixed and are difficult to predict.

Suppose an investor had put $10,000 into a regular bond in the 1970s. During the life of his bond, he would have unhappily watched escalating inflation. During the time he held the bond and by the time his bond matured, he would have witnessed the erosion of the purchasing power of his $700 of annual interest and $10,000 of returned principal.

Enter the inflation-indexed Treasury bond. Say you have $10,000 to invest and you buy a 10-year, inflation-indexed bond that pays you a *real rate of return* (this is the return above and beyond the rate of inflation) of, say, 3 percent.

This portion of your return is paid out in interest. The other portion of your return is from the inflation adjustment to the principal you invested. The inflation portion of the return gets put back into principal. So if inflation were running at about 3 percent, as it has in recent years, your $10,000 of principal would be indexed upwards after one year to $10,300. In the second year of holding this bond, the 3 percent real return of interest would be paid on the increased ($10,300) principal base.

If inflation skyrocketed and was running at, say, 10 percent rather than 3 percent per year, your principal balance would grow 10 percent per year, and you'd still get your 3 percent real rate of return on top of that. Thus, an inflation-indexed Treasury bond investor would not see the purchasing power of his invested principal or annual interest earnings eroded by unexpected inflation.

The inflation-indexed Treasuries can be a good investment for conservative, inflation-worried bond investors, as well as taxpayers who want to hold the government accountable for increases in inflation. The downside: Inflation-indexed bonds can yield slightly lower returns, since they are less risky compared to regular Treasury bonds.

Table 12-6	Recommended State-and-Federal-Tax-Free Bond Funds		
Fund	*Investments*	*Operating Expenses*	*Minimum to Open*
Intermediate-term			
Vanguard CA Tax-Free Insured Intermediate Term	CA Municipals	0.2%	$3,000

Fund	Investments	Operating Expenses	Minimum to Open
Long-term			
Vanguard CA Tax-Free Insured Long-Term	Insured CA Municipals	0.2%	$3,000
Fidelity Spartan CT Muni Income	Lower-quality CT Municipals	0.5%	$10,000
Vanguard FL Insured Tax-Free	FL Municipals	0.5%	$3,000
Fidelity Spartan MA Muni Income	Lower-quality MA Municipals	0.5%	$10,000
Fidelity Spartan MI Muni Income	Lower-quality MI Municipals	0.5%	$10,000
Fidelity Spartan MN Muni Income	MN Municipals	0.5%	$10,000
Vanguard NJ Tax-Free Insured Long-Term	Insured NJ Municipals	0.2%	$3,000
Vanguard NY Insured Tax-Free	Insured NY Municipals	0.2%	$3,000
Vanguard OH Tax-Free Insured Long-Term	Insured OH Municipals	0.2%	$3,000
Vanguard PA Tax-Free Insured Long-Term	Insured PA Municipals	0.2%	$3,000
USAA TX Tax-Free Income		0.5%	$3,000
USAA VA Tax-Free Income		0.4%	$3,000

A number of states do not have bond fund options listed in Table 12-6 (some that do may have minimums that are too high for you). In some cases, none exists. In other cases, the funds that are available for that state (and not on the recommended list) have such high annual operating expenses, and therefore such low yields, that you would be better off in the more competitively run federal-tax-free-only funds listed in Table 12-7. If a bond fund is not listed for your state, or if you're only in a high federal tax bracket, check out Table 12-8 for recommended federal-tax-free bond funds.

Federal-tax-free-only bond funds

Federal-tax-free-only bond funds (the dividends on them are state-taxable) are appropriate when you're in a high federal bracket (31 percent and up) but lower state bracket (less than 5 percent) or when you live in a state that doesn't have state- and-federal-tax-free funds available (refer to Table 12-6 to make sure).

Table 12-7	Federal-Tax-Free-Only Bond Funds		
Fund	**Investments**	**Operating Expenses**	**Minimum to Open**
Short-term			
Vanguard Muni Short-Term	Municipals	0.2%	$3,000
Vanguard Muni Limited-Term	Municipals	0.2%	$3,000
Intermediate-term			
Vanguard Muni Intermediate-Term	Municipals	0.2%	$3,000
Long-term			
Vanguard Muni Insured Long-Term	Insured Municipals	0.2%	$3,000
Vanguard Muni Long-Term	Municipals	0.2%	$3,000

Certificates of deposit (CDs)

For many decades, bank CDs have been the investment of choice for folks with some extra cash that is not needed in the near-term. The attraction is that you get a higher rate of return on a CD than on a bank savings account. And unlike bond funds, your principal does not fluctuate in value.

Compared to bonds, however, CDs have a number of drawbacks.

- ✔ First, in a CD, your money is not accessible unless you cough up a fairly big penalty — typically six months' interest. With a no-load (commission-free) bond fund, if you need some or all of your money next week, month, or year, you can access it without penalty.

- ✔ A second, and less-often noted drawback, is that CDs come in only one tax flavor — taxable. Bonds, on the other hand, come in tax-free (federal and/or state) and taxable flavors. So if you're a higher-tax-bracket investor, bonds offer you a tax-friendly option that CDs can't.

In the long run, you should earn more — perhaps one to two percent more per year — and have better access to your money in bond funds than in CDs. Bond funds make particular sense when you're in a higher tax bracket and would benefit from tax-free income on your investments. If you're not in a high tax bracket (15 percent federal), and you have a bad day whenever your bond fund takes a dip in value, then consider CDs. Just make sure that you shop around to get the best interest rate.

Stock funds

Listed in Table 12-8 are stock funds, which are appropriate if you don't want current income or are in a high federal tax bracket (28 percent and up). Note that *all* the funds in Table 12-8 are intended as long-term investments. That's because funds that avoid bonds and dividend-producing stocks focus on growth stocks.

If you're not in a high tax bracket (less than 28 percent federal), you can also consider some of the stock funds recommended in Chapter 12 in the section "Great Investment Recipes."

Table 12-8	Relatively Tax-Friendly Stock Funds	
Parent	*Fund*	*Operating Expenses*
U.S. funds		
Vanguard	Tax-Managed Capital Appreciation	0.2%
Vanguard	Tax-Managed Small Capitalization	0.2%
Vanguard	Total Stock Market Index	0.2%
International funds		
Vanguard	International Growth	0.5%
Vanguard	Tax-Managed International	0.4%
Vanguard	Total International	0.4%

Annuities

As I discuss in Chapter 11, *annuities* are accounts that are partly insurance but mostly investment. You should only consider contributing to an annuity after you've exhausted contributions to all your available retirement accounts. Because annuities carry higher annual operating expenses than

Don't buy CDs for the FDIC insurance

Much is made, particularly by bankers, of the FDIC insurance that comes with bank CDs. The lack of this insurance on high-quality bonds shouldn't be a big concern. High-quality bonds rarely default; even if a fund held a bond that defaulted, it would probably be a tiny fraction (less than 1 percent) of the value of the fund, so it would have little overall impact.

Besides, the FDIC itself is no Rock of Gibraltar. Banks have failed and will continue to fail. Yes, you are insured if you have less than $100,000 in a bank, but in reality, if the bank crashes, you may have to wait a long time and settle for less interest than you thought you were getting. You are not immune from harm, FDIC or no FDIC.

If the U.S. government backing through FDIC insurance allows you to sleep better, you can invest in Treasuries (see the discussion earlier in this chapter), which are government-backed bonds.

comparable mutual funds, you should only consider them if you plan to leave your money invested preferably for 15 or more years. Even if you have that long, the tax-friendly funds discussed in the previous sections of this chapter can allow your money to grow without excessive annual taxation.

The best annuities can be purchased from no-load (commission-free) mutual fund companies — specifically Vanguard (800-662-7447) and T. Rowe Price (800-638-5660).

Real estate

Real estate can be a financially and psychologically rewarding investment. It can also be a money pit and a real headache if you buy the wrong property or get a tenant from hell. (I discuss real estate as an investment in Chapter 9 and the nuts and bolts of buying real estate in Chapter 14.)

Small-business investments

Investing in your own business or someone else's established small business can be a high-risk but potentially high-return investment. The best options are those you understand well. Please refer to Chapter 9 for more information about small-business investments.

Chapter 13

Investing for Educational Expenses

*I*f you're like most parents or potential future parents, just turning to this chapter makes you anxious. Such trepidation is understandable. Much of what you read about educational expenses, particularly college expenses, says that if costs keep rising at the current rate, you'll have to spend upwards of a million dollars to give your youngster a quality education.

Quality education for your child need not, and probably won't, cost you as much as those gargantuan projections suggest. Whether you've already started saving or are about to begin a regular college investment plan, your emotions may lead you astray. The hype about educational costs may scare you into taking a path that is less financially beneficial than others that are available.

The Big Mistake Nonwealthy Parents Make when Saving for College Costs

When little Homer and Gwendolyn are filling out their college applications, you don't want to have to say that you can't afford to send them to their dream school. Being considerate and thoughtful parents, you may start investing money in a separate custodial account for them, or through some other financial product, such as a life insurance policy. Doing so is usually a major financial mistake in both the short- and long-term.

Although a small amount of the interest earned on custodial accounts in your child's name is taxed at the child's income tax rate rather than yours, you receive no tax deduction on your contributions to these accounts. And, as I discuss later in this chapter, the more money you accumulate outside your tax-sheltered retirement accounts, the less financial aid you're likely to qualify for.

You should provide for your own financial security *before* saving for your child. You should be saving and investing through retirement accounts, such as a 401(k), SEP-IRA, Keogh, or other retirement account (described in Chapter 11), that give you significant tax benefits. Some people may think that my advice sounds selfish. Please allow me to explain.

Think back to your most recent trip by airplane. Remember what the flight attendants instructed you to do in an emergency? In the event of a loss of air pressure that necessitates the use of oxygen masks, you are instructed to put your oxygen mask on *first*. Only then should you help your children with their oxygen masks.

Consider for a moment why airlines recommend this approach. Although your instinct may be to ensure that your children are safe before taking care of yourself, by taking care of yourself first, you are stronger and better able to help your children.

How the Financial Aid System Works

Just as your child shouldn't choose a college based solely on whether she thinks she can get in, she shouldn't choose a college on the basis of whether you think you can afford it. Except for the affluent who have plenty of cash available to pay for the full cost of college, everyone else should apply for financial aid. More than a few parents who don't think that they qualify for financial aid are pleasantly surprised to find that they have access to loans as well as grants (grants, unlike loans, aren't repaid).

Mary paid for the full cost of her daughter's first year at an expensive private college. In her 50s, Mary had little put away for retirement. "I didn't bother applying for financial aid," she says, adding, "with the value of my home and savings, I thought I was too rich to qualify."

Mary was wrong. In fact, for her daughter's junior year, Mary, who most would consider middle-class, was delighted and shocked to learn that her daughter would receive nearly $9,000 in grants as well as access to moderate-interest loans. Two things did the trick. First, Mary applied for aid, and second, before she did, she invested a hefty chunk of savings into an annuity, which is a type of retirement account. In a moment, you'll see why this worked.

The first step in the financial aid process is to complete the Free Application for Federal Student Aid (FAFSA), which is available from any high school or college. (Internet users can fill out the form online at www.fafsa.ed.gov.) As its name makes clear, you pay nothing for submitting this application other than the time you take to complete the paperwork (completing the application takes more time than watching a TV sitcom but probably less time than getting a driver's license). Some private colleges also require that you complete the Financial Aid Form (FAF), which asks for more information than the FAFSA.

States have their own financial aid programs, so check with your local high school or college financial aid office to get the forms to apply to these as well if you're planning on attending an in-state college. Some colleges also require submission of supplementary forms directly to them.

The data you supply through student aid forms is run through a *financial needs analysis,* a standard methodology approved by the U.S. Congress. The needs analysis considers a number of factors, such as parents' income and assets, age and need for retirement income, number of dependents, number of family members in college, and unusual financial circumstances, which you explain on the application.

The needs analysis calculates how much money you as the parent(s) and your child as the student can be expected to contribute toward educational expenses. Even if the needs analysis determines that you don't qualify for *needs-based* financial aid, you may still have access to loans that are *not* based on need if you go through the financial aid application process. So make sure that you apply for financial aid!

Treatment of retirement accounts

Under the current needs analysis, the value of your retirement plans is *not* considered an asset. By contrast, money that you save *outside* retirement accounts, including money in the child's name, is counted as an asset and reduces your eligibility for financial aid.

Therefore, forgoing contributions to your retirement savings plans in order to save money in a taxable account for Junior's college fund doesn't make sense. When you do, you pay higher taxes both on your current income and on the interest and growth of this money. In addition to paying higher taxes, you are expected to contribute more to your child's educational expenses.

So while your children are years away from applying to college, make sure that you fully fund your retirement accounts such as 401(k)s, SEP-IRAs, and Keoghs. In addition to getting an immediate tax deduction in the year you contribute money, future growth on your earnings will grow without taxation while you're maximizing your child's chances of qualifying for aid.

Comparing the plans of the Selfish family and the Good Intentions family

Imagine two families, the Selfish family and the Good Intentions family, who both live in identical neighborhoods. They own identical homes that they purchased at exactly the same cost. They have identical mortgages and identical jobs that pay the same salaries.

Both families give birth to a child on the same day. The only financial difference between these two families is that the Good Intentions family wants to start saving $100 per month in a nonretirement account when their child is born to help pay for the child's future college expenses. (Because they have to pay income tax on this money, however, the Good Intentions family is actually putting only about $63 per month to work.)

The Selfish family saves the same amount, $100 per month, in their retirement savings plans. Because they pay no federal and state income tax on this money, all of their contributions go to work in the retirement savings plan.

Assuming that both families' investments average an 8-percent-per-year rate of return before taxes, the Good Intentions family ends up with about $22,100 when their kid turns 18. The Selfish family, on the other hand, has more than $48,500 when their child celebrates his 18th birthday. (Later in the chapter, I discuss how you can help pay for Junior's college expenses if you're socking money away into retirement accounts.)

Apart from deciding where to invest money for college, these two families continue to live parallel financial lives in every other way. When the children of the two families apply for financial aid, however, the Selfish family kid qualifies for a good deal more aid. The Selfish family actually holds higher assets, but given the current financial aid criteria and regulations, the Good Intentions family looks wealthier on paper because they hold more money outside their retirement accounts.

Let me stress the need to get an early start on saving. If you read about Mary earlier in the chapter, you remember that she waited until the last minute — with her daughter already in college, you could say she waited even beyond the last minute. She then had to resort to an annuity (explained in Chapter 11) because it was the only avenue open to her to put tens of thousands of dollars away at once into a retirement account. Her procrastination cost her thousands of dollars in tax-deductions she could have had over the years as well as the financial aid she missed out on during her daughter's earlier years in college.

In recent years, some schools have begun to use "Profile" forms to supplement the FAFSA described earlier in the chapter. This form is mainly used by costly private schools to differentiate need among financial aid applicants. Individual schools may attach their own questions, which may require you to list information about retirement accounts. The information on this form is used to help determine how much money you will receive from the school's privately endowed funds. Does this mean you should ignore retirement accounts? Not at all. The vast majority of schools don't consider retirement account funds at all when making financial aid determinations. And even if your child ends up going to one of the schools that does examine such accounts, it's not at all clear that the reduction in your financial aid offer will outweigh the tax benefits gained from the accounts.

Treatment of money in the kids' names

If you plan to apply for financial aid, save money in your name rather than in your children's names (such as via custodial accounts). Colleges expect a much greater percentage of money in your child's name (35 percent) to be used annually for college costs than money in your name (about 6 percent).

If you're affluent enough that you expect to pay for your kid's entire educational costs, investing through custodial accounts can save you on taxes. Prior to your child reaching age 14, the first $1400 of interest and dividend income is taxed at your child's income tax rate rather than yours. After age 14, *all* income generated by investments in your child's name is taxed at your child's rate.

Another option, which, like a traditional custodial account, generally makes the most sense for affluent parents who don't expect to apply for or need any type of financial aid, is the relatively new Education IRA. (As with regular custodial accounts, parents expecting their kids to apply for financial aid will likely be penalized by college financial aid offices for having Education IRA balances.) Subject to eligibility requirements, you can put up to $500 per child per year into an Education IRA. Single taxpayers with adjusted gross incomes (AGIs) of $110,000 or more and couples with AGIs of $160,000 or more may not contribute to an Education IRA (although another individual such as a grandparent may make the contribution to the child's account). While the contribution is not tax-deductible, the future investment earnings compound without taxation. Upon withdrawal, unlike a traditional retirement account, the investment earnings are not taxed as long as the money is used for qualified higher education expenses and, in the year of withdrawal, the HOPE or Lifetime Learning tax credit is not claimed for the student.

The HOPE Scholarship credit and the Lifetime Learning credit are available to couples with an adjusted gross income less than $80,000 ($40,000 for single filers). The maximum annual HOPE credit is $1,500, and it is available to families with students in the first two years of post-secondary education. The Lifetime Learning credit, capped at $1,000, is available at any year for both undergraduate and graduate level education, as well as course work that improves job skills.

State-sponsored college savings plans

Section 529 plans (named after Internal Revenue Code Section 529 and also known as qualified state tuition plans) are among the newest educational savings plans around. A parent or grandparent can put up to $100,000 per beneficiary into one of these plans for each child. Up to $50,000 may be placed in a child's college savings account immediately, and that counts for the next five years' worth of $10,000 tax-free gifts allowed under current gifting laws. (Money contributed to the account is not considered part of the donor's taxable estate. However, if the donor dies before five years are up after gifting $50,000, a pro-rata amount of that gift will be charged back to the donor's estate.)

The biggest attraction of these plans is that money inside the plan compounds tax-deferred, and if withdrawn to pay for college tuition, room and board, and other related higher education expenses, the investment earnings and growth are taxed at the student's rate.

In addition to paying college costs, the money in Section 529 plans may also be used for graduate school expenses. Some states provide tax benefits on contributions to their state-sanctioned plan whereas other states induce you to invest at home by taxing profits from out-of-state plans.

Unlike contributing money into a custodial account with which a child may do with as he pleases when he reaches either the age of 18 or 21 (the age varies by state), these state tuition plans must be used for higher education expenses. Some state plans even allow you to change the beneficiary and take the money back if you change your mind (you will, however, owe tax on the withdrawn earnings plus a penalty — typically 10 percent).

A big potential drawback — especially for families hoping for some financial aid — is that college financial aid offices may treat assets in these plans as the child's, which can greatly diminish financial aid eligibility.

Another potential drawback is that you can't control how the money is invested in state tuition plans. The investment provider(s) for each state plan decides how to invest the money. In most plans, the more years your child is away from college age, the more aggressive the investment mix is. As your child approaches college age, the investment mix is tilted more to conservative investments. Most state plans have somewhat high investment management fees, and some plans don't allow transfers to other plans.

Please also be aware that a future Congress could change the tax laws affecting these plans and diminish the tax breaks or increase the penalties for non-qualified withdrawals. A child cannot have both an Education IRA and Section 529 plan contribution in the same year (even from different contributors).

Clearly, there are pros and cons to these plans. They generally make the most sense for affluent parents (or grandparents) to establish for children who don't expect to qualify for any financial aid. Do a lot of research and homework before investing in any plan. Check out the investment track record, allocations, and fees in each plan as well as restrictions on transferring to other plans or changing beneficiaries. These plans are relatively new and the market for them is evolving fairly rapidly, so take your time committing to one of them.

The need to reform the financial aid system

To some, structuring your finances to maximize financial aid seems, well, a bit underhanded. Let me discourage you from this type of thinking. The government has set up both a financial aid and a tax system that encourage you to save for retirement. Therefore, retirement saving is not selfish — it's financially responsible for you and your children (and the government that doesn't want to get stuck caring for you if you don't save for retirement). Because so many parents — probably including you before you read this chapter — do not understand this, they are not receiving the financial aid that they deserve.

Perhaps we can criticize the government for not publicizing its intentions more effectively. But compare financial aid to the tax system. The tax system also rewards certain types of behavior, but if you ask the IRS for help, they will not tell you *how* to reduce your taxes. The same is true of financial aid: It is *your* responsibility to understand the system in order to receive the financial aid that your child deserves.

Of course, the system is far from perfect, but it is also our responsibility to work for changes. For example, one inequity in the current financial aid determination process is that it makes no allowance for differences in the cost of living across the country. If you live in a high-cost urban area, such as New York, Los Angeles, or San Francisco, the financial aid system makes the erroneous assumption that you are able to contribute the same amount for college costs as someone with equivalent income who lives in a low-cost rural area. Some adjustment for differences in cost of living should be considered in the system.

Treatment of home equity and other assets

Your family's assets may also include equity in real estate and businesses that you own. Although the federal financial aid analysis no longer counts equity in your primary residence as an asset, many private (independent) schools continue to ask parents for this information when making their own financial aid determinations. Thus paying down your home mortgage more quickly instead of funding retirement accounts can harm you financially. You may end up with less financial aid and a higher tax bill.

How Will I Pay for Educational Expenses?

Now you may be wondering how you'll come up with the money to pay for educational expenses if you stash money into retirement accounts. I don't have just one correct solution because how you'll help pay for your child's college costs depends on your own unique situation. However, in most cases, even if you have some available cash that can be directed to pay the college bills as they come in, you will probably have to borrow *some* money.

Some tips: Loans, grants, and scholarships

When you're a homeowner, you may be able to borrow against the equity (market value less the outstanding mortgage loan) in your property. This is a useful option because you can borrow against your home at a reasonable interest rate, and the interest is generally tax-deductible. Some company retirement plans — for example, 401(k)s — allow borrowing as well.

Parents are allowed to make penalty-free withdrawals from Individual Retirement Accounts if the funds are used for college expenses. Although you will not be charged an early-withdrawal penalty, the withdrawal amount will be treated by the IRS as income, and your income taxes will increase accordingly. On top of that, the financial aid office will look at your beefed-up income and assume that you don't need as much financial aid.

A host of financial aid programs, including a number of loan programs, allow you to borrow at fair interest rates. As with some mortgage loans on real estate, federal government educational loans have variable interest rates — which means that the interest rate you're charged floats, or varies, with the overall level of interest rates. Most programs add 3.1 percent to the current interest rates on three-month to one-year Treasury bills. Thus, current rates on educational loans are in the vicinity of 9 percent. The rates are also capped so that the interest rate on your loan can never exceed a few percent more than the initial rate on the loan.

A number of loan programs, such as *Unsubsidized Stafford Loans* and *Parent Loans for Undergraduate Students (PLUS),* are available even when your family is not deemed financially needy. Only *Subsidized Stafford Loans,* on which the federal government pays the interest that accumulates while the student is still in school, are limited to students deemed financially needy.

Most loan programs limit the amount that you can borrow per year as well the overall total you can borrow for a student's educational career. If you need more money than your limits allow, PLUS loans can fill the gap: Parents can borrow the full amount needed after other financial aid is factored in. The only obstacle is that you must go through a credit qualification process. Unlike privately funded college loans, federal loans' main qualification stipulation is that you don't have negative credit (recent bankruptcy, more than three debts over three months past due, and so on). For more information from the federal government about these student loan programs, call the Federal Student Aid Information Center at 800-433-3243.

In addition to loans, a number of grant programs are available through schools and the government as well as independent sources. You can apply for federal government grants via the FAFSA. Grants available through state government programs may require a separate application. Specific colleges and other private organizations (including employers, banks, credit unions, and community groups) also offer grants and scholarships.

Many scholarships and grants don't require any extra work on your part — simply apply for financial aid through colleges. Other programs need seeking out — check directories and databases at your local library, your child's school counseling department, and college financial aid offices. Also try local organizations, churches, employers, and so on. You have a better chance of getting scholarship money through these avenues.

College scholarship search services are generally a waste of money; in some cases, they are actually scams. Some of these services charge up to $100 just to tell you about scholarships that either you're already being considered for or that you're not even eligible for. The legitimate services may tell you about scholarships for, say, $500 that require you to obtain and complete an application and essays. Most people who lack the initiative to use the free references that I describe earlier in this chapter probably won't take the time to apply for these small-potato scholarships.

Your child can work and save money during high school and college. In fact, if your child qualifies for financial aid, he or she is expected to contribute a certain amount to education costs from savings and from employment during the school year or summer breaks. Besides giving Junior a stake in his or her own future, this training encourages sound personal financial management down the road.

The borrowing-versus-saving debate

More than a few investment firms and financial planners argue that, in the long run, saving for your children's college expenses is far cheaper than borrowing for them. This claim is not true. If you are able to save in retirement accounts and choose decent investments and then separately borrow the money needed for college costs later, you can come out ahead, thanks to the tax benefits that retirement accounts provide and the increased financial aid you may receive.

The conflict of interest of these organizations and planners is that they can't sell you investments if you channel your savings into your employer's retirement plan. They have every reason to scare you into action (and into their hands).

What's college going to cost?

College can cost a lot. The total costs vary substantially from school to school. The average annual cost (including tuition, fees, books, supplies, room, board, and transportation) at private colleges is running around $24,000 per year and around $11,000 at public colleges and universities. The more expensive schools can cost up to one-third more. Ouch!

Is all this expense worth it? Although many critics of higher education claim that the cost of a college education should not be rising faster than inflation and that costs can, and should, be contained, denying the value of going to college is hard. Whether it is a local community college, your friendly state university, or a selective Ivy League institution, investing in education is usually worth the effort and the cost.

The definition of an *investment* is an outlay of money for an expected profit. Unlike a car that depreciates in value each year that you drive it, an investment in education yields monetary, social, and intellectual profit. A car is more tangible in the short term, but an investment in education (even if it means borrowing money) gives you more bang for the buck in the long run.

Colleges are now finding themselves subject to the same types of competition that for-profit companies confront. As a result, schools are having to clamp down on rising costs. As with any other product or service purchase, it pays to shop around. You can find good values — colleges that offer competitive pricing *and* provide a quality education.

Setting realistic savings goals

If you have money left over *after* taking advantage of retirement accounts, by all means try to save for your children's college costs. As discussed earlier, you should ideally save in your name unless you know that you won't need or want to apply for financial aid, including those loans that are available regardless of your economic situation.

Be realistic about what you can afford for college expenses given your other financial goals, especially saving for retirement (refer to Chapter 3). Being able to pay the full cost of a college education or anything approaching the full cost, especially at a four-year private college, is a luxury of the affluent. If you're not a high-income earner, consider trying to save enough to pay a third or at most half of the cost. You can make up the balance through loans, your child's employment before and during college, and the like.

Use Table 13-1 to help get a handle on how much you should be saving.

Table 13-1	How Much to Save for College*
Figure Out This	*Write It Here*
1. Cost of school you think your child will attend.	$ _____
2. Percent of costs you'd like to pay (for example, 20% or 40%).	x _____ %
3. Line 1 times line 2 is amount you'll pay (in today's dollars).	= $ _____
4. Number of months until your child reaches college age.	÷ _____ months
5. **Amount to save per month (today's dollars). Line 3 answer divided by line 4 answer.	= $ _____ / month

* Don't worry about correcting the overall analysis for inflation. This worksheet takes care of that through the assumptions made on the returns of your investments as well as the amount that you save over time. This way of doing the calculations works because you assume that the money you're saving will grow at the rate of college inflation. (In the happy event that your investment return exceeds the rate of college inflation, you'll end up with a little more than you had expected.)

**The amount you need to save (calculated in line 5) needs to be increased once per year by the increase in college inflation — 5 or 6 percent should do.

If your child has expensive taste in schools, you may want to tack on 20 to 30 percent to the following average figures:

✔ Average cost of a four-year private college education today: $96,000.

✔ Average cost of a four-year public college education today: $44,000.

Investments for Educational Funds

Financial companies pour millions of dollars into advertising for investment and insurance products that they claim are the best ways to make your money grow for your little gremlins — I mean, children. Don't get sucked in by the ads.

What makes for good and bad investments in general applies to investments for educational expenses, too. Stick with basic, proven, lower-cost investments (Chapter 9 explains what generally to look for and beware of). This section focuses on considerations specific to college funding.

Good investments: No-load mutual funds

As I discuss in Chapter 10, the professional management and efficiency of the best no-load mutual funds makes them a tough investment to beat. Chapters 11 and 12 provide recommendations for investing money in funds both inside and outside tax-sheltered retirement accounts.

The important issue is to gear the investments to the time frame involved until your children need to use the money. The closer your child gets to attending college and using the money saved, the more conservatively the money should be invested.

Bad investments

Life insurance policies that have cash values are some of the most oversold investments to fund college costs. The usual pitch is: Because you need life insurance to protect your family, why not buy a policy that you can borrow against to pay for college?

The reason you shouldn't is that you're better off contributing to retirement accounts. These investments give you an immediate tax deduction that saving through life insurance does not. Because life insurance that comes with a cash value is more expensive, parents are more likely to make a second mistake — not buying enough coverage. If you need and want life insurance, you're better off buying lower-cost term life insurance (see Chapter 16).

Another poor investment for college expenses is one that fails to keep you ahead of inflation, such as savings or money market accounts. You need your money to grow to afford educational costs down the road.

Prepaid tuition plans should generally be avoided. A few states have developed plans to allow you to pay college costs at a specific school (calculated for the age of your child). The allure of these plans is that by paying today, you eliminate the worry of not being able to afford rising costs in the future.

This logic doesn't work for several reasons. First, odds are quite high that you don't have the money today to pay in advance. If you have that kind of extra dough around, you're better off using it for other purposes (and you're unlikely to worry about rising costs anyway). You can invest your own money — that's what the school's going to do with it anyway.

Besides, how do you know which college your child will want to attend and how long it might take Junior to get through? Coercing your child into the school you've already paid for is a sure ticket to long-term problems in your relationship with your teenager.

Overlooked investments

Too often, I see parents knocking themselves out to make more money so that they can afford a bigger home, costlier cars, and vacations and to send their kids to more expensive (and therefore supposedly better) private high schools and colleges. Sometimes families want to send younger children to costly elementary schools, too. Families stretch themselves with outrageous mortgages or complicated living arrangements to get into neighborhoods with top-rated public schools or to send their kids to expensive private elementary schools that they can barely afford.

The best school in the world for your child is you and your home. The reason many people I know, including me and my siblings, were able to attend some of the top educational institutions in this country is that concerned parents worked hard, not just at their jobs, but at spending time with the kids while they were growing up. Rather than working to make more money (with the best of intentions to buy educational games or trips or to send the kids to better schools), in my humble opinion, some parents could do more for their kids by focusing more time on the child.

I see parents scratching their heads about their child's lack of academic interest and achievement — they blame the school or TV or society at large. These factors may contribute to the problem, but education begins in the home. Schools can't do it alone.

Living within your means not only allows you to save more of your income, but it also can free more of your time to raise and educate your children. Don't underestimate the value of spending more time with your kids and giving them your attention.

Chapter 14

Real Estate

• •

In This Chapter

▶ To buy or not to buy

▶ Determining how much to spend and what to buy

▶ Understanding mortgages

▶ Finding a great property

▶ How to work with real estate agents

▶ Putting a deal together

▶ Issues after you buy

• •

*B*uying a home or investing in real estate can be a financially and psychologically rewarding experience. On the other hand, owning real estate
can be a real pain in the butt. Purchasing and maintaining property can be
time-consuming, emotionally draining, and financially painful.

Perhaps you are looking to escape your rented apartment and buy your first
home. Or maybe you're interested in cornering the local real estate market
and making millions in investment property. In either case, you can learn
many lessons from real estate buyers who have traveled before you.

Note: Although this chapter focuses primarily on real estate in which you
would live — otherwise known by those in the trade as *owner-occupied property* — much of what is in the chapter is relevant to real estate investors. For
additional information on buying investment real estate — property that you
rent out to others — see Chapter 9.

To Buy or Continue Renting?

You may be tired of moving from rental to rental. Perhaps your landlord
doesn't adequately keep up the place, or you have to ask permission to hang
a picture on the wall. You may desire the financial security and rewards that
seem to come with home ownership. Or maybe you just want a place to call
your own.

The advantages of renting

Renting has its advantages. Some financially successful renters who I've seen include people who pay low rent, either because they've made housing sacrifices or live in a rent-controlled building. If you're consistently able to save 10 percent or more of your earnings, you're probably well on your way to achieving your future financial goals.

As a renter, you can also enjoy your free time not worrying about or being responsible for fixing up the property — that's your landlord's responsibility. You also have more financial and psychological flexibility as a renter. If you want to move, you can generally do so a lot easier as a renter than as a homeowner.

Another problem that you won't have in renting over the long haul is having a lot of your money tied up in your home. Some people enter their retirement years with a substantial portion of their wealth in their homes. As a renter, you have all your money in financial assets that you can probably tap into more easily.

Any one of these reasons is a good enough reason to *want* to buy a home. But you should take stock of your life and your financial health *before* you know whether you can or should buy a home and how much you can really afford to spend. It's time to ask yourself some bigger questions.

What's your timeline?

From a financial standpoint, you really shouldn't buy a place unless you can anticipate being there for at least three years and preferably five or more. Buying and selling a property entails a lot of expenses, including the cost of getting a mortgage (points, application, and appraisal fees), inspection expenses, moving costs, real estate agents' commissions, and title insurance. To cover these transaction costs plus the additional costs of ownership, a property needs to appreciate about 15 percent.

If you may need or want to move in a couple of years, counting on that kind of appreciation is risky. If you're lucky and happen to buy before a sharp upturn in housing prices, you may get it. If you're not, you will probably lose money on the deal.

Some people are willing to invest in real estate even when they don't expect to live in it for long and would consider turning their home into a rental. Doing so can work well financially in the long haul, but don't underestimate the responsibilities that come with being a landlord. Also, most people need to sell their first home in order to tap all the cash that they have in it to buy the next one.

Can you afford to buy?

Although buying and owning your own home can be a wise financial move in the long run, it is a major purchase that can and probably will send shock waves through the rest of your personal finances. You will probably take out a 15- to 30-year mortgage to finance your purchase. The home you buy will need maintenance over the years. Owning a home is a bit like running a marathon: Just as you have to be in good physical shape to successfully run a marathon, you should be in good financial health when you buy a home. For as long as you own the home, you will be paying for something or other all the time.

Don't let your home control your financial future. I have seen too many people fall in love with a home and make a rash decision without taking a hard look at the financial ramifications. Take stock of your overall financial health, especially where you stand in terms of retirement planning, *before* you buy property or agree to a particular mortgage.

Lenders look primarily at annual income when determining how much a potential home buyer can borrow; they pay no attention to a borrower's overall financial situation. Whether you have no money already tucked away into retirement savings or have several children to clothe, feed, and help pay for college, you qualify for the same size loan as other people with the same income (assuming equal outstanding debts).

So don't trust the lender when he tells you what you can afford according to some formulas that the bank uses to determine what kind of a credit risk you are. Only you can figure out how much you can afford, because only you know what your other financial goals are and how important they are to you.

Here are some important financial questions no lender will ask you or care about but that you should ask yourself before buying a home:

- Are you saving enough monthly to reach your retirement goals?

- How much do you spend (and want to continue spending) on fun things such as travel and entertainment?

- How willing are you to budget your expenses in order to meet your monthly mortgage payments and other housing expenses?

- How much of your children's expected college educational expenses do you want to be able to pay for?

The other chapters in this book can help you answer these important questions. Chapter 3 in particular will help you think through saving for important financial goals.

Many new homeowners run into financial trouble because they don't know their spending needs and priorities and don't know how to budget for them. Some of these owners have trouble curtailing their spending despite the large amount of debt they just incurred; in fact, some spend even more because all sorts of furniture and remodeling expenditures can be made for their home. Many people prop up their spending habits with credit. For this reason, a surprisingly large percentage — some studies say about half — who borrow additional money against their home equity use the funds to pay consumer debts.

How much will lenders allow you to borrow?

All mortgage lenders want to know your ability and the likelihood of your repaying the money you borrow. So you have to pass a few tests that calculate the maximum amount the lender is willing to lend you. For a home in which you will reside, lenders total up your monthly housing expenses. They define your housing costs as:

```
Mortgage Payment + Property Taxes + Insurance
```

Lenders typically loan you up to about 33 percent of your monthly gross (before taxes) income for the housing expense. If you're self-employed, take your net income from the bottom line of your federal tax form Schedule C and divide by 12 to get your monthly gross income.

Lenders also consider your other debts when deciding how much to lend you. A lot of other debt diminishes the funds available to pay your housing expenses. To your monthly housing expense, lenders add the amount you need to pay down your other consumer debt (auto loans, credit cards). The monthly total costs of these debt payments plus your housing costs typically cannot exceed 38 percent.

An old rule of thumb says that you can borrow up to three times (or two and one-half times) your annual income when buying a home. But this is a really rough estimate. The maximum that a mortgage lender loans you depends on interest rates. If rates fall (as they have during much of the past decade), the monthly payment on a mortgage of a given size also drops.

Table 14-1 gives you a ballpark idea of the maximum that you're probably eligible to borrow. Multiply your gross annual income by the number in the second column to determine the maximum size mortgage you can get. For example, if you're getting a mortgage with a rate around 7 percent and your annual income is $50,000, multiply 3.5 × $50,000 to get $175,000, the approximate maximum mortgage allowed. Lower interest rates make buying real estate much more affordable.

Table 14-1 What's the Approximate Maximum You Can Borrow?

When Mortgage Rates Are	Multiply Your Gross Annual Income* by This Figure to Determine the Maximum You May Be Able to Borrow
4%	4.6
5%	4.2
6%	3.8
7%	3.5
8%	3.2
9%	2.9
10%	2.7
11%	2.5

*If you're self-employed, this is your net income (after expenses but before taxes).

What's the cost of owning versus renting?

An important financial consideration for many renters is the cost of owning a home. Some people assume that owning costs more. In fact, owning a place doesn't have to cost a truckload of money. It may even cost less than renting.

On the surface, buying a place seems a lot more expensive than renting. You're probably comparing your monthly rent (a couple hundred dollars to more than $1,000, depending on where you live) to the purchase price of a property, which is usually a much larger number — $100,000, $200,000, or more. When you consider a home purchase, you're forced to think about your housing expenses in one huge chunk rather than in small monthly installments like a rent check.

Tallying up the costs of owning a place can be a useful and not-too-complicated exercise. To make fair the comparison between ownership and rental costs, you need to figure what it would cost on a *monthly basis* to buy a place you desire versus what it would cost to rent a *comparable* place. The worksheet in Table 14-2 enables you to do such a comparison. **Note:** In the interest of reducing the number of variables, all this "figuring" assumes a fixed-rate mortgage, *not* an adjustable (I discuss mortgages later in this chapter).

Also, I have ignored what economists call *the opportunity cost of owning.* In other words, when you buy, the money that you put into your home can't be invested elsewhere, and the foregone investment return on that money, say some economists, should be considered a cost of owning a home. I choose to ignore this for two reasons. First, and most importantly, I don't agree with this line of thinking. When you buy a home, you are investing your money — in real estate — which as I discuss Chapter 9, historically has offered solid long-term returns. Secondly, I have you ignore opportunity cost because it greatly complicates the analysis.

Table 14-2	Monthly Expenses: Renting Versus Owning	
Figure Out This		*Write It Here ($ per month)*
1. Monthly mortgage payment (see "Mortgage")		$
2. Plus monthly property taxes (see "Property taxes")	+	$
3. Equals total monthly mortgage plus property taxes	=	$
4. Your income tax rate (see Table 7-1)		%
5. Minus tax benefits (line 3 multiplied by line 4)	–	$
6. Equals after-tax cost of mortgage and property taxes (subtract line 5 from line 3)	=	$
7. Plus insurance ($30 to $150/mo., depending on property value)	+	$
8. Plus maintenance (1% of property cost divided by 12 months)	+	$
9. Equals total costs of owning (add lines 6, 7, and 8)	=	$

Now, compare Line 9 in Table 14-2 with the monthly rent on a comparable place to see which comes out (roughly) ahead, owning or renting.

Mortgage

To determine the monthly payment on your mortgage, simply multiply the relevant number ("Multiplier") from Table 14-3 by the size of your mortgage expressed in (divided by) thousands of dollars. For example, if you are taking out a $100,000, 30-year mortgage at 8 percent, then multiply 100 by 7.34 for a $734 monthly payment.

Table 14-3	Your Monthly Mortgage Payment "Multiplier"	
Interest Rate	*15-Year Mortgage*	*30-Year Mortgage*
4.0%	7.40	4.77
4.5%	7.65	5.07
5.0%	7.91	5.37
5.5%	8.17	5.68
6.0%	8.44	6.00
6.5%	8.71	6.32
7.0%	8.99	6.65
7.5%	9.27	6.99
8.0%	9.56	7.34
8.5%	9.85	7.69
9.0%	10.14	8.05
9.5%	10.44	8.41
10.0%	10.75	8.78

Property taxes

Ask a real estate person, mortgage lender, or your local assessor's office what your annual property tax bill would be for a house of similar value to the one you are considering buying (the average is 1.5 percent of your property's value). Divide this amount by 12 to arrive at your monthly property tax bill.

Tax savings in home ownership

The following shortcut works quite well in determining your tax savings in home ownership. Multiply your federal tax rate (refer to Chapter 7) by the total amount of your property taxes and mortgage. Technically speaking, not all of your mortgage payment is tax-deductible — only the portion of the mortgage payment that goes to interest is tax-deductible. In the early years of your mortgage, the portion that goes toward interest is nearly all of it. On the other hand, your property taxes will probably rise over time. You may earn state tax benefits as well from your deductible mortgage interest and property taxes.

If you want to know more precisely how home ownership may affect your tax situation, get out your tax return and try plugging in some reasonable numbers to "guesstimate" how your taxes will change. You can also speak with a tax advisor or pick up a copy of *Taxes For Dummies,* which I co-wrote.

Consider the long-term cost of renting

When you crunch the numbers to see what owning rather than renting a comparable place may cost you on a monthly basis, you may discover that owning isn't as expensive as you thought. Or you may find that owning costs somewhat more than renting. This discovery may tempt you to think that, financially speaking, renting is cheaper than owning.

Be careful not to jump to conclusions. Remember that you're looking at the cost of owning versus renting *today*. What about 5, 10, or 30 years from now? As an owner, your biggest monthly expense — the mortgage payment — does not increase (assuming that you buy your home with a fixed-rate mortgage). Your property taxes, homeowner's insurance, and maintenance expenses — which are generally far less than your mortgage payment — are the items that increase with the cost of living.

When you rent, however, your entire monthly rent is subject to the vagaries of inflation. The exception to this rule is when you live in a rent-controlled unit, where the annual increase allowed in your rent is capped. Rent control does not eliminate price hikes; it just limits them.

Suppose that you are comparing the costs of owning a home that costs $160,000 to renting that home for $800 a month. Table 14-4 compares the cost of owning the home per month (after factoring in tax benefits) to your rental costs over 30 years. This assumes that you take out a mortgage loan equal to 80 percent of the cost of the property at a fixed rate of 7 percent and that the rate of inflation of your homeowner's insurance, property taxes, maintenance, and rent is 4 percent per year. I further assume that this person is in a moderate combined 35 percent federal and state tax bracket.

Table 14-4	Cost of Owning versus Renting over 30 Years	
Year	*Ownership Cost per Month*	*Rental Cost per Month*
1	$920	$800
5	$980	$940
10	$1,080	$1,140
20	$1,360	$1,690
30	$1,800	$2,500

As you can see in Table 14-4, it costs a little more in the first few years to own the home than to rent it. In the long run, however, owning becomes less expensive. This is because more of your rental expenses increase with inflation. And don't forget that you're building equity in your property as a homeowner, and that equity will be quite substantial by the time that you have your mortgage paid off.

If you've been paying attention, you may be thinking that if inflation doesn't rise 4 percent per year, renting could end up being cheaper. This is not necessarily so. Suppose there's no inflation. Your rent shouldn't escalate, but home ownership expenses (property taxes, maintenance, and insurance) shouldn't, either. And with no inflation, you can probably refinance your mortgage at a rate lower than 7 percent. If you do the math, owning should still cost less in the long run with lower inflation, but the advantage compared to renting is less than during periods of higher inflation. Also, in case you're wondering what happens in the analysis if you're in a different tax bracket, owning still costs less in the long run — the cost savings widens a bit for people in higher tax brackets and lessens a bit for those in lower tax brackets.

Financing Your Home

Once you've looked at your financial health, figured out your timeline, and compared renting to owning costs, you're partway to owning your own home. Unless you're independently wealthy, now you need to confront acquiring a hunk of debt to buy a home. A mortgage loan from a bank or other source makes up the difference between the cash you intend to put into the purchase and the agreed-upon selling price of a piece of real estate. Without a mortgage, most people can't buy the home they want.

The monthly mortgage payments, which consist of interest and principal to repay your loan balance, are huge expenses. Did you know that you may end up paying more for the *interest* on your mortgage than you will for your humble abode itself?

Assume that your new pad costs $150,000. To buy it, you borrow $120,000 and contribute $30,000 from your savings for the down payment. If you borrow that $120,000 with a 30-year fixed-rate mortgage at 7 percent, you end up paying more than $167,000 *in interest* over the life of your loan. (Although you'll pay back some of these interest dollars many years from now when the dollar will likely, thanks to inflation, be worth less than it is today, you're still going to spend a truckload of dollars in interest.)

So taking the time to educate yourself about how to get the best possible deal on a mortgage and ancillary fees is a very wise financial move. More importantly, you won't be able to buy your dream home unless you can finance its purchase.

Understanding the two types of mortgages

Like many other financial products, zillions of different mortgages are available to choose from. The differences can be important or trivial, expensive or cost-free. First, the big differences. Two major types of mortgages exist — those with a *fixed interest rate* and those with a *variable* or *adjustable rate*.

Usually issued for a 15- or 30-year period, fixed-rate mortgages have interest rates that never, ever change. The interest rate you pay the first month is the same one that you pay the last month and every month in between.

Because the interest rate stays the same, your monthly mortgage payment amount does not change. You have no uncertainty or interest rate worries.

Fixed-rate loans are not without risks, however. If interest rates fall significantly after you obtain your mortgage, you face the danger of being stuck with your higher-cost mortgage if you're unable, because of a deterioration in your financial situation or a decline in the value of your property, to *refinance* your mortgage (refinancing is discussed later in this chapter). And, even if you are eligible to refinance, you'll probably have to spend significant time and money to complete the process.

In contrast to a fixed-rate mortgage, an *adjustable-rate mortgage* (ARM) carries an interest rate that varies over time. Like a fidgeting child, it rises, falls, and otherwise can't sit still.

Some ARMs are more hyperactive and tend to get you into more trouble than others — again, like kids. You can start with one interest rate this year and have different ones for every year, possibly every month, during a 30-year mortgage. Thus, the size of your monthly payment fluctuates. Because a mortgage payment makes an unusually large dent in most homeowners' checkbooks anyway, signing up for an ARM without understanding its risks is dangerous.

The attraction of ARMs is the potential interest savings. For the first few years of an adjustable loan, the interest rate is typically lower than on a comparable fixed-rate loan. After that, it depends on the overall trends in interest rates. When interest rates drop, stay level, or rise just a little, you continue to pay less for your adjustable. On the other hand, when rates rise more than a percent or two and stay elevated, the adjustable should cost you more than a fixed-rate loan.

Choosing between fixed- and adjustable-rate mortgages

Ideally, you should weigh the pros and cons of each mortgage type and decide what's best for your situation *before* you go out to purchase a piece of real estate or refinance a loan. In the real world, most people ignore this advice. The excitement of purchasing a home tends to cloud one's judgment. My experience has been that few people look at their entire financial picture before making major real estate decisions. You may end up with a mortgage that could someday seriously overshadow your delight in your little English herb garden out back.

Consider the issues that I discuss in this section before you decide which kind of mortgage — fixed or adjustable — is right for you.

How willing and able are you to take on financial risk?

Take stock of how much risk you can take with the size of your monthly mortgage payment. You can't afford much risk, for example, if your job and income are unstable and you need to borrow a lot. I define *a lot* as close to the maximum that a bank is willing to lend you. *A lot* can also mean that you have no slack in your monthly budget — that is, you're not regularly saving money. If you're in this situation, stick with a fixed-rate loan.

Don't take an adjustable simply because the initially lower interest rates allow you to afford the property you want to buy (unless you're absolutely certain that your income will rise to meet future payment increases). Try setting your sights on a property that you can afford — with a fixed-rate mortgage.

If interest rates rise, a mushrooming adjustable mortgage payment may test the lower limits of your checking account balance. When you don't have emergency savings that you can tap to make the higher payments, how can you afford the monthly payments — much less all the other expenses of home ownership?

And don't forget to factor in reasonably predictable future expenses that may affect your ability to make payments. For example, are you planning to start a family soon? If so, your income may fall while your expenses will surely rise.

If you can't afford the highest allowed payment on an adjustable-rate mortgage, don't take it. You shouldn't take the chance that the interest rate might not rise that high — it could, and you could lose your home! Ask your lender to calculate the highest possible *maximum monthly payment* on your loan. That's the payment you would face if the interest rate on your loan went to the highest level allowed, or the *lifetime cap*.

Consider also your stress level. If you have to start checking interest rates daily, it's probably not worth gambling on rates. Life is too short!

On the other hand, maybe you're in a position to take the financial risks that come with an adjustable-rate mortgage. An adjustable places more (but not all, as most adjustables limit, or *cap,* the rise in the interest rate allowed on your loan) of the risk of fluctuating rates on you. In return, lenders cut you a deal — an adjustable's interest rate starts lower and stays lower if the overall level of interest rates doesn't rise substantially. Even if rates go up, they will probably come back down over the life of your loan. So if you can stick with your adjustable for better and for worse, you may still come out ahead in the long term. Typical caps are 2 percent per year and 6 percent over the life of the loan.

You might feel financially secure in choosing an adjustable loan if you have a hefty financial cushion that is accessible in the event that rates go up, if you take out a smaller loan than you're qualified for, or if you're saving more than 10 percent of your income.

How long do you plan to keep the mortgage?

A mortgage lender takes extra risk in committing to a constant interest rate for 15 to 30 years. Lenders generally don't know any better than you or me what may happen in the intervening years, so they charge you a premium for their risk.

Savings on most adjustables is usually guaranteed in the first two or three years because an adjustable-rate mortgage starts at a lower interest rate than a fixed one. If rates rise, you can end up giving back or losing the savings you achieve in the early years of the mortgage. In most cases, if you aren't going to keep your mortgage more than five to seven years, you're probably paying unnecessary interest costs to carry a fixed-rate mortgage.

Another mortgage option is a *hybrid loan,* which combines features of fixed- and adjustable-rate mortgages. For example, the initial rate may hold constant for a number of years — three to five years is common — and then adjust once a year or every six months thereafter. These hybrid loans may make sense for you if you foresee a high probability of keeping your loan seven to ten years or less but want some stability in your monthly payments. The longer the initial rate stays locked in, the higher the rate is.

Fixed-rate mortgages

Of the two major types of mortgages I discuss earlier in this chapter, fixed-rate loans are generally easier to shop for and to compare. Here's what you need to know.

Trading off interest rate and points

The *interest rate* is the rate of interest that a lender charges you for borrowing its money. Unlike credit-card interest rates, which are usually in the double digits, fixed-rate loans are much lower.

Just as a seesaw doesn't work with one rider missing, an interest rate quote on its own is completely meaningless. The interest rate on a fixed-rate loan must always be quoted with the points on the loan.

Points are up-front fees paid to your lender when you close on your loan. Points are actually percentages: One point is equal to 1 percent of the loan amount. So when a lender tells you that 1.5 points are on a quoted loan, you pay 1.5 percent of the amount you borrow as points. On a $100,000 loan, for example, 1.5 points cost you $1,500.

If one lender offers 30-year mortgages at 7.75 percent and another lender offers them at 8 percent, the 8-percent loan is not necessarily worse. You need to know how many points each lender charges, too.

The seesaw analogy explains how the interest rate and points on a fixed-rate loan go together and move in opposite directions. On a given loan, if you are willing to pay more points (one end of the seesaw goes up), the lender is usually willing to reduce the interest rate (the other end of the seesaw goes down). Paying more in up-front points can save you a lot of money in interest because the interest rate on your loan determines your payments over a long, long time — 15 to 30 years. If you want to pay fewer points, your interest rate increases. Paying less in points might appeal to you if you don't have much cash to close on your loan.

Suppose Lender X quotes you 7.75 percent on a 30-year fixed-rate loan and charges one point (1 percent). Lender Y, who quotes 8 percent, doesn't charge any points. Which is better? The answer depends mostly on how long you plan to keep the loan.

The 7.75-percent loan is 0.25 percent less than the 8-percent loan. Year in and year out, the 7.75-percent loan saves you 0.25 percent. But because you have to pay 1 percent (one point) up front on the 7.75-percent loan, you take about four years to earn back the savings to cover the cost of that point. So if you expect to keep the loan less than 4 years, go with the 8 percent option.

To perform an apples-to-apples comparison of mortgages from different lenders, get interest rate quotes at the same point level for each mortgage. For example, ask each lender for the interest rate on a loan for which you pay one point.

Be wary of lenders advertising no-point loans as though they're offering something for nothing. Remember, if a loan has no points, it's *guaranteed* to have a higher interest rate. That's not to say that it's better or worse than comparable loans from other lenders. But don't get sucked in by a no-points sales pitch. Most lenders who spend big bucks on advertising these types of loans rarely have the best deals anyway.

Understanding other lender fees

In addition to charging you points and the ongoing interest rate, lenders tack on all sorts of other up-front fees in processing your loan. You should know the total of all lender fees so that you can determine how much completing your home purchase will cost you and can compare different mortgages.

Lenders can nickel and dime you with a number of fees other than points. Actually, you pay more than nickels and dimes — $300 here and $50 there adds up in a hurry! Here are the main culprits:

- ✓ **Application and processing fees.** Most lenders charge several hundred dollars to complete your paperwork and process it through their under-writing (loan evaluation) department. The justification for this fee is that if your loan is rejected or you decide not to take it, the lender needs to cover the costs. Some lenders return this fee to you upon closing when you go with their loan (after you're approved).

- ✓ **Credit report.** Many lenders charge a modest fee to pay for the cost of obtaining a copy of your credit report. This report tells the lender whether you've been naughty or nice to other lenders in the past. If you have problems on your credit report, clean them up before you apply (see my discussion of this issue later in this chapter).

- ✓ **Appraisal.** The property for which you are borrowing money needs to be valued. If you default on your mortgage, a lender doesn't want to get stuck with a property worth less than you owe. The appraisal cost is typically several hundred dollars for most residential properties.

- ✓ **Title and escrow charges.** These not-so-inconsequential costs are discussed later in this chapter in the section, "Title insurance and escrow fees."

Get a written itemization of charges from all lenders you are seriously consid-ering so that you have no surprises when you close on your loan and so that you can more readily compare different lenders' mortgages. And to minimize your chances of throwing money away on a loan for which you might not qualify, ask the lender whether you might not be approved for some reason. Be sure to disclose any problems on your credit report or problems with the property that you are aware of.

Some lenders offer loans without points or other lender charges. Remember: Lenders aren't charities. If they don't charge points or other fees, they have to make up the difference by charging a higher interest rate on your loan. Only consider such loans when you lack cash for closing or when you're plan-ning to use the loan for just a few years.

Beware prepayment penalties

Avoid loans with prepayment penalties. You pay this charge, usually 2 to 3 percent of the loan amount, when you pay off your loan before you're supposed to.

Typically, prepayment penalties don't apply when you pay off a loan because you sell the property. But if you refinance such a loan in order to take advantage of lower interest rates, you'll almost always get hit by the prepayment penalties.

The only way to know whether a loan has a prepayment penalty is to ask. If the answer is yes, find yourself another mortgage.

Shun balloon loans

Be wary of balloon loans, which look like fixed-rate loans but really aren't. With a *balloon loan,* the large remaining loan balance becomes fully due at a predetermined time — typically within three to ten years. Balloon loans are dangerous because you may not be able to refinance into a new loan to pay off the balloon loan when it comes due. What if you lose your job or your income drops? What if the value of your property drops, and the appraisal comes in too low to qualify you for a new loan? What if interest rates rise and you can't qualify for the higher rate on a new loan? Taking a balloon loan is a high-risk maneuver that can backfire.

You should take such a loan *only* if the following three conditions are true: You *really, really* want a certain property; the balloon loan is your *only* financing option; and you're *positive* that you'll be able to refinance when the balloon comes due. If you take a balloon loan, get one with as much time as possible before it comes due.

Adjustable-rate mortgages (ARMs)

While sorting through myriad fixed-rate mortgage options is enough to give most people a headache, comparing the bells and whistles of ARMs will give you a mortgage migraine. *Caps, indexes, margins,* and *adjustment periods* — you can spend weeks figuring it all out. If you're clueless about personal finances — or just think that you are — shopping for adjustables scores a 9.9 degree of difficulty on the financial frustration scale.

Unfortunately, you have to wade through a number of details to understand and compare one adjustable to another. Bear with me. And remember throughout this discussion that calculating exactly which ARM should cost you the least is impossible, because the cost depends on so many variables. Selecting an ARM has a lot in common with selecting a home to buy. You have to make trade-offs and compromises based upon what's important to you.

Start rate

Just as the name implies, the *start rate* is the interest rate that your ARM begins with. Don't judge a loan by this rate alone. You won't be paying this attractively low rate for long. The interest rate will rise as soon as the terms of the mortgage allow.

Start rates are probably one of the least important items to focus on when comparing adjustables. You'd never know this from the way some lenders advertise adjustables — you see ads with the start rate in 3-inch bold type and everything else in microscopic footnotes!

The formula (which includes index and margin) and rate caps are far more important in determining what a mortgage is going to cost you in the long run. Some people have labeled the start rate a *teaser rate* because the initial rate on your loan is set artificially low to entice you. In other words, even if the market level of interest rates doesn't change, your adjustable is destined to increase — 1 to 2 percent is not uncommon.

The formula

You'd never (I hope) agree to a loan if your lender's whim and fancy determined your future interest rate. You need to know exactly how a lender figures how much your interest rate increases. All adjustables are based on the following formula, which specifies how the future interest rate on your loan is set:

```
Index + Margin = Interest Rate
```

The *index* measures the overall level of interest rates from which the lender chooses to calculate the specific interest rate on your loan. Indexes are generally (but not always) widely quoted in the financial press. For example, the six-month Treasury bill rate is an index used on some mortgages.

The *margin* is the amount added to the index to determine the interest rate you pay on your mortgage. Most loans have margins of around 2.5 percent.

So, for example, the interest rate of a mortgage driven by the following formula

```
Six-month Treasury bill rate + 2.5 percent
```

is set at the going rate for six-month Treasuries plus 2.5 percent. For example, if six-month Treasuries are yielding 5.5 percent, the interest rate on your loan should be 8 percent. This figure is known as the *fully indexed rate*. If this loan starts at 5 percent and if the rate on six-month Treasuries stays the same, your loan should eventually increase to 8 percent.

Avoid loans with negative amortization

As you make mortgage payments over time, the loan balance you still owe is gradually reduced — this process is known as *amortizing* the loan. The reverse of this process — increasing your loan balance — is called *negative amortization.*

Negative amortization is allowed by some ARMs. Your outstanding loan balance can grow even though you're continuing to make mortgage payments when your mortgage payment is less than it really should be.

Some loans cap the increase of your monthly payment but not that of the interest rate. The size of your mortgage payment may not reflect all the interest that you owe on your loan. So rather than paying the interest that is owed and paying off some of your loan balance (or *principal*) every month, you're paying off some but not all of the interest you owe. Thus the extra unpaid interest you still owe is added to your outstanding debt.

Taking on negative amortization is like paying only the minimum payment required on a credit card bill. You keep racking up greater interest charges on the balance as long as you make only the artificially low payment. Doing so defeats the whole purpose of borrowing an amount that fits your overall financial goals. And you may never get the mortgage paid off!

Avoid ARMs with negative amortization. The only way to know whether a loan includes it is to ask. Some lenders aren't forthcoming about telling you. You'll find it more frequently on loans that lenders consider risky. If you're having trouble finding lenders willing to deal with your financial situation, be especially careful.

The margin is greatly important. When you are comparing two loans that are tied to the same index and are otherwise the same, the loan with the lower margin is better. The margin determines the interest rate for every year you hold the mortgage.

Representatives at one large mortgage lender told me that their market research shows that most borrowers care more about the start rate than the margin on their mortgage. So they happily jacked up their loans' margins and lowered the start rates. Rather than educating their borrowers about the longer-term importance of the margin, they chose to pursue short-term profits.

Indexes differ mainly in how rapidly they respond to changes in interest rates. The following are the more common indexes:

- ✔ **Treasury bills (T-bills).** These indexes are based upon government IOUs (Treasury bills), and there are a whole lot of them are out there. Most adjustables are tied to the interest rate on 6-month or 12-month T-bills.

- ✔ **Certificates of deposit (CDs).** Certificates of deposit are interest-bearing bank investments that lock you in for a specific period of time. ARMs are usually tied to the average interest rate banks are paying on six-month CDs. Like T-bills, CDs tend to respond quickly to changes in the market level of interest rates. Unlike T-bills, CD rates tend to move up a bit more slowly when rates rise and come down faster when rates decline.

✔ **11th district cost of funds.** This index tends to be among the slower moving. ARMs tied to 11th district cost of funds tend to start out at a higher interest rate. A slower-moving index has the advantage of moving up less quickly when rates are on the rise. On the other hand, you must be patient to realize the benefit of falling interest rates.

Adjustment period or frequency

Every so many months, the mortgage-rate formula is applied to recalculate the interest rate on an adjustable-rate loan. Some loans adjust monthly. More typical is an adjustment every 6 or 12 months.

In advance of each adjustment, the lender should send you a notice telling you what your new rate is. All things being equal, the less frequently your loan adjusts, the less financial uncertainty you have in your life. Less-frequent adjustments usually indicate that your loan starts at a higher interest rate, though.

Rate caps

Once the initial interest rate expires, the interest rate fluctuates based on the formula of the loan. Almost all adjustables come with rate *caps.* The *adjustment cap* limits the maximum rate change (up or down) allowed at each adjustment. On most loans that adjust every six months, the adjustment cap is 1 percent.

Loans that adjust more than once per year usually limit the maximum rate change allowed over the entire year as well. On most such loans, 2 percent is the annual rate cap.

Finally, almost all adjustables come with *lifetime caps,* which limit the highest rate allowed over the entire life of the loan. ARMs commonly have lifetime caps 5 to 6 percent higher than the initial start rate. Before taking an adjustable, figure out the maximum possible payment at the lifetime cap to be sure that you can handle it.

Other ARM fees

Just as with fixed-rate mortgages, ARMs can carry all sorts of additional lender-levied charges. See the section "Understanding other lender fees" in the fixed-rate mortgage section earlier in this chapter for details.

How to buy with less money down

When you buy a home, ideally you should make a down payment of at least 20 percent of the purchase price of the property. Why? Because you'll generally be able to qualify for the most favorable terms on a mortgage with such a down payment, and you'll also be able to avoid the added cost of private mortgage insurance (PMI). To protect against their losing money in the event you default on your loan, lenders usually require PMI, which on a typical mortgage costs several hundred dollars per year.

Many people don't have the equivalent of 20 percent or more of the purchase price in savings to buy a home without private mortgage insurance. Here are a number of solutions for coming up with that 20 percent faster or buying with less money down and solving the down-payment blues:

- **Go on a spending diet.** One sure way to come up with a down payment is to raise your savings rate by slashing your spending. Take a tour through Chapter 6 to learn strategies for doing so.

- **Consider lower-priced properties.** Some buyers want their first home to be a palace. Smaller properties and ones that need some work can help to keep down the purchase price and, therefore, the required down payment.

- **Find partners.** You can usually get more home for your money when you buy a building in partnership with one, two, or a few people. Make sure that you write up a legal contract to specify what will happen if a partner wants out.

- **Seek reduced-down-payment financing.** Some property owners or developers may be willing to finance your purchase with as little as 5 to 10 percent down. You can't be as picky about properties because not as many are available under these terms — many need work or haven't yet sold for other reasons.

- **Get assistance from family.** If your parents, grandparents, or other relatives have money dozing away in a savings or CD account, they may be willing to lend (or even give) you the down payment. You can pay them a higher rate of interest than they have been earning (but still lower than what you would pay to borrow from a bank) and thus be able to buy a home — a win/win situation.

- **Obtain private mortgage insurance (PMI).** Some lenders may offer you a mortgage even though you may be able to put down only 5 to 10 percent of the purchase price. Once the property rises enough in value or you pay down the mortgage enough to have 20 percent equity in the property, you can drop the PMI.

15-year versus 30-year mortgages

Many people don't have a choice between 15- and 30-year mortgages. To afford the monthly payments on their desired home, they need to spread the loan payments over a longer period of time, and a 30-year mortgage is the only answer. A 15-year mortgage has higher monthly payments because you pay it off faster. With fixed-rate mortgages hovering around 8 percent, a 15-year mortgage comes with payments that are about 30 percent higher than those for a 30-year mortgage.

If you can afford these higher payments, taking the 15-year option is not necessarily better. The money for making extra payments doesn't come out of thin air. You might have better uses, which I discuss later in this section, for your excess funds.

And, if you opt for a 30-year mortgage, you maintain the flexibility to pay it off faster (except in those rare cases where there is a prepayment penalty). By making additional payments, you can create your own 15-year mortgage. But you can fall back to making only the payments required on your 30-year schedule when the need arises.

There's risk in locking yourself into higher monthly payments with a 15-year mortgage. If money gets too tight in the future, you can fall behind in your mortgage payments. You might be able to refinance your way out of the predicament, but you can't count on it. If your finances worsen or your property declines in value, you may have trouble qualifying for a refinance.

Should you consider faster mortgage payoff?

Suppose that you can qualify for a 15-year mortgage and you're financially comfortable with the higher payments. The appeal of paying off your mortgage 15 years sooner is enticing. Besides, the interest rate is lower — generally up to ½ percent lower — on a 15-year mortgage. So if you can afford the higher payments on the 15-year mortgage, you'd be silly not to take it, right? Not so fast. You're really asking whether you should pay off your mortgage slowly or more quickly. And the answer isn't simple — it depends.

You need to think through this decision despite the fact that entire books have been written extolling the virtues of owning your home without mortgage debt as soon as possible. Those books come complete with endless rows and columns of numbers so that you can look up how much you save through a faster payback.

If you have the time and inclination (and a good financial calculator), you can calculate how much interest you can save or avoid through a faster payback. I have a friendly word of advice about spending hours crunching numbers: *don't*. You can make this decision by considering some qualitative issues.

Consider alternative uses for savings

First, think about *alternative uses* for the extra money you'd be throwing into the mortgage paydown. What's best for you depends on your overall financial situation and what else you can do with the money. If you would end up blowing the extra money at the racetrack or on an expensive car, pay down the mortgage. That's a no-brainer.

But suppose that you take the extra $100 or $200 per month that you were planning to add to your mortgage payment and contribute it to a retirement account instead. That step may make financial sense. Why? Because contributions to 401(k)s, SEP-IRAs, Keoghs, and other types of retirement accounts (discussed in Chapter 11) are tax-deductible.

When you add an extra $200 to your mortgage payment to pay off your mortgage faster, you get no tax benefits. Zero, *nada,* zippo! When you dump that $200 into a retirement account, you get to subtract that $200 from the income on which you pay taxes. If you're paying 35 percent in federal and state income taxes, you shave $70 (that's $200 multiplied by 35 percent) off your tax bill.

In most cases, you get to deduct your mortgage interest on your tax return. So if you're paying 8 percent interest, your mortgage may really only cost you around 5 percent after you factor in the tax benefits. If you think you can do better by investing elsewhere (stocks, investment real estate), go for it. Investments such as stocks and real estate have generated better returns over the long haul. These investments carry risk, though, and are not guaranteed to produce any return.

If you're uncomfortable investing and would otherwise leave the extra money sitting in a money market fund or savings account, you're better off paying down the mortgage. Paying down the mortgage is investing your money in a sure thing with a modest return.

If you have pre-college-age kids, you have an even greater reason to fund your retirement accounts before you consider paying down your mortgage quickly. Under current rules for determining financial aid for college expenses, money in your retirement accounts is not counted as an asset. Equity in your home (the difference between its market value and your loan balance), by contrast, is still counted by many schools as an asset.

When you pay down your mortgage balance faster, you build more equity in your home. On paper, you appear wealthier to financial aid officers than when you save the money in a retirement account. Your reward for paying down your mortgage balance may be less financial aid! (See Chapter 13 for more details about financing educational expenses.)

Paying down your mortgage faster, especially when you have children, is rarely a good financial decision when you haven't exhausted contributions to retirement accounts. Save first in retirement accounts and get the tax benefits.

Finding the best lender

As with other financial purchases, you can save a lot of money by shopping around. It doesn't matter whether you do so on your own or hire someone to help you. Just do it!

On a 30-year, $120,000 mortgage, for example, getting a mortgage that costs 0.5 percent less per year saves you about $14,000 in interest over the life of the loan (given current interest rate levels). That's enough to buy a decent car! On second thought, save it!

Doing it yourself

You can find many mortgage lenders in most areas. Although having a large number to choose from is good for competition, it also makes shopping a chore.

Large banks whose names you recognize from their advertising usually don't offer the best rates. Make sure that you check out some of the smaller lending institutions in your area as well. Also, check out mortgage bankers, which, unlike banks, only do mortgages. The better ones offer some of the most competitive rates.

Real estate agents can also refer you to lenders with whom they've done business. Those lenders don't necessarily offer the most competitive rates — the agent simply might have done business with them in the past.

Look also in the real estate section of one of the larger Sunday newspapers in your area for charts of selected lender interest rates. These tables are by no means comprehensive or reflective of the best rates available. In fact, many of them are sent to newspapers for free by firms that distribute mortgage information to mortgage brokers. Use them as a starting point by calling the lenders who list the best rates.

HSH Associates (800-873-2837; www.hsh.com) publishes mortgage information for most metropolitan areas. For $20, the company will send you a list of dozens of lenders' rate quotes. You need to be a real data junkie to wade through these multipage reports full of numbers and abbreviations, though.

Hiring a mortgage broker

Insurance agents peddle insurance, real estate agents sell real estate, and mortgage brokers deal in mortgages. They buy mortgages at wholesale from lenders and then mark them up to retail to you. The difference, or *spread,* is their income. The terms of the loan obtained through a broker are generally the same as you would obtain from the lender directly.

A mortgage broker gets paid a percentage of the loan amount — typically 0.5 to 1 percent. This commission is negotiable, especially on larger loans that are more lucrative. Ask a mortgage broker what his cut is. Many people don't, so some brokers may act taken aback when you inquire. Remember, it's your money!

The chief advantage of using a mortgage broker is that the broker can shop among various lenders to get you a good deal. If you're too busy or disinterested to shop around for a good deal on a mortgage, a competent mortgage broker can probably save you money. A broker can also help you through the tedious process of filling out all those horrible documents lenders demand before giving you a loan. And if you have credit problems or an unusual property, a broker may be able to match you with a hard-to-find lender willing to offer you a mortgage.

In evaluating a mortgage broker, be on guard for those who are lazy and don't continually shop the market looking for the best mortgage lenders. Some brokers place their business with the same lenders all the time, and those lenders don't necessarily offer the best rates. Also watch out for those who are salespeople who earn big commissions pushing certain loan programs that are not in your best interests. They aren't interested in taking the time to understand your needs and discuss your options. Check a broker's references.

Even if you plan to shop on your own, talking to a mortgage broker may be worthwhile. At the very least, you can compare what you find with what brokers say they can get for you. Just be careful. Some brokers tell you what you want to hear and then aren't able to deliver when the time comes.

When a loan broker quotes you a really good deal, make sure to ask who the lender is. (Most brokers refuse to reveal this information until you pay the few hundred dollars to cover the appraisal and credit report.) You can check with the actual lender to verify the interest rate and points the broker quotes you and make sure that you're eligible for the loan.

Increasing your approval chances

A lender can take several weeks to complete your property appraisal and evaluation of your loan package. When you're under contract to buy a property, having your loan denied after waiting several weeks could mean that you lose the property as well as the money you spent applying for the loan and having the property inspected. Some property sellers may be willing to give you an extension, but others won't.

Here's how to increase your chances of having your mortgage approved:

> ✔ **Get your finances in shape before you shop.** You're not going to have a good handle on what you can afford to spend on a home until you whip

your personal finances in shape. Do so before you begin to make offers on properties. This chapter and book can help you. If you have consumer debt, get rid of it — the more credit card, auto loan, and other consumer debt you rack up, the less mortgage you qualify for. In addition to the high interest rate on consumer debt and the fact that it encourages you to live beyond your means, you now have a third reason to get rid of it. Hang onto the dream of a home and plug away at paying off consumer debts.

✔ **Clear up credit report problems.** Late payments, missed payments, or debts that you never bothered to pay can come back to haunt you. If you think there are problems on your credit report, get a copy before you apply for your mortgage. The major credit bureaus are Equifax (800-685-1111), Experian (888-397-3742), and Trans Union (800-632-1765). They generally charge less than $10 for a copy of your report (you may obtain a free copy if you ask within 60 days of being denied credit, employment, or insurance based upon information in your credit report).

Mistakes crop up on credit reports. The only way to fix them, unfortunately, is to get on the phone with the credit bureaus and start squawking. When specific creditors have reported erroneous information, call them, too. If the customer service representatives you talk with are no help, dash off a nice letter to the president of each company. For bona fide problems documented on your credit report, try explaining them to your lender. Should the lender be unsympathetic, try calling other lenders. Tell them your credit problems up front and see whether you can find one willing to give you a loan. Mortgage brokers (discussed earlier) can also help you shop for lenders in these cases.

✔ **Get preapproved or prequalified.** *Prequalified* means that you've spoken with a lender about your financial situation and they've calculated the maximum they will lend you based upon what you've told them. *Preapproval* is more in-depth and includes a lender's actual review of your financial statements. Although neither is binding upon a lender to actually make you a mortgage loan, preapproval means more, especially in qualifying you financially in the eyes of a seller. Just be sure not to waste your time and money getting preapproved if you're not really ready to get serious about buying.

✔ **Be up-front about problems.** The best defense against loan rejection is to avoid it in the first place. You can sometimes head off potential rejection by disclosing to your lender anything that may cause a problem before you apply for the loan. That way, you have more time to correct problems and find alternate solutions.

✔ **Work around low/unstable income.** When you're self-employed or have been changing jobs, your recent economic history may be as unstable as a communist country trying out capitalism. One way around this problem is to make a larger down payment. If you put down 30 percent or more, you may be able to get a no-income verification loan. You may try getting a cosigner such as a parent, another relative, or even a rich friend. As long as they aren't borrowed up to their eyeballs, they can help you qualify for a larger loan than you can get on your own. Be sure that all parties understand the terms of the agreement, including who is responsible for monthly payments!

✔ **Consider a backup loan.** You certainly should shop among different lenders, and you may even want to apply to more than one for a mortgage. Although applying for a second loan means additional fees and work, it can increase your chances of getting a mortgage if you're attempting to buy a difficult-to-finance property or your financial situation makes some lenders leery. Also be sure to disclose what you're doing to each lender — the second lender to pull your credit report will see that another lender has been there already.

Finding the Right Property and Location

Shopping for a home can be fun. You get to peek inside other people's refrigerators and drawers. But for most people, finding the right house at the right price can take a lot of time. It can also entail a lot of compromise when you're buying with partners or a spouse (or children, if you choose to share the decision-making with them).

A good agent (or several in different areas) can help with the legwork. Here are the main things to consider:

Condo, townhouse, co-op, or detached home?

Some people's image of a home is a single-family dwelling — a stand-alone house with a lawn and white picket fence. In some areas, however, particularly in higher-cost neighborhoods, non-single-family housing is more common. *Condominiums* (you own the unit and a share of everything else), *townhomes* (attached or row houses), and *cooperatives* (you own a share of the entire building) are higher-density housing units.

The allure of non-single-family housing is that it is generally less expensive. In some cases, as an owner, you don't have to worry about some of the general maintenance because the owner's association (which you pay for, directly or indirectly) takes care of it.

If you don't have the time, energy, or desire to keep up a property, shared housing can make sense. Shared housing may also provide you with better security than a stand-alone home, and you generally get more living space for your dollar.

As investments, however, single-family homes generally do better in the long run. Shared housing is easier to build and hence easier to overbuild; on the other hand, single-family houses are harder to put up because more land is required. But most people, when they can afford it, still prefer a stand-alone home.

That said, you should remember that a rising tide raises all boats. In a good real estate market, all types of housing appreciate, although single-family homes tend to do better. Shared housing values tend to increase best in densely populated urban areas with little available land for new building.

If you can afford a smaller single-family home instead of a larger shared-housing unit, buy the single-family home. Be especially wary of buying shared housing in suburban areas with lots of developable land.

Cast a broad net

Before you start your search, you may have an idea about the type of property and location that you are interested in or think you can afford. You may think, for example, that you can afford only a condominium in the neighborhood you want. But if you take the time to check out other communities, you may be surprised to find one that meets most of your needs and has affordable single-family homes. You'd never know that, though, if you narrowed your search too quickly.

Even if you've lived in an area for a while and think that you know it well, look at different types of properties in a number of different areas before you start to narrow your search. Be open-minded and be sure to know which of your many criteria for a home you *really* care about. You may have to be flexible on some of your preferences.

Find out actual sale prices

Don't look at just a few homes listed at a particular price and get depressed because they're all dogs or you can't afford what you really want. Before you decide to renew your apartment lease, remember that properties often sell for less than the price at which they are listed.

Find out what the places you look at end up selling for. Doing so gives you a better sense of what you can really afford as well as what places are really worth. Ask the agent or owner who sold the property what the sales price was or contact the town's assessors' office about how to obtain property sales price information.

Research the neighborhood and area

Even (and especially) if you fall in love with a house at first sight, go back to the neighborhood at different times of day and on different days of the week. Travel to and from your prospective new home during commute hours to see how long your commute will really be. Knock on a few doors and meet your potential neighbors. You may discover, for example, that a flock of chickens lives in the backyard next door or that the street and basement flood every other winter.

What are the schools like? Go visit them. Don't rely on statistics about test scores. Talk to parents and teachers — what's really going on at the school? Even if you don't have kids, the quality of the local school has direct bearing on the value of your property. Is crime a problem? Call the local police department. Will future development be allowed? If so, what type? Talk to the planning department. What will your property taxes be? Is the property located in an area susceptible to major risks, such as floods, mud slides, fires, or earthquakes? Consider these issues even if they are not important to you, because they can affect the resale value of your property.

Once you buy a home, you're stuck with it. Make sure that you know what you're getting yourself into *before* you buy.

Working with Real Estate Agents

When you buy (or sell) a home, you'll probably work with a real estate agent. Real estate agents, like many people who call themselves "financial consultants," earn their living on commission. As such, their incentives are different from yours and can be at odds with what's best for you.

Unlike commission-based financial consultants, who are really salespeople with a loftier sounding title, real estate agents do not hide the fact that they get a cut of the deal. Property buyers and sellers usually understand the real estate commission system. I credit the real estate profession for calling its practitioners "agents" and not coming up with some silly title such as "housing consultants."

A top-notch real estate agent can be of significant help in your purchase or sale of property. On the other hand, a mediocre, incompetent, or greedy agent can be a real liability. Real estate agents don't have as bad a reputation as used car salespeople, but it's not great, either. The following quotations capture some fundamental problems among real estate agents:

> ". . . Commissions are overpriced, quality of service bears no relation to commission levels, agents face serious conflicts of interest, most buyers are inadequately represented by agents, and agents dominate most state regulatory bodies. The residential real estate industry functions as a cartel that overcharges home buyers and sellers over $10 billion a year."
>
> — Consumer Federation of America
> (a nonprofit consumer advocacy group)

> "For the most part agents look out for themselves. The problem . . . is the commission. The only way you're going to get someone to really look out for your interests is to pay him an hourly fee. If he gets a commission, his overwhelming motivation is to see that the deal closes with a minimum of effort on his part."
>
> — John T. Reed, *Residential Property Acquisition Handbook*

Real estate agents' top conflicts of interest

Real estate agents, because they work on commission, face numerous conflicts of interest. Some agents may not even recognize the conflicts in what they're doing. This section discusses what to watch out for in recognizing agents' most common conflicts of interest.

Buy now, sell now

"You must buy now! Prices and interest rates are low, but they could rise any day."

"The market could worsen before it gets better — you'd better sell now."

Because agents work on commission, it costs them when they spend time with you and you don't buy or sell. They want you to complete a deal, and they want that deal as soon as possible — otherwise, they don't get paid.

Don't expect an agent to give you objective advice about what you should do given your overall financial situation. Examine your overall financial situation *before* you decide to begin working with an agent.

Spend more (and take an adjustable mortgage)

Because real estate agents get a percentage of the sales price of a property, they have a built-in incentive to encourage you to spend more. Adjustable-rate mortgages (discussed earlier in this chapter) allow you to spend more because the interest rate starts at a lower level than that of a fixed-rate mortgage. Thus real estate agents are far more likely to encourage you to take an adjustable. But adjustables are a lot riskier — you must understand these drawbacks before signing up for one.

Buy my company's listings

Agents often receive a higher commission selling listings belonging to other agents in their office. Beware.

Especially problematic are cases in which the same agent represents both the property seller and the property buyer in the transaction. Agents holding open houses for sale may try to sell to an unrepresented buyer whom they meet at the open house. There's no way one person can represent the best interests of both sides.

I don't waste my time working with small fries like you

Because agents work on commission and get paid a percentage of the sales price of the property, many are not interested in working with you if you can't or simply don't want to spend a lot. Some agents may reluctantly take you on as a customer but then give you little attention and time. Before you hire an agent, check references to make sure that he has worked well with buyers like you.

Buy in my area

Real estate agents typically work a specific territory. As a result, they usually can't objectively tell you the pros and cons of the surrounding region. Most won't admit that you may better meet your needs by looking in another town (or some other part of town) where they don't normally work. Before you settle on an agent (or an area), spend time on your own learning the pros and cons of different territories. If you do want to look seriously in more than one area, find an agent in each who specializes in that area.

Get your loan from my favorite lender

If you don't get approved for a mortgage loan, your entire real estate deal will unravel. So it's a good thing that real estate agents want you to get approval for a loan. But it may cause them to refer you to a more expensive lender who has the virtue of high approval rates. Be sure to shop around — you can probably get a loan and get it more cheaply.

Also, beware of agents who may refer you to mortgage lenders and mortgage brokers who pay agents referral fees. Such payments clearly bias a real estate agent's "advice."

Buyer's brokers

Increasing numbers of agents are marketing themselves as *buyer's brokers.* Supposedly, they represent your interests as a property buyer exclusively.

Legally speaking, buyer's brokers may sign a contract saying that they represent your — and only your — interests. Before this enlightened era, all agents contractually worked for the property seller.

The title, buyer's broker, is one of those things that sounds better than it really is. Agents representing you as buyer's brokers still get paid only when you buy. And they still get paid on commission as a percentage of the purchase price. So they still have an incentive to sell you a piece of real estate, and the more expensive it is, the more commission they make.

Use this inspector — he's easy

Home inspectors are supposed to be objective third parties who are hired by prospective buyers to evaluate the condition of a property. The inspector's job is to uncover problems that your novice eye can't see. I've heard of tougher (nitpicky) inspectors referred to as "deal killers" by disgruntled real estate agents. Some inspectors get more referrals from agents because they aren't tough. But you'll be the one who's sorry if your newly acquired home has undiscovered problems due to an inadequate inspection.

I'm helping the seller cover up problems

Some agents, under pressure to get a house listing for sale, agree to be accomplices and not disclose known defects or problems with the property. In most cases, it seems, the seller may not explicitly ask an agent to help cover up a problem, but the agent may look the other way or not tell the whole truth. Never buy a home without having a home inspector look it over from top to bottom.

They scratch my back and I scratch theirs

Some agents refer you to lenders, inspectors, and title insurance companies that have referred business to them. A referral, of course, should first and foremost be based on the competence of the person to whom you're being referred. Too often in referrals, this criterion is minor or, in some cases, nonexistent. Some agents also solicit and receive referral fees (or bribes) from mortgage lenders, inspectors, and contractors to whom they refer business.

Qualities to look for in real estate agents

Whether you're hiring an agent to work with you as a buyer or seller, you want someone who is competent and with whom you can get along. Working with an agent costs you a lot of money — make sure that you get your money's worth.

Interview several agents. Check references. Ask agents for the names and phone numbers of at least three clients with whom they've worked in the past six months in the geographical area in which you are looking. You should look for these traits in any agent you work with:

- ✔ **Full-time employment.** Some agents work in real estate as a second or even third job. Information in this field changes constantly. The best agents work at it full-time to stay on top of the market.

- ✔ **Experience.** Hiring someone with experience doesn't necessarily mean looking for an agent who's been kicking around for decades. Many of the best agents come into the field from other occupations, such as business or teaching. Some sales, marketing, negotiation, and communication skills can certainly be learned in other fields, but experience in this field does count.

- ✔ **Honesty and integrity.** You're trusting your agent with a lot. If the agent doesn't level with you about what a neighborhood or particular property is really like, you suffer the consequences.

- ✔ **Interpersonal skills.** An agent has to be able to get along not only with you but also with a whole host of other people involved in a typical real estate deal: other agents, property sellers, inspectors, mortgage lenders, and so on. An agent doesn't have to be Mr. or Ms. Congeniality, but he or she should be able to put your interests first without upsetting others.

- ✔ **Negotiation skills.** Putting a real estate deal together involves negotiation. Is your agent going to exhaust all avenues to get you the best deal possible? Be sure to ask the agent's references how well the agent negotiated for them.

- ✔ **High quality standards.** Sloppy work can lead to big legal or logistical problems down the road. If an agent neglects to recommend an inspection, for example, you may be stuck with undiscovered problems after the deal is done.

Agents sometimes market themselves as *top producers,* which means that they sell a relatively larger volume of real estate. This title doesn't count for much for you, the buyer. It may be a red flag for an agent that focuses on completing as many deals as possible. When you're buying a home, you need an agent who has the following additional traits:

✓ **Patience.** When you're buying a home, the last thing you need or want is an agent who tries to push you into making a deal. You need an agent who is patient and willing to allow you the necessary time to get educated and make the best decision for yourself.

✓ **Local market and community knowledge.** When you're looking to buy a home in an area in which you're not currently living, an informed agent can have a big impact on your decision.

✓ **Financing knowledge.** As a buyer, especially a first-time buyer or someone with credit problems, you should look for an agent who can refer you to lenders who can handle your type of situation, which can save you a lot of legwork.

Buying and selling real estate require somewhat different skills. Few agents can do both equally well. No law or rule says that you must use the same agent when you sell a property as when you buy. Don't feel obliged to sell through the agent who worked with you as a buyer just because he sends you holiday cards every year asking how the garden is growing. Remember, he works on commission.

Putting Your Deal Together

Once you've done your homework on your personal finances, understood how to choose a mortgage, and researched neighborhoods and home prices, you'll hopefully soon close in on your goal. Eventually you'll find a home you'd like to buy. Before you make that first offer, though, you need to understand the importance of negotiations, inspections, and other elements of a real estate deal.

Negotiating 101

When you work with an agent, the agent usually handles the negotiation process. But you need to have a plan and strategy in mind — otherwise, you might overpay for your home. Here are some recommendations for getting a good deal:

✓ **Never fall in love with a property.** If you have money to burn and you can't imagine life without the home you've just discovered, then pay what you will. Otherwise, always remind yourself that other good properties are out there. Having an actual backup property in mind never hurts.

WARE

Games real estate agents play to get a deal done

The thirst for a commission brings out the worst in some agents. They'll tell you fibs to motivate you to buy on the seller's terms. One common one is to say that other offers are coming in on the property you're interested in. Or they'll say that the seller already turned down an offer for *x* dollars because he is holding out for a higher offer.

Another tactic is the car dealer trick — blaming the office manager for not allowing them to reduce their commission. The bottom line is that if it's not in writing, be skeptical. Be sure to spend the time needed to find a good agent and to understand an agent's potential conflicts of interest (see the section on agents earlier in the chapter).

✔ **Learn about the property and owner before you make your offer.** How long has the property been on the market? What are its flaws? Why is the owner selling? For example, if the seller is moving because she got a job in another town where she's about to close on a home purchase, she may be eager to get her money out and may be willing to reduce the price. The more you understand about the property that you want to buy and the seller's motivations, the better able you will be to draft an offer that meets both parties' needs.

✔ **Get comparable sales data to support your price.** Too often, home buyers and their agents pick a number out of the air when making an offer. But if the offer has no substance behind it, the seller will hardly be persuaded to lower his asking price. Pointing to recent and comparable home sales to justify your offer price strengthens your case.

✔ **Remember that price is only one of several negotiable items.** Sometimes sellers get fixated on selling their homes for a certain amount. Perhaps they want to get at least what they paid for it themselves several years ago. You may be able to get a seller to pay for certain repairs or improvements or to offer you an attractive loan without all the extra loan fees that a bank would charge. Likewise, the real estate agent's commission is negotiable, too.

Inspect, inspect, inspect

When you buy a home, you're probably making one of the biggest (if not *the* biggest) purchases of your life. Unless you've built homes and done contracting work yourself, you probably have no idea what you're getting yourself into when it comes to furnaces and termites.

Spend the money and time to hire inspectors and other experts to evaluate the major systems and potential problem areas of the home. Areas that you want to check include

- Overall condition of the property
- Electrical, heating, and plumbing systems
- Foundation
- Roof
- Pest control and dry rot
- Seismic/slide/flood risk

Inspection fees often pay for themselves. When problems are uncovered that you weren't aware of, the inspection reports give you the information you need to go back and ask the property seller to fix the problems or reduce the purchase price of the property to compensate you for correcting the deficiencies yourself.

As with other professionals whose services you retain, interview a few inspection companies. Ask which systems they inspect and how detailed a report they will prepare for you (ask for a sample copy). Ask them for names and phone numbers of three people who used their service within the past six months.

Never accept a seller's inspection report as your only source of information. When a seller hires an inspector, he may hire someone who won't be as diligent and critical of the property. What if the inspector is buddies with the seller or agent selling the property? By all means, review the seller's inspection reports if available, but get your own as well.

And here's one more inspection for you to do: The day before you close on the purchase of your home, do a brief walk-through of the property to make sure that everything is still in good order and that all the fixtures, appliances, curtains, and other items that were to be left as per the contract are still there. Sometimes, sellers (and their movers) "forget" what's to be left or try to test your powers of observation.

Title insurance and escrow fees

Mortgage lenders require *title insurance* to protect against someone else claiming legal title to your property. This can happen, for example, when a husband and wife split up and the one who remains in the home decides to sell and take off with the money. If both spouses were listed as owners on the title, the spouse who sold the property (possibly by forging the other's signature) had no legal right to do so.

Both you and the lender could get stuck holding the bag if you bought the home that this divided couple was selling. But title insurance will be the salvation for you and your lender. Title insurance protects you against the risk in a case like this that the other spouse (whose name was forged to sell the home) could come back and reclaim rights to the home after it was sold.

If you're in the enviable position of paying cash for a property, you should still buy title insurance even though a mortgage lender won't prod you to do so. You need to protect your investment.

Escrow charges pay for neutral third-party services to ensure that the instructions of the purchase contract or refinance are fulfilled and that everyone gets paid.

Many people don't seem to know that title insurance and escrow fees vary from company to company. As a result, they don't bother to shop around and simply use the company that their real estate agent or mortgage lender suggests.

When you call around for title insurance and escrow fee quotes, make sure that you understand all the fees. Many companies tack on all sorts of charges for things such as courier fees and express mail. If you find a company with lower prices and want to use it, it doesn't hurt to ask for an itemization in writing so that you don't have any surprises.

Real estate agents and mortgage lenders can be a good starting point for referrals because they usually have a broader perspective on cost and service quality of different companies. Call other companies as well — agents and lenders may be biased toward certain companies simply because they are in the habit of using them or have referred clients to them before.

After You Buy

After you buy a home, over the months and years ahead, you'll make a number of important decisions regarding your castle (or shoe box). This section discusses key issues and what you need to know to make the best decision for each.

Refinancing your mortgage

Three reasons motivate people to *refinance* — obtaining a new mortgage to replace your old one. One is obvious — to save money because interest rates have dropped. Refinancing also can be a way of raising capital for some other purpose. A final reason is to get out of one type of loan and into another. The following discussion should help you to decide upon the best option in each case.

Spending money to save money

If your current loan has a higher rate of interest than comparable new loans now available, you may save money by refinancing. Because refinancing usually costs money, whether you can save enough to justify the cost is open to question. You should be able to save money if by refinancing you can obtain a new loan for at least one percent less than your current loan and you're planning to keep the property for at least five years. If you can recover the costs of the refinance within a few years, go for it. If it takes longer, refinancing may still make sense if you anticipate keeping the property and mortgage that long.

Be wary of mortgage lenders or brokers who brag about how soon your refinance will pay for itself; they usually oversimplify their calculations. For example, if the refinance costs you $2,000 to complete (accounting for appraisals, loan fees and points, title insurance, and so on) and reduces your monthly payment by $100, the lender or broker typically says that it takes 20 months for you to recoup the refinance costs. This isn't accurate, however, because you lose some tax write-offs if your mortgage interest rate and payment are reduced. You can't simply look at the reduced amount of your monthly payment (mortgage lenders like to look at it, however, because it makes refinancing more attractive). And your new mortgage will be reset to a different term than the number of years remaining on your old one.

If you want a better estimate of your likely cost savings but don't want to spend hours crunching numbers, take your tax rate — for example, 28 percent — and reduce your monthly payment savings on the refinance by this amount (see Chapter 7). Continuing with the example in the preceding paragraph, if your monthly payment drops by $100, you're *really* only saving around $72 a month after factoring in the lost tax benefits. So it takes 28 months ($2,000 divided by $72) — not 20 — to recoup the refinance costs.

Note that not all refinances cost tons of money. So-called *no-cost* refinances or *no-point* loans minimize your out-of-pocket expenses but, as discussed earlier in this chapter, may not be your best long-term options. Such loans usually come with higher interest rates.

Using money for another purpose

Refinancing to pull out cash from your home for some other purpose can make good financial sense because, under most circumstances, mortgage interest is tax-deductible. A common reason for borrowing against a home is to pay off other higher-interest consumer debt — such as on credit cards or on an auto loan. The interest on consumer debt is not tax-deductible and is generally at a much higher interest rate than what mortgages charge you.

If you're starting a business, consider borrowing against your home to finance the launch of your business. You can usually do so at a lower cost than on a business loan.

The most critical question is whether a lender is willing to lend you more money against the equity in your home (which is the difference between the market value of your house and the loan balance). Use Table 14-1 to estimate the maximum loan for which you may qualify.

Changing loans

You might want to refinance even though you aren't forced to raise cash or can save money. Perhaps you're not comfortable with your current loan — holders of adjustable-rate mortgages often face this problem. You may find out that a fluctuating mortgage payment makes you a nervous wreck in addition to wreaking havoc on your budget. The certainty of a fixed-rate mortgage may be your salvation.

Paying money to go from an adjustable into a fixed is a lot like buying insurance. The cost of the refinance is "insuring" you a level mortgage payment. Consider this option only if you want peace of mind and you plan to stay with the property for a number of years.

Sometimes jumping from one adjustable to another makes sense. Suppose you can lower the maximum lifetime interest rate cap and the refinance won't cost much. Your new loan should have a lower initial interest rate than the one you're paying on your current loan. Even if you won't save megabucks, the peace of mind of a lower ceiling can make refinancing worth your while.

Mortgage life insurance

Shortly after you buy a home or close on a mortgage, you'll start getting mail from all kinds of organizations who keep track of publicly available information about mortgages. Most of these organizations want to sell you something, and they don't tend to beat around the bush.

"What will your dependents do if you meet with an untimely demise and they are left with a gargantuan mortgage?" they ask. Fair enough. In fact, this is a good financial-planning question. If your family is dependent upon your income, can they survive financially if you and your income disappear from life as we know it?

Don't waste your money on mortgage life insurance. You may need life insurance to provide for your family and help meet large obligations such as mortgage payments or educational expenses for children. But mortgage life insurance is grossly overpriced. (Read the life insurance section in Chapter 16 for advice about term life insurance.) You should consider mortgage life insurance only if you have a health problem and the mortgage life insurer does not require a physical examination. Be sure to compare it with term life options.

Is getting a reverse mortgage a good idea?

Increasing numbers of homeowners are finding, particularly in their later years of retirement, that they lack cash. Their largest asset is usually the home in which they live. Unlike other investments, such as bank accounts, bonds, or stocks, a home does not provide any income to the owner unless he or she decides to rent out a room or two.

A *reverse mortgage* allows a homeowner who's low on cash to tap into home equity. For an elderly homeowner, this can be a difficult thing to do psychologically. Most people work hard to feed a mortgage month after month, year after year, until finally it is all paid off. What a feat and what a relief after all those years!

Taking out a reverse mortgage reverses this process. Each month, you get a check from the reverse mortgage lender that you can spend on food, clothing, travel, or whatever suits your fancy. The money you receive each month is really a loan from the bank against the value of your home, which makes the monthly check free from taxation. Other advantages of a reverse mortgage are that it allows you to stay in your home and use its equity to supplement your monthly income.

The main drawback is that a reverse mortgage can deplete the estate that you may want to pass onto your heirs or use for some other purpose. Also, some loans require repayment within a certain number of years. The fees and the effective interest rate you are charged to borrow the money can be quite high.

Because some loans require the lender to make monthly payments to you as long as you live in the home, lenders assume that you will live long so that they don't lose money in making these loans. If you end up keeping the loan for only a few years because you move, for example, the cost of the loan is extremely high.

You may be able to create a reverse mortgage within your own family network. This technique can work if you have family members who are financially able to provide you with monthly income in exchange for ownership of the home when you pass away.

There are also other alternatives to tapping home equity. One is to simply sell your home and buy a less expensive property or rent a place. Under current tax laws, qualifying house sellers can exclude a sizable portion of their profits from capital gains tax: up to $250,000 for single taxpayers and $500,000 for married couples.

Selling your house

The day will someday come when you will want to sell your house. If you're going to sell, make sure that you can afford to buy the next home you desire. Be especially careful if you're a trade-up buyer — that is, you're going to buy an even more expensive home. All of the affordability issues discussed at the beginning of this chapter apply. Also consider the following issues.

Selling through an agent

Selling and buying a home demand agents with different strengths. When you're selling a property, you want an agent who can get the job done efficiently and for as high a price as possible. As a seller, you should seek agents who have marketing and sales expertise and are willing to put in the time and money necessary to sell your house. Don't necessarily be impressed by an agent who works for a large company. What matters more is what the agent is going to do to market your property.

When you list your house for sale, the contract that you sign with the listing agent includes specification of the commission to be paid if the agent is successful in selling your house. In most areas of the country, agents usually ask for a 6 percent commission. In an area that has lower-cost housing, they may ask for 7 percent.

Regardless of the commission an agent says is "typical," "standard," or "what my manager requires," *always* remember that commissions are negotiable. Because the commission is a percentage, you have a much greater ability to get a lower commission on a higher-priced house. If an agent makes 6 percent selling both a $200,000 house and a $100,000 house, the agent makes twice as much on the $200,000 house. Yet selling the higher-priced house does not take twice as much work. (Selling a $400,000 house certainly doesn't take four times the effort of selling a $100,000 house.)

If you live in an area with higher-priced homes (above $250,000), you have no reason to pay more than a 5 percent commission. For expensive properties ($500,000 and up), a 4 percent commission is reasonable. You may find, however, that your ability to negotiate a lower commission is greatest when an offer is on the table. Because you don't want to give other agents (working with buyers) a reason not to sell your house, have your listing agent cut his take rather than reducing the commission that you advertise that you're willing to pay to an agent who brings you a buyer.

In terms of the length of the listing sales agreement you make with an agent, three months is reasonable. When you give an agent too long a listing (6 to 12 months), the agent may simply toss your listing into the multiple listing book and expend little effort to get your property sold. Practically speaking, you can fire your agent whenever you want, regardless of the length of the listing agreement. But a shorter listing may be more motivating for your agent.

Selling without a real estate agent

The temptation to sell without an agent is usually to save the commission that an agent deducts from your house's sale price. If you have the time, energy, and marketing experience, you can sell your house and possibly save some money.

The major problem with attempting to sell your house on your own is that you can't generally list it in the *multiple listing service* (MLS), which only real estate agents can access. Some people have said, and I concur, that the MLS functions as an effective near monopoly over the selling of houses. And if you're not listed in the MLS, many potential buyers will never know that your house is for sale. Agents working with buyers don't generally look for or show their clients properties that are for sale by owner.

Besides saving you time, a good agent can help ensure that you're not sued for failing to disclose known defects of your property. If you decide to sell your house yourself, make sure that you have access to a legal advisor who can review the contracts. Whether you sell through an agent or not, be sure to read *House Selling For Dummies,* which I co-wrote with real estate expert Ray Brown.

Should you keep your home until prices go up?

Many homeowners are tempted to hold onto their properties when they need to move if the property is worth less than when they bought it or if the real estate market is soft. It's probably not worth the hassle of renting out your property or the financial gamble of holding onto it. If you need to move, you're better off in most cases selling your house.

You may reason that in a few years, the real estate storm clouds will clear and you can sell your property at a much higher price. Here are three risks associated with this way of thinking:

- ✔ You can't know what's going to happen to property prices in the next few years. They might rebound, but they could stay the same or drop even further. A property generally needs to appreciate at least a few percent per year just to make up for all the costs of holding and maintaining it.

- ✔ If you haven't been a landlord, don't underestimate the hassle and headaches associated with this job.

- ✔ Once you convert your home into a rental property, you need to pay capital gains tax on your profit when you sell it if it does appreciate. This tax wipes out much of the advantage of having held onto the property until prices recovered. (If you want to be a long-term rental property owner, you can do a *tax-free exchange* into another rental property once you sell.)

A good reason to hold onto a home that has plunged in value is that you would realize little cash from selling *and* lack other money to come up with the down payment to purchase your next property.

Should you keep your home as investment property if you move?

It's worth considering converting your home into rental property if you need to or want to move. Don't consider doing so unless it really is a long-term proposition (ten or more years). As discussed in the preceding section, selling rental property has tax consequences.

One advantage to keeping your current home as an investment property after you move is that you already own it. Locating and buying investment property takes time and money. You also know what you have with your current home. If you go out and purchase a property to rent, you're starting from scratch.

If your property is in good condition, consider what damage renters might do — few renters will take care of your home the way that you will. Also consider whether you're cut out to be a landlord. For more information, read the section in Chapter 9 that discusses real estate as an investment.

Part IV
Protecting What You've Got

"I'm sorry, Mr. Binkman, but if you look closely, your policy with us is for otter insurance, not auto insurance. By the way, your otter wasn't hurt in the accident, was he?"

In this part . . .

1 show you how to obtain the right kind of insurance to shield you from the brunt of unexpected major expenses and protect your assets and future earnings. Just because insurance is boring doesn't mean you can ignore it! I reveal which types of insurance you do and do not need, what to include and what not to include in your policies, and how much of which things you should insure. Plus, you finally face other creepy but important stuff such as wills, probate, and estate planning.

Chapter 15

Insurance Basics

● ●

In This Chapter

▶ How the insurance industry works

▶ My three laws of buying insurance

▶ How to get the insurance coverage you need at the best price

▶ What to do if you are denied coverage

▶ How to get your claim money

● ●

*U*nless you work in the industry (by choice), insurance is, for most people, a dreadfully boring topic. Most people associate insurance with disease, death, and disaster and would rather do just about anything other than review or spend money on insurance. But because you don't want to deal with money hassles when you are coping with catastrophes — illness, disability, death, fires, floods, earthquakes — you must take care of insurance well before you need it.

Insurance is probably the least understood and least monitored area of personal finance. Studies by the nonprofit National Insurance Consumer Organization show that more than nine in ten Americans purchase and carry the wrong types and amounts of insurance coverage. My own experience as a financial counselor confirms this statistic. Most people are overwhelmed by all the jargon in sales and policy statements. As a result, people get insurance from the wrong companies, pay more than is necessary for their policies, or get insured through companies with poor reputations for servicing customers with claims on their policies.

Insurance: A Big, Inefficient Business

Consider these tantalizing tidbits about the insurance industry: More than 35,000 insurance companies employ more than 1.5 million people, half of whom are the agents and brokers who sell the stuff. Nearly 1 in every 12 dollars spent in our economy goes to pay for insurance.

In *The Invisible Bankers,* an insightful book on the insurance industry, author Andrew Tobias makes the observation that the insurance industry, like the IRS and postal service, interacts with all Americans. However, to accomplish their goals, the insurance companies need 20 times more employees than the IRS and 3 times more employees than the U.S. Postal Service!

Unlike mutual funds, which are often available directly from the companies that issue them, virtually all insurance is sold through insurance agents who work on commission. Because of the commission structure, shopping around for the best deal and figuring out — and buying — policies and features that are in your best interests are difficult tasks.

One of the primary reasons that the insurance industry is so inefficient is that it enjoys a unique (and unfair) exemption from federal antitrust regulations. The McCarran-Ferguson Act of 1945, a little-known piece of legislation, allows insurance companies to dictate a fixed price for a specific policy and effectively eliminate competition among their commission-based agents. That makes shopping for a specific insurance policy different from shopping for a Sony 19-inch color television set or a Ford Taurus. Although some auto dealers or stereo stores will cut you a better deal than others, an insurance policy "model" will have the same price from every agent who sells it. (Please note that although price competition does not exist among different agents of a specific policy, it does exist among different insurance companies.)

Equally problematic is the fact that insurers exert tremendous control and influence, through lobbying and representation on state insurance regulatory boards, over the entities that are supposed to oversee them — the state governments.

Why all these details about the insurance industry? Because understanding the industry will help you comprehend the weird stuff on policies, the high costs of many policies, and the inefficiency of most insurers. And, hopefully, you will also become informed enough to make your voice heard when you speak to insurers and government regulators about ways to improve insurance for consumers.

Eric's Three Laws of Buying Insurance

I know your patience and interest in learning about insurance may be limited, so I've boiled it down to three fairly simple but powerful concepts that can easily save you thousands of dollars over the rest of your insurance-buying years. And while you're saving money, you can still get the coverage you need to avoid a financial catastrophe.

Law 1: Insure for the big, not the small stuff

Imagine, for a moment, that you're offered a chance to buy insurance that reimburses you for the cost of a magazine subscription in the event the magazine folds and you don't get all the issues you paid for. Because a magazine subscription doesn't cost much, I don't think you would buy that insurance.

What if you could buy insurance that pays for the cost of a restaurant meal if you get food poisoning? Even if you're splurging at a fancy restaurant, you don't have a lot of money at stake, so you'd probably decline that coverage as well.

The point of insurance is to protect against losses that would be financially catastrophic to you, not to smooth out the bumps of everyday life. The examples above are silly, but some people buy equally silly policies without knowing it, as I illustrate in this section.

Avoid small-potato policies

A good insurance policy can seem expensive. A policy that doesn't cost much, on the other hand, can fool you into thinking that you're getting something for next to nothing. Policies that cost little also cover little — they are priced low because they aren't covering large potential losses.

The following are examples of common, "small potato" insurance policies that are generally a waste of your hard-earned dollars. As you read through this list, you may find examples of policies that you yourself have bought and that you feel paid for themselves. I can hear you saying, "But I collected on that policy you're telling me not to buy!" Sure, getting the satisfaction (the revenge?) of being "reimbursed" for the hassle of something being lost or going wrong is always nice. But consider all such policies that you have bought or could buy over the course of your life. You're not going to come out ahead in the aggregate — if you did, insurance companies would lose money! These policies aren't worth the cost relative to the small potential benefit. On average, insurance companies pay out just 60 cents in benefits on every dollar collected. Many of the following policies pay you back even less — around 20 cents in benefits (claims) for every insurance premium dollar spent.

Extended warranty and repair plans

Isn't it ironic that right after the salesperson persuades you to buy a television, computer, or car — in part by saying how reliable the goods are — he tries try to convince you to spend more money to insure against the failure of the item? If the stuff is so good, why do you need insurance?

Product manufacturers' warranties typically cover any problems that occur in the first three months to a year. After that, should you need to pay for a repair out of your own pocket, it won't be a financial catastrophe. Extended warranty and repair plans are expensive and unnecessary insurance policies.

Home warranty plans

If your real estate agent or the seller of the home wants to pay the cost of a home warranty plan for you, turning down the offer would be ungracious (as grandma would say, you shouldn't look a gift horse in the mouth). But don't buy this type of plan for yourself. In addition to requiring some sort of fee (around $30 to $50) if you need a contractor to come out and look at a problem, home warranty plans limit how much they'll pay for problems.

Your money is much better spent on hiring a competent inspector to uncover problems and fix them *before* you buy the home. Everyone buying a house should expect to spend money on repairs and maintenance. Buying insurance for the smaller repairs and maintenance is a waste of money.

Dental insurance

If your employer pays for dental insurance, take advantage of it. But you shouldn't pay for this coverage on your own. Dental insurance generally covers a couple of teeth cleanings each year and limits payment for more expensive work.

Credit life and credit disability policies

Many direct-mail firms try to sell policies that pay a small benefit in case you die with an outstanding loan (a credit life policy) or that pays a small monthly income in the event of a disability (a credit disability policy). Credit card companies usually sell these policies. Some companies sell insurance to pay off your credit card bill in the event of your death or disability.

The cost of such insurance seems low, but that's because the potential benefits are small. In fact, given what little insurance you're buying, these policies are extraordinarily expensive. When you need life or disability insurance, purchase it. But get enough coverage and buy it in a separate, cost-effective policy (see Chapter 16 for more details).

One exception to the above rule is if you are in poor health and you can buy these insurance policies without a medical evaluation. In that case, these policies may be the only ones you have access to. This is another reason that these policies are expensive. If you're in good health, you are paying for the people with poor health who can enroll without a medical examination and who undoubtedly make more claims.

Daily hospitalization insurance

Hospitalization insurance policies that pay a certain amount per day, such as $100, are often sold to older people. These policies prey on people's fears of running up big hospital bills. Health care is expensive — there's no doubt about that.

But what you really need is a comprehensive (major medical) health insurance policy. One day in the hospital can lead to several thousand dollars in charges, so that $100 per day policy might pay for less than an hour of your 24-hour day! These policies don't offer coverage for the big-ticket expenses. If you don't have a comprehensive health insurance policy, get one (see Chapter 16)!

Insuring packages in the mail

You buy a $40 gift for a friend, and when you go to the post office to ship it, the friendly postal clerk asks if you want to insure it. For a couple of bucks, you think, why not? The U.S. Postal Service may have a bad reputation for many reasons, but it rarely loses or damages things. Go spend your money on another gift instead!

Contact lens insurance

The things that people in this country come up with to waste money on just astound me. Contact lens insurance really does exist! The money goes to replace your contacts if you lose or tear them. Lenses are cheap. Don't waste your money on this kind of insurance.

Little stuff riders

Many policies that are worth buying, such as auto and disability insurance, have all sorts of add-on riders. These are extra bells and whistles that insurance agents and companies like to sell because of the high profit margin (for *them*). On auto insurance policies, for example, you can buy a rider for a few bucks per year that pays you $25 each time your car needs to be towed. Having your vehicle towed isn't going to bankrupt you, so it isn't worth insuring against.

Likewise, small insurance policies that are sold as add-ons to bigger insurance policies are usually unnecessary and overpriced. For example, you can buy some disability insurance policies with a small amount of life insurance added on. If you need life insurance, purchasing a sufficient amount in a separate policy is less costly.

Take the highest deductible you can afford

Most insurance policies have *deductibles* — the maximum amount you must pay in the event of a loss before your insurance coverage kicks in. On many policies, such as auto and homeowner's/renter's coverage, most folks opt for a $100 to $250 deductible.

Here are two benefits to taking a higher deductible:

- ✔ **You save premium dollars.** Year in and year out, you can enjoy the lower cost of an insurance policy with a high deductible. You may be able to shave 15 to 20 percent off the cost of your policy. Suppose, for example, that you can reduce the cost of your policy by $150 per year by raising your deductible from $250 to $1,000. That $750 worth of coverage is costing you $150 per year. Thus, you would need to have a claim of $1,000 or more every five years — highly unlikely — to come out ahead. If you are that accident-prone — guess what? — the insurance company will crank up your premiums.

- ✔ **You don't have the hassles of filing small claims.** If you have a $300 loss on a policy with a $100 deductible, you need to file a claim to get your $200 (the amount you're covered for after your deductible). Filing an insurance claim can take hours of time and can be an aggravating experience. In some cases, you may even have your claim denied after jumping through all the necessary hoops.

When you have low deductibles, you may file more claims (although this doesn't necessarily mean that you'll get more money). After filing more claims, you may be rewarded with higher premiums — in addition to the headache of preparing those blasted forms! Filing too many claims may even cause cancellation of your coverage!

Buy insurance to cover financial catastrophes

You should insure against what could be a huge financial loss for you or your dependents. The price of insurance isn't cheap, but it is relatively small in comparison to the potential total loss.

The beauty of insurance is that it spreads risks over millions of other people. Should your home burn to the ground, paying the rebuilding cost out of your own pocket probably would be a financial catastrophe. If you have insurance, the premiums paid in by you and all the other homeowners collectively can easily pay the bills.

Think for a moment about what your most valuable assets are. (No, they're not your dry wit and your charming personality.) Also consider potential large expenses.

- ✔ During your working years, your most valuable asset is probably your future earnings. If you were disabled and unable to work, what would you live on? That's why long-term disability insurance exists. If you have a family that is financially dependent on your earnings, how would your family manage financially if you died? Life insurance can fill the financial void left by your death.

✔ If you're a business owner, what would happen if you were sued for $1,000,000 for negligence in some work that you messed up? Liability insurance can bail you out.

✔ In this age of soaring medical costs, you can easily rack up a $100,000 hospital bill in short order. That's why you need major medical health insurance coverage. And, yet, a surprising number of people don't carry any health insurance, particularly those who work in small businesses. (See Chapter 16 for more on health insurance.)

Psychologically, buying insurance coverage for the little things that are more likely to occur is tempting. You don't want to feel like you're wasting your insurance dollars. You want to get some of your money back, darn it! You are more likely to get into a fender bender with your car or have a package lost in the mail than you are to lose your home to fire or suffer a long-term disability. But if the fender bender costs $500 (which you end up paying out of your pocket because you took my advice to take a high deductible), it isn't going to be a financial disaster.

On the other hand, should you lose your ability to earn an income because of a disability or are sued for $1,000,000 but are not insured against such catastrophes, you will not only be extremely unhappy but you will also face financial ruin. "Yes, but what are the odds," I hear people rationalize, "that I'll suffer a long-term disability or that I'll be sued for $1,000,000?" I agree that the odds are quite low, but the risk is there. The problem is that you just don't know what bad luck will befall you or when.

And don't make the mistake of thinking that you can figure the odds any better than the insurance companies can. The insurance companies predict the probability of your making a claim, large or small, with a great deal of accuracy. That's why they employ armies of number-crunching actuaries to calculate the odds of bad things happening and the frequency of current policyholders making particular types of claims. The companies price their policies accordingly.

So buying or not buying insurance based on your perception of the likelihood of needing the coverage is foolish. Insurance companies aren't stupid; in fact, they are ruthlessly smart! When insurance companies price policies, they look at a number of factors to determine the likelihood of your filing a claim. Take the example of auto insurance. If you're a single male, age 20, living the fast life in a high-crime city, driving a macho, turbo-sports car, and having two speeding tickets in the past year, you're gonna pay a whole lot more than a couple in their 40s, living in a low-crime area, driving a four-door sedan, and having a clean driving record.

Our misperceptions of risks

How high do you think are your risks of expiring prematurely if you're exposed to toxic wastes or pesticides or if you live in a dangerous area that has a high murder rate? Well, actually these risks are quite small when compared to the risks you're subjecting yourself to when you get behind the wheel of a car or light up yet another cigarette.

ABC reporter John Stossel was kind enough to share with me the results of a study done for him by physicist Bernard Cohen who compared different risks. Cohen's study showed that our riskiest behaviors are smoking and driving. Smoking whacks an average of seven years off a person's life, whereas driving a car results in a bit more than half a year of life lost on average. Toxic waste shaves an average of one week off an American's life span.

Knowing what's risky and what isn't is part of what you need to know. Unfortunately, you can't buy a formal insurance policy to protect yourself against all of life's great dangers and risks. But that does not mean that you must face these dangers as a helpless victim. Simple changes in behavior can help you fight the odds.

Personal health habits are a good example. If you're overweight, eat fatty, high-cholesterol foods, drink excessively, and don't exercise, you're asking for trouble, especially during post-middle age. Engage in these habits, and you're dramatically increasing your risk of heart disease and cancer.

So does this mean that we should all eat bean sprouts, stay out of cars, never light up, and cease being concerned about toxic waste? No. But you should understand the consequences of your behaviors before you engage in them and minimize big risks accordingly.

If you're reading this chapter, you obviously want to find out about insurance. My point is this: You can buy all the types of traditional insurance that I recommend in this book and still not be well-protected for the simple reason that you're overlooking uninsurable risks. But just because you can't buy formal insurance to protect against some risks doesn't mean that you can't drastically reduce your exposure to such risks by modifying your behavior.

Law 11: Buy broad coverage

Another major mistake people make when buying insurance is purchasing coverage that is too narrow. Such policies often seem like cheap ways to put their greatest fears to rest. For example, instead of buying life insurance, some folks buy flight insurance at an airport self-service kiosk. They seem to worry more about their mortality when getting on an airplane than they do when getting into a car. If they die on the flight, their beneficiaries collect. But should they die the next day in an auto accident or get some dreaded disease — which is statistically far more likely than going down in a jumbo jet — the beneficiaries don't collect anything from flight insurance.

The medical equivalent of flight insurance is cancer insurance. Older people, fearful of having their life savings depleted by a long battle with this dread disease, are easy prey for unscrupulous insurance salespeople pitching this narrow insurance. If you get cancer, cancer insurance pays the bills. But what if you get heart disease, diabetes, AIDS, or some other disease? Cancer insurance won't pay these costs.

Our fears in life are natural and inescapable; they are also often arbitrary and irrational. Although we may not have control over the emotions that our fears invoke, we must often ignore those emotions in order to make rational insurance decisions. In other words, getting shaky in the knees and sweaty in the palms when boarding an airplane is okay, but letting your fear of flying cause you to make poor insurance decisions is not okay, especially when those decisions affect the lives of your loved ones.

You can't possibly predict what's going to happen to you. You want to get the broadest possible coverage that you can. Buy life insurance, not flight insurance. Buy major medical coverage, not cancer insurance.

Law III: Shop around and buy direct

Whether you're looking at auto, home, life, disability, or other types of coverage, some companies may charge double or triple the rates that other companies charge for the same coverage. The companies charging the higher rates may not be better about paying claims, however. You may even end up with the worst of both possible worlds — high prices *and* lousy service.

Most insurance is sold through agents and brokers who earn commissions based on what they sell. This, of course, tends to bias what they recommend that you buy. A study done by Cummins and Weisbart and cited in Andrew Tobias's book *Invisible Bankers* confirms this bias: ". . . 48% of the time, an agent's decision on where to place a customer's business was based on which insurer paid the highest commission."

Not surprisingly, policies that pay agents the biggest commissions also tend to be more costly. In fact, insurance companies compete for the attention of agents by offering bigger commissions than other insurers. When I browse through magazines and other publications targeted to insurance agents, I often see ads in which the largest text is the commission percentage offered to agents who sell the advertiser's products.

Besides the attraction of policies that pay higher commissions, agents also get hooked, financially speaking, to companies whose policies they sell frequently. Once an agent has sold a certain amount of a company's insurance policies, he is rewarded with higher commission percentages on any future sales. Just as airlines bribe frequent fliers with mileage bonuses, insurers bribe agents with fatter commissions for their loyalty.

The financial health of your insurers

In addition to the price of a policy and the insurer's reputation and track record for paying claims, an insurer's financial health is an important consideration when you choose a company. If you faithfully pay your premium dollars year after year, you'll be upset if the insurer goes bankrupt right before you have a major claim.

Insurance companies can fail just like any other companies, and dozens do in a typical year. A number of organizations evaluate and rate, with some sort of letter grade, the financial viability and stability of insurance companies. The major rating agencies include A. M. Best, Moody's, Standard & Poor's, Duff & Phelps, and Weiss Research.

The rating agencies' letter-grade system works just the way it does in high school: A is better than B or C. Each company uses a different scale. Some companies have as their highest rating AAA, and then AA, A, BBB, BB, and so on. Others use A, A–, B+, B, B–, and so on. Just as some teachers grade more easily, some firms, such as A. M. Best, have a reputation for giving out a greater number of high grades. Others, such as Weiss Research, are tough graders. Unlike in school, however, you want the tough critics when researching where to put your money and future security.

Just as it is a good idea to get more than one medical opinion, two or three financial ratings can give you a better sense of the safety of an insurance company. Stick with companies that are in the top two — or, at worst, three — levels on the different rating scales.

You can obtain current rating information about insurance companies, free of charge, by asking your agent for a listing of the current ratings. Ask the insurer itself if you are interested in a policy sold without the involvement of an agent.

Although the financial health of an insurance company is important, it's not as big a deal as some insurers (usually those with the highest ratings) and agents make it out to be. Just as financially unhealthy banks are taken over and merged into viable ones, sickly insurers usually follow a similar path under the direction of state insurance regulators.

In most insurance company failures, claims still get paid. The people who usually lose out are those who had money invested in life insurance or annuities with the failed insurer. Even then, you'll typically get back 80 or 90 cents on the dollar of your account value with the insurer, but you may have to wait years to get it.

Shopping around is a challenge not only because most insurance is sold by agents working on commission but also because insurers set their rates in mysterious ways. Every company has a different way of analyzing how much of a risk you are; one company may offer low rates to me but not to you and vice versa.

Despite the obstacles, several strategies exist for obtaining low-cost, high-quality policies. The following tips offer smart ways to shop for insurance. (Chapters 16 and 17 recommend how and where to get the best deals on specific types of policies.)

Employer and other group plans

When you buy insurance as part of a larger group, you generally get a lower price because of the purchasing power of the group. Most health and disability policies that you can access through your employer are less costly than equivalent policies that you can buy on your own.

Likewise, many occupations have professional associations through which you may be able to obtain lower-cost policies. Not all associations offer better deals on insurance, so make sure to compare what they offer (policy features and costs) with other options available to you.

One exception to the rule that group policies offer better value than individual policies is with life insurance. Group life insurance plans usually aren't cheaper than the best life insurance policies that you can buy individually. However, group policies may have the attraction of convenience (ease of enrollment and avoidance of lengthy sales pitches from life insurance salespeople). Group life insurance policies that allow your enrollment without a medical evaluation will probably be more expensive because such plans attract more people with health problems who couldn't get coverage on their own. If you're in good health, you should definitely shop around for life insurance (see Chapter 16 to find out how).

Insurance agents who want to sell you an individual policy can come up with 101 reasons why buying from them is preferable to buying through your employer or some other group. In most cases, agents' arguments for buying an individual policy from them include a lot of self-serving marketing hype. In some cases, agents tell outright lies (which are hard to detect if you're not insurance-savvy).

One valid issue agents will raise is that, if you leave your job, you'll lose your group coverage. Sometimes that may be true. For example, if you know that you'll be leaving your job to become self-employed, securing an individual disability policy before you leave your job makes sense. However, your employer's health insurer may allow you to convert your health insurance policy into an individual one when you leave.

In the chapters that follow, I explain what you need in the policies that you are looking for so that you can determine whether a group plan meets your needs. In most cases, group plans, especially through an employer, offer good benefits. So as long as the group policy is cheaper than a comparable individual policy, you'll save money buying through the group plan.

Insurance without sales commissions

Your best bet for getting a good insurance value is to buy policies from the increasing number of companies that are selling their policies directly to the public without the insurance agent and the agent's commission. Just as you can purchase no-load mutual funds directly from an investment company without paying any sales commission (refer to Chapter 10), you also can buy no-load insurance. Be sure to read Chapters 16 and 17 for more specifics on how to buy insurance directly from insurance companies.

Annuities, investment/insurance products traditionally sold through insurance agents, are also now available directly to the customer, without sales commission. Simply contact some of the leading no-load mutual fund companies such as Vanguard and T. Rowe Price (refer to Chapter 11).

In the late 1990s, legislation before Congress was aimed at repealing the insurance industry's federal antitrust exemption and allowing agents in all 50 states to compete on the pricing of the policies that they sell and to allow agents to rebate commissions to consumers. Few people knew about the legislation or how it could benefit them, and the insurance companies and agents maneuvered stealthily to defeat it. If you would like to see the insurance industry opened up to the same competitive forces as other industries (which would save us all big bucks), write a letter to your state insurance commissioner or congressperson today.

The straight scoop on commissions and how insurance is sold

The commission paid to an insurance agent is never disclosed through any of the documents or materials that you receive in the process of buying insurance. This information ought to be disclosed by insurers and agents, just as sales charges on mutual funds are disclosed through a prospectus.

The only way you can know what the commission is on a policy and how it compares with other policies is to ask the agent. Nothing is wrong or impolite about asking. It's your money, after all, that pays the commission. You need to know whether a particular policy is being pitched harder because of its higher commission.

Commissions are typically paid as a percentage of the first year's premium on the insurance policy. (Many policies pay smaller commissions on subsequent years' premiums.) On life and disability insurance policies, for example, a 50 percent commission on the first year's premium is not unusual. On life insurance policies that have a cash value, commissions of 80 to 100 percent of your first year's premium are possible. Commissions on health insurance are lower, but generally not as low as commissions on auto and homeowner's insurance.

Dealing with Insurance Problems

When you seek out insurance or have insurance policies, sooner or later you're bound to hit a roadblock. Although insurance problems can be among the more frustrating in life, in the sections ahead, I explain how to successfully deal with the more common obstacles.

Help! I've been denied coverage!

Just as you can be turned down when you apply for a loan, you can also be turned down when applying for insurance. For medical, life, or disability insurance, a company may reject you if you have an existing medical problem (a preexisting condition) and are therefore more likely to file a claim. When it comes to insuring assets such as a home, you may have difficulty getting coverage if the property is deemed to be in a high-risk area.

Here are some strategies to employ if you are denied coverage:

✔ **Ask the insurer why you were denied.** Perhaps the company made a mistake or misinterpreted some information that you provided in your application. Should you be denied coverage because of a medical condition, see what information the company has on you and whether the information is accurate.

✔ **Request a copy of your medical information file.** Many people don't know that just as you have a credit report file that details your use (and misuse) of credit, you also have a medical information report. You can request a current copy of your medical information file by writing to the Medical Information Bureau at P.O. Box 105, Essex Station, Boston, MA 02112. You can also call the bureau at 617-426-3660 or visit its web site at www.mib.com. If a mistake is on your report, you have the right to request that it be fixed. However, the burden is on you to prove that the information in your file is incorrect. This can be a major hassle — you may even need to contact physicians that you've seen in the past because their medical records could be the source of the incorrect information.

✔ **Shop other companies.** Just because one company denies you coverage doesn't mean that all insurance companies will. Some insurers better understand certain medical conditions and are more comfortable accepting applicants with those conditions. Most insurers, however, charge a person with a blemished medical history a higher rate than a person with a perfect health record, but some companies penalize you less than others. An agent who sells policies from multiple insurers, called an *independent agent,* can be helpful because he or she can shop among a number of different companies.

✔ **Learn about state high-risk pools.** Check with your state department of insurance (see the "Government" section of your local white pages phone directory) if you're turned down for health or property insurance. A number of states act as the insurer of last resort and provide insurance for those who can't get it from insurance companies. State high-risk pool coverage is usually bare bones, but it beats going without any coverage.

✔ **Check for coverage availability before you buy.** If you're considering buying a home, for example, and you can't get coverage, the insurance companies are trying to tell you something. What they are effectively saying is, "We think that property is so high-risk, we're not willing to insure it even if you pay a high premium."

Help! My insurer is hassling me about paying a claim

In the event that you suffer a loss and file an insurance claim, you may hold the happy belief that your insurance company will cheerfully and expeditiously pay your claims. Given all the money that you've shelled out for coverage and all the hoops you jumped through to be approved for coverage in the first place, that's a reasonable expectation.

Insurance companies may refuse to pay you what you think you are owed for many reasons, however. In some cases, they may actually be right — your claim may not be covered under the terms of the policy. At a minimum, the insurer wants documentation and proof of your loss. Other people who have come before you have been known to cheat, so insurers won't simply take your word, no matter how honest and ethical you are.

In other cases, though, you're right, and the insurance company is just jerking you around. Some companies view paying claims as an adversarial situation and take a "negotiate tough" stance. Thinking that all insurance companies are going to pay you a fair and reasonable amount unless you make your voice heard is a mistake.

The tips that I discuss in this section help you to ensure that you get paid everything your policy entitles you to.

Document your assets and case

When you're insuring assets, such as your home and its contents, having a record of what you own helps your case. A videotape is the most efficient record, but a handwritten list detailing your possessions works, too. Just remember to keep this record away from your home — if your home burns to the ground, you'll lose your documentation, too!

If you are robbed or are the victim of an accident, get the names, addresses, and phone numbers of witnesses. Take pictures of property damage and solicit estimates for the cost of repairing or replacing what's lost or damaged. File police reports if appropriate, if for no other reason than to bolster your documentation for the insurance claim.

The best offense is a good defense. If you've kept records of valuables and can document their cost, you should be in better shape.

Prepare your case

Filing a claim should be viewed the same way as preparing for a court trial or an IRS audit. Any information that you provide verbally or in writing can and will be used against you to deny your claim. First, you should understand whether the policy you bought covers your claim (this is why getting the broadest coverage possible helps). Unfortunately, the only way to find this out is by getting out the policy and reading it. Policies are hard to read because they use legal language in non-user-friendly ways.

A possible alternative is to call the claims department and, *without* providing your name, ask a representative whether a particular loss (such as the one that you just suffered) is covered under its policy. You have no need to lie to the company, but you have no need to tell the representative who you are and that you're about to file a claim, either. Your call is informational so that you can understand what your policy covers. Some companies are not willing to provide detailed information, however, unless a specific case is cited.

After you initiate the claims process, keep records of all conversations and all copies of documents that you have given to the insurer's claims department. If you have problems down the road, this "evidence" may bail you out.

For property damage, you should get at least a couple of reputable contractors' estimates. Demonstrate to the insurance company that you're trying to shop for a low price, but don't agree to use a low-cost contractor without knowing that he or she can do quality work.

Remember, your claim is a negotiation

To get what you're owed on an insurance claim, you must approach most claims' filings for what they are — a negotiation that is often not cooperative. And the bigger the claim, the more your insurer will play the part of adversary.

A number of years ago, when I filed a homeowner's insurance claim after a winter storm significantly damaged my backyard fence, I was greeted on a weekday by a perky, smiley adjuster. Once the adjuster entered my yard and started to peruse the damage, her demeanor changed dramatically. She had a combative, hard-bargainer type attitude that I last witnessed during my days as a consultant when I worked on some labor-management negotiations.

While standing on my back porch a good distance away from the fences in my yard that had been blown over by wind and crushed by two large trees, the adjuster said that my insurer preferred to repair damaged fences rather than replace them. "With your deductible of $1,000, I doubt this will be worth filing a claim for," she said.

The fence that had blown over, she reasoned, could have new posts set in concrete. As we had already begun to clean up some of the damage for safety reasons, I presented to her some pictures of what the yard looked like right after the storm; she refused to take them. She took some measurements and said she'd have her settlement check to us in a couple of days. The settlement she faxed was for $1,119, nowhere near what it would cost me to fix the damage that was done.

Be persistent

When you take an insurance company's first offer and don't fight for what you're due, you could be leaving a lot of money on the table. To make my long fence-repair story somewhat shorter, after *five* rounds of haggling with the adjusters, supervisors, and finally managers, I was awarded payment to replace the fences and clean up most of the damage. Although all the contractors I had contacted recommended that the work be done this way, the insurance adjuster discredited their recommendations by saying, "Contractors try to jack up the price and recommended work once they know an insurer is involved."

My final total settlement came to $4,888, more than $3,700 higher than the insurer's first offer. Interestingly, my insurer backed off its preference for repairing the fence when the contractor's estimates for doing that work exceeded the cost of a new fence.

I was disappointed with the behavior of my insurance company. Having faithfully paid my premiums for years and having never filed a claim, I expected they would be cooperative and not combative. Boy, was I naive. I know from conversations with others that my homeowner's insurance company is not unusual in its adversarial strategy, especially with larger claims. And to think that my insurer has one of the "better" track records for paying claims!

Enlist support

If you do your homework and you're not making progress with the insurer's adjuster, ask to speak with supervisors and managers. That's what I had to do to get the additional $3,700 that was needed to get things back to where they were before the storm.

The agent who sold you the policy may be helpful in preparing and filing the claim. A good agent can help increase your chances of getting paid and getting paid sooner. When you're having difficulty with a claim for a policy obtained through your employer or other group, speak with the benefits department or a person responsible for interacting with the insurer. These folks have a lot of clout because of the potential threat to the agent and/or insurer of losing the entire account.

For policies that you buy on your own, if you're having problems getting a fair settlement from the insurer, try contacting the state department of insurance. You can find the phone number in the state government white pages of your phone book or possibly in your insurance policy.

Another option is to hire a public adjuster who, for a percentage of payment (typically 5 to 10 percent), can negotiate with insurers on your behalf.

When all else fails and you have a major claim at stake, try contacting an attorney who specializes in insurance matters. You can find these specialists in the yellow pages of your phone directory under "Attorneys — Insurance Law." Expect to pay around $100 or more per hour. Consider looking for a lawyer who is willing to negotiate on your behalf, help draft letters, and so on, on an hourly basis without filing a lawsuit. Your state department of insurance, the local bar association, or other legal, accounting, or financial practitioners also may be able to refer you to someone.

The possible headache in filing a claim is another reason to take the highest insurance deductibles you're comfortable with. Remember that insurance is to protect against large, not small, losses. With a high deductible and a small loss, you'll save yourself some haggling.

Chapter 16

Insurance on You

• •

In This Chapter

▶ Life insurance

▶ Disability insurance

▶ Health insurance

▶ Long-term care insurance

▶ Overlooked personal insurance

• •

*M*ultiply your typical annual income by the number of remaining years you plan to work — you come up with a pretty big number, don't you? That dollar amount equals probably your most valuable asset — your ability to earn an income — and you probably need to protect it. You need to buy some insurance on you.

This chapter explains the ins and outs of buying insurance that protects your income: life insurance, in case of death, and disability insurance, in case of an accident or illness that prevents you from working. I tell you what coverage you should have, where to look for it, and what to avoid.

In addition to protecting your income, you also need to insure against financially catastrophic expenses. I am not talking about December's credit card bill; you're on your own with that one. I am talking about the type of bills that are racked up from a major surgery and a six-week stay in the hospital. Medical expenses today can make even the most indulgent shopping mall spending spree look dirt-cheap. To protect yourself from potentially astronomical medical bills, you also need to have comprehensive health insurance.

Life Insurance

You generally only need life insurance when other people depend on your income.

BEWARE

Don't waste your money on life insurance for children

You've surely heard of Gerber baby food. Well, the folks at Gerber knew that their brand name had clout with parents, so they sat around racking their brains about what else they could pitch to parents.

So Gerber established a life insurance company that now has billions of dollars of life insurance in force. The only problem is that the company specializes in selling life insurance policies on individuals who don't need it: children.

Gerber's "Grow-Up" policy provides $5,000 of life insurance for children. The marketing materials say, "Life insurance for the child you love . . . $1 a week at most ages. . . ."

Sounds like such a deal, but it's really a rip-off that contradicts the entire logic of life insurance. Unless your kid was the star of the *Home Alone* movies, you are not financially dependent on any of your children; your children are dependent on you! As any parent knows, kids cost a good deal of money — kids don't earn money!

And if a person does need life insurance coverage, of what use is a piddling $5,000 worth of

coverage? And a buck a week is hardly a deal — for that cost, a young adult could buy about ten times as much coverage ($50,000)!

Insurance agents love to prey on the emotional bond between parents and children. In a written sales pitch an agent made to one of my counseling clients, the agent said, ". . . as long as the policies remain in-force, your signature(s) will always be there as a reminder of your very thoughtful financial gift."

Agents also love to sell cash value life insurance on kids because such policies pay the agent a hefty commission (25 percent of all cash value policies sold are on children). Part of the supposed allure is that the huge premiums that you pump into such policies partly go into a savings account for the child's future. As you see later in this chapter, cash value life insurance is a costly life insurance and investment choice. If you want to secure your children's financial future, follow the advice in this book and pass this information on to your children. Don't waste money on life insurance on your kids — they don't need it.

That means that a lot of people don't need life insurance to protect their incomes: single people, working couples who could maintain an acceptable lifestyle if one of the incomes was gone, independently wealthy people who don't need to work, and retired people who are living off of their retirement nest egg.

But if others are either fully or partly dependent on your paycheck (usually a spouse and/or children), you should buy life insurance, especially if you have major financial commitments such as a mortgage or years of child rearing ahead. Also consider life insurance if an extended family member is currently or likely to be dependent on your future income.

How much do you need?

When you need life insurance, deciding how much to buy is as much a subjective thing as it is a quantitative decision. I've seen some worksheets that are incredibly long and tedious (some are worse than your tax returns). There's no need to get fancy. If you're like me, your eyes start to glaze over if you have to complete 20 plus lines of calculations. Figuring out how much life insurance you need doesn't have to be that complicated.

The main purpose of life insurance is to provide a lump sum payment that replaces the deceased person's income. The question you need to ask yourself is how many years of income do you want to replace? Table 16-1 provides a simple way to calculate how much life insurance you should consider purchasing. To replace a certain number of years of income, simply multiply the appropriate number in the table by the person's annual after-tax income.

Table 16-1	Life Insurance Need Calculation
Years of Income to Replace	*Multiply Annual After-Tax Income* By*
5	4.5
10	8.5
20	15
30	20

*You can roughly determine your annual after-tax income in one of two ways. You can get out last year's tax return (and Form W-2) and calculate it by subtracting the federal, state, and Social Security taxes you paid from your gross employment income. Or you can estimate it by multiplying your gross income by 80 percent if you're a low-income earner, 70 percent if you're a moderate-income earner, or 60 percent if you're a high-income earner. (You need to replace only after-tax, not pre-tax, income because life insurance policy payouts are not taxed.)

Another way to determine the amount of life insurance to buy is to think about how much you will need to pay for major debts or expenditures, such as your mortgage, other loans, and college for your children. For example, if you'd like your spouse to have enough of a life insurance death benefit to be able to pay off half of your mortgage and pay for half of your children's college education, then simply add half of your mortgage amount to half of their estimated college costs (refer to Chapter 13 for approximate numbers) and buy that amount of life insurance.

Social Security, if you're covered, can provide *survivors'* benefits to your spouse and children. However, if your surviving spouse earns more than about $20,000 per year, he or she is not going to get any coverage (so you can skip the rest of this section). If either you or your spouse anticipates earning less than $20,000 per year, however, you may want to factor this into how much life insurance to buy. Contact the Social Security Administration at 800-772-1213 (or visit its web site at www.ssa.gov) and request Form 7004, which gives you an estimate of your Social Security benefits.

The Social Security Administration can tell you how much your survivors will receive per month in the event of your death. You should factor this benefit into the amount of life insurance that you calculate in Table 16-1. For example, suppose that your annual after-tax income is $15,000 and Social Security should provide $8,000 annually. Therefore, for purposes of Table 16-1, you should determine the amount of life insurance needed to replace $7,000 annually ($15,000 – $8,000), not $15,000.

"Other" life insurance

Contemplating the possibility of your untimely demise is surely depressing. You'll likely feel some peace of mind in purchasing a life insurance policy to provide for your dependents.

However, let's take things a step further. Suppose you (or your spouse) do pass away. Do you think simply buying a life insurance policy will be sufficient "help" for the loved ones you leave behind? Probably not. Surely your contribution to your household involves far more than being a breadwinner.

For starters, you should make sure that all of your important financial documents — investment account statements, insurance policies, employee benefits materials, small-business accounting records, and so on — are kept in one place (such as a file drawer) that your loved ones know about.

Do you have a will? See Chapter 17 for more details on wills and other estate planning documents.

You might also consider providing a list of key contacts — such as who you recommend calling (or what you recommend reading) in the event of legal, financial, or tax quandaries.

So, in addition to trying to provide financially for your dependents, you should also take some time to reflect upon what else you can do to help point them in the right direction on matters you've historically handled. In most couples, it's natural for one spouse to take more responsibility, say, for money management. That's fine; just make sure to talk about what's being done so that in the event the responsible spouse dies, the remaining person knows how to jump into the driver's seat.

If you have kids, and even if you don't, how about giving thought to philosophical leave-behinds for your loved ones? It could be something like a short note telling them how much they meant to you and what you'd like them to remember about you.

Term versus cash value life insurance

I'm going to tell you how you can save hours of time and thousands of dollars. Ready? *Buy term life insurance.* (The only exception is if you have a high net worth — a couple million bucks or more — in which case you may want to consider other options. See the estate-planning section in Chapter 17.) If you've already figured out how much life insurance to purchase and this is all the advice you need to go ahead, skip the rest of this section and jump to the "Buying term insurance" section that follows.

The following information is for the rest of you who want the details behind my recommendation for term insurance. Or maybe you've heard (and have already fallen prey to) the sales pitches from life insurance agents, most of whom love selling cash value life insurance because of its huge commissions.

Let me start with some background. Despite the variety of names that life insurance marketing departments have cooked up for policies, life insurance comes in two basic flavors:

- **Term insurance** is pure life insurance: You pay an annual premium for which you receive a predetermined amount of life insurance protection. If the insured person passes away, the beneficiaries collect; otherwise, the premium is gone. In this way, term life insurance is similar to auto or homeowner's insurance.

- **Cash value insurance.** All other life insurance policies (whole, universal, variable, and so on) combine life insurance with a supposed savings feature. Your premiums not only pay for life insurance, but some of your dollars are also credited to an account that grows in value over time, assuming you keep paying your premiums. On the surface, this sounds potentially attractive. People don't like to feel that all their premium dollars are getting tossed away.

  But there's a big catch. For the same amount of coverage (for example, for $100,000 of life insurance benefits), cash value policies cost you about eight times (800 percent) more than comparable term policies.

Insurance salespeople know the buttons to push to get you interested in buying the wrong kind of life insurance. Here are typical arguments that they make for purchasing cash value polices, followed by my perspective.

"It's all paid up after × years. You don't want to be paying life insurance premiums for the rest of your life, do you?"

Agents pitching cash value life insurance show you all sorts of projections that imply that after the first ten or so years of paying your premiums, you won't need to pay more premiums to keep the life insurance in force. The only reason that you may be able to stop paying premiums is that you've poured so much extra money into the policy in the early years of payment. Remember that cash value life insurance costs about eight times as much as term.

Imagine that you're currently paying $500 a year for auto insurance and an insurance company comes along and offers you a policy for $4,000 per year. The representative tells you that after 10 years, you can stop paying and still keep your same coverage. I'm sure that you wouldn't fall for this sales tactic, but many people do when they buy cash value life insurance.

You also need to be wary of the projections because they often include unrealistic and lofty assumptions about the investment return that your cash balance can earn. When you stop paying into a cash value policy, the cost of each year's life insurance is deducted from the remaining cash value. If the rate of return on the cash balance is not sufficient to pay the insurance cost, the cash balance begins sliding, and eventually you will receive notices saying that your policy needs more funding to keep the life insurance in force.

"You won't be able to afford term insurance when you're older."

As you get older, the cost of term insurance increases because the probability of your dying rises. But life insurance is not something you need all your life! It's typically bought in a person's younger years when financial commitments and obligations outweigh financial assets. Twenty or thirty years later, the reverse should be true.

When you retire years from now, you probably won't need life insurance to protect your employment income because there won't be any to protect! You might have needed life insurance when you were raising a family and/or had a substantial mortgage you were responsible for, but by the time you retire, the kids should be out on their own (you hope!) and the mortgage should be paid down.

In the meantime, term insurance saves you a tremendous amount of money. For most people, it takes 20 to 30 years for the premium they are paying on a term insurance policy to finally catch up to (equal) the premium they've been paying all along on a comparable amount of cash value life insurance purchased today.

"You can borrow against the cash value at a low rate of interest."

Such a deal! It's your money in the policy, remember? If you deposited money in a savings or money market account, how would you like to pay for the privilege of borrowing your own money back? Borrowing on your cash value policy is potentially dangerous: You increase the chances of the policy exploding on you — leaving you with nothing to show for your premiums.

"Your cash value grows tax-deferred."

Ah, a glimmer of truth at last. The fact that the cash value portion of your policy grows without taxation until you withdraw it is true. But if you want tax-deferral of your investment balances, you should first take advantage of such savings plans as 401(k)s, 403(b)s, SEP-IRAs, and Keoghs. Such accounts give you an immediate tax deduction for your current contributions in addition to growth without taxation until withdrawal.

Money paid into a cash value life policy gives you *no* up-front tax deductions. If you've exhausted the tax-deductible plans, then variable annuities or a nondeductible individual retirement account (IRA) can provide access to better investment options and tax-deferred compounding of your investment dollars (refer to Chapter 11 for details on retirement accounts).

Life insurance tends to be a mediocre investment. The insurance company quotes you an interest rate for the first year only. After that, the company pays you what it wants. If you don't like the future interest rates, you can be penalized for quitting the policy. Would you ever invest your money in a bank account that quoted an interest rate for the first year only and then penalized you for moving your money within the next seven to ten years?

"It's forced savings."

Many agents argue that a cash value plan is better than nothing — at least it's forcing you to save. This is silly reasoning because so many people drop cash value life insurance policies after just a few years of paying into them.

You can accomplish "forced savings" without using life insurance. Any of the retirement savings accounts mentioned in Chapter 11 can be set up for automatic monthly transfers. Employers offering such a plan can deduct contributions from your paycheck — and it doesn't take a commission! You can also set up monthly electronic transfers from your bank checking account to contribute to mutual funds (see Chapter 10).

"Life insurance is not part of your taxable estate."

If the ownership of a life insurance policy is properly structured, it's true that the death benefit is free of estate taxes. This part of the sales pitch is about the only sound reason that exists for buying cash value life insurance. Under current federal laws, a person can pass on $675,000 free of federal estate taxes (for tax year 2000). But even if you're expecting such an estate, you have numerous other ways to reduce your taxable estate (see Chapter 17).

Summary

Insurance salespeople aggressively push cash value policies because of the high commissions that insurance companies pay them. Commissions on cash value life insurance range from 50 to 100 percent of your first year's premium.

An insurance salesperson, therefore, can make *eight to ten times more money* (yes, you read that right) selling you a cash value policy than he can selling you term insurance.

You are ultimately paying the high commissions that are built into these policies when you purchase cash value life insurance. As you can see in a policy's cash value table, you won't get back any of the money that you dump in the policy if you quit the policy in the first two to three years. The insurance company can't afford to give you any of your money back in those first few years because so much of it has been paid to the selling agent as commission. That's why these policies explicitly penalize you for withdrawing your cash balance within the first seven to ten years.

Because of the high cost of cash value policies relative to the cost of term, you are more likely to buy less life insurance coverage than you need — that's the sad part of the insurance industry's pushing of this stuff. *The vast majority of life insurance buyers need more protection than they can afford to buy with cash value coverage.*

Cash value life insurance is the most oversold insurance and financial product in the history of the financial services industry. Cash value life insurance makes sense for a small percentage of people such as a small-business owner who owns a business worth more than one to two million dollars and who would not want his heirs to be forced to sell the business to pay estate taxes in the event of his death. (See "If you need cash value life insurance," later in this chapter.)

Purchase low-cost term insurance and do your investing separately. Life insurance is rarely a permanent need; over time, you can gradually reduce the amount of term insurance that you carry as you accumulate more assets.

Buying term insurance

Term insurance policies have several features to choose from. So that you can make an informed decision about purchasing term insurance, I cover the important elements in this section.

How often your premium adjusts

As you get older, the risk of dying increases, so the cost of your insurance goes up. Term insurance can be purchased so that your premium adjusts (increases) annually or every 5, 10, 15, or 20 years. The less frequently your premium adjusts, the higher the initial premium and its incremental increases will be.

The advantage of a premium that locks in for, say, 15 years is that you have the security of knowing how much you'll be paying each year for the next 15 years. You also don't need to go through medical evaluations as frequently to qualify for the lowest rate possible.

The disadvantage of a policy with a long-term rate lock is that you'll be paying more in the earlier years than you would on a policy that adjusts more frequently. In addition, you may want to change the amount of insurance you carry as your circumstances change, so you would be throwing money away if you dump a policy with a long-term premium guarantee before its rate is set to change.

Policies that adjust the premium every five to ten years offer a happy medium between price and predictability.

Guaranteed renewability

This feature guarantees that the policy cannot be canceled because of poor health. Guaranteed renewability is standard practice on better policies. Do not buy a life insurance policy without this feature unless you expect that your life insurance needs will disappear when the policy is up for renewal.

Where to buy term insurance

A number of sound ways to obtain high-quality, low-cost term insurance are available. If you choose to buy through a local agent — because you know her or because you'd prefer to buy from someone close to home — you should invest a few minutes of your time to get quotes from one or two of the following sources to get a sense of what's available in the insurance market. Gaining familiarity with the market can prevent an agent from selling you an overpriced, high-commission policy.

Here are some sources for high-quality, low-cost term insurance:

- ✔ **USAA** sells low-cost term insurance directly to the public (800-531-8000).

- ✔ **Insurance agency quotation services** provide proposals from the highest-rated, lowest-cost companies available. Like other agencies, the services receive a commission if you buy a policy from them, which you're under no obligation to do. Unlike local insurance agents, they don't hound you (don't give them your phone number if you don't want to be called, however). They'll ask you your date of birth, whether you smoke, and how much coverage you'd like. The best quotation services in terms of customer service, pricing, and presentation of information are **SelectQuote** (800-343-1985; www.selectquote.com) and **Waterhouse Insurance Services** (800-622-3699; www.waterhouse.com). See Chapter 19 for more on how to use your computer when making life insurance decisions.

How to get rid of cash value life insurance

If you were snookered into buying a cash value life insurance policy and want to part ways with it, do so. *But don't cancel the coverage until you first secure new term coverage.* When you need life insurance, you don't want to leave open a period when you're not covered (Murphy's Law says *that's* when disaster will strike).

Ending a cash value life insurance policy has tax consequences. For most of these policies, you must pay tax on the amount you receive that is in excess of the premiums you paid over the life of the policy. Because some life insurance policies feature tax-deferred retirement savings, you may incur a 10-percent penalty on earnings withdrawn before age 59½, just as you would with an IRA. If you want to withdraw the cash balance in your life insurance policy, consider checking with the insurer or a tax advisor to clarify what the tax consequences may be.

You can avoid early withdrawal penalties and taxation on accumulated interest in a life insurance policy by doing a tax-free exchange into a no-load (commission-free) *variable annuity.* The no-load mutual fund company through which you buy the annuity takes care of transferring your existing balance. (Refer to Chapter 12 for more information about annuities.)

If you're considering cash value life insurance

Don't expect to get objective information on this important decision from anyone who sells cash value life insurance. Beware of insurance salespeople masquerading under the guise of self-anointed titles, such as estate planning specialists or financial planners.

As I discuss earlier in the chapter, purchasing cash value life insurance may make sense if you expect to have an estate tax problem. However, cash value life insurance is just one of numerous ways to reduce your estate taxes. Read the section in Chapter 17 on estate planning.

Among the best places to shop for cash value life insurance policies are:

- ✔ **USAA** (800-531-8000).
- ✔ **Ameritas** (800-552-3553).
- ✔ **Insurance quotation services** (see the section, "Where to buy term insurance" earlier in this chapter).

TIP

If you want to obtain some cash value life insurance, avoid local insurance agents, especially while you're in the learning stage. Agents aren't as interested in educating as they are in selling (big surprise). Besides, the best cash value policies can be obtained free of most (or all) sales commissions if you buy from the preceding sources. The money saved on commissions is reflected in a much higher cash value for you — up to several thousand dollars' worth.

Disability Insurance

As with life insurance, the purpose of disability insurance is to protect your income. The only difference is that you're protecting the income for yourself (and perhaps also your dependents). If you're completely disabled, you still have living expenses, but you probably can't earn employment income.

I'm talking here about long-term disabilities. If you throw out your back while reliving your athletic glory days with your aging adult body and wind up in bed for a couple of weeks, that won't be as much of a disaster to your finances as it is to your ego! What would be a financial disaster, however, is if you're disabled in such a way that you can't work for several years.

Most large employers offer disability insurance to their employees. Many smaller company employees and all self-employed people are left to fend for themselves and don't have disability coverage. Being without disability insurance is a risky proposition, especially if, like most working people, you need your employment income to live on.

If you're married and your spouse earns a large enough income that you can make do without yours, then you may consider skipping disability coverage. The same is true if you've already accumulated enough money for your future years (you're financially independent). Keep in mind, though, that your expenses may go up if you are disabled and require specialized care.

For most people, dismissing the need for disability coverage is easy. The odds of suffering a long-term disability seem so remote — and they are. But if you meet up with bad luck, disability coverage can relieve you (and possibly your family) of a major financial burden.

Most disabilities are caused by medical problems, such as arthritis, heart conditions, hypertension, and back/spine or hip/leg impairments. Some of these ailments are caused by advancing age, but more than a third of disabilities are suffered by people under age 45. The vast majority of these medical problems cannot be predicted in advance, particularly those caused by random accidents.

If you think that you have good disability coverage through government programs, you'd better think again:

- **Social Security disability.** Social Security pays long-term benefits only if you are not able to perform any substantial, gainful activity for more than a year or if your disability is expected to result in death. In fact, 70 percent of all applicants for Social Security disability benefits coverage are turned down. Furthermore, Social Security disability payments are quite low because they are intended to provide only for basic, subsistence-level living expenses.

- **Worker's compensation.** Worker's compensation, if you have such coverage through your employer, pays you if you're injured on the job but does not pay any benefits if you get disabled away from your job. You need coverage that pays regardless of where and how you are disabled.

- **State disability programs.** A few states have disability insurance programs, but the coverage is typically not extensive enough because benefits are paid over too short a period of time (rarely more than a year). State programs are also generally not good values because of the cost for the small amount of coverage they provide.

How much disability insurance do you need?

You need enough disability coverage to provide you with sufficient income to live on until other financial resources are available. If you don't have much saved in the way of financial assets and you would want to continue with the lifestyle supported by your current income, get enough disability coverage to replace your entire take-home (after-tax) monthly pay.

The benefits you purchase on a disability policy are quoted as dollars per month that you receive if disabled. So if your job provides you with a $2,000-per-month income after payment of taxes, then seek a policy that provides a $2,000-per-month benefit.

If you pay for your disability insurance, the benefits are tax-free (but hopefully you won't ever have to collect them). Should your employer pick up the tab, your benefits are taxable, so you need a higher amount of benefits.

In addition to the monthly coverage amount, you also need to select the duration of time you want a policy to pay you benefits. You need a policy that pays benefits until an age at which you become financially self-sufficient. For most people, that's age 65 or so when their Social Security benefits kick in. You may want to obtain disability coverage that pays you until a later age if you anticipate needing your employment income past your mid-60s.

On the other hand, if you've crunched some numbers (refer to Chapter 3) and see that you expect to be financially independent by age 55, you can get a policy that pays benefits up to that age — it'll cost you less than one that pays benefits to you until age 65. If you're within five years of being financially independent or able to retire, five-year disability policies are available, too. You might also consider such short-term policies because you're sure that someone (for example, a family member) can support you financially over the long-term.

Other features you need in disability insurance

Disability insurance policies have many confusing features. Here's what to look for — and look out for — when purchasing disability insurance:

- **Definition of disability.** An *own-occupation* disability policy provides benefit payments if you cannot perform the work you normally do. Some policies pay you only if you're unable to perform a job for which you are *reasonably trained*. Other policies revert to this definition after a few years of being own-occupation.

  Own-occupation policies are the most expensive because there's a greater chance that the insurer will have to pay you. The extra cost may not be worth it for you unless you're in a high-income or specialized occupation, and you'd have to take a big pay cut to do something else (and you wouldn't be happy about a reduced income and the required lifestyle changes).

- **Noncancelable and guaranteed renewable.** These features guarantee that your policy cannot be canceled because of poor health conditions. With policies requiring periodic physical exams, you can lose your coverage just when you're most likely to need it.

- **Waiting period.** This is the "deductible" on disability insurance — the lag time between the onset of your disability and the time you begin collecting benefits. As with other types of insurance, you should take the highest deductible (longest waiting period) that your financial circumstances allow. The waiting period significantly reduces the cost of the insurance and eliminates the hassle of filing a claim for a short-term disability. The minimum waiting period on most policies is 30 days, and the maximum can be up to one to two years. Try a waiting period of three to six months if you have sufficient emergency reserves.

- **Residual benefits.** This option pays you a partial benefit if you have a disability that prevents you from working full-time.

- ✔ **Cost-of-living adjustments (COLAs).** This feature automatically increases your benefit payment by a set percentage or in accordance with changes in inflation. The advantage of a COLA is that it retains the purchasing power of your benefits. A modest COLA, such as 4 percent, is worth having.

- ✔ **Future insurability.** A clause that many agents encourage you to buy, future insurability allows you, regardless of health, to buy additional coverage. For most people, paying for the privilege of buying more coverage later is not worth it if the income that you earn today fairly reflects your likely long-term earnings (except for cost-of-living increases). Disability insurance is sold only as a proportion of your income. People who may benefit from the future insurability option are those whose income is artificially low now and who not only are confident of its rising significantly in the future but also need to protect it. (For example, you just got out of medical school and are earning a low salary while being enslaved as a resident.)

- ✔ **Insurer's financial stability.** As I discuss in Chapter 15, you should choose insurers that will be here tomorrow to pay your claim. But don't get too hung up on the safety of the company; benefits are paid even if the insurer fails because the state or another insurer almost always bails the insurer out.

Where to buy disability insurance

The best place to buy disability insurance is through your employer or professional association. Unless these groups have done a lousy job shopping for coverage, group plans offer better value than you can purchase on your own. Just make sure that the plan that's offered meets the specifications discussed in the preceding section.

Don't trust an insurance agent to be enthusiastic (or even honest) about the quality of a disability policy your employer or other group is offering. Agents have a huge conflict of interest when they criticize these options because your group insurance cuts them out of the picture.

If you don't have access to a group policy, then check with your agent or a company you already do business with. Also call USAA (800-531-8000), which offers competitively priced disability policies.

Tread carefully when purchasing disability insurance through an agent. Some agents try to load down a policy with all sorts of extra bells and whistles to pump up the premium and their own commission.

Other "insurance" to protect your income

Life insurance and disability insurance replace your income if you die or suffer a disability. But you could also see your income reduced or completely eliminated if you lose your job. Although no formal insurance exists to protect you against the forces that can cause this to happen, you can do some things to reduce your exposure to such risk.

Make sure that you have an emergency reserve of money that you can tap into if you lose your

job. (Chapter 3 offers specific guidelines for deciding how much money is right for you.)

Another form of "insurance" is to continually attend to your skills and professional development. Not only does upgrading your education and skills ensure that you are employable if you have to hit the streets to look for a new job, but it may also help you keep your old one and earn a higher income.

If you buy disability insurance through an agent, use a process called *list billing.* With list billing, you sign up with several others for coverage at the same time and are invoiced together for your coverage. It can knock up to 15 percent off an insurer's standard prices. Ask your insurance agent how this works.

Health Insurance

Almost everyone (except the super-wealthy) needs health insurance, but not everyone has it. Some people who can afford it choose not to buy it, believing that they're healthy and are not going to need it. Others who opt not to buy health insurance figure that if they ever really need it, they'll get care even if they can't pay. To a large extent, they're right. However, the care is usually a lot more expensive by the time they seek it (due to advanced illness, emergency room visits, and so on). People without health insurance generally put off getting more routine care, which can lead to small problems turning into big ones.

Choosing the best health plan

Before Medicare, the government-run insurance program for the elderly, kicks in at age 65, odds are you will obtain your health insurance through your employer. Be thankful if you do. Employer-provided coverage eliminates the headache of shopping for your own coverage and is usually cheaper than coverage bought on your own.

Health insurers: Bigger is usually better

With health insurance plans, you should give preference to plans that insure large numbers of people and that have been around longer. Larger plans can negotiate better rates from providers, and older plans are more likely to be here tomorrow.

Many insurers operate in a bunch of different insurance businesses. You want those that are the biggest in the health insurance arena and are committed to that business. If your coverage is canceled, you might have to search for coverage that allows an existing medical problem. Other health insurers won't want to insure you. (Find out whether your state department of insurance offers a plan for people unable to get coverage.)

Nationally, Blue Cross, Blue Shield, Kaiser Permanente, Aetna, United Healthcare and Cigna are the older and larger health insurers.

Whether you have options through your employer or need to hunt for a plan on your own, here are the major issues to consider when selecting among the health insurance offerings in the marketplace.

Major medical coverage

You need a plan that covers the *big* potential expenses: hospitalization, physician, and ancillary charges, such as X-ray and laboratory work. For women, if you are entering or are already in your child-bearing years and may want to have children, make sure that your plan has maternity benefits.

Choice of health care providers

Increasing numbers of health insurance plans contract with specific health care providers, which restricts your choices. Health maintenance organizations (HMOs) and preferred provider organizations (PPOs) are the main plans that restrict your choices. They keep costs down because they negotiate lower rates with selected providers.

HMOs and PPOs are more similar than they are different. The main difference is that PPOs still pay the majority of your expenses if you use a provider outside their approved list. If you do this with an HMO, you typically won't be covered at all.

Plans that allow you to use any health care provider you want are becoming less common and more expensive in most areas. If you have your heart set on particular physicians or hospitals, find out which health insurance plans they accept as payment. Ask yourself whether the extra cost of the open-choice plan is worth being able to use their services should particular providers not be part of a restricted-choice plan. Also be aware that some plans allow you to go outside their network of providers as long as you pay a portion of the incurred medical costs. If you're interested in being able to use alternative types of providers such as acupuncturists, find out whether the plans that you're considering cover these services.

Don't be deterred from HMO and PPO plans by stories of how hard getting an appointment with a doctor is or other logistical hassles. This can happen in plans with open choice, too — some doctors are always running late or are overbooked. It is also a myth that doctors who can't get patients on their own are the only ones who sign up with restricted-choice plans. Although HMO and PPO plans do offer less choice of providers, customer surveys show that customer satisfaction with these plans is as high as in plans that offer more choice.

Lifetime maximum benefits

Health insurance plans specify the maximum total benefits that they'll pay over the course of your time insured by their plan. Although a million dollars may be more money than you could ever imagine being spent on yourself, that's the minimally acceptable level of total benefits. With the cost of health care today, you can blow through that in short order if you develop major health problems. Ideally, choose a plan that has no maximum or that has a maximum of at least several million dollars.

Deductibles and copayments

To reduce your health insurance premiums, choose a plan with the highest deductible and copayment that you can afford. As with other insurance policies, the more you are willing to share in the payment of your claims, the less you will have to pay in premiums. Most policies have annual deductible options, such as $250, $500, $1,000, and so on, as well as copayment options, typically 20 percent or so.

When choosing a copayment percentage, don't let your imagination run wild and unnecessarily scare you. A 20-percent copayment does not mean that you would have to come up with $20,000 for a $100,000 claim. Insurance plans generally set a maximum out-of-pocket limit on your annual copayments (usually around $1,000); the company will cover 100 percent of any medical expenses that go over that cap.

With insurance provided by your employer, consider plans with low out-of-pocket expenses if you know you have health problems. Being part of a group, they won't increase your individual rates just because you're filing more claims.

Most HMO plans don't have deductible and copayment options. Most just charge a set amount — $5 to $25 — for a physician's office visit.

Saving on your taxes when spending on health care

If you expect to have out-of-pocket medical expenses, find out whether your employer offers a flexible spending or health care reimbursement account. These accounts enable you to pay for uncovered medical expenses with pretax dollars. If, for example, you're in a combined 35-percent federal and state income tax bracket, these accounts allow you to pay for needed health care at a 35-percent discount. In addition to your out-of-pocket health care costs, these accounts can be used to pay for vision and dental care.

Be forewarned of some major stumbling blocks to saving through medical reimbursement accounts. First, you need to elect to save money from your paycheck prior to the beginning of each plan year. The only exception is at the time of a "life change" such as a family member's death, marriage, spouse's job change, divorce, or birth of a child. You also need to use the money within the year saved because these accounts contain a "use or lose it" feature.

Effective 1997, the federal government authorized what is called a Medical Savings Account (MSA) for the self-employed and for people who work for small firms (50 or fewer employees). To qualify, you must have a high-deductible individual health insurance policy; then you can put money earmarked for medical expenses into an investment account that offers the tax benefits — deductible contributions and tax-deferred compounding — of a retirement account (see Chapter 3). And, unlike a flexible spending account, you don't have to deplete an MSA by the end of the year: Money can compound tax-deferred inside the MSA for years.

Because MSAs are still in their infancy, the best investment companies mentioned in this book are holding back from offering them. Stay tuned for future developments.

Another way that you may be able to save on taxes is if you have a substantial amount of health care expenditures in a year. You can deduct medical and dental expenses as an itemized deduction on Schedule A to the extent that they exceed 7.5 percent of your adjusted gross income (refer to Chapter 7). Unless you're a low income earner, you would need to have substantial expenses, usually caused by an accident or major illness, to take advantage of this tax break.

Guaranteed renewable

You want a health insurance plan that keeps renewing your coverage without your needing to prove continued good health.

Buying health insurance

You can buy many health plans through agents and some directly from the insurer. When it's sold both ways, buying through an agent usually won't cost more.

If you're self-employed or work for a small employer that doesn't offer health insurance as a benefit, get proposals from Blue Cross, Blue Shield, Kaiser, or other large health insurers in your area. Also check with professional or other associations that you belong to. A competent independent insurance agent who specializes in health insurance can help find insurers willing to offer you coverage.

Health insurance agents have a conflict of interest common to all financial salespeople working on commission: The higher the premium plan they sell you, the bigger the commission they earn. So an agent may try to steer you into higher-cost plans and not suggest some of the strategies discussed in the previous section to reduce your cost of coverage.

If you're denied insurance

When you try to enroll in a particular health insurance plan, you may be turned down because of health problems you currently have or previously had. Your *medical information file* (the medical equivalent of a credit report) may contain information explaining why you were turned down. (Read Chapter 15 to learn about steps you can take if you're denied coverage.)

If you have a so-called *preexisting condition* (current or prior medical problems), you have several options to pursue to secure health insurance:

- ✔ **Try health insurance plans that don't "discriminate."** A few plans — typically Blue Cross, Blue Shield, and some HMO plans such as Kaiser Permanente — will sometimes take you regardless of your condition.

- ✔ **Find a job with an employer whose health insurer doesn't require a medical exam.** Of course, this shouldn't be your only reason for seeking new employment, but it can be an important factor. Likewise, if you're married, you may be able to get into an employer group plan if your spouse takes a new job.

- ✔ **Find out whether your state offers a plan.** A number of states maintain pools that insure people with preexisting conditions who are unable to find coverage elsewhere. Try contacting your state's insurance department (see the state government section of your phone book) to see if your state offers such plans. I suppose, in a drastic situation, if your state doesn't offer one of these plans, you could move to a nearby state that does.

Dealing with medical claims headaches

If you sign up for a health plan that has deductibles and copayments, be sure to review the benefits statements that your insurer sends you. Errors often pop up on these statements and in the claims filing process. Not surprisingly, the errors are rarely in your favor and are usually at your expense.

Be sure that your insurer has kept accurate track of your contributions toward meeting your plan's annual deductible and maximum out-of-pocket charges. Also, don't pay any health care providers who send you bills until you've received proper notification from the insurance company detailing what you are obligated to pay those providers according to the terms of your plan. Because most insurance companies have negotiated discounted fee schedules with health care providers, the amount that a provider bills you is often higher than the amount they are legally due as per the terms of their contract with your insurer. Your insurer's benefit statement should detail what is the approved and negotiated rate.

And don't let providers try to bully you into paying them the difference between what they've billed you for and what the insurer says they are due. Providers are only due what discounted fees they've agreed to with your insurer.

Haggling with your health insurer is a real pain, and it usually happens after you have racked up significant medical expenses and still may not be feeling well. But if you don't stay on top of your insurer, you can end up paying thousands of dollars in overpayments.

If you're overwhelmed with an avalanche of claims and benefits statements, you might consider using a health insurance claims processing service. You can get a referral to firms in your area that are engaged in this line of work by contacting the Alliance of Claims Assistance Professionals (630-588-1260; www.claims.org).

Retiree medical care insurance

Medicare, the government-run health insurance plan for the elderly, is a two-part major medical plan. Enrollment in Part A (hospital expenses) is automatic. Part B, which covers physician and other charges including home health care coverage, is optional. Supplemental insurance policies might be of interest to help you pay for those costs that Medicare doesn't.

Medigap insurance

Medigap coverage generally pays the deductibles and copayments that Medicare charges. For the first 60 days of a hospitalization, you'll pay $768 out of your own pocket. If you have an unusually long continuous hospitalization, you'll pay $192 per day for the 61st through 90th day, $384 per day for the 91st through 150th day, and all costs beyond 150 days. Clearly, if you stay in a hospital for many months, your out-of-pocket expenses could escalate.

However, the longest hospitalizations tend to not last past a couple of months. Also note that Medicare's hospitalization benefits refresh once a person is out of the hospital for 60 consecutive days.

If the costs from a long hospital stay would be a financial catastrophe for you and if you're unable to pay for the deductibles and copayments because your income is low, Medicaid, the state-run medical insurance program for low-income people, may help pay your bills. Alternatively, Medigap insurance can help close the gap.

Check with your physician(s) to see that he or she does not charge a fee higher than that listed on Medicare's fee schedule. If so, you should consider going to another physician if you can't afford the fee or want to save yourself some money. Medicare often pays only 80 percent of the physician charges that the program allows on its fee schedule. Some physicians charge higher fees than those allowed by Medicare; others don't.

The biggest fear and reason that elderly people consider extra health insurance is that Medicare only pays for the first 100 days in a skilled nursing facility. Anything over that is your responsibility. But Medigap policies also don't address this issue.

Nursing-home insurance

Insurance agents, eager to earn a hefty commission from selling you a policy, will tell you that *nursing-home insurance* is the solution to your concerns about an extended stay in a nursing home. Don't get your hopes up. Policies are complicated and filled with all sorts of exclusions and limitations. On top of all that, they're expensive, too.

The decision to purchase nursing-home insurance is a trade-off. Do you want to pay thousands of dollars annually from age 60 onward to guard against the possibility of a long-term nursing-home stay? If you live into or past your mid-80s, you could pay more than $50,000 to $100,000 or more on a nursing-home policy (not to mention the lost investment earnings on these insurance premiums).

Those who end up in a nursing home for years on end might come out ahead financially buying nursing-home insurance. The majority of people are in homes less than a year, though, because they either pass away or move out.

Medicare pays for the bulk of the first 100 days' cost of nursing-home stays as long as certain conditions are satisfied. Medicare pays for all basic services (telephone, television, and private room charges excluded) for the first 20 days and then requires $96 per day copayment for the next 80 days. First, the nursing-home stay must follow a hospitalization within 30 days, and the nursing-home stay must be for the same medical condition that caused the hospitalization. Once discharged from a nursing home, you can qualify for an additional 100-day benefit period if you have not been hospitalized or in a nursing home the prior 60 days.

If you have relatives or a spouse who would probably care for you in the event of a major illness, you should definitely *not* waste your money on nursing-home insurance. Also bypass this coverage if you have and don't mind using retirement assets to help pay nursing-home costs.

Even if you do deplete your assets, remember that you have a backup: *Medicaid* (state-provided medical insurance) can pick up the cost if you can't. You should, however, be aware of a number of potential drawbacks to getting coverage for nursing-home stays under Medicaid:

- ✓ **Medicaid patients are at the bottom of the priority list.** Most nursing homes are interested in the bottom line, so those patients who bring in the least revenue — namely Medicaid patients — get lowest priority on nursing-home waiting lists.

- ✓ **Some nursing homes don't take Medicaid patients.** Check with your preferred nursing homes in your area to see if they accept Medicaid.

- ✓ **The states might squeeze Medicaid further.** What medical conditions warrant coverage is up to your state. With the budget noose tightening in some states, some are disallowing certain types of coverage: for example, mental problems for elderly people who are otherwise in good physical health. Also, the federal government finances part of Medicaid, and the federal trend these days is to give states blocks of money and let them decide what they want to do with it. In such an environment, more states might restrict Medicaid access.

If you're concerned about having your stash of money wiped out by an extended nursing-home stay and you strongly desire to pass money onto family or a favorite charity, you could start giving it away while you're still healthy. (If you're already in poor health, legal experts can do Medicaid planning, which is strategizing to preserve your assets and keep them from being used to pay nursing-home costs.)

Consider buying nursing-home insurance if you want to retain and protect your assets and it gives you peace of mind to know that a long-term nursing-home stay is covered. But do your homework. Comparison-shop policies and be sure to buy a policy that pays benefits for the long-term. A year's worth or even a few years of benefits won't protect your assets if your stay lasts longer. Also be sure to get a policy that adjusts the daily benefit amount for increases in the cost of living. Watch out for policies that restrict benefits to limited types of facilities and settings. Get a policy that covers care in your home or other settings if you don't need to be in a high-cost nursing home and one that does not require prior hospitalization for benefits to kick in.

You might also consider retirement communities if you're willing to live as a younger retiree in such a setting. After paying an entrance fee, you pay a monthly fee, which usually covers your rent, care, and meals. Be sure that any such facility you're considering guarantees care for life and accepts Medicaid in case you deplete your assets.

The Most Overlooked Form of Insurance

You buy health insurance to cover large medical expenses, disability insurance to replace your income in the event of a long-term disability, and perhaps life insurance to provide money to those dependent on your income in the event of your death. Many people buy all the right kinds of personal insurance, spending a small fortune over the course of their lives in the process. Yet they overlook the obvious, virtually free protection: taking care of themselves.

If you work all day at a desk and use many of life's modern conveniences, you could end up being the Great American Couch Potato. Odds are that you've heard of most of these forms of "life insurance," but if you're still on the couch, the advice apparently didn't sink in.

So, for you sofa spuds, here are seven healthful tips:

- Don't smoke.
- Drink alcohol in moderation, if you drink at all.
- Get plenty of rest.
- Exercise regularly.
- Eat healthfully (refer to Chapter 6 for diet tips that improve your health and save you money).
- Get regular health care checkups to detect medical, dental, and vision problems.
- Take time to smell the roses.

Chapter 17

Insuring Your Assets

●●

In This Chapter

▶ Homeowner's/renter's insurance

▶ Automobile insurance

▶ Planning your estate

●●

*I*n Chapter 16, I discuss the importance of protecting your future income from the possibilities of disability, death, or large, unexpected medical expenses. But you also need to insure major assets that you have acquired in the past: your home, your car, and your personal property.

You need to protect some of these assets for two reasons:

✔ **Your assets are valuable.** If you were to suffer a loss, replacing the assets with money out of your own pocket could be a financial catastrophe.

✔ **A lawsuit could drain your finances.** This reason is less well-known. If someone were injured or killed in your home or because of your car, a lawsuit could be even more financially devastating than an outright loss of the asset.

Homeowner's/Renter's Insurance

When you buy a home, most lenders require that you purchase homeowner's insurance. But even if they don't, you are wise to do so because your home and the personal property within it are worth a great deal and would cost a bundle to replace.

As a renter, damage to the building in which you live is not your financial concern, but you still have personal property that you may want to insure. And there's also the possibility, albeit remote, that you could be sued by someone who is injured in your rental.

When shopping for a homeowner's or renter's policy, you should consider the important features that I cover in this section.

Dwelling coverage: The cost to rebuild

How much would you have to spend to *rebuild* your home if you lost it completely in a fire, an attack of locusts, or whatever? The cost to rebuild should be based on the size (square footage) of your home. Neither the purchase price nor the size of your mortgage has anything to do with how much *dwelling coverage* you need.

If you're a renter, rejoice that you don't need this coverage. If you're a condominium owner, find out whether the coverage that the condo association has bought for the entire building is sufficient.

Be sure that your homeowner's policy includes a *guaranteed replacement cost* provision. This useful feature ensures that the insurance company will rebuild the home even if the cost of construction is more than the policy coverage. If the insurance company underestimates your dwelling coverage, then *it* has to make up the difference.

Unfortunately, insurers define guaranteed replacement cost differently. Some companies pay for the full replacement cost of the home, no matter how much it ends up costing. Other insurers set limits. For example, some insurers may only pay up to 25 percent more than the dwelling coverage on your policy. Ask your insurer how it defines guaranteed replacement cost.

If you have an older property that has many costly-to-replace features that do not meet building codes, consider buying a rider that pays for code upgrades. This covers the cost of rebuilding your home to comply with building codes that are more stringent today than when your home was built. Ask your insurance company what your basic policy covers and what it doesn't cover. Some companies include a certain amount (for example, 10 percent of your dwelling coverage) for code upgrades in the base policy.

Personal property coverage

On a homeowner's policy, the amount of personal property coverage is typically derived from the amount of dwelling coverage you carry. Generally, you get personal property coverage of 50 to 75 percent of the dwelling coverage. This is usually more than enough.

I am not a fan of riders that you can buy to cover jewelry, computers, furs, and other somewhat costly items that may not be fully covered by typical homeowner's policies. Ask yourself if your out-of-pocket expense from the loss of such items would constitute a financial catastrophe. Unless you have tens of thousands of dollars worth of jewelry or computer equipment, for example, skip such riders.

Some policies come with *replacement cost guarantees,* which pay you for the cost to replace an item. This payment can be considerably more than what a used item was worth before it was damaged or stolen. When this feature is not part of the standard policy sold by your insurer, you may want to purchase it as a rider, if available.

As a renter or condominium owner, you need to choose a dollar amount of the personal property that you want covered. Tally it up instead of guessing — the total cost of replacing all your personal property may surprise you.

Make a list — or even better, take pictures or make a video — of your belongings with an estimate of what they're worth. Keep this list updated; you'll need it if you have to file a claim. Keeping receipts for major purchases may also help your case. No matter how you document your belongings, don't forget to keep the documentation somewhere besides your home — otherwise, it could be destroyed along with the rest of your house in a fire or other disaster.

Liability insurance

Liability insurance protects you financially against lawsuits arising from bad things that happen to others on your property, including wounds inflicted by the family pit bull or terrible tabby (of course, you should keep Bruno restrained during guests' visits, even those from your in-laws). At a minimum, get enough insurance to cover your financial assets — covering two times your assets is better. Buying extra coverage is inexpensive and well worth the cost.

The probabilities of being sued are low, but if you *are* sued and lose, you could owe big bucks. If you have substantial assets to protect, you might consider an umbrella or excess liability policy (which I discuss later in this chapter).

Liability protection is one of the side benefits of purchasing a renter's policy — you protect your personal property as well as insure against lawsuits. (But don't be reckless with your banana peels if you get liability insurance!)

Flood and earthquake insurance

As I recommend in Chapter 15, purchase the broadest possible coverage when buying any type of insurance. The problem with homeowner's insurance is that it is not comprehensive enough — it doesn't typically cover losses due to earthquakes and floods. You must buy such disaster coverage piecemeal.

If an earthquake or flood struck your area and your home was destroyed, you would be out tens, if not hundreds, of thousands of dollars without proper coverage. Yet, many people don't carry these important coverages, often due to misconceptions:

- ✔ **"Not in my neighborhood."** Many people mistakenly believe that earthquakes, for example, occur only in California. I wish this were true for those of you who live in the other 49 states, but it's not. In fact, one of the strongest earthquakes in the last century happened in the Midwest, and known (though not very active) fault lines lie along the East coast. The cost of earthquake coverage is based on insurance companies' assessment of the risk of your area and property type, so you shouldn't decide whether to buy insurance based on how small you think the risk is. The risk is already built into the price.

  An estimated 20,000 communities around the country face potential flood damage. Like earthquakes, floods are not a covered risk in standard homeowner's policies, so you need to purchase a flood insurance rider. Check with your current homeowner's insurer or with those recommended in this chapter. The federal government flood insurance program (800-638-6620; www.fema.gov/nfip) provides background information on flood insurance policies.

- ✔ **"The government will bail me out."** The vast majority of government financial assistance is through low-interest loans. Loans, unfortunately, need to be repaid, and the money comes out of your pocket.

- ✔ **"In a major disaster, insurers would go bankrupt anyway."** This is highly unlikely given the reserves that insurers are required to keep and the fact that the insurance companies *reinsure* — that is, they buy insurance to back up the policies they write.

The only homeowners at risk who might consider not buying earthquake or flood coverage are people who have little equity in their property and who are willing to walk away from the property and the mortgage in the event of a major quake or flood. Keep in mind that doing so damages your credit report because you will have essentially defaulted on your loan.

You may be able to pay for much of the cost of earthquake or flood insurance by raising the deductibles on the main part of your homeowner's/renter's insurance and other insurance policies, such as those for autos. You can more easily afford the smaller claims, not the big ones. If you think flood or earthquake insurance is too costly, compare those costs with the costs you will incur to completely replace your home and personal property. Buy this insurance if you live in an area that has a chance of being affected by these catastrophes. To help keep the cost of earthquake insurance down, consider taking a 10 percent deductible. Most insurers offer deductibles of 5 or 10 percent of the cost to rebuild your home. Ten percent of the rebuilding cost is a good chunk of money. But what you want to insure against is losing the other 90 percent.

Deductibles

As I discuss in Chapter 15, the point of insurance is to protect against catastrophic losses, not the little losses. By taking the highest deductibles you're comfortable with, you'll save on insurance premiums year after year, and you won't have to go through the hassle of filing small claims.

Special discounts

You may qualify for special discounts. Companies and agents that sell homeowner's and renter's insurance don't always check to see if you're eligible for discounts. After all, the more you spend on policy premiums, the more money they make! If your property has a security system, if you are older, or if you have other policies with the same insurer, you may qualify for a lower rate. Don't forget to ask.

Where to buy homeowner's or renter's insurance

Each insurance company prices its homeowner's and renter's policies based on its own criteria. So the lowest-cost company for your friend's property might not be so for yours. You have to shop around at several companies to find the best rates. The following is a list of companies that historically offer lower-cost policies for most people and that have decent track records with customer satisfaction and payment of claims:

- **Amica.** Call the company (800-242-6422). Although Amica does have good customer satisfaction, in some areas, the company's prices are high.

- **Erie Insurance.** This company does business primarily in the Midwest and Mid-Atlantic. Check your local phone directory for agents or call (800-458-0811) for a referral to a local agent.

- **GEICO.** Call the company (800-841-3000).

- **Liberty Mutual.** Check your local phone directory for agents.

- **Nationwide Mutual.** Check your local phone directory for agents.

- **State Farm.** Check your local phone directory for agents.

- **USAA.** This company provides insurance for military officers and their family members. Call the company for specifics to see if you qualify (800-531-8080).

Don't worry that some of these companies require you to call an 800 number for a price quote. This doesn't mean they are unreachable. This process saves you money because these insurers don't have to pay commissions to local agents hawking their policies. These companies have local claims representatives to help you if and when you do have a claim.

A number of the previously named companies sell other types of insurance (for example, life insurance) that are not as competitively priced. Be sure to check out the relevant sections in this book for the best places to buy these other coverages if you need them.

You may have access to more specific information for your state. Some state insurance departments conduct surveys of insurers' prices and tabulate complaints received. Look up your state's department of insurance phone number in the government section of your local phone directory or visit the National Association of Insurance Commissioner's web site at `www.naic.org/consumer/state/usamap.htm` to find links to each state's department of insurance site.

Auto Insurance

Over the course of your life, you'll probably spend tens of thousands of dollars on auto insurance. Much of the money that people spend on auto insurance is not spent where it is most needed. In other cases, it is simply wasted. You should look for the following important features when searching for an auto insurance policy.

Bodily injury/property damage liability

As with homeowner's liability insurance, auto liability insurance provides insurance against lawsuits. Especially in a car, accidents happen. Make sure that you have enough bodily injury liability insurance to cover your assets. (Coverage of double your assets is preferable.)

If you are just beginning to accumulate assets, do not mistakenly assume that you do not need liability protection. Many states require a minimum amount — insurers should be able to fill you in on the details for your state. Also, don't forget that your future earnings, which are an "asset," can be garnished in a lawsuit.

Property damage liability insurance covers damage done by your car to other people's cars and property. The amount of property damage liability coverage in an auto insurance policy is usually determined as a consequence of the bodily injury amount selected. $50,000 is a good minimum to start with.

Coping with teen drivers

If you have a teenage driver in your household, in addition to worrying a lot more, you are going to be spending a lot more on auto insurance. Try to keep your teenager out of your car as long as possible. It's the best advice I can offer.

If you allow your teenager to drive, you can take a number of steps to avoid spending all of your take-home pay on auto insurance bills:

✔ Make sure that your teen does well in school. Some insurers offer discounts if your child is a high-academic achiever and has successfully completed a nonrequired driver's education class.

✔ Get price quotes from several insurers to see how adding your teen driver to your policy affects the cost.

✔ Have your teenager share in the costs of using the car. If you pay all the insurance, gas, oil changing, and maintenance bills, your teenager won't value the privilege of using your "free" car.

Of course, letting teens drive shouldn't just be about keeping your insurance bills to a minimum. Auto accidents are the number one cause of death for teens. So, before you let your teen drive, be sure to educate him about the big risks of driving and the importance of not riding in a car driven by someone who is intoxicated. Also be sure that your teens drive in safe cars.

Uninsured or underinsured motorist liability

When you are in an accident with another motorist and he doesn't carry his own liability protection or doesn't carry enough, *uninsured or underinsured motorist liability coverage* allows you to collect for lost wages, medical expenses, and pain and suffering incurred in the accident.

Should you already have comprehensive health and long-term disability insurance, then uninsured or underinsured motorist liability coverage is largely redundant. You do give up the ability to sue for general pain and suffering if you drop this coverage and to insure passengers in your car who may lack adequate medical and disability coverage.

To provide a death benefit to those financially dependent on you in the event of a fatal auto accident, buy term life insurance (see Chapter 16).

Deductibles

To keep your auto insurance premiums down and to eliminate the need to file small claims, take the highest deductibles you are comfortable with (most people should consider $500 to $1,000). On an auto policy, two deductibles exist: *collision* and *comprehensive*. Collision applies to claims arising from collisions (note that you can generally bypass collision coverage when you rent a car if you have collision coverage on your own policy). Comprehensive applies to other claims for damages not caused by collision (for example, a window broken by vandals).

As your car ages and is worth less, you can eventually eliminate your comprehensive and collision coverages altogether. The point at which you do this is up to you. Remember that the purpose of insurance is to compensate you for losses that are financially catastrophic to you. For some people, this amount may be as high as $5,000 or more — others would choose $1,000 as their threshold point. Insurers won't pay more than the book value of your car, regardless of what it costs to repair or replace it.

Special discounts

You may be eligible for special discounts on auto insurance. Don't forget to tell your agent or insurer if your car has a security alarm, air bags, or antilock brakes. If you're older or have other policies or cars insured with the same insurer, you may also qualify for discounts. And make sure that you're given appropriate "good driver" discounts if you've been accident- and ticket-free in recent years.

And here's another idea: *Before* you buy your next car, call insurers and ask for insurance quotes for the different models that you're considering. The cost of insuring a car should factor into your decision as to which car you buy because the insurance costs will be a major portion of your car's ongoing operating expenses.

Little-stuff coverage to skip

Auto insurers have dreamed up all sorts of riders, such as towing and rental car reimbursement. On the surface, these riders appear to be inexpensive. But the riders are expensive given the little that you'd collect from a claim plus the hassle of filing.

Riders that waive the deductible under certain circumstances make no sense, either. The point of the deductible is to reduce your policy cost and the hassle of filing small claims.

Medical payments coverage typically pays a few thousand dollars for medical expenses. If you and your passengers carry major medical insurance coverage, this rider isn't really necessary. Besides, a few thousand dollars of medical coverage doesn't protect you against catastrophic expenses.

Overlooked auto insurance: safe driving

A pipe bomb explodes in a crowded park and kills a person. An airplane crashes and several dozen people die.

Such tragic events are well-covered by our media, but the number of deaths that make the front pages of our newspapers pales in comparison to the approximately 40,000 people who die on America's roads every year.

I'm not suggesting that our national media should start reporting every automobile fatality. Even 24 hours of daily CNN coverage probably could not keep up with all the accidents on our roads. But the real story with auto fatalities lies not in the who, what, and where of specific accidents but in the why. When we ask that question, we see how many of them are preventable.

No matter what kind of car you drive, you can and should drive safely. Stay within the speed limits and don't drive while intoxicated or tired, or in adverse weather conditions. Wear your seat belt — a U.S. Department of Transportation study found that 60 percent of auto passengers killed were not wearing their seat belts. And don't try to talk on your cell phone and write notes on a pad of paper attached to your dashboard while balancing your coffee cup between your legs!

You can also greatly reduce your risk of dying in an accident by driving a safe car. You don't need to spend buckets of money to get a car with airbags, reinforced sides, front and rear-impact resistance, and good visibility. The *Consumer Reports* annual auto buying guide has lots of good information on individual car model safety.

Roadside assistance, towing, and rental car reimbursement coverage will only pay small dollar amounts and aren't worth buying. In fact, if you belong to an automobile club, you may already have some of these coverages.

Where to buy auto insurance

You can use the same list presented earlier in this chapter for homeowner's insurers to obtain quotes for auto insurance. In addition, contact Progressive at 800-288-6776; or if you live in the great state of California, consider checking with Mercury Insurance (check your local phone directory for agents).

Umbrella Insurance

Umbrella or *excess liability* insurance is additional liability insurance that is added on top of the liability protection on your home and car(s). If you are fairly affluent and have, for example, $700,000 in assets, you can buy a one-million-dollar umbrella liability policy for around $200 per year to add to the $300,000 liability insurance that you have on your home and car. This is a small cost for big protection. Each year, thousands of people suffer lawsuits of more than one million dollars related to their cars and homes.

Investment insurance

Insurance companies do not sell policies that protect the value of your investments. But you can shield your portfolio from many of the dangers of a fickle market through diversification.

If all of your money is invested in bank accounts or bonds, you're exposed to the risks of inflation, which can erode your money's purchasing power. Conversely, if the bulk of your money is invested in one high-risk stock, your financial future could go up in smoke if that stock explodes.

Chapter 9 discusses the benefits of diversification and how to choose investments that do well under different conditions. Chapter 10 discusses why mutual funds are powerful investment vehicles that make diversification easy and cost-effective.

Umbrella or excess liability insurance is generally sold in increments of one million dollars. So how do you decide how much you need if you have a lot of assets? As I've said with other insurance coverages, you should have at least enough liability insurance to protect your assets and preferably enough to cover twice the value of those assets.

Purchasing umbrella or excess liability insurance through your existing homeowner's or auto insurance company is usually necessary.

Estate Planning

Estate planning is the process of determining what will happen to your assets after you die. Thinking about this in the context of insurance may seem a bit odd. But the time and cost of various estate-planning maneuvers is really nothing more than buying insurance: You are insuring that after you die, everything will be taken care of as you wish and that taxes will be minimized. Thinking about it in this way can help you to better evaluate whether certain options make sense at particular points in your life.

Depending upon your circumstances, you may eventually want to contact an attorney who specializes in estate-planning matters. However, educating yourself first about the different options is worth your time. More than a few attorneys have their own agendas (increased fees) about what you should do, so be careful. And most of the estate-planning strategies that you're likely to benefit from do not require hiring an attorney.

Wills, living wills, and medical powers of attorney

When you have children who are minors (dependent), a *will* is a necessity. A will names the guardian to whom you entrust your children if both you and your spouse die. Should you and your spouse both die without a will (called *intestate*), the state (courts and social-service agencies) decides who will raise your children. Therefore, even if you cannot decide at this time who would raise your children, you should *at least* appoint a trusted guardian who could decide for you.

A will still makes good sense even if you don't have kids because it gives instructions on how to handle and distribute all your worldly possessions. When you die without a will, your state decides how to distribute your money and other property, according to state law. Therefore, your friends, more-distant relatives, and favorite charities will probably receive nothing. Without any living relatives, your money could go to the state government!

And without a will, your heirs are legally powerless, and the state may appoint an administrator to supervise the distribution of your assets at a fee of around 5 percent of your estate. A bond typically must also be posted at a cost of several hundred dollars.

Living wills and a medical power of attorney are useful additions to a standard will. A *living will* tells your doctor what, if any, life-support measures you would prefer or not want. A *medical power of attorney* grants authority to someone you trust to make decisions with a physician regarding your medical care options.

The simplest and least costly way to prepare a will, a living will, and a medical power of attorney is to use the high-quality, user-friendly software packages that I recommend in Chapter 19. Be sure to give copies of these documents to the guardians and executors named in the documents.

You don't need an attorney to make a legal will. Most attorneys, in fact, prepare wills and living trusts using software packages! What makes a will *valid* is that it is witnessed by three people.

If doing it all yourself seems overwhelming, another option (besides hiring an attorney) is to use a paralegal typing service to help you prepare the documents. These services generally charge 50 percent or less of what an attorney charges.

Probate and living trusts

Because of our quirky legal system, even if you have a will, some or all of your assets must go through a court process known as probate. *Probate* is the legal process for administering and implementing the directions in a will. Property and assets that are owned in joint tenancy or inside retirement accounts, such as IRAs or 401(k)s, generally pass to heirs without having to go through probate. Most other assets pass through probate.

A *living trust* effectively transfers assets into a trust. You control those assets and can revoke the trust whenever you desire. The advantage of a living trust is that upon your death, assets can pass directly to your beneficiaries without going through probate. Probate can be a lengthy, expensive hassle for your heirs — with legal fees tallying around 5 to 7 percent of the value of the estate. In addition, your assets become a matter of public record as a result of probate.

Living trusts are likely to be of greatest value to people who meet the following criteria:

- ✔ Age 60 and older
- ✔ Single
- ✔ Assets worth more than $100,000 that must pass through probate (including real estate, nonretirement accounts, and small business)

As with a will, you do *not* need an attorney to establish a legal and valid living trust. (See my software recommendations in Chapter 19 and consider the paralegal services that I mention in the previous section on wills.) Attorney fees to establish a living trust can range from $700 to $2,000. A competent attorney who charges reasonable fees is of greatest value to people with large estates (see the next section) who do not have the time, desire, and expertise to maximize the value derived from estate planning.

Note: Living trusts keep assets out of probate but have nothing to do with minimizing estate or inheritance taxes.

Estate planning to minimize estate taxes

For tax year 2000, an individual can pass $675,000 to beneficiaries without federal estate taxes. (This exclusion will continue increasing until it hits $1,000,000 in 2006.) Whether or not you will have an estate tax "problem" depends on several issues.

First and most important is how much of your assets you will use up during your life. This depends on how much your assets grow over time, as well as how rapidly you spend money. During retirement, you will (hopefully) be utilizing your money.

I've seen too many affluent individuals worrying about estate taxes on their money throughout their retirements. If your intention is to leave your money to your children, grandchildren, or a charity, why not start giving while you're still alive so that you can enjoy the act? You can give $10,000 annually to each of your beneficiaries, *tax-free*. By giving away money, you reduce your estate and, therefore, the estate taxes owed on it.

In addition to gifting, a number of trusts allow you to minimize estate taxes. For example, if you're married, both you and your spouse can each pass on up to $675,000 to your heirs (for a total of $1,350,000), free of federal estate taxes. This can be accomplished by your each establishing a *bypass trust*. Upon the death of the first spouse, assets held in his or her name go into the bypass trust, which effectively removes those assets from the remaining spouse's taxable estate.

Buying cash value life insurance is another estate planning tool but one which, unfortunately, is overused. People who sell cash value insurance — that is, insurance salespeople and others masquerading as financial planners — too often advocate life insurance as the one and only way to reduce estate taxes. Other methods are superior in most cases because they don't require wasting money on life insurance.

Small-business owners whose businesses are worth $1,000,000 or more may want to consider cash value life insurance under specialized circumstances. If you lack the necessary additional assets to pay expected estate taxes and you don't want your beneficiaries to be forced to sell the business, you can buy cash value life insurance to pay expected estate taxes.

To learn more about how to reduce your estate (and other) taxes, pick up a copy of the latest edition of *Taxes For Dummies* (IDG Books Worldwide, Inc.), which I co-wrote.

Part V
Where to Go for More Help

The 5th Wave   By Rich Tennant

"You may want to talk to Phil—he's one of our more aggressive financial planners."

In this part . . .

1 help you sift through the morass of financial resources competing for your attention and dollars. Many people who call themselves financial planners claim to be able to make you rich, but I show you how you may end up poorer if you don't choose an advisor wisely. I also cover software and internet resources and name the best. Finally, I discuss how to benefit from the financial coverage in print and on the air while sidestepping problematic advice in those media.

Chapter 18

Financial Planners

• •

In This Chapter

▶ Your financial management options

▶ Why it's hard to find good financial help

▶ Deciding whether you need help and how to find it if you do

▶ Financial planners' conflicts of interest

▶ Questions to ask financial planners you may hire

• •

*"T*he financial planning business has two problems. One is credibility, and the other is conflict of interest."

— Fortune *magazine*

"When I was a child, my father told me to pick a field where you only need to be mediocre to be great. I chose personal financial planning."

— *financial planner Jim Schwartz, as quoted in* The Wall Street Journal

Hiring a competent, ethical, and unbiased financial planner or advisor to help you make and implement financial decisions *can* be money well spent. But if you pick a poor advisor or someone who really isn't a financial planner but a salesperson in disguise, things could get worse instead of better. So before we talk about the different types of help to hire, let's take a little journey with Alice to give you an idea of what you're up against in the land of financial planners.

Alice in Financial-Planner Land

Alice is a client who once landed on my doorstep. She struck out the first four times she sought financial help. Her story illustrates many of the pitfalls in finding a good financial planner.

Alice's adventures

First, on the recommendation of her accountant, Alice called a *financial consultant,* who was a *certified financial planner* (CFP) at a well-known investment (brokerage) firm. Although Alice explained that she wanted a conservative investment, the broker sold her a mutual fund that, unbeknowst to Alice, primarily held *aggressive growth* (volatile) stocks.

After buying the fund and getting her first account statement a few days later, Alice noticed that there were several thousand dollars less in the fund than she had invested. The broker had told her he earned a 4-percent commission but assured her that she need not concern herself with it because the fund paid him and it wouldn't affect her investment.

After a little investigation, Alice discovered that the fund had, in fact, paid the broker out of her investment — a hefty 6.5-percent commission. Thus, the broker had not only lied about where the commission dollars came from (all such commissions come from the investors' money), but he had also understated the size of his commission.

Understandably steamed, Alice called the Securities and Exchange Commission (SEC), and after she jumped through many hoops, the brokerage firm coughed up nearly $2,000 for the broker's fib about the commission amount.

Thinking that perhaps men and women simply don't communicate well, Alice next turned to a female financial planner on the recommendation of a friend. The planner told Alice: "Women need to stick together." Then she promptly tried to sell Alice a limited partnership that, the planner said, was *sure* to return upward of 20 to 40 percent per year.

Alice took a gander at the *prospectus* — a delightfully long document written by attorneys — and saw in black and white on page 2 that the partnership paid the selling broker a 10 percent sales commission (which, she now knew, would be deducted from her investment).

Because Alice is a conscientious investor, she did more research in financial books and magazines and learned that limited partnerships are also handicapped by high, ongoing management fees. Alice did not return the dozen or so follow-up calls ("to see how you are doing") from her "sister" financial planner and fortunately passed on the partnership.

Wanting to learn more before her next attempt to get help, Alice enrolled in an "adult education class" at a local college. Alice, a student eager to learn, attended all the classes but soon felt only more confused. The world of finance and investments, her teacher said, is *very, very complicated.* Unless, of course, you're a financial expert.

The teacher, a "certified financial planner," told the class that he was just such an expert. He offered a free, one-hour consultation to all his students at the end of his "course." During her free session, Alice was told that she should invest in an *annuity*. Investigation, however, revealed (you guessed it) high sales commissions and management fees.

Alice was also uncomfortable because planner number three hadn't inquired about other aspects of her situation and seemed intent only on selling her an annuity. Annuities did not make sense for her, she later learned, because she was nearly retired and in a low tax bracket.

At this point, most people probably would have bought a good financial book or put their money in a mattress or the next best place — their local bank — but Alice really wanted to talk to someone about her money issues and ideas.

After listening to a financial planner on a radio call-in program, Alice had the planner mail his background materials to her. In addition to a certified financial-planning credential, *this* planner had a seemingly endless list of other, lofty-sounding credentials, such as RIA, BSCE, LLB, and MBA.

 Quite wary of sales commissions by now, Alice also liked the sound of the planner's fee: $350 for his time to help with her investment decisions and to discuss her other financial questions. Partway through their two-hour, $350 consultation, however, planner number four tried to persuade Alice that what she really needed was to hire him as an ongoing manager of her money. For just $2,000 per year for the service (commissions and management fees were extra), he would trade her in and out of investments based on his economic analyses and expert prognostications.

That seemed like a lot of money to Alice, who had $150,000 to invest, and she did not like the thought of turning over her money to someone who could move it around among various investments without her approval. Besides, she was interested in learning more about finance, and this "planner" kept telling her how complicated it is to make investing and other financial decisions. Alice therefore declined planner number four's sales pitch for managing her investments, whereupon the moody planner stormed out of her house, complaining that she had wasted his time (for which he had his $350 check in hand for a mere two hours of his time!).

Lessons learned from Alice's journey

Alice's case highlights four major problems that people often encounter when hiring financial help:

- ✔ First, you absolutely, positively *must* do your homework before hiring any financial advisor. Just look at Alice: Despite enthusiastic recommendations from her accountant and a friend, Alice ended up with bad advice from biased advisors.

✔ Second, the financial planning and brokerage fields are minefields for consumers. The fundamental problem is the enormous conflict of interest that is created when "advisors" sell products that earn them sales commissions to people who believe they are getting unbiased advice. Selling ongoing money management services, as Alice learned from the last "advisor," creates conflicts of interest as well.

As an analogy, imagine that you have flu symptoms. Would you be comfortable seeing a physician who didn't charge for office visits but made money only by selling you drugs? Maybe you don't *need* the drugs — or at least not so many expensive ones. Maybe what you really need is Mom's chicken soup and 16 hours of sleep.

In its review of the financial planning industry, *Consumer Reports* said, "Financial planners often end up being wolves in sheep's clothing with hidden agendas to sell mutual funds, for example, or life insurance." Respected financial columnist Jane Bryant Quinn of *Newsweek* says, "Planners are supposed to pull apart your finances and suggest better ways of meeting your goals. They purport to be objective. But they can't be if they work for brokerage firms or insurance companies or if their income depends on sales commissions from the products they sell."

✔ Third, financial advisors often like to make things far more complicated than need be, and they're generally not interested in educating you. As others have observed, financial planning is hardly the only occupation guilty of this. As author George Bernard Shaw put it, "All professions are conspiracies against the laity."

The more you know and the more you realize that investing and other financial decisions needn't be complicated, the more you'll realize you don't need to spend gobs of money, or any money at all, on financial planners and advisors. If you look in the mirror, you see the person who is most qualified to be your best financial advisor and who has your best interests at heart.

✔ Fourth, don't place a whole lot of faith in credentials, especially the Certified Financial Planning (CFP) moniker, which *Forbes* magazine columnist Gretchen Morgensen called a "meaningless label," adding, "When picking a financial planner, pay a lot of attention to how the planner is compensated. Pay no attention to CFPs. . . ."

What's truly amazing about Alice's situation is that none of the so-called financial "planners" ever bothered to ask about her insurance and debt situation. As it turns out, I learned that Alice not only lacked adequate homeowner's insurance, but she also amazingly had no health insurance!

Alice also had some relatively high-interest consumer debt that none of the "planners" ever asked about, probably because paying off her debt would have diminished the funds that Alice would have available for investment. Alice could afford both the insurance and debt payoff. In short, no one had taken the time to explain to Alice the costs and risks of not getting her financial house in order.

The credentialization of America: What credentials qualify a financial advisor?

It seems that everywhere I turn today, more and more people carry credentials after their names. We have certified lactation consultants, certified foot reflexologists, and registered dietitians.

Among sales people, especially in the financial services industry, the use of dubious credentials and self-anointed and misleading titles is on the rise. Stockbrokers are no longer called stockbrokers — they are "financial consultants" and "financial advisors." Some life insurance agents now call themselves "estate planning specialists." Next thing I know, when I visit an auto dealer, I'll speak with a certified transportation consultant, and when I buy my next home, it will be through a certified housing consultant rather than a real estate agent. It seems that everything today is *certified* — even the once "used car" is now referred to by some dealers as "certified pre-owned!"

Speaking of "certified," tens of thousands of people have earned the Certified Financial Planning credential. This is basically a home-study course that, unlike gaining entrance into medical, law, or business school, virtually anyone can undertake. The test itself isn't difficult to pass — an astounding 74 percent of people recently enrolled in the College for Financial Planning passed the CFP test. Gaining admission to a top professional school and becoming an architect, attorney, or doctor is exponentially more difficult and demanding.

The CFP Board of Standards, which licenses the CFP credential, claims that the combination of passing a test and meeting continuing education requirements ensures that their profession is doing the best that it can. To that, I and others who regularly observe CFP incompetence and conflicts of interest, politely say "Bunk!"

- The CFP tests nothing of a planner's business ethics or how the planner earns income.

- The CFP exam covers arcane financial details, which are rarely encountered by consumer-oriented planners and could easily be contained in a handy reference book.

- The CFP curriculum has little practical information on the important topics of asset allocation and mutual fund selection.

- And the few individuals who don't pass the CFP exam on the first try are told what answers they got wrong so that they can focus their time memorizing the trivial details and pass the exam on the second try.

Boston Globe columnist Charles Jaffe took the CFP exam and concluded that ". . . financial planning is a long way from qualifying as a profession."

Unfortunately, the vast majority of people with CFPs work on commission and are employed by securities and insurance brokerage firms, so they're not really financial planners so much as salespeople with a "credential." Most of the rest sell ongoing money management services.

Meeting the CFP continuing education requirements is a sham. CFPs can attend what amount to sales presentations by companies pitching financial products to earn continuing education credit hours. Another method is for CFPs to read financial planning journals, which have multiple choice and true-false questions in the back. The planner can take the test on his or her own time and even refer to the relevant articles to find the answers!

If you are interested in hiring financial help, be sure to read "Interviewing a Potential Financial Advisor," later in this chapter, where I detail questions you should ask a financial advisor before you hire him or her, including how to make sense of all the credential gobbledygook.

Finally, in case you're wondering, Alice did happily invest her money in a nice portfolio of commission-free mutual funds (see Chapter 10), which have been performing just swimmingly for her over the years.

Your Financial Management Options

Everyone has three basic choices about how to approach managing money: You can do nothing, you can do it yourself, or you can hire someone to help you.

Doing nothing

The *do-nothing* approach has a large following (and you thought you were the only one!). People who fall into this category may be leading terribly exciting, interesting lives and are therefore too busy to attend to something as mundane as dealing with their personal finances. Or they may be leading terribly mundane lives but are too busy fantasizing about more appealing ways to spend their time. For both types, everything from a major UFO sighting to taking out the garbage captures the imagination more than thinking about financial management.

But the dangers of doing nothing are many. Problem areas, left to themselves, get worse. Putting off saving for retirement or ignoring your buildup of debt eventually comes back to haunt you. Not carrying adequate insurance can be devastating when an accident occurs. Fires and earthquakes in California, flooding in the Midwest, and hurricanes in the South and East all show how precariously we live in paradise.

Even if the do-nothing approach has been yours all your life, you are now officially promoted out of it! You bought this book to learn more about personal finance and to make changes in your money matters, right? So take control and keep reading!

Doing it yourself

The do-it-yourselfers learn enough about financial topics to make informed decisions on their own. Doing anything yourself, of course, requires you to invest some time to learn the basic concepts and keep up with changes. For some, personal financial management becomes a challenging and absorbing interest. Others focus on what they need to do to get the job done efficiently.

It's a myth that if you self-direct your finances and make your own decisions, you will spend endless hours doing so. The harder part for most people is catching up to where they should be and correcting past mistakes. After you get things in order, which you can easily do with this book as your companion, you should not need to spend more than an hour or two every few months on your personal finances (unless a major issue, like a real estate purchase, comes up).

Some in the financial advisory business like to make things seem so complicated that they compare what they do to brain surgery! Their argument goes, "You wouldn't perform brain surgery on yourself, so why would you manage your money yourself?" Well, to this I say, personal financial management *ain't* brain surgery — not even close. You can manage on your own and, in fact, you can do better than what most advisors can do for you. Why? Because, you're not subject to conflicts of interest, and you care the most about your money.

Hiring financial help

Realizing that you need to hire someone to help you make and implement financial decisions can be a valuable insight. Spending a few hours and several hundred dollars to hire a competent professional can be money well spent, even if you have a modest income or assets. But you need to know what your money is buying.

Financial planners or advisors make money in one of three ways:

- ✔ They earn commissions based on sales of financial products.
- ✔ They can charge a percentage of your assets that they are investing.
- ✔ They can charge by the hour.

As you can see from Alice's journey into this area at the beginning of this chapter, hiring financial assistance can be anything but a tea party. The following sections help you differentiate among the three main types of financial planners.

Commission-based "planners"

Commission-based planners aren't really planners, advisors, or counselors at all — they are salespeople. Many *stockbrokers* and *insurance brokers* of prior decades are now called *financial consultants* or *financial service representatives* in order to glamorize the profession and obscure how they are compensated. Ditto for insurance salespeople calling themselves *estate planning specialists.*

That's like a Honda dealer calling himself a *transportation consultant.* A Honda dealer is a salesperson who makes a living selling Hondas, period. He's definitely not going to tell you nice things about Ford, Chrysler, or Toyota cars — unless, of course, he happens to sell those, too. He also has no interest in educating you about money-saving public transit possibilities!

As I discuss earlier in this chapter, salespeople and brokers masquerading as planners can have an enormous self-interest when they push certain products, particularly those products that pay generous commissions. Being paid on commission tends to skew their recommendations toward certain strategies (such as buying investment or life insurance products) and causes the salespeople to ignore or downplay other aspects of your finances. For example, they'll gladly sell you an investment rather than persuade you to pay off your high-interest debts or to save and invest through your employer's retirement plan, thereby reducing your taxes.

Table 18-1 gives you an idea of the commissions that a financial planner/salesperson can earn through selling particular financial products.

Table 18-1	Financial Product Commissions
Product	*Commission*
Life Insurance ($250,000, age 45):	
Term Life	$140 to $565
Universal/Whole Life	$1,020 to $2,580
Disability Insurance:	
$4,000/month benefit, age 35	$345 to $1,200
Investments ($20,000):	
Mutual Funds	$800 to $1,700
Limited Partnerships	$1,400 to $2,000
Annuities	$1,000 to $1,800

Percentage-of-assets-under-management advisors

A generally better choice than a commission-based planner is a financial advisor who charges a percentage of the assets that are being managed or invested. This compensation system removes the incentives to sell you products with high commissions and to initiate lots of transactions to generate more of those commissions.

Although it is an improvement over product-pushers working on commission, the fee-based system has flaws, too. First off, suppose that you're trying to decide whether to invest in stocks, bonds, or real estate. A planner who earns her living managing your money likely won't recommend real estate because that would deplete your investment capital. The planner also won't recommend paying down your mortgage for the same reason — she'll claim that you can earn more investing your money (with her help, of course) than it will cost you to borrow.

Fee-based planners are also only interested in managing money for those who have already accumulated a fair amount of it — which rules out most people. According to the Boston Company, an economics research firm, the median household (*median* means half have more, half have less) headed by a person aged 35 to 49 has just $6,000 in financial assets — far below the six-figure minimums of most fee-based advisors.

Hourly-based advisors

Your best bet for professional help with your personal finances is an advisor who charges for his time. Because he doesn't sell any financial products, his objectivity is maintained. He doesn't perform money management, so he can help you make comprehensive financial decisions dealing with loans, retirement planning, and selecting good investments including real estate, mutual funds, and small business.

The primary risk in selecting an hourly-based planner is incompetence. You can address this by checking references and learning enough yourself to discern between good and bad financial advice. Another risk comes from not clearly defining the work to be done and the approximate total cost before you begin. You should also review some of the other key questions outlined later in this chapter.

A drawback of an entirely different kind occurs when you don't follow through on the recommendations of your advisor. You paid for her work but didn't act on it, so you didn't capture its value. If part of the reason that you hired the planner in the first place was that you're too busy or not interested enough to make changes to your financial situation, then you should look for this support in the services you buy from the planner.

Should you just need someone as a sounding board for ideas or to recommend a specific strategy or product, you can hire an hourly based planner for one or two sessions of advice. You save money doing the legwork and implementation on your own. Just make sure that the planner is willing to give you specific enough advice that you can implement it.

Should You Hire a Financial Planner?

Most people reading this book don't need to hire a financial planner. But just because you're financially savvy, you shouldn't be too quick to write off the value of hiring help.

Good reasons for hiring a financial planner can be the same reasons for hiring someone to clean your home or do your taxes. If you're too busy or don't enjoy doing it or you're terribly uncomfortable making decisions on your own, using a planner for a second opinion makes good sense. And if you shy away from numbers and bristle at the thought of long division, a good planner can help you.

How a good financial planner can help

The following gives you a rundown of some of the important things a competent financial planner can assist you with.

- ✔ **Identifying problems and goals.** Many otherwise intelligent people have a hard time being objective about their financial problems. They may ignore their debts or have unrealistic goals and expectations given their financial situations and behaviors. And many are so busy with other aspects of their lives that they never take the time to think about what their financial goals are. A good financial planner can give you the objective look you need.

  Surprisingly, some people are in better financial position than they thought in relation to their goals. Good counselors really enjoy this aspect of their jobs — good news is easier and much more fun to deliver.

- ✔ **Identifying strategies to reach your financial goals.** Your mind may be a jumble of various plans, ideas, and concerns, along with a cobweb or two. A good counselor can help you sort out your thoughts and can propose alternative strategies for you to consider in accomplishing your financial goals.

- ✔ **Setting priorities.** You could be doing dozens of things to improve your financial situation, but making a few key changes could probably have the greatest value. Equally important is to identify the changes that fit your overall situation and that won't keep you awake at night fretting about them. Good planners help you prioritize.

- ✔ **Saving research time and hassle.** Even if you know what major financial decisions are most important to you, doing the research can be time-consuming and frustrating if you don't know where to turn for good information and advice. A good planner does research to match your needs to the best available strategies and products. So much lousy information is out there on various financial topics that you can easily get lost, discouraged, sidetracked, or swindled. A good advisor can prevent you from making a bad decision based on poor or insufficient information.

✔ **Purchasing commission-free financial products.** When you hire a planner who charges for her time, you can easily save hundreds or thousands of dollars by avoiding the cost of commissions in the financial products you buy. This commission-free situation is especially valuable when it comes to purchasing investments and insurance.

✔ **Providing an objective voice for major decisions.** Deciding when to retire, how much to spend on a home purchase, and where to invest your money are big decisions. Getting swept up in the emotions of these issues can cloud your perspective and objectivity. A competent and sensitive advisor can cut through this cloud to raise issues and provide sound counsel.

✔ **Helping you to just do it.** Deciding what you need to do is not enough — you have to actually do it, too. And although you can use a planner for advice and make all the changes on your own, a good counselor can help you follow through with your plan as well. After all, part of the reason you hired the advisor in the first place may be that you're too busy or uninterested to manage your finances.

✔ **Mediating.** If you have a spouse or partner, financial decisions can produce real fireworks, particularly with financial decisions involving the extended family. Although a counselor can't be a therapist, a good one can be sensitive to the different needs and concerns of each party and can try to find middle ground on the financial issues you're grappling with.

✔ **Making you money and allowing you peace of mind.** The whole point of professional financial planning is to help you make the most of your money and help you plan for and attain your financial and personal goals. In the process, the financial planner should show you how to enhance your investment returns; reduce your spending, taxes, and insurance costs; increase your savings; improve your catastrophic insurance coverage; and achieve your financial independence goals. And last but not least: Putting your financial house in order should take some weight off your mind — like that clean, light-headed feeling after a haircut.

Why financial planners aren't for everyone

As I discuss in the next section, finding a good financial planner ain't easy. That's a good reason why you should be sure you want to hire an advisor before you venture out in search of a competent one.

Although some people can benefit from the advice of a knowledgeable and ethical financial planner, you should also consider your personality type before you decide to hire help. My experience has been that some people (believe it or not) enjoy the research and number-crunching. If this is you or if you're not really comfortable taking advice, you'd be better off doing your own homework and creating your own plan.

Likewise, if you have a specific tax or legal matter, you're better off hiring a good professional who specializes in that field rather than a financial planner.

The Frustrations of Finding Good Financial Planners

Overwhelmed and undereducated consumers like Alice, especially those in low- and middle-income brackets, have few attractive options if they want to hire financial help. The vast majority of the people who call themselves *financial planners* and *financial consultants* sell products and work on commission, which, as Alice found in the previous section, creates enormous conflicts of interest. Those conflicts stem from the fact that the broker has an incentive to recommend strategies and sell products that pay generous commissions and to ignore strategies and products that pay no or low commissions.

The few financial advisors who are *fee-only* make most of their fees from money-management services. (*Fee-only* or *fee-based* means that the advisors' fees are paid by their clients, not by companies whose products they recommend.) Thus, fee-based advisors tend to focus on those who have already accumulated significant wealth. Fee-based advisors may also have conflicts of interest in that they gravitate toward strategies and recommendations that involve their ongoing management of your money and may ignore or dismiss tactics that diminish the pool of investment money that they can manage for you for an ongoing fee.

The following sections describe some of the problems associated with finding a good planner.

Regulatory problems

A pretty basic problem of oversight afflicts the financial planning field. Oversight is minimal *at best.* In many states, anyone can hang out a shingle and call him- or herself a financial planner. The U.S. Securities and Exchange Commission (SEC) polices only those who provide investment advice; they must register with the SEC as registered investment advisors (RIAs). The SEC provides no oversight of noninvesting advice provided.

Several studies have shown that, because the SEC has so few investigators to police so many RIAs, the typical RIA is investigated on the order of every 15 years or so. The SEC believes that the states should police the hundreds of thousands of people who call themselves financial planners. But most states have done little to monitor planners and protect consumers. Thus, as the nonprofit Consumer Federation of America said in its assessment of the industry: "Today's investors go up against a deadly combination of abusive securities industry practices and regulatory inattentiveness when investing their money."

Financial planners *should* have to disclose in writing, prior to working with a client, how they are compensated. This would make it easier for people to know how the planner earns a living. And it would eliminate much of the need for more formal government regulation. Several bills with this sort of common-sense provision that were introduced in state and federal government have been squashed. Financial planners, insurance brokers, and others selling products with commissions that are hidden from the public have lobbied successfully (by spending and contributing money to politicians' campaigns) to kill such bills.

Letting the Big Bad Wolf guard the Three Little Pigs

The International Association of Financial Planners (IAFP) and the Institute of Certified Financial Planners (ICFP) are the two primary trade associations (and are in the process of merging) that represent most financial planners. Unfortunately, these organizations tend to promote the status quo in the industry because they *are* the industry. Their membership and leadership are policing themselves.

In fact, the associations have lobbied government to defeat laws aimed at regulation of their membership's sales practices rather than advocating what's ethical or best for the public. Other sources to be wary of are "educational" materials produced by the National Endowment for Financial Education, which is funded by the College for Financial Planning that grants CFPs.

Financial planners' top conflicts of interest

All professions have conflicts of interest. Some fields have more than others, and the financial planning field is one of those fields. Knowing where some of the land mines lie can certainly help. Here, then, are the most common reasons that planners may not have 20/20 vision when giving financial directions.

Selling and pushing products that pay commissions

If a financial planner isn't charging you a fee for his time, you can rest assured he is earning commissions on the products he'll try to sell you. In order to sell financial products, this planner must have a broker's license. A person who sells financial products and earns commissions from those products is a salesperson, *not* a financial planner. Financial planning involves taking an objective, holistic look at your financial puzzle to find the pieces that fit it well, something that brokers are neither trained nor financially motivated to do.

To make it even harder for you to discern planners' agendas, you can *not* assume that planners who do charge fees for their time don't also earn commissions selling products. Sadly for people seeking financial advice, compensation *double-dipping* is becoming more common.

Selling products that provide a commission tends to skew a planner's recommendations. Products that carry commissions mean that you have fewer of your dollars working in the investments and insurance you buy. Because a commission is earned only when a product is sold, such a product or service is inevitably more attractive in the planner's eyes than any other option. For example, if the planner sells disability insurance that you could obtain at a lower cost through your employer or a group trade association (see Chapter 16), he may overlook or criticize your most attractive option (buying through your employer) and focus on *his* most attractive option — selling you a higher-cost disability policy on which he derives a commission.

Another danger of trusting the recommendation of a commission-based planner is that she may steer you toward the products that have the biggest payback for her. These products are among the *worst* for you because they siphon off even more of your money up front to pay the commission. They also tend to be among the costliest and riskiest financial products available.

Planners who are also commission-greedy may try to *churn* your investments. They encourage you to buy and sell at the drop of a hat, attributing the need to changes in the economy or the companies you've invested in. More trading means more commissions for the broker.

"Financial planning" in banks

Over the past couple of decades, banks have witnessed an erosion of the money in their coffers and vaults. The reason is simple — increasing numbers of investors realized that banks are generally lousy places to build wealth. The highest yielding bank savings accounts and certificates of deposit barely keep an investor ahead of inflation. If you factor in both inflation and taxes, these bank "investments" provide no real growth on your investment dollars.

Increasingly, banks have "financial representatives" and "investment specialists" sitting in their branches waiting to pounce on bank customers with big balances. In many banks, these "financial planners" are simply brokers who are out to sell investments that pay them (and the bank) hefty sales commissions.

Although you may expect your bank account balances to be confidential and off-limits to the eager eyes of investment salespeople in a bank, numerous studies have demonstrated that banks are betraying customer trust.

✔ First, many customers have no idea that these bank reps are earning commissions and that those commissions are being siphoned out of customers' investment dollars.

✔ Second, many customers are mistaken (partly due to the banks' and salespeople's poor disclosure) in believing that these investments, like bank savings accounts, are FDIC-insured and cannot lose value.

✔ Finally, many of the reps in banks are inexperienced and don't understand what they are selling and what is suitable for particular customers.

Taking a narrow view

Because of the way they earn their money, many planners are biased in favor of certain strategies and products. As a result, they do not typically keep your overall financial needs in mind. For example, if you have a problem with accumulated credit card debts, some planners may never know (or care) because they're focused on selling you an investment product. Likewise, a planner who sells a lot of life insurance tends to develop recommendations that require its purchase.

Not recommending saving through your employer's retirement plan

One of your best financial options is to take advantage of saving through your employer's retirement savings plan(s). Although this method of saving may not be as exciting as risking your money in cattle futures, it's not as dull as watching paint dry — and, most importantly, it is tax-deductible. Planners are reluctant to recommend taking full advantage of this option: It doesn't leave much money for the purchase of their commission-laden investment products.

Ignoring debts

Sometimes, your best investment is to pay off outstanding loans, whether credit card, auto, or even mortgage debts. But most financial planners don't recommend this strategy because paying down debts depletes the capital with which you could otherwise buy investments — the investments that the broker may be trying to sell you to earn a commission or the advisor would like to manage for an ongoing fee.

Not recommending real estate and small-business investments

Like paying off debts, investing in real estate and small business takes away from your interest and ability to invest elsewhere. Most planners won't help with these choices. They may even tell you tales of real-estate and small-business-investing disasters to give you cold feet.

Sure, the value of real estate can go down just like any other investment. But over the long haul, owning a home makes good financial sense for most people. With small business, the risks are higher, but so are the potential returns. Don't let a financial planner convince you that these options are foolish — in fact, if you do your homework and know what you're doing, you can make higher rates of returns investing in real estate and small business than you can in traditional securities such as stocks and bonds. See Part III to read more about your investing options.

Selling ongoing money-management services

The vast majority of financial planners/advisors who don't work on commission make their money by managing your money for an ongoing fee percentage (typically 1 to 3 percent annually of your investment). Although this removes the incentive to *churn* your account (frequently trade your investments) to run up more commissions, it's a service that you're unlikely to need.

An ongoing fee percentage still creates a conflict of interest; the financial planner will tend to steer you away from beneficial financial strategies that reduce the asset pool from which he derives his percentage. Financial strategies such as maximizing contributions to your employer's retirement savings plan, paying off debts like your mortgage, investing in real estate or small business, and so on may make the most sense for you but are rarely recommended by an advisor who works on a percentage of assets under management basis.

The latest rage, particularly among brokerage firms, is the *wrap account* (also known as the *managed account*). Wrap accounts can cost you upward of 3 percent of your assets annually. As I explain in Part III, you can hire *professional money managers* for 1 percent per year or less.

Selling legal services

More and more planners are getting into the business of drawing up *trusts* and providing other estate planning services for their clients. Although these and other legal documents may be right for you, far lower-cost options are available if your situation is not complicated (see Chapter 17).

If you want advice on whether you need these legal documents, do a little investigating: Do some additional reading or consult an advisor who won't actually perform the work. Legal matters are complex enough that the competence of someone who doesn't specialize in it full-time should be carefully scrutinized. If you do ultimately hire someone to perform estate planning services for you, hire someone who specializes and works at it full-time. Read the section in Chapter 17 to learn more about estate planning.

Scaring you unnecessarily

Some planners put together nifty computer-generated projections showing that you will need millions of dollars by the time you retire to maintain your standard of living. Or that tuition will cost hundreds of thousands of dollars by the time your two-year-old is ready for college.

Waking up a client to the realities of his or her financial situation is an important and difficult job for a good financial planner. But some unscrupulous planners take this task to an extreme, deliberately scaring you into buying what they're selling. They paint a bleak picture and imply that you can fix your problems only if you do what they say. Don't let them scare you — read this book and get your financial life in order.

Creating dependency

Another conflict-of-interest issue: Financial planners have a tendency to create dependency, making things seem so complicated that their clients feel as though they could never manage their finances on their own. If your advisor is reluctant to tell you how you can educate yourself about personal money management, or if she advises you that your time would be better spent learning yoga, you've probably found a *self-perpetuating consultant.*

How to Find a Good Financial Planner

Locating a good financial planner who is willing to work with the not-yet-rich-and-famous and who doesn't have conflicts of interest can be like finding a needle in a haystack. Two methods that can serve as good starting points are personal referral and associations.

Personal referrals

One of the best ways to find a good financial planner is to get a personal referral from a satisfied customer who is someone you trust. A referral from an accountant or an attorney whose judgment you've tested can help as well.

Word-of-mouth is how the best financial planners continue to build their practices. Satisfied customers are any professional's best and least costly marketers.

However, never *ever* take a recommendation from anyone as gospel. I don't care *who* is making the referral — even if it's your mother or the Pope. You must do your homework: Ask the planner the interview questions I list later in this chapter. I've seen people get into real trouble because of blindly accepting someone else's recommendation. Remember: The person making the recommendation is (probably) not a financial expert. He or she could be just as bewildered as you are.

You may get referred to a planner or broker who returns the favor by sending business to the tax, legal, or real estate person who referred you. On more than a few occasions, professionals in other fields have made it clear that they would refer business to me if I referred business to them. I refused, of course. Good professionals don't do tit for tat. Hire professionals who make referrals to others based on their competence and ethics.

Associations

Associations of financial planners are more than happy to refer you to planners in your area. But as I discuss earlier in this chapter, the major trade associations are composed of planners who sell products and work on commission.

Two better places to start include the following:

> ✔ **The National Association of Personal Financial Advisors**
> 355 West Dundee Rd., Suite 200
> Buffalo Grove, IL 60089
> 888-333-6659; www.napfa.org
>
> The NAPFA is made up of fee-only planners. Its members are not supposed to earn commissions from products they sell. However, most planners in this association earn their living by providing money-management services and charging a fee that is a percentage of assets under management.

✔ **The American Institute of Certified Public Accountants (AICPA)**
1211 Avenue of the Americas
New York, NY 10036
888-999-9256; www.cpapfs.org

The AICPA is the professional association of CPAs that can provide names of members who have completed the Institute's Personal Financial Specialist (PFS) program. Many, but certainly not all, of the CPAs who have completed the PFS program provide financial advice on a fee basis. Competent CPAs have the advantage of understanding the tax consequences of different choices, which are important components of any financial plan. On the other hand, it is hard for a professional to keep current in two broad fields.

Ways that planners of dubious distinction cultivate clients

The channel through which you hear of a planner may provide clues to a planner's integrity and way of doing business. Beware of planners you find (or that find you) through these avenues:

✔ **Cold calling.** You've just come home after a hard day. No sooner has your posterior hit the recliner to settle in for the night when the phone rings. It's Joe the financial planner, and he wants to help you achieve all your financial dreams. *Cold calling* (the salesperson calls you, without an appointment) is the most inefficient way a planner can get new clients. It's also intrusive and is typically used by aggressive salespeople who work on commission.

Keep a log beside your telephone. Record the date, time, name of organization, and name of caller every time you receive a cold call. Tell cold callers to never call you again. Then, if they do call you again, you can sue them for $500 in small claims court!

✔ **Adult education classes.** Here's what often happens at adult education classes given at local universities: You pay a reasonable fee for the course. You go to class giddy at the prospect of learning how to manage your finances. And then the instructor ends up being a broker or financial planner hungry for clients. He confuses more than he conveys. He's short on specifics. But he'll be more than happy to show you the way if you contact (and hire) him outside of class.

Instructors for these courses are paid to teach. They don't need to solicit clients in class, and, in fact, it's unethical for them to do so. I should note, however, that part of the problem is that some universities take advantage of the fact that they know such "teachers" want to solicit business. So the universities set the pay at a low level, thinking, erroneously, that they'll save money. So, *never* assume that someone who is teaching a financial-planning course at a local college is ethical, competent, or looking out for your best interests. Although I may sound cynical in so saying, assume that these people are none of the above until they clearly prove otherwise.

Ethical instructors who are there to teach do *not* solicit clients and may actively discourage students from hiring them. Smart

(continued)

(continued)

universities pay their instructors well and weed out the instructors who are more interested in building up their client base than teaching.

✔ **"Free" seminars.** This is a case of "you get what you pay for." Because you don't pay a fee to attend "free seminars," and the "teachers" don't get paid, either, these events tend to be more clear-cut sales pitches. The "instructor" may share some information, but smart seminar leaders know that the goal of a successful seminar is to establish himself or herself as an expert and to whet the prospects' appetites.

Note: Be *especially* wary of seminars targeted at selected groups, such as special seminars for people who have received retirement plan distributions or those touting "Financial Planning for Women." Financial planning is not specific to gender, ethnicity, or marital status.

Don't assume that the financial planner giving a presentation at your employer's office is the right planner for you, either. It's surprising how little investigation some corporate benefits departments conduct on the people they let in. In most cases, planners are accepted simply because they don't charge. One organization I'm familiar with gave preference to planners who, in addition to doing free presentations, also brought in a catered lunch! Guess what — this attracted lots of the brokers who sell high-commission products.

Interviewing a Potential Financial Advisor

Don't consider hiring a financial advisor until you have read the rest of this book. If you're not educated about personal finance, how can you possibly evaluate the competence of someone you might hire to help you make important financial decisions?

I firmly believe that you are your own best financial advisor. However, I know that some people don't want to make financial decisions without getting assistance. Perhaps you're busy, or you simply can't stand making money decisions.

But recognize that when you hire a financial advisor, you have a lot at stake. Besides the cost of his services, which generally don't come cheaply, you're placing a lot of trust in the advisor's recommendations. The more you know, the better the advisor you'll end up working with and the fewer services you'll need to buy.

These ten questions get to the core of an advisor's competence and professional integrity. Get answers to these questions *before* you decide to hire a financial advisor.

What percentage of your income comes from fees paid by your clients versus commissions from the products that you sell?

Asking this question first may save you the trouble and time of asking the next nine. The right answer is, "100 percent of my income comes from fees paid by clients." Anything less than 100 percent means the person you're speaking to is a salesperson with a vested interest in recommending certain strategies and product purchases.

Sadly, more than a few "financial advisors" don't tell the truth. In an under-cover investigation done by *Money* magazine, nearly one-third of advisors who claimed they were fee-only turned out to be brokers who sold invest-ment and insurance products on a commission basis. How can you ferret these people out?

All advisors who provide investment advice must register with the U.S. Securities and Exchange Commission (SEC). They must file Form ADV, other-wise known as the Uniform Application for Investment Advisor Registration. This lengthy document asks for very specific information from investment advisors, such as

✔ A breakdown of where their income comes from

✔ Relationships and affiliations with other companies

✔ Each advisor's educational and employment history

✔ The types of securities the firm recommends

✔ The firm's fee schedule

In short, Form ADV provides — in black and white — answers to all the ques-tions. In a pitch over the phone or in marketing materials sent in the mail, a planner is much more likely to gloss over or avoid certain issues. Although an advisor can lie to the SEC on Form ADV (it has happened on numerous occasions), an advisor will likely be more truthful on this form than in her own marketing to you.

You can ask the advisor to send you a copy of the Form ADV. You can also check to see that the advisor is registered and whether he or she has a track record of problems by calling the SEC at 800-732-0330, visiting the SEC web site at www.sec.gov, or writing to the SEC at 450 Fifth St. NW, Washington, D.C. 20549. You might also check with the department in your state that over-sees investment advisors (nearly all states have one).

What percentage of fees paid by your clients is for ongoing money management versus hourly financial planning?

The answer to how the advisor is paid provides a big clue as to whether the planner has an agenda to convince you to hire him to manage your money. If what you want are objective and specific financial planning recommendations, you should seek advisors who derive their income from hourly fees. Many counselors and advisors call themselves "fee-based," which usually means they make their living managing money for a percentage.

Some advisors do not tell you the truth. Reviewing the advisor's Form ADV generally helps you get closer to the truth. Also be aware that some advisors have been known to operate two separate companies. One company claims to give advice on a fee-basis. However, the other (generally hidden) company sells products or manages money.

If you want a money manager, you can hire the best quite inexpensively through a mutual fund or, if you have substantial assets, you can hire an established money manager (refer to Chapter 10).

What is your hourly fee?

Rates, as with legal and tax advisors, vary all over the map. I've seen and heard of fees as low as $50 per hour all the way up to several hundred dollars per hour. If you shop around, you can find terrific planners who charge around $100 per hour and who work faster than a snail's pace.

Because good planners spend a reasonable portion of their time researching and running their business, don't assume they're getting rich at your expense at this rate. Running a business is costly, but you shouldn't pay hundreds of dollars per hour unless you're wealthy and want an advisor who works only with people like you. Also, be aware that a number of planners who manage money or sell products charge very high hourly rates because they don't really want to work with people on an hourly fee basis.

Do you also perform tax or legal services?

Be wary of someone who claims to be an expert beyond one area. The tax, legal, and financial fields are vast in and of themselves and are difficult for even the best and brightest advisor to cover simultaneously. One exception is the accountant who also performs some basic financial planning by the hour. Likewise, a good financial advisor should have a good grounding in tax and legal issues that relate to your personal finances. Larger firms may have specialists available in different areas.

What work and educational experience qualifies you to be a financial planner?

There's no one right answer here. Ideally, a planner should have experience in the business or financial services field. Some say to look for planners with at least five or ten years experience. I've always wondered how planners earn a living their first five or ten years if folks won't hire them until they reach these benchmarks! A good planner should also be good with numbers, speak in plain English, and have good interpersonal skills.

Education is sort of like food. Too little leaves you hungry. Too much might leave you feeling stuffed and uncomfortable. And less of high quality is better than a lot of low quality.

As I discuss earlier in this chapter, don't place too much value in the CFP (certified financial planner) degree. Most advisors with this "credential," which can be earned by taking a self-study course at home, sell investments.

Because investing decisions are a critical part of financial planning, take note of the fact that the most common designations of educational training among professional money managers are MBA (master of business administration) and CFA (chartered financial analyst). And some tax advisors who work on an hourly basis have earned the "Personal Financial Specialist" credential.

Have you ever sold limited partnerships? Options? Futures? Commodities?

The correct answers here are *no, no, no, no.* If you don't know what these disasters are, refer to Chapter 9. Also, be wary of any financial advisor who once dealt in these areas but claims to have seen the light and reformed his ways.

Professionals with poor judgment may not repeat the same mistakes, but they're more likely to make some new ones at your expense. My experience is that even advisors who have "reformed" are unlikely to be working by the hour. Most work on commission or want to manage your money for a hefty fee.

Do you carry liability insurance?

You wouldn't (or shouldn't) let contractors into your home to do work without knowing they have insurance to cover any mistakes they make, should they cause your home to look like the one in the movie *The Money Pit*. Likewise, you should insist on hiring a planner who carries protection in case she makes a major mistake for which she is liable. Make sure that she carries enough coverage given what she is helping you with.

Some counselors may be surprised by this question or may think you're a problem customer looking for a lawsuit. On the other hand, accidents happen; that's why insurance exists. So if the planner doesn't have liability insurance, she missed one of the fundamental concepts of planning: Insure against risk. Don't you make the same mistake by hiring her.

Can you provide references of clients with needs similar to mine?

Take the time to ask other people who have used the planner what the planner did for them. Inquire what the advisor's greatest strengths and weaknesses are. You can learn a bit about the planner's track record as well as style. And because you want to have as productive a relationship as possible with your planner, the more you learn about the planner, the easier it will be for you to hit the ground running if you hire him.

Some financial advisors offer a "free" introductory consultation. If this is offered to allow you to check out the advisor and it makes you feel more comfortable about hiring that planner, fair enough. But be careful: Most "free" consultations are offered by planners who work on commission or who will try to sell you ongoing money management services. So the "free" consultation ends up being a big sales pitch for certain products or services offered through the advisor.

The fact that a planner doesn't offer a "free" consultation may be a good sign. Counselors who work strictly by the hour and are busy can't afford to burn an hour of their time for an in-person "free" session. They also need to be careful of folks seeking "free" advice. Such advisors usually are willing to spend some time on the phone answering background questions. They should also be able to send background materials by mail and provide references.

Will you provide specific strategies and product recommendations that I can implement on my own if I choose?

This is an important question. Some advisors may indicate that you can hire them by the hour. But then they provide only generic advice without many specifics. Some planners even *double dip* — they charge an hourly fee to make you feel like you're not working with a salesperson. Then they try selling commission-based products. Also be aware that some advisors say you can choose to implement their recommendations on your own, but then recommend financial products that carry commissions.

How is implementation handled?

Ideally, find an advisor who lets you choose whether you want to hire him to help with implementation after the recommendations have been presented to you. If you know that you will follow through on the advice and can do so without further discussions and questions, don't buy the planner's time to implement.

On the other hand, if you hired the counselor in the first place because you lack the time, desire, and/or expertise to manage your financial life, building implementation into the planning work makes good sense. If you're the type of person who needs to tie a string around a finger to remember to do something but then forgets why the string is there, pay for the necessary hand-holding.

Chapter 19

PC Money Management

● ●

In This Chapter

▶ Understanding the different types of "content"

▶ Internet virtues and pitfalls

▶ Using your computer for money tracking, planning, investing, and insuring

● ●

Soon, everybody is going to own a computer. And every business is soon to have an internet site. So shouldn't you just join up with everyone else in the cyber-universe?

The short answer is *no*. And, I know plenty of people who don't own a computer or who use one sparingly and who do an excellent job of managing their money.

Although a computer may be able to assist you with your personal finances, it's simply one of many tools. Computers are really best at performing routine tasks faster: processing lots of bills or performing many calculations.

Computers aren't smart, and computers and all the accompanying paraphernalia, while cheaper than years ago, certainly aren't cheap. And never assume that just because you're accessing something financial through your computer, the information you're accessing is any good or that it's even information at all.

Software and Internet Sites

You can access two major repositories of personal finance stuff through your computer. Although the lines are sometimes a bit blurry between these two categories, they are roughly defined as software and the internet:

- ✔ *Software* is a computer program that is either packaged in a box about as big as a hardcover book such as *War and Peace* or can be downloaded online. Most of the mass-marketed financial software packages sell for under $100. If you've ever used a word-processing program such as Word or WordPerfect, or a spreadsheet program such as Excel or Lotus 1-2-3, then you've used software.

- ✔ *The internet* is a vast ocean of stuff that you can generally access via a modem, which allows your computer to talk with other computers over phone lines. To access the internet, you need some sort of web browser which you can obtain through an internet service provider. Most of the financial stuff on the internet is supplied by companies marketing their wares and, hence, is available for free.

The benefits of using financial software

Although the number of personal finance software packages and online sites is mushrooming rapidly, quality is having a hard time keeping up, especially among the free internet sites. Most of the best financial tools for your computer fall into the software category and can help you in the following ways:

- ✔ Good software can guide you to better organization and management of your personal finances.

- ✔ Good software can help you complete mundane tasks or complex calculations more quickly and easily and provide basic advice in unfamiliar territory.

- ✔ Good software can make you feel in control of your life.

Mediocre and bad software, on the other hand, can make you feel stupid or, at the very least, make you want to tear your hair out. Lousy packages usually end up in the software graveyard.

Having reviewed many of the packages available, I can assure you that if you are having a hard time with some of the programs out there (even sometimes the more useful ones), you are not at fault. Too many packages assume that you already know things such as your tax rate, your mortgage options, and the difference between stock and bond mutual funds. Much of what's out there isn't user-friendly and is too technically oriented. Some of it is even flawed in its financial accuracy.

A good software package, like a good tax or financial advisor, should be your partner in helping you better manage your finances. It should simply and concisely explain financial terminology and provide a road map to help you make decisions by offering choices and recommendations so that you can "play" with alternatives before following a particular course of action.

With increasing regularity, financial software packages are being designed to do more than one task or to address more than one area of personal finances. But no package covers the whole range of issues in your financial life.

Tread carefully on the web

"Go surfing!"

"Cool!"

No, you're not eavesdropping on a southern California beach conversation. To hear promoters of companies with sites on the globe's largest computer network known as the internet, you may think that the internet is not only a hip place to be but *The Place to Be*.

I'm increasingly asked questions like, "How do I research investments through the internet?" or, "How can I use the internet to manage my personal finances?"

My answer — "very carefully."

Like information from any medium, you have to sift out the good from the bad. If you blindly navigate the internet and naively think that everything out there is useful "information," "research," or "objective advice," you will be in for a rude awakening.

Most personal finance sites on the internet are free, which — guess what — means that these sites are basically advertising or are dominated and driven by advertising. If you're looking for written material by unbiased experts or journalists — well — you can find some on the web, but there's far more biased and uninformed stuff.

Consider the source

A report on the internet published by a leading investment-banking firm provides a list of the "coolest finance" sites. On the list is the web site of a major bank. Because it's been a long time since I was in junior high school, I'm not quite sure what cool means anymore. If cool can be used to describe a well-organized and graphically pleasing web site, then I guess I could say that the bank's site is cool.

However, if you are looking for sound information and advice, then the bank's site is decidedly "uncool." It steers you in a financial direction that benefits, not surprisingly, the bank and not you. For example, in the real estate section, users are asked to plug in their gross monthly income and down payment, which are used to spit out the supposed amount that users can "afford" to spend on a home. No mention is given to other financial goals and concerns — such as saving for retirement — that affect one's ability to spend a particular amount of money on a home.

Consider this advice in the lending area: "Maybe you *can* have it now. When you don't have the cash on hand for important purchases, we can help you borrow what you need. From a new car, to that vacation you've been longing for, to new kitchen appliances, you can make these dreams real now." Click on a button on the bottom of this screen — and presto, you're on your way to racking up credit card and auto debt. Why bother practicing delayed gratification, living within your means, or buying something used if getting a loan is "easy" and comes with "special privileges?"

Watch out for "sponsored" content

Another problem to watch out for on internet sites is "sponsored" content, a euphemism for advertising under the guise of editorial content. Often buried in small print in an obscure part of the web page or site, you'll find a disclaimer or note saying that an article is sponsored by (in other words, paid advertising by) the "author."

For example, one mutual fund site states that its "primary purpose is to provide viewers with an independent guide that contains information and articles they can't get anywhere else." The "content" of the site suggests otherwise. In the "Expert's Corner," material is reprinted from a newsletter that advocates frequent trading in and out of mutual funds to time market moves. Turns out that the "article" is "sponsored by the featured expert": In other words, it's a paid advertisement. (The track record of the newsletter's past recommendations, which isn't discussed, is poor.)

Steer clear of biased financial planning advice

I also suggest skipping the financial planning advice offered by financial service companies with financial products to sell. Such companies cannot take the necessary objective, holistic view required to render useful advice. Investment companies, for example, will prod you into establishing college savings accounts with them without pointing out the benefits of funding your employer's retirement savings plan instead or the deleterious effect that college accounts have on your child's ability to qualify for financial aid (refer to Chapter 13 for more details).

For example, on a major mutual fund company's web site, there's a good deal of material on its mutual funds. The site's college planning advice is off the mark because it urges parents to put money in a custodial account in the child's name. Ignored is the fact that this will undermine your child's ability to qualify for financial aid and that you're likely best off funding your employer's retirement plan. If you did that, though, you couldn't set up a college savings plan account at the fund company, which this area prods you to do.

Shun short-term thinking

Many financial internet sites provide real-time stock quotes as a hook to some site that is cluttered with advertising. My experience working with individual investors is that the more short-term they think, the worse they do, and checking your portfolio during the trading day certainly promotes short-term-ism.

Also, beware of tips offered around the electronic water cooler — message boards. As in the real world, chatting with strangers and exchanging ideas is fine. However, if you don't know the identity and competence of message board posters or chat room participants, why would you follow their financial advice or stock tips? Getting ideas from various sources is okay, but educate yourself and do your homework before making personal financial decisions.

If you want to best manage your personal finances and learn more, remember that there's a grain of truth in the old expression, "You get what you pay for." Free information on the internet, especially that which is provided by companies in the financial services industry, is largely self-serving. Stick with information providers who have proven themselves offline or who don't have anything to sell, except objective information and advice. Where appropriate in this chapter, I recommend useful internet sites that meet these criteria.

Computer Money Tasks

In the remainder of this chapter, I detail important personal financial tasks that your computer can help you accomplish. I also provide my recommendations for the best software and web sites where appropriate to help you accomplish these chores.

Pay your bills and track your money

Every month, you write out by hand a bunch of checks to the same organizations and people you wrote checks to last month and the month before that. Checkbook software automates the process of paying your bills. When you have to make your monthly payment to the phone company, for example, your monthly check, already made payable to the phone company, pops up on-screen at your command. All you have to do is fill in the new amount that you have to pay and print your check on your computer's printer. (As I discuss later in this section, for a small monthly fee, you also can pay your bills electronically, completely eliminating the process of writing and mailing in checks.)

Checkbook programs can track your check writing and prepare reports that detail your spending by category — so that you can get a handle on where the fat is in your budget. One drawback of using these programs to track your spending is that it only captures what is entered. So the amount and spending category of your individual credit card and cash purchases, which for most people are substantial, are omitted unless you enter such data (or get a credit card from the software company, which allows you to download your credit card transactions via your computer's modem). For a complete discussion on how to track your spending, please see Chapter 4.

Kiplinger's Simply Money, Quicken, and Microsoft's Money are good programs that I've reviewed in this category. In addition to offering the printed checks and electronic bill-payment features, each of these packages is a financial organizer. The programs allow you to list your investments and other assets and your loans and other financial liabilities.

In addition to a significant investment of your time to learn a software program, another drawback is cost — computer checks are pricey. If you order checks directly from the software manufacturers (order forms come with your software), expect prices of about $75 for 500 checks. You can beat those prices by ordering from other companies. PC Checks and Supplies (www.pcchecks.com), for example, sells 500 checks for $43.

You can avoid dealing with any paper checks at all — written or printed — if you sign up for *online bill payment*. With such services, you save on stamps and envelopes, and the cost of the service may be comparable to what you are spending on those supplies (the cost for most online bill paying services is around $10 per month). Such services are available through increasing numbers of banks, credit unions, and brokerage firms as well as the checkbook programs to anyone with a checking account. An intermediary company that receives your electronic instructions and pays the bill for you enacts the service. No more stamp licking and envelope stuffing. You can even set up regularly recurring bills to be paid automatically.

You don't need a checkbook program to pay your bills online. Simply sign up through a financial institution offering the service. CheckFree's web site (www.checkfree.com) can direct you to firms that offer their bill-paying service. Because most online bill payment services charge a minimum monthly fee, there are cheaper ways to avoid check writing and stamp licking. For example, some businesses you must pay monthly will allow you to establish a monthly electronic payment service directly with them.

Online bill-paying should not be confused with *online banking*, which is a direct, two-way electronic avenue between you and your particular bank. You can make transfers online, get up-to-date check-clearing information, and download your current balance and account statement. This eliminates the need to enter such transactions as ATM withdrawals into your checkbook program, makes reconciling your account a snap, and is offered by some banks for free.

Tracking your investment returns often isn't worth the headache

Accurately tracking the return on your investments can be an extremely complicated, tedious, and time-consuming task — exactly the type of chore that computers were designed to relieve us of. Although you would think that a number of excellent investment tracking software packages would be on the market today, I feel that such available packages are . . . well . . . complicated, tedious, and time-consuming. At this point anyway, these programs are often not any more efficient than the old-fashioned method of pencil, paper, and a calculator.

My big gripe with the investment tracking software programs is that most of them don't allow you to determine your investment's total return. And the programs that do require lots of your time to get to that point. Your effective or *internal rate of return* (IRR), which compares your original amounts invested to the current market value, is the best way to measure the success of your investments over time.

Most of the other packages calculate your *cost basis,* which is your original investment plus reinvested dividends and capital gains, for which you would have already paid taxes in a nonretirement account. When you sell a nonretirement account investment, you need to know the cost basis for tax purposes (refer to Chapter 7). Cost basis reports make your returns look less generous because reinvested distributions increase your original investment and seemingly reduce your returns. I know from direct experience that investors often look at the cost basis reports — which are sometimes misleadingly named "investment performance" or "investment analysis" — and assume that the reports tell them what their total investment returns are. Using software for cost basis calculations is generally not worthwhile because most investment companies provide cost basis information to you upon request or when you sell an investment.

If you want to analyze your historic returns, you need to gather all your old account statements (if you can find them) and enter every investment you made as well as all reinvestments of dividends, interest, and capital gains distributions.

For buy-and-hold mutual fund investors, investment-tracking software has limited benefit given the time required to enter your data. Mutual funds and many other published resources tell you what the funds' total return was for the past year, so you don't need to enter every dividend and capital gain distribution for yourself.

As for calculating the return of your overall portfolio with the old-fashioned method of paper and pencil mentioned above, simply weight the return of each investment by the portion of your portfolio invested in it. For example, with a simple portfolio equally divided between two investments that returned 10 percent and 20 percent respectively, your overall portfolio return would be 15 percent.

Investment tracking software can be more useful for stock traders. In my experience, stock traders don't usually track their overall returns. If they actually used one of these programs, they could at least see how all their trading depresses their returns. (I've never worked with a stock picker who went through this exercise with me and beat the market indexes over the long term.)

Plan for retirement

Good retirement planning software and online calculators can help you to plan for retirement by crunching the numbers for you. But they can also teach you how particular changes — such as your investment returns, rate of inflation, or your savings rate — can affect when, and in what style, you can retire. The biggest time savings aspect of retirement planning software and internet sites is that they let you more quickly play with and see the consequences of changing the assumptions.

Some of the major investment companies that I profile in Part III of this book are the sources for some high-quality, low-cost retirement planning tools. Here are some good ones to consider:

- ✔ T. Rowe Price's Retirement Planning Analyzer software helps those more than five years from retirement to determine how much they should be saving to meet a given retirement goal. When ordered by phone (800-638-5660) the software costs $19.95; when downloaded from the company's web site (www.troweprice.com), it costs $9.95. T. Rowe Price also offers some excellent workbooklets to help you plan for retirement. The company's Retirement Planning Kit is for those more than five years from retirement, and the Retirees Financial Guide is intended for people who are already retired or within five years of retirement. Expect some marketing of T. Rowe Price's mutual funds in these booklets and software.

- ✔ Vanguard's Online Planner on Vanguard's Web site (www.vanguard.com) can help with figuring savings goals to reach retirement goals as well as with managing your budget and assets in retirement. Vanguard also offers a downloadable version of the online planner in the form of a software program called Navigator.

Prepare your taxes

Properly used, good tax preparation software can save you time and money. The best programs "interview" you to gather the necessary information and select the appropriate forms based on your responses. Of course, you're still the one responsible for locating all the information needed to complete your return. More experienced taxpayers can bypass the interview and jump directly to the forms they know they need to complete. These programs also help flag overlooked deductions and identify other tax-reducing strategies.

Among the better tax preparation programs I've reviewed are TurboTax and Kiplinger Taxcut.

In addition to the federal tax packages, tax preparation programs are available for state income taxes, too. Many state tax forms are fairly easy to complete because they are based on information from your federal form. If that's your situation, you may just skip buying the state income tax preparation packages and prepare your state return by hand.

If you're mainly after tax forms, you can get them without charge in tax preparation books or through the IRS web site (`www.irs.gov`).

Research investments

Much of the better information in the online world is geared toward investing in individual stocks. So if you have given up on being the next Warren Buffett and instead invest in mutual funds, the online world will be of less use to you.

The advantage of going online isn't that you profit from getting news sooner or from tapping into the latest predictions of yet more gurus, but that you can access useful resources more quickly and more cheaply than you could before (that is, if your modem is speedy and you know where to look). Rather than schlepping off to the library and fighting over the favorite investing reference manuals, ponying up hundreds of dollars to buy print versions for your own use, or slogging through voice mail hell when you call government agencies, you can access a variety of materials with your computer. You can also usually pay for just what you need:

- `Disclosure-investor.com`. This site supplies information from Securities and Exchange Commission filings and other sources on public companies. Disclosure is a useful place to start if you already have particular stocks in mind and want to learn more about the companies' businesses and financials. Disclosure holds your hand through the process of navigating and understanding the various documents. To sidestep the commercial online service's charges, you can access SEC documents directly via the SEC's internet site (`www.sec.gov`), but be aware that navigating this site takes patience. All public corporations, as well as mutual funds, file with the agency.

- `Morningstar.net`. This site provides access to Morningstar's individual stock and mutual fund reports. The reports are free, but they are watered-down versions of the company's comprehensive software and paper products. If you want to buy Morningstar's unabridged fund reports online, you can do so for $3 each at the web site.

- `Vanguard.com`. Although I'm leery of financial service company "educational" materials because of bias and self-serving advice, some companies do a worthy job. The investor-friendly, penny-pinching Vanguard Group of mutual funds has an online university on its internet site where investors can learn the basics of fund investing. Additionally, investors in Vanguard's funds can access up-to-date personal account information through the site.

If you are an investing and mutual fund novice, you probably won't succeed using the major mutual fund software programs in the marketplace published by Morningstar, Value Line, and a few other companies. None of the programs I've reviewed offer enough guidance on mutual fund basics, such as how to analyze annual operating expense ratios, the merits of no-load versus load funds, how to construct a portfolio, and how to allocate assets. And they're not cheap. The best programs cost several hundred dollars.

Trade online

If you've done your investing homework, trading securities online may save you money and perhaps some time. For years, discount brokers (which I discuss in Chapter 8) had been heralded as the low-cost source for trading. Now, online brokers such as Brown & Company (800-822-2021; www.brownco.com) and Waterhouse (800-934-4443; waterhouse.com) have set a new lower-cost standard.

A number of the newer discount brokers have built their securities brokerage business around online trading. By eliminating the overhead of branch offices, and by accepting and processing trades by computer, online brokers keep their costs and brokerage charges to a minimum. Cut-rate electronic brokerage firms are for people who want to direct their own financial affairs and don't want or need to work with a personal broker. However, some of these brokers have limited products and services. For example, some do not offer many of the best mutual funds. And, my own experience with reaching live people at some online brokers has been trying — I've had to wait more than ten minutes on hold before a customer service representative answered the call.

While online trading may save you on transaction costs, it can also encourage you to trade more than you should, resulting in higher total trading costs, lower investment returns, and higher income tax bills. Following investments on a daily basis encourages you to think short term. Remember that the best investments are bought and held for the long haul (see Part III for more information).

Read and search periodicals

Many business and financial publications are going online to offer investors news and financial market data. *The Wall Street Journal* offers an online personalized edition of the paper (update.wsj.com). You can tailor the content to meet your specific needs. The cost is $59 per year ($29 if you're already a *Journal* subscriber).

Leading business publications such as Forbes (www.forbes.com) and Business Week (www.businessweek.com) put their magazines' content on the web, which also allows you to conduct searches for articles on specific topics that interest you. Be careful, though, as I discuss in the next chapter, to take with many grains of salt what you read and hear in the mass media. Much of the content revolves around tweaking people's anxieties and dwelling on the latest crises and fads.

Buy life insurance

If loved ones are financially dependent upon you, you probably know that you need some life insurance. But, add together the dread of life insurance salespeople and a fear of death, and you have a recipe for procrastination. While your computer can't stave off the grim reaper, it can help you find a quality, low-cost policy that can be more than 80 percent less costly than the most expensive options, without having to deal with high-pressure sales tactics.

The best way to shop for term life insurance online is through one of the online agency quotation services such as SelectQuote (www.selectquote.com), InstantQuote (www.instantquote.com), or Waterhouse Insurance Services (www.waterhouse.com). At each of these sites, you fill in your date of birth, whether you smoke, how much coverage you'd like, and for how long you'd like to lock in the initial premium. A new web page pops up with a list of low-cost quotes (based on assumed good health) from highly rated (for financial stability) insurance companies.

Invariably, the quotes are ranked by how cheap they are. While cost is certainly an important factor, many of these services don't do as good a job explaining what other important factors to consider when doing your comparison shopping. For example, the projected and maximum rates after the initial term has expired are sometimes not covered. Be sure to ask about these other future rates before you agree to a specific policy.

If you decide to buy a policy from one of these online agencies, you can fill in an online application form. The quotation agency will then mail you a detailed description of the policy and insurer, and your completed application. And, I'm sorry to say, in addition to having to deal with snail mail, you're also going to have to deal with a "medical technician" who will drop by your home to check on your health status . . . at least until some computer genius figures out a way for you to give a blood and urine sample online!

Prepare legal documents

Just as you can prepare a tax return with the advice of a software program, you can also prepare common legal documents. This type of software may save you from the often-difficult task of finding a competent and affordable attorney.

Using legal software is generally preferable to using fill-in-the-blank documents. Software has the built-in virtues of directing and limiting your choices and preventing you from making common mistakes. Quality software also incorporates the knowledge and insights of the legal eagles who developed the software. And it can save you money.

When your situation isn't unusual, legal software may work well for you. As to the legality of documents that you create with legal software, remember that a will, for example, is made legal and valid by your witnesses; the fact that an attorney prepares the document is *not* what makes it legal.

An excellent package for preparing your own will is WillMaker, published by Nolo Press, a name synonymous with high quality and user-friendliness in the legal publishing world. In addition to allowing you to prepare wills, WillMaker can also help you prepare a *living will* and medical power of attorney document (refer to Chapter 17).

Nolo's Living Trust software allows you to create a living trust that serves to keep property out of probate in the event of your death (see Chapter 17). Like wills, living trusts are fairly standard legal documents that you can properly create with the guidance of a top-notch software package. The Living Trust package also advises you to seek professional guidance for your situation, if necessary.

Chapter 20

On Air and in Print

. . . .

In This Chapter:

▶ Recognizing the mass media's impact on investors

▶ Deciding whether to tune in or tune out radio and television investing coverage

▶ Surfing safely for investing information on the internet

▶ Evaluating newspapers and magazines

▶ Finding the best investing books

. . . .

*Y*ou won't lack for options when it comes to finding radio and television news, internet sites, newspapers, magazines, and books that talk about money (explicitly and implicitly) and purport to help you get rich. Tuning out poor sources and focusing upon the best is the real challenge.

Since you probably don't consider yourself a financial expert, more often than not, you won't know who to believe and listen to. This chapter helps you solve that problem.

The Mass Media

For better and for worse, America's mass media has had profound influences on our culture. On the good side, news is widely disseminated these days so if a product is recalled or a dangerous virus breaks out in your area, you'll probably hear about it, perhaps more than you want to, through the media — and perhaps from tuned-in family members!

The downsides are plenty, though.

Alarmists

Imagine sitting down to watch the evening news and hearing the following stock market report:

"On Wall Street today, stock prices dropped a bit less than one percent, extending the market's decline of the past week. The reason: There were more people wanting to sell than those wanting to buy. For the year, the U.S. market is still up 15 percent, which is well above the historic average annual return of 10 percent."

Now, contrast that report with the following report for the same day:

"Stocks plunged sharply today as the Dow Jones Industrial Average plummeted more than 100 points to close at its lowest level in the past 168 hours. Dell Computer saw its shares get creamed 10 percent as the company issued a profit warning that third-quarter revenues would take a big hit due to the Taiwan earthquake. Banking stocks got hammered again, and the sector is now off more than 20 percent from its peak this past spring."

While the second news report goes into more detail, it is meant to be more provocative and anxiety-producing. Most of the daily stock market reports I hear in the media are like this rather than the mundane, calming first report. News producers, in their quest for ratings and advertising dollars, seek to be alarming.

Poor values

Daily doses of American mass media, including all the advertising that comes with it, essentially communicate the following messages to us:

- Your worth as a person is directly related to your physical appearance (including quality of clothing and jewelry you wear) and your material possessions — cars, homes, electronics, and other gadgets.

- The more money you make, the more "successful" you clearly are.

- The more famous you are (especially movie and sports stars), the more you're worth listening to and admiring.

- Don't bother concerning yourself with the consequences of your behavior before engaging in it.

- Delaying gratification and making sacrifices is for boring losers.

So bad is some of the programming in the mass media that Former U.S. Secretary of Education and Republican William J. Bennett teamed up with Democratic Senator Joseph Lieberman to create the Silver Sewer Award to be presented each year to a deserving media organization in recognition of its outrageous contribution to the degradation and coarsening of our culture and its unswerving dedication to the pursuit of profit above principle.

The latest Silver Sewer Award dishonored recipient was the Fox Television Network and its CEO, Rupert Murdoch. Lieberman and Bennett said Murdoch had ". . . led one of America's largest, most successful, most powerful television networks into the gutter. He is now responsible for what is perhaps the worst — the most crude, cynical and insulting — material ever to be broadcast to the American public over network television airwaves . . .There seems to be almost nothing that Fox will not broadcast. Its shows are filled with vulgarity, lewdness, promiscuity, violence and overall decadence."

 Continually inundating yourself with poor messages absolutely can cause you to behave in a way that undermines your long-term happiness and financial success. Don't support (by watching) media that don't reflect your values and morals.

Worship of prognosticating pundits

Perhaps the only thing the media loves more than hyping short-term news events is to quote and interview experts. What's the economy going to do next quarter? What's stock XYZ going to do next month? What's the stock market going to do in the next hour? No, I'm not kidding about that last one — stock market cable channel CNBC regularly interviews floor traders from the New York Stock Exchange late in the trading day to get their opinions about what the market will do in the last hour before closing!

 Prognosticating pundits keep many people tuned in since their advice is constantly changing (and therefore entertaining and anxiety-producing) and gives investors hope that they can maneuver their investments in advance to outfox future financial market moves. Common sense suggests, though, that no one has a working crystal ball, and if they did, they certainly wouldn't share such insights gratis with the mass media. (For more on experts who purport to predict the future, see Chapter 8.)

Radio and Television

Over the years, money issues have received increased coverage through the major media of television and radio. Is that because managing your money is so much more complicated than it was a generation ago? Not really — while we have more financial products and services to choose from these days, the best of these can simplify rather than complicate your financial life. For example, while there are far more mutual funds to choose from today than in decades past, many of the better fund companies offer funds of funds to simplify the process of building a portfolio of mutual funds.

Particular topics gain more coverage in radio and television because it helps draw more advertising dollars (which follow what people are watching). When you click on the radio or television, you don't pay a fee to tune in (pay cable channels being an exception). Advertising won't necessarily prevent a medium from delivering objective, in-your-best-interests coverage of a topic, but it sure doesn't help.

Can you imagine, for example, a financial radio or television correspondent saying:

> "We've decided to stop providing financial market updates every five minutes because we've found it causes some investors to become addicted to tracking the short-term movements in the markets and to lose sight of the bigger picture. We don't want to encourage people to make knee-jerk reactions to short-term events."

Another problem with both of these media is soundbite-itis. Producers and network executives believe that if you go into too much detail, viewers and listeners will change channels.

Now, as I discuss elsewhere in this chapter and book, radio and television are hardly the only media that offer some poor advice and cause investor myopia. The internet can be even worse, for example. And, I've read plenty of lousy money books over the years.

The Internet

Are you tired of hearing about the internet? I'm finding more and more people who are — and who can blame them? Sure, the internet is changing the world, but certainly not always for the better and not always in such a big way.

Consider the way we shop. Okay, you can buy things online that in the past you couldn't. Big deal — what's the difference between calling an 800 number and doing mail order, which many of us did for years before the internet got commercialized, and clicking your computer mouse to buy an object you desire? Purchasing things online simply broadens the avenues through which you can spend money. I see a big downside here: Overspending is easier for some who surf the internet a lot.

How about the way we invest? Some of the best web sites allow you to more efficiently access information that may help you make important investing decisions. However, this doesn't mean your computer and modem allow you to compete at the same level as a professional money manager. No, the playing field ain't level. The best pros work at their craft full-time and have far more expertise and experience than the rest of us. Some nonprofessionals have been fooled into believing that investing online makes them better investors. My experience has been that people who spend time online daily dealing with investments tend to trade and react more to short-term events and have a harder time keeping the bigger picture and their long-term goals and needs in focus.

If you know where to look, you can more easily access some types of information. However, there's a lot of crappola online — just as on other advertiser dominated media like television and radio. In Chapter 19, I explain how to safely navigate online to the best of what's out there.

Newspapers and Magazines

Despite the internet and other supposed sources of competition, financial print publications have also mushroomed in recent years. Compared with radio and television, print publications generally offer lengthier discussions of topics. And, in the more financially focused publications, the editors who work on articles generally have more background in the topics they write about.

Even within the better publications, I find a wide variety of quality, so don't instantly believe what you read, even if you read a piece in a publication you like. Here's how to get the most from financial periodicals:

- ✔ **Read some back issues**. At your local library or perhaps through the publication's web site, read some issues that are at least one to two years old. While reading old issues may seem silly and pointless, it can actually be enlightening. By reviewing a number of past issues at a sitting, you can begin to get a flavor for a publication's style, priorities, and philosophies. You can also generally get old content gratis.

- ✔ **Look for solid information and perspective**. Headlines reveal a lot about how a publication perceives its role. Publications with cover stories such as "10 hot stocks to buy now!" and "Funds that will double your money in the next three years!" are probably best avoided. Look for articles that seek to educate with accuracy, not predict.

- ✔ **Note bylines**. Over time, as you read a given publication, you should begin to make note of the different writers. As you get to know who the better ones are, you can skip over the ones you don't care for and spend your limited free time reading the best.

- ✔ **Don't react**. Here's a common example of how not to use information and advice you glean from publications. I had a client who had some cash he wanted to invest. He would read an article about investing in real estate investment trusts and then go out the next week and buy several. Then he'd see a mention of some technology stock funds and invest in some of those. Eventually, his portfolio was a mess of investments that reflected the history of what he had read rather an orchestrated, well-thought-out investment portfolio.

Books

One of my favorite ways to get a crash course on a given financial topic is to read a good book. As with the other types of resources discussed in this chapter, you definitely have to choose carefully — there's plenty of mediocrity and garbage out there (please see my discussion in Chapter 2 about the publishing and book business).

Good books can go into depth on a topic in a way that simply isn't possible in other resources. Books also aren't cluttered with advertising and the conflicts inherent therein.

Here's a list of some of my favorite financial titles:

- ✔ *The Ultimate Credit Handbook: How to Double Your Credit, Cut Your Debt, and Have a Lifetime of Great Credit* by Gerri Detweiler (Plume)

- ✔ *A Random Walk Down Wall Street* by Burton Malkiel (Norton)

- ✔ *Stocks for the Long Run* by Jeremy Siegel (McGraw Hill)

- ✔ *Bogle on Mutual Funds* by John C. Bogle

- ✔ *Built to Last: Successful Habits of Visionary Companies* by James Collins and Jerry Porras (Harper Business)

- ✔ *Paying for College Without Going Broke* by Kalman A. Chany (Princeton Review)

- ✔ *Don't Miss Out: The Ambitious Student's Guide to Financial Aid* by Anna and Robert Leider (Octameron Associates)

- ✔ Nolo Press's legal titles

- ✔ And, not surprisingly, my books on investing, mutual funds, taxes, home buying, house selling, mortgages, and small business, all published by IDG Books

Part VI
The Part of Tens

The 5th Wave   By Rich Tennant

"I can always tell when Philip is working on family finances. A 'cursor' appears on both sides of the computer screen."

In this part . . .

You find some fun and useful chapters that will help you with financial strategies for ten life changes and remind you of ten things more important than money. Why "tens"? Why not?

Chapter 21

Eric's Tips for Ten Life Changes

· ·

Some of life's changes come unexpectedly, like earthquakes. Others you can see coming when they are still far off on the horizon, like a big storm moving in off the ocean. Whether a life change is predictable or not, your ability to navigate successfully through its challenges and to adjust quickly to its new circumstances depends largely on your degree of preparedness.

Perhaps you find my comparison of life changes to earthquakes and storms to be a bit negative. After all, some of the changes I discuss in this chapter should be occasions for joy, and here I am comparing them to natural disasters. But realize that what one defines as a "disaster" has everything to do with his or her preparedness. To the person who has stored no emergency rations in his basement, the big snowstorm that has trapped him in his home could mean problems. But to the prepared person with plenty of food and water, that same storm could mean a vacation from work and a relaxing week in the midst of a winter wonderland.

Before I discuss critical financial issues for you to deal with before and during major life changes, here are some general tips that apply to all life changes:

- ✔ **Stay in financial shape.** An athlete is best able to withstand physical adversities during competition by training and eating well in advance. Likewise, the more sound your finances are to begin with, the better able you'll be to deal with life changes.

- ✔ **Changes require change.** Even if your financial house is in order, a major life change — starting a family, buying a home, starting a business, divorcing, retiring — should prompt you to review your personal financial strategies. Why? Because life changes often affect your income, spending, insurance needs, and ability to take financial risk.

- ✔ **Make changes sooner rather than later.** Being human, most of us procrastinate. But with a major life change on the horizon, procrastination can be costly. You (and your family) might overspend and accumulate high-cost debts, lack proper insurance coverage, or take other unnecessary risks. Early preparation can save you from these pitfalls.

    ✔ **Manage stress and your emotions.** Life changes often are accompanied by stress and other emotional upheavals. During changes, don't make knee-jerk decisions. Take the time to become fully informed and recognize and acknowledge your feelings. Educating yourself is key, and you may want to hire experts to help (refer to Chapter 18). Don't abdicate decisions and responsibilities to advisors — the advisors may not have your best interests at heart or fully appreciate your needs.

Here, then, are the major life changes that you may have to deal with at some point in your life. I wish you more of the good changes than the bad.

Starting Out: Your First Job

If you've just graduated from college or some other program, or are otherwise entering the workforce, your increased income and reduction in educational expenses are probably a welcome relief. You would think, then, that more young adults wouldn't have financial trouble and challenges. But they do, largely because of poor financial habits picked up at home or from the world at large. Here's how to get on the path to financial success:

    ✔ **Don't use consumer credit.** The use and abuse of consumer credit can cause financial pain and hardship well into adult life. You'd like furniture, a new television, and lots of fun vacations, but all these things cost money. To get off on the right financial foot, young workers should shun the habit of making purchases on credit cards that they can't pay for in full when the bill arrives in the mail. The simple solution if you overspend and run up outstanding credit card balances: Don't carry a credit card. Cash and checks worked fine for decades before credit cards arrived on the scene. If you need the convenience of making purchases with a piece of plastic instead of cash or checks, get a debit card (see Chapter 5).

    ✔ **Get in the saving and investing habit.** Should you hope to someday own a home and cease full-time work, you'll need to save over many years. Ideally, your savings should be directed into retirement accounts that offer tax benefits unless you want to accumulate down-payment money for a home or small-business purchase (see Chapter 3). Thinking about a home purchase or retirement is usually not in the active thought patterns of first-time job seekers. I'm often asked, "At what age should a person start saving?" To me, that's similar to asking at what age you start brushing your teeth. Well, when you have teeth to brush! So I say you should start saving and investing money from your first paycheck. Try starting to save 5 percent and then eventually 10 percent of every paycheck. If you're having trouble saving money, track your spending and make cutbacks as needed (refer to Chapters 4 and 6).

✔ **Get insured.** Many people starting out are able to rationalize themselves out of buying insurance. When you're young and healthy, it's hard to imagine life otherwise. Many twentysomethings give little thought to the potential for health care expenses. But because accidents and unexpected illnesses can strike at any age, forgoing coverage can be financially devastating. Buying disability coverage, which replaces income lost to a long-term disability, in a first full-time job with more limited benefits is wise as well. And as you begin to build your assets, consider making out a will so that your assets go where you want in the event of your death.

✔ **Continue your education.** Once you're out in the work force, you (like many other people) may realize how little you've learned in formal schooling that can be used in the real world and, conversely, how much you need to learn (like personal financial management) that school never taught you. Read, learn, and continue to grow. Continuing education will help you to advance in your career and enjoy the world around you.

Changing Jobs or Careers

During your adult life, you will almost surely change jobs — perhaps as often as several times a decade. I hope that most of the time you'll be changing by your own choice. But let's face it: Job security is not what it used to be. Corporate downsizing has made victims of even the most talented workers.

Always be prepared for a job change. No matter how happy you are in your current job, knowing that your world won't fall apart if you are not working tomorrow will give you an added sense of security and encourage an openness to possibility. Whether it's a job change by choice or necessity, the following financial maneuvers will ease the transition:

✔ **Structure your finances to afford an income dip.** Spending less than you earn always makes good financial sense, but if you're coming up to a possible job change, this is even more important, particularly if you are entering a new field or starting your own company and you expect a short-term income dip. Many people view a lifestyle of thriftiness as restrictive, but ultimately those thrifty habits can give you *more* freedom to do what you want to do. Be sure to keep an emergency reserve fund (refer to Chapter 8).

If you lose your job, batten down the hatches. Normally, when you lose your job through no choice of your own, you get little advance warning. That does not mean, however, that you can't do anything financially. Evaluating and slashing your current level of spending may be necessary. Everything should be fair game, from how much you spend on housing to how often you eat out to where you do your grocery shopping. Avoid at all costs the temptation to maintain your level of spending by accumulating consumer debt.

- ✔ **Evaluate the total financial picture when relocating.** At some point in your career, you may have the option of relocating. But don't call the moving company until you understand the financial consequences of such a move. You can't simply compare salaries and benefits between the two jobs. Also compare the cost of living between the two areas: That includes housing, commuting, state income and property taxes, food, utilities, and all the other major expenditure categories that I discuss in Chapter 4.

- ✔ **Track your job search expenses for tax purposes.** If you are seeking a new job in your current (or recently current) field of work, your job search expenses may be tax-deductible. Even if you don't get a job you seek, you can deduct the expenses related to your search and interviews. Remember, however, that if you are moving into a new career, your job search expenses are not tax-deductible. See Chapter 7 for details.

Getting Married

Ready to tie the knot with the one you love? Congratulations — I hope that you'll have a long, healthy, and happy life together. In addition to the emotional and moral commitments that you and your spouse make to one another, you'll probably be merging many of your financial decisions and resources. It would be highly unusual for you and your spouse to have identical money personalities; after all, opposites often attract. Even if you are largely in agreement about your financial goals and strategies, managing as two is different than managing as one.

- ✔ **Take a compatibility test.** Too many couples never discuss their goals and plans before marriage; failing to do so breaks up way too many of these marriages. Finances are just one of many issues to discuss. Others include expectations for having and raising children, dealing with in-laws, career goals, and so on. A good way to minimize your chances for heartache is to ensure that you know what you're getting yourself into. Ministers, priests, and rabbis sometimes offer premarital counseling to surface issues and differences. Don't let romance blind you to important issues vital to the long-term health of your marriage.

- ✔ **Consider taxes.** Some couples are depressed to learn that their joint income tax bill will be higher, perhaps significantly higher, once married. More than a few couples actually allow their joint tax burdens to influence when and even if they marry. You're more likely to be hit with a higher combined tax bill when married if both you and your partner earn above-average incomes and/or are high-income earners. The only way to know what will happen to your tax bill is to get out a tax return and plug in the relevant numbers and see what the IRS will do to you after you're married. If you're flexible in terms of the timing of your wedding and a late-in-the year wedding will cause you to pay much more in taxes, consider waiting until early the following year.

✔ **Discuss and set joint goals.** Once you are married, you and your spouse should set aside time once a year or every few years to discuss personal and financial goals for the years ahead. If for no other reason, talking about where you want to go helps ensure that you're rowing your financial boat in the same direction.

✔ **Decide whether to keep finances separate or jointly managed.** Some couples choose to keep separate financial accounts, whereas others pool resources. Philosophically, I like the idea of pooling better. After all, marriage is a partnership and shouldn't be a "his" versus "hers" affair. In some marriages, however, spouses choose to keep some money separate, particularly for spending purposes so that they don't feel the scrutiny of a spouse with different spending preferences. Spouses who have been through divorce may choose to keep the assets they bring into the new marriage separate in order to earmark and protect their assets in the event they divorce again. As long as you're jointly accomplishing what you need to, some separation of money is okay. But for the health of your marriage, don't hide money from one another, and, if you're the higher-income spouse, don't assume power and control over your joint income.

✔ **Coordinate and maximize employer benefits.** If one or both of you have access to a package of employee benefits through an employer, understand how best to make use of those benefits. Coordinating and using the best that each package has to offer is like giving yourselves a pay raise. For example, if you both have access to health insurance, compare which of you has better benefits. Likewise, one of you may have a better retirement savings plan — one that matches and offers superior investment options. Unless you can afford to save the maximum through both your plans, saving more in the better plan will increase your combined assets. (**Note:** If you're concerned about what happens if you save more in one of your retirement plans and then divorce, in most states that money is considered part of your joint assets to be divided equally.)

✔ **Discuss life and disability insurance needs.** If you and your spouse can make do without each other's income, you might not need any income-protecting insurance. However, if, like many husbands and wives, both spouses depend upon each other's incomes, or if one spouse depends fully or partly on the other's income, you may each need to have long-term disability and term life insurance policies (refer to Chapter 16).

✔ **Update your wills.** When you marry, you should update your wills. If you haven't gotten around to making a will, having a will is potentially more valuable when you're married, especially if you want to leave money to others in addition to your spouse, or if you have children for whom you should name a guardian. See Chapter 16 for more on wills.

✔ **Reconsider beneficiaries on investment and life insurance.** With retirement accounts and life insurance policies, you name beneficiaries to whom the money or value in those accounts will go in the event of your passing. When you marry, you will probably want to rethink beneficiaries.

Starting a Small Business

Many people aspire to be their own bosses, but far fewer people actually leave their jobs in order to achieve that dream. Psychologically and financially, giving up the apparent security of a job with benefits and a built-in network of coworkers is difficult for most people. Going into small business is not for everyone, but don't let inertia stand in your way. Here are some tips to help get you started and increase your chances for long-term success:

✔ **Prepare to ditch your job.** Do you spend all or nearly all that you earn while employed and haven't banked a war chest? Many people in such a situation never leave their jobs behind to pursue their entrepreneurial dreams because they feel dependent upon their paychecks. Live as spartan a lifestyle as you can while you are employed to maximize your ability to save money; you will simultaneously be developing thrifty habits that will help you weather the reduced income and increased expenditure period that comes with most small-business start-ups. You might also consider easing into your small business by working at it part-time in the beginning, with or without cutting back on your normal job.

✔ **Develop a business plan.** If you research and think through your business idea, you'll not only reduce the likelihood of your business failing and increase its success if it thrives, but you'll also feel more comfortable taking the entrepreneurial plunge. A good business plan should be a blueprint for how you expect to build the business. It should describe in detail the business idea, the marketplace you'll be competing in, your marketing plans, and expected revenue and expenses.

✔ **Replace your insurance coverage.** Before you finally decide to leave your job, set the wheels in motion to get proper insurance coverage. With health insurance, employers allow you to continue your existing coverage (at your own expense) for 18 months and then convert. Thanks to a relatively new law, individuals with existing health problems are allowed to purchase an individual policy at the same price that a healthy individual can. With disability insurance, securing coverage before you leave your job is best so that you have income to qualify for coverage. If you have life insurance through your employer, you should secure new individual coverage as soon as you know you're going to leave your job (refer to Chapter 16 for more details).

✔ **Establish a retirement savings plan.** Once your business is making a profit, consider establishing a retirement savings plan such as a SEP-IRA or Keogh. As I explain in Chapter 11, such plans allow you to shelter up to 20 percent of your business income from federal and state taxation.

Buying a Home

Most Americans end up buying a home. To be a financial success, you need not own a home, but home ownership certainly offers financial rewards. Over the course of your adult life, the real estate that you own should appreciate in value. Additionally, someday you should have your mortgage paid off, which will greatly reduce your housing costs. As a renter, on the other hand, your full housing costs will increase over time with inflation.

If you're considering buying a home:

✔ **Get your overall finances in order.** Before you consider buying a home, you need to analyze your current budget, your ability to afford debt, and your future financial goals. Make sure that your expected housing expenses still allow you to save properly for retirement and other long- or short-term objectives. Don't buy a home based upon what lenders are willing to lend. Read and digest the relevant portions of this book to get your financial house in order before you buy.

✔ **Determine if now's the time.** Especially if you're a first-time home buyer, buying if you don't see yourself staying put three to five years rarely makes financial sense. Buying and selling a home gobbles up a good deal of money in transaction costs — you'll be lucky to recoup all those costs even within a five-year period. Also, if your income is likely to drop or you have other pressing goals, such as starting a business, you might wait to buy.

To learn more about buying a home, be sure to read Chapter 14.

Budgeting for life changes

One thing is certain about life: It changes — marriage, buying a home, family expansion, starting a business, divorce, retirement, or the death of a spouse. Although some life events bring joy and others sorrow, all bring financial change. If you don't manage this change, it may end up managing and ruling you.

I've witnessed the best of savers turn into deficit financiers due to the financial upheaval and shock waves from a major life event — even those events that were anticipated. You should budget ahead for life changes.

For example, if you'd like to take the entrepreneurial plunge and leave your full-time job, you should know whether you can afford to do that and what impact changed expenses and income would have on your ability to save money. Wannabe parents, likewise, should consider how increased expenses and a likely reduction in income would affect their monthly budget.

Going through this exercise is a great way to estimate what impact a child or other significant life change will have on your financial situation. I advised some nervous expectant parents to go through this budgeting exercise because they were wondering what financial impact having a baby would have on their household finances. Their findings: Given their expected spending, the parents would go from saving 12 percent of their annual incomes to spending 5 percent more than they earned. But the lower-income spouse was also surprised to see that, by working half-time rather than full-time, the couple's net savings would actually increase thanks largely to lower taxes, child-care, and work-related expenses.

In Chapter 4, I provide suggested categories for tallying your expenses — such as housing, clothing, auto, cable TV, furniture, insurance, telephone, other utilities, education, and so on. You can adjust and create new spending and income categories to match your personal financial situation.

As you plan for your next life change, remember the limitations of quantitative analysis. It can't factor in the nonfinancial considerations such as how you feel about working more or less because of a life change. Crunching numbers may also mistakenly give you the illusion of control. Those expectant parents that I told you about earlier learned that they were having three new additions to their family and not just one!

Having Children

If you thought being a responsible adult, holding down a job, paying your bills on time, and preparing for your financial future was tough, wait 'til you add kids to the equation. Most parents find that, with kids in the family, the already precious commodities of free time and money become even more precious — sometimes even extinct. The more efficiently you learn how to manage your time and money, the better able you will be to have a sane, happy, and financially successful life as a parent.

Here are some key things to recognize and to do both before and after you begin your family:

✔ **Set your priorities: You can't do it all and have it all.** As with many other financial decisions, starting or expanding a family requires that you financially plan ahead. Set your priorities and structure your finances and living situation accordingly. Is it more important to have a bigger home in a particular community, or would you rather have less pressure to work and spend more time with your family? Keep in mind that a less hectic work life not only gives you more free time but also often reduces your cost of living by decreasing meals out, dry cleaning costs, day care expenses, and so on.

✔ **Take a hard look at your budget.** If you've had a hard time living within your means before children, then you definitely should take an honest look at how your income and spending will change after your family grows. In addition to diaper changes and less sleep at night, children mean increased spending. At a minimum, expenditures for food and clothing will increase. But you're also likely to spend more on housing, insurance, day care, and education. On top of that, if you want to play an active role in raising your children, working at a full-time job won't be possible. So while you consider the added expenses, you may also need to factor in a decrease in income.

No simple rules of thumb exist for estimating how children will affect your household's income and expenses. On the income side, figure out how much you'll want to cut back on work. On the expense side, government statistics show that the average household with school-age children spends about 20 percent more than those without. A more scientific approach would be for you to go through your budget category by category and estimate how kids will change your spending (use the worksheets in Chapter 4).

✔ **Boost insurance coverages *before* getting pregnant.** Before you try to have a baby, be sure that your health insurance plan offers maternity benefits (ask about waiting periods that may exclude coverage for a pregnancy within the first year or so of the insurance). With disability insurance, pregnancy is considered a preexisting condition, so a woman lacking such coverage should secure it before getting pregnant. And most families-to-be should buy life insurance. Buying life insurance *after* the bundle of joy comes home from the hospital is a risky proposition — if Mom or Dad develops a health problem, she or he could be denied coverage. Also consider buying life insurance for a stay-at-home parent. Even though that parent is not bringing in income, if he or she were to pass away, hiring assistance could cripple the family budget.

✔ **Check maternity leave with your employers.** Many larger employers offer some maternity leave for women and, in rare but thankfully increasing cases, for men. At some employers, the leaves are paid and with others, they're not. Understand the options and the financial ramifications before you consider the leave and ideally before you get pregnant.

✔ **Update your will.** If you had a will before starting a family, you'll need to do a new one. If you don't have a will, make one now. With children in the picture, name a guardian in your will who will be responsible for raising your children should you and your spouse both pass away. Although choosing a guardian is a daunting decision, even more frightful is the thought of letting courts decide who would raise your children.

✔ **Enroll the baby in your health plan.** Once he or she is welcomed into this world, enroll your newborn in your health insurance plan. Most insurers give you about a month or so to enroll. New parents tend to forget to do things amidst the whirlwind of time-consuming parenting responsibilities. Also get Junior a Social Security number, which comes in handy for many occasions — especially when filing your next income tax return. Without a Social Security number, you can't claim your child as a dependent (and get that tax break).

✔ **Understand child care tax benefits.** For every one of your children with an official Social Security number, you get a $2,800 deduction from your income taxes (tax year 2000). So if you're in the 28 percent federal tax bracket, each child saves you a cool $784 in federal taxes. On top of that, you may be eligible for a $500 tax credit for each child under the age of 17. That should certainly motivate you to take the two minutes to apply for your kid's Social Security number!

If you and your spouse both work (full- or part-time) and you have children under the age of 13, you can also claim a tax credit for child care expenses. Or, you may work for one of the increasing numbers of employers who offer flexible benefit or spending plans. These plans allow you to put money away from your paycheck on a pre-tax basis, up to $5,000 per year, which you can then use to pay for child care expenses. For many parents, especially those in higher income tax brackets, these plans can save a lot of taxes. Keep in mind, however, that if you take advantage of one of these plans, you cannot also claim the child care tax credit mentioned earlier, and you must deplete the entire account every tax year or you forfeit any money not used.

✔ **Ignore saving in custodial accounts.** New parents often feel the weight of new responsibilities on their shoulders. One common concern is how to sock away enough money to pay for the ever-rising cost of a college education. If you start saving money in your child's name in a so-called custodial account, however, you might not only be harming your child's future ability to qualify for financial aid but you might also be missing out on the tax benefits that come with investing elsewhere. See Chapter 13.

✔ **Don't indulge the children.** Toys, art classes, sports, field trips, and the like can rack up big bills, especially if not controlled. Some parents exercise little control over children's programs. Most parents don't set guidelines or limits on extracurricular activities. Some put their children's desires ahead of all other financial needs and goals. Others mindlessly follow the example of peers' families. Introspective parents have shared with me that they feel some insecurity about providing the best for their children. The parents (and kids) that seem happiest and most financially successful are those who clearly distinguish between material luxuries and family necessities.

As children get older and become indoctrinated into the world of shopping, all sorts of other purchases come into play. Consider giving your kids a weekly allowance and letting them learn how to spend and manage it. And when they're old enough, having your kids get a part-time job helps teach financial responsibility as well.

Caring for Aging Parents

There comes a time for many of us when we reverse roles with our parents. Instead of being the one who is cared for, you become the caregiver or the caretaker. As your parents age, they may need help with a variety of issues and living tasks. Although it's unlikely that you'll have the time or ability to perform all these functions yourself, you may well end up being the coordinator of service providers who can.

Here are some things to consider when caring for aging parents:

✔ **Get help where possible.** In most communities, a variety of nonprofit organizations offer information and sometimes even counseling to families grappling with caring for elderly parents. You might best find your way to such resources through your state's department of insurance as well as recommendations from local hospitals and doctors. You'll especially want to get assistance and information if your parents may need some sort of home care, nursing home care, or assisted living arrangement.

✔ **Get involved in their health care.** Your aging parents may already have a lot on their minds or simply may not be able to coordinate and manage all the health care providers giving them medications and advice. Try, as best as you can, to be their advocate. Speak with their doctors to understand their current medical condition and need for various medications and to help coordinate caregivers. Visit nursing homes and speak with prospective care providers.

✔ **Understand tax breaks.** If you are financially supporting your parents, you may be eligible for a number of tax credits and deductions for elder care. Some employers' flexible benefit plans, for example, allow you to put away money on a pre-tax basis to pay for the care of your parents. Also explore the dependent care tax credit, which you can take on your federal income tax Form 1040. And if you provide half or more of the support costs for your parents, you may be able to claim them as dependents on your tax return.

✔ **Discuss getting the estate in order.** Parents don't like talking and thinking about their demise and usually feel awkward discussing it with their children. But opening a dialogue between you and your folks about such issues can be healthy in many ways. Discussing wills, living wills, living trusts, and estate planning strategies (refer to Chapter 17) can not only make you aware of your folks' situation but can also improve their plans to both their benefit and yours.

✔ **Take some time off.** Caring for an aging parent, particularly one who is having health problems, can be time-consuming and emotionally draining. If you were already juggling the responsibilities of a job, marriage, and parenthood before your parents needed help, you now may well feel completely overwhelmed. Do yourself and your parents a favor and use some vacation time to help get things in order. Although not the kind of vacation you probably envisioned, the time should reduce your stress and help you get more on top of things.

Divorcing

Sadly, half of all marriages end in divorce. In most marriages destined to split up, there are early warning signs that both parties recognize; sometimes, however, one spouse surprises the other with an unexpected request for divorce.

Whether planned or unexpected, here are some key things to consider when getting a divorce:

✔ **Question the divorce.** Some say that divorcing in America is too easy, and I tend to agree. Although some couples are indeed better off to part their ways, others give up too easily, thinking that the grass is greener elsewhere only to later discover that all lawns have weeds and crabgrass. Just as with a lawn that isn't watered and fertilized, relationships can wither without nurturing.

Money and disagreements over money are certainly a contributing factor to marital unhappiness. Unfortunately, in many relationships, money is wielded as power by the spouse who earns more of it. Try talking things over, perhaps with a marital counselor; invest in making your relationship stronger, and reap the dividends for years to come.

✔ **Separate your emotions from the financial issues.** Separating your feelings from your finances is easier said than done. Feelings of revenge may be common in some divorces, but they will probably only help to ensure that the attorneys get rich at your expense as the two of you butt heads. If you really want a divorce, work at doing it efficiently and harmoniously so that you can get on with your lives.

✔ **Detail resources and priorities.** Draw up a list of all the assets and liabilities that you and your spouse have. Be sure that you get all the financial facts, including investment account records and statements. Once you know the whole picture, begin to think about what is and is not important to you financially and otherwise.

✔ **Educate yourself about personal finance and legal issues.** Divorce sometimes forces nonfinancially-oriented spouses to get a crash course in personal finance at a difficult emotional time. Hopefully, this book can help educate you financially. In terms of the legal issues of divorce, visit a bookstore and pick up a good legal guide or two about divorce.

✔ **Choose advisors carefully.** Odds are that you will retain the services of one or more specialists to assist you with the myriad issues, negotiations, and concerns of your divorce. Legal, tax, and financial advisors can help, but recognize their limitations and conflicts of interest. Attorneys, unfortunately, benefit financially the more complicated things become and the more you haggle with your spouse. Don't use your divorce attorney for financial or tax advice — your lawyer probably knows no more than you do in these areas. Also, realize that you don't need an attorney to get divorced. As for choosing tax and financial advisors, if you think you need that type of help, refer to Chapters 7 and 18 for how to find good advisors.

✔ **Analyze your spending.** When you go back to being single, although your "household" expenses will surely be less, you'll probably have to make do with less income. Some divorcees find themselves financially squeezed in the early years following a divorce. In addition to helping you to adjust to a new budget, analyzing your spending needs pre-divorce will help you negotiate a fairer settlement with your spouse.

✔ **Review needed changes to insurance.** If you are covered under your spouse's employer insurance plan, be sure to set the wheels in motion to get those coverages replaced (refer to Chapter 16). If you or your children will still be financially dependent upon your spouse post-divorce, be sure that the divorce agreement mandates life insurance coverage. And you should revise your will (see Chapter 17).

✔ **Revamp your retirement plan.** With changes to your income, expenses, assets, liabilities, and future needs, your retirement plan will surely need an overhaul post-divorce. Refer to Chapter 3 for a reorientation.

Receiving a Windfall

Whether through inheritance, stock options, small-business success, or lottery winnings, you may receive a financial windfall at some point in your life. Like many who are totally unprepared psychologically and organizationally for their sudden good fortune, you may well find that a flood of money can create more problems than it solves. If you're saying, "I should have such problems," fair enough. Who wouldn't rather be rich than poor?

Here are a few tips to help you make your financial windfall the pleasant experience that it should be:

- **Take the time to educate yourself.** If you've never had to deal with significant wealth, there's no reason that I'd expect you to know how to handle it. Don't rush and pressure yourself to invest it as soon as possible. Leaving the money where it is or stashing it in one of the higher-yielding money market funds recommended in Chapter 12 is a far better short-term solution than jumping into investments that you don't understand and haven't taken the time to research.

- **Beware the sharks.** You may begin to wonder if someone has posted your net worth, address, and home telephone number in the local newspaper and on the internet. Brokers and financial advisors may flood you with marketing materials, telephone solicitations, and lunch date requests. These folks who pursue you do so for a reason: They want to convert your money into their income either by selling you investment and other financial products or by managing your money. Stay away from the sharks, educate yourself, and take charge of your own financial moves. Decide on your own terms whom to hire and seek them out. Most of the best advisors that I know don't have the time or philosophical orientation to chase after prospective clients.

- **Recognize the emotional side of coming into a lot of money.** One of the side effects of accumulating wealth quickly is that you may have feelings of guilt or otherwise be unhappy, especially if you expected money to solve your problems. Getting a big inheritance from your folks may make you feel guilty if you didn't invest in your relationship with them and now, with their passing, you regret how you interacted with them. As another example, if you poured endless hours into a business venture that finally paid off, all that money sitting in your investment accounts may leave you with a hollow feeling if you divorced and lost friends through neglecting your relationships.

- **Pay down debts.** One of the simplest and best investments you can make if you come into wealth is to pay off your debts. I had a counseling client come to me who was frustrated because he didn't know how to invest several million dollars he had. Partly because he had worked so hard in his business to build his wealth, he was worried about losing money on investments. He had a decent-size home mortgage at 8 percent interest, which made complete sense for him to pay off. We generally borrow money to buy things that we otherwise couldn't buy in one fell swoop. When you have plenty of money, getting rid of debts is an especially good move.

✔ **Diversify.** To protect your wealth, don't keep it all in one pot. Mutual funds (refer to Chapter 10) are an ideally diversified, professionally managed investment vehicle to consider. And if you want your money to continue growing, consider the wealth-building investments — stocks, real estate, and small-business options — that I discuss in Part III of this book.

✔ **Make use of the opportunity.** Most people work their whole lives for a paycheck in order to pay a never-ending stream of monthly bills. Although I'm not advocating a hedonistic lifestyle, why not take some extra time to travel, spend time with your family, and enjoy the hobbies you've long been putting off? And how about trying a new career that you'd find more fulfilling and that might make the world a better place? Many people have little flexibility. Don't waste it if you do.

Retiring

If you've spent the bulk of your adult life working, retiring can be a challenging life transition. Most Americans have an idealized vision of how wonderful a retired life would be. No more irritating bosses and pressure of work deadlines. Unlimited time to travel, play, and lead the good life. Sounds good, huh? Well, the reality for most Americans is far different, especially for those who don't plan ahead financially and otherwise.

Here are some tips to help you through retirement:

✔ **Plan both financially and personally.** Leaving behind a full-time job and career creates even bigger challenges, such as what to do with all your free time — the opposite problem that new parents have. You can get too much of a good thing, which is why planning for your time and activities in retirement is even more important than planning financially. If your focus during your working years is solely on your career and saving money, you may lack interests, friends, and the ability to know how to spend money once you do retire.

✔ **Take stock of your resources.** Many people worry and wonder if they have sufficient assets to cut back on work or retire completely, yet they haven't crunched any numbers to see where they stand. Sometimes in life, ignorance can be blissful, but this is a case where ignorance might cause you to misunderstand how little or much you really have accumulated for retirement versus what you need. See Chapter 3.

✔ **Reevaluate your insurance needs.** During your working years, you carried disability and perhaps some life insurance to protect you and your dependents should you not be able to earn an income. Once you have sufficient assets to retire, you won't need to retain insurance to protect your employment income any longer. On the other hand, as your assets have grown over the years, you may be underinsured with regards to liability insurance (refer to Chapter 17).

✔ **Decide on health care/living options.** Medical expenses in your retirement years, particularly the cost of nursing home care, can be daunting. Which course of action you take — supplemental insurance, buying into a retirement community, or not doing anything — depends upon your financial and personal situation. Early preparation increases your options. If you wait until you have major health problems, it may be too late to choose certain paths. See Chapter 16 for more details.

✔ **Decide what to do with your retirement plan money.** When you're set to retire, you may have to elect what to do with your retirement plan money and which of your employer's pension options you'd like. If you have money in a retirement savings plan, many employers will offer you the option of leaving the money in the plan rather than rolling it over into your own retirement account. Brokers and financial advisors clearly prefer that you do the latter since it means more money for them. Read Part III of this book to learn about investing and evaluating the quality of your employer's retirement plan investment options.

✔ **Pick a pension option.** Selecting a pension option (plans that pay a monthly benefit during retirement) is similar to choosing a good investment — each pension option carries different risks, benefits, and tax consequences. Pensions are structured by actuaries based on reasonable life expectancies. The younger the age when you start collecting your pension, the less you'll get per month. Check to see if the amount of your monthly pension stops increasing past a certain starting age. You obviously wouldn't want to delay access to your pension benefits past that age because you will receive no reward for waiting any longer, and you'll collect the benefit for fewer months.

If you know that you have a health problem that shortens your life expectancy, drawing your pension sooner is usually to your benefit. Should you plan to continue working in some capacity and earning a decent income once you leave your employer, waiting for higher pension benefits when you'll be in a lower tax bracket is probably wise.

As for your other choices that affect what pension amount your surviving spouse receives should you die first, at one end of the spectrum you have the risky single life option, which pays benefits until you pass away and provides no benefits thereafter for your spouse. This option maximizes your monthly take while you are alive. Only consider this option if your spouse could do without this income. The least risky option and thus least financially rewarding while the pensioner is still living is the *100 percent joint and survivor option,* which pays your survivor the same amount that you received while still alive. The other joint and survivor options fall somewhere in between these two extremes and generally make sense for most couples who desire decent pensions early in retirement but want a reasonable amount to continue should the pensioner die first.

✔ **Get your estate in order.** Confronting your mortality is never a joy, but when you're considering retiring or are retired, getting your estate in order makes all the more sense. Learn about wills and trusts that might benefit you and your heirs. Also consider gifting if you have more than you need. You can't take it with you, and if you are worried about estate taxes, gifting money yearly to your heirs will reduce your taxable estate.

Chapter 22

Ten Things More Important than Money

• •

*T*hroughout this book, I provide information and advice that should enable you to make the most of your money. Whether you have stuck with me since Chapter 1 or have simply skimmed a few chapters, you probably know that I take a holistic approach to money decisions.

Although I hope my financial advice serves you well, I also want to be sure that you remember the many things in life (I chose my ten favorite) that are far more important than the girth of your investment portfolio or the size of your latest paycheck. Too often in our capitalistic society, we place too much emphasis on financial success and status and too little importance on living with a higher purpose. I hope this chapter makes a small contribution to keeping you on the best path.

Family

In our culture, men especially and increasingly women see their primary role as "providing" financially for their families. Such a focus seems to permit people to feel comfortable with making sacrifices for the sake of their work and careers. We also seem to psychologically justify placing work before family because we've been taught the virtues of a strong work ethic.

Some employees rightfully fear that their bosses may not be sympathetic to the needs of their families, especially when those needs get in the way of getting the job done as efficiently as an impatient boss would like. However, others put their companies first because that's what peers do and because they don't want to rock the boat.

Your spouse, your parents, and your kids, of course, should come first. They're much more important than your next promotion, and you should treat them that way. Balance is key. Should your boss not respect or value the importance of family, then perhaps it's time to find a new boss. With the strong economy and low unemployment rate, I can't imagine a better time to be more aggressive in making time for your family. Just be sure that you have a sufficient emergency reserve (see Chapter 3).

Friends

The older some people get, the less time they seem to have for friends. People too busy climbing the career ladder may not even make time for friends.

So many items in our consumer-oriented society are disposable, and unfortunately, friends too often fall into that category. Friends aren't really friends as much as they are acquaintances who can further our careers, and once that function has passed, they're tossed aside.

What friends do you really care for? Do you have friends you can turn to in a time of need who can really listen and be there for you? Take the time to invest in your friendships, both old and new.

Your health

Stress, poor diet, lack of exercise, poor relationships within your family — all of these bad habits can have adverse personal health consequences. People neglect their health for different reasons. In some cases, as with money management, people lack the knowledge as to the keys to good personal health. Getting too caught up in one's career and working endless hours also often leads to neglect of one's health.

Some people don't fully realize what the downside may be to their neglect of their bodies. Worst case, of course, is your untimely demise. But plenty of people suffer from ongoing conditions that damage the body and can make them feel far less well than they could. Unless you believe in reincarnation, you only get one body — take care of it and treat it with the respect it deserves!

Kids

Investing in your children is absolutely one of the best investments you can make. Understanding how to relate to and care for kids can help make you a better and more fulfilled person. (And I think that understanding kids can help you better understand what makes grown-ups tick, too!)

Our future is our children. You should care about children even if you don't have any. Why? Do you care about the quality of our society? Have any concerns about crime? Do you care about the economy? How about entertainment and the arts? What about your Social Security and Medicare benefits?

All of these issues depend to a large extent on our nation's children and what kind of teenagers and adults our children someday become. I know that many parents struggle to balance the demands of work and raising kids. I think everyone benefits when parents find ways to work at their careers less and spend more time with their children. Find ways to make do with what money you have. When your children are grown, they won't remember — nor appreciate — if by working harder at your career, you were able to buy them more computer software or Pokémon cards. They *will* remember — and won't appreciate — a lack of attention.

Your neighbors

Your neighbors can be sources of friendship, happiness, and comfort. Too often, I see people caught up in their daily routines neglecting their neighbors.

Of course, you may not want to get to know all your neighbors better. But give them a chance. Don't write them off because they aren't the same age, race, or occupation as you. Part of our coherence with our greater society comes from where we live, and our neighbors are an important piece of that connection. Don't miss out on that.

Appreciating what you do have

In my work as a financial counselor and writer, I have the opportunity to interact with many people from all walks of life. Despite the overall level of affluence in our society, I continue to be struck by how many people focus upon and lament the material things they lack (a bigger house, more costly cars, and so on) rather than appreciating the material and nonmaterial things they do have.

Right now, make a list of at least ten things that you appreciate. Periodically (daily, weekly, or monthly), make a similar list. Our culture sometimes causes us to dwell on what we don't have (which is usually not nearly as important as what we do have).

Your reputation

What do you think of when I say William Jefferson Clinton, Ivan Boesky, or Michael Milken? All of these people would be deemed successful in a career and monetary sense, but is that what first came to your mind?

One of my professors once said, "It can take a lifetime to build a reputation but only moments to lose it." The Tenth Commandment is, "You shall not covet." As people chase after more fame, power, money, and possessions, they often devalue and underinvest in relationships and breach the other commandments along the way.

Think of the people you most admire in your life. Although I'm sure that none of them are perfect, I bet each has a superior reputation with you.

Education

Education is a lifelong process — it's not just about attending a fancy college and perhaps getting an advanced degree. Whether it's related to your career or a newfound hobby, there's always something to learn. As long as you have your mental capacities, you can keep learning and building on what you already know.

And, who knows, maybe someday you'll gain an understanding of the meaning of life. The older we get, the more we have to reflect upon and learn from.

Having fun

In the quest to earn more, save more, and invest smarter, some people get so caught up in society's money game that money becomes the purpose of their existence. Whether you call it an addiction or obsession, having such a financial focus will surely steer you from the good things in life. I've known plenty of people who realize too late in life that sacrificing personal relationships and one's health isn't worth any amount of financial success.

Therapists' offices are filled with unhappy people who spend too much time and energy chasing promotions and money. These same people come to me as well. Often, they seem to worry about having enough money, and when I tell them that they have "enough," the conversation usually turns to the personal things lacking in their lives.

Solving social problems

Although we may well have the greatest economy on the face of the earth and the highest per capita income of any country, by other more important measures, we Americans have a good deal of room for improvement. Among industrialized countries, we have some of the highest rates of infant mortality, poverty, gun violence, divorce, and suicide. We have more than our fair share of problems.

Why not be part of the solution rather than part of the problem? You can find plenty of causes worthy of your volunteer time or donations such as Big Brothers/Big Sisters, which partners adults with children for informal mentoring, and Habitat for Humanity, which helps build affordable housing.

Glossary

● ●

adjustable-rate mortgage (ARM): A mortgage whose interest rate and monthly payments vary throughout its life. ARMs typically start with an artificially low interest rate that gradually rises over time. The interest rate is determined by a formula: margin (which is a fixed number) plus index (which varies). Generally speaking, if the overall level of interest rates drops, as measured by a variety of different indexes, the interest rate of your ARM generally follows suit. Similarly, if interest rates rise, so does your mortgage's interest rate and monthly payment. The amount that the interest can fluctuate is limited by caps. Before you agree to an ARM, be certain that you can afford its highest possible payments.

adjusted cost basis: For capital gains tax purposes, the adjusted cost basis is how the IRS determines your profit or loss when you sell an asset such as a home or a security. For an investment such as a mutual fund or stock, your cost basis is what you originally invested plus any reinvested money. For a home, you arrive at the adjusted cost basis by adding the original purchase price to the cost of any capital improvements (expenditures that increase your property's value and life expectancy).

adjusted gross income (AGI): The sum of your taxable income (such as wages, salaries, and tips) and taxable interest less allowable adjustments (such as retirement account contributions and moving expenses). AGI is calculated before subtracting your personal exemptions and itemized deductions, which are used to derive your taxable income.

after-tax contributions: Some retirement plans allow you to contribute money that has already been taxed. Such contributions are known as after-tax contributions.

alternative minimum tax (AMT): The name given to a sort of shadow tax system that may cause you to pay a higher amount in federal income taxes than you otherwise would. The AMT was designed to prevent higher income earners from lowering their tax bills too much through large deductions.

American Stock Exchange (AMEX): The second largest stock exchange in the United States, it typically lists mid-sized firms.

annual percentage rate (APR): The figure that states the total yearly cost of a loan as expressed by the actual rate of interest paid. The APR includes the base interest rate and any other add-on loan fees and costs. The APR is thus inevitably higher than the rate of interest that the lender quotes.

annuity: An investment that is essentially a contract backed by an insurance company and is frequently purchased for retirement purposes. Its main benefit is that it allows your money to compound and grow without taxation until withdrawal. Selling annuities is a lucrative source of income for insurance agents and "financial planners" who work on commission, so don't buy one of these until you're sure it makes sense for your situation.

asset allocation: When you invest your money, you need to decide how to proportion it between risky, growth-oriented investments (such as stocks) whose values fluctuate and more stable, income-producing investments (like bonds). How soon you will need the money and how tolerant you are of risk are two important determinants when deciding how to allocate your money.

audit: IRS examination of your financial records, generally at the IRS offices, to substantiate your tax return. Among life's worst experiences.

bank prime rate: See **prime rate**.

bankruptcy: Legal action that puts a halt to creditors' collection actions against you. If you have a high proportion of consumer debt to annual income (25 percent or greater), it may be your best option.

bear market: A period when the stock market experiences a strong downward swing and is usually accompanied by and sometimes precedes an economic recession. Imagine a bear in hibernation, because this is what happens in a bear market: Investors hibernate, and the market falters. During a bear market, the value of stocks can decrease significantly. Usually the market must drop at least 20 percent to be considered a bear market.

beneficiaries: In the event of your death, the people to whom you desire to leave your assets or, in the case of life insurance or a pension plan, your benefits. For each retirement account, you denote beneficiaries.

blue chip stock: The stock of the largest and most consistently profitable corporations. This term comes from poker, where the most valuable chips are blue. The list of these stocks is unofficial and changes.

bond: A loan investors make to a corporation or government. Bonds generally pay a set amount of interest on a regular basis. They are an appropriate investment vehicle for conservative investors who do not feel comfortable with the risk involved in investing in stocks and who want to receive a steady income. All bonds have a maturity date when the bond issuer must pay back at par (full) value the bond holders (lenders). Bonds should not be your primary long-term investment vehicle because they produce little real growth on your original investment after inflation is factored in.

bond rating: See **Standard & Poor's ratings** and **Moody's ratings**.

bond yield: How much a bond will yield to an investor depends on two important factors: creditworthiness of the bond's issuer and the maturity date of the bond. The better the rating a bond receives, the less risk involved and, thus, the lower the yield. As far as the maturity date is concerned, the longer you loan your money, the higher the risk (because it is more likely that rates will fluctuate) and the higher your yield generally will be. A yield is quoted as an annual percentage rate of return that a bond will produce if the bond makes its promised interest payments.

broker: An intermediary. When you buy a house, insurance, or stock, you will most likely do so through a broker. Most brokers are paid on commission, which creates a conflict of interest with their clients. The more the broker sells, the more he or she makes. But more is not necessarily better for you. Some insurance companies let you buy their policies directly, and many mutual fund families bypass stockbrokers. If you're going to work with a broker, a discount broker can help you save on commissions.

bull market: A period when the stock market experiences a strong upward swing, usually accompanied and driven by a growing economy and increasing corporate profits.

callable bond: A bond for which the lender can decide to pay the holder earlier than the previously agreed-upon maturity date. If interest rates are relatively high when a bond is issued, lenders may prefer issuing callable bonds because it gives them the flexibility to call back these bonds and issue new, lower-interest rate ones if interest rates decline. Callable bonds are risky for investors, because if interest rates decrease, the bond holder will get his investment money returned early and may have to reinvest his money at a lower interest rate.

capital gain: One way investors make money with an investment, such as stock. A capital gain is the profit from selling your stock at a higher price than the price for which it was purchased. For example, if you bought 50 shares of Rocky and Bullwinkle stock at $20 per share, and two years later you sold your shares when the price had risen to $25 per share, your profit or capital gain is $5 per share, or $250. If you held this Rocky and Bullwinkle stock outside of a tax-sheltered retirement account, you would owe federal tax on this profit when you sold the stock. In addition to the federal government, many states also levy such a tax.

capital gains distribution: Taxable distribution by a mutual fund or a real estate investment trust (REIT) created by securities that are sold within the fund or REIT at a profit. These distributions may either be short-term (assets held a year or less) or long-term (assets held more than one year).

cash value insurance: A type of life insurance that is extremely popular with insurance salespeople because it commands a high commission. In a cash value policy, you buy life insurance coverage but also get a savings-type account. Unless you are looking for ways to limit your taxable estate (if you are extremely wealthy, for example), avoid cash value insurance. The investment returns tend to be mediocre, and your contributions are not tax-deductible.

Certificate of Deposit (CD): A specific term loan that you make to your banker. The maturity date for CDs ranges from a month up to several years. The interest paid on CDs is fully taxable, thus making CDs inappropriate for higher tax-bracket investors investing outside tax-sheltered retirement accounts.

closed-end mutual fund: A **mutual fund** that decides up front exactly how many shares it will issue to investors. Once all the shares are sold, an investor seeking to invest in the closed-end fund can only do so by purchasing shares from an existing investor. Shares of closed-end funds trade on the major stock exchanges and therefore can sell at either a discount if there are more sellers than buyers or at a premium if demand exceeds supply.

COBRA: Name of the federal legislation that requires health insurers and larger employers to continue to offer health insurance, at the employee's expense, for 18 months after coverage would otherwise end — for example, when an employee is laid off.

commercial paper: A short-term debt or IOU issued usually by larger, stable companies to help make their businesses grow and prosper. Credit worthy companies can sell this debt security directly to large investors and thus bypass borrowing money from bankers. Money market funds invest in soon-to-mature commercial paper.

commission: The percentage of the selling price of a house, stock, bond, or other investment that is paid to agents and brokers. Because most agents and brokers are paid by commission, understanding how the commission can influence their behavior and recommendations is important for investors and home buyers. Agents and brokers make money only when you make a purchase, and they make more money when you make a bigger purchase. Choose an agent carefully, and take your agent's advice with a grain of salt because this inherent conflict of interest can often set an agent's visions and goals at odds with your own.

commodity: A form of derivatives, a financial instrument whose value is derived from the performance of an underlying security such as a stock or bond. Raw materials (gold, wheat, sugar, and gasoline, for example) are commodities traded on the futures market.

common stock: Shares in a company that do not offer a guaranteed amount of dividend to investors; the amount of dividend distributions, if any, is at the discretion of company management. While they may or may not make money through dividends, common stock investors hope the stock price will appreciate as the company expands its operations and increases its profits. Common stock tends to offer you a better return (profit) than other investments, such as bonds or preferred stock. However, if the company falters, you could lose some or all of your original investment.

comparable market analysis (CMA): A written analysis, usually completed by a real estate agent, of similar houses currently being offered for sale and which have recently sold.

consumer debt: Debt on consumer items that depreciate in value over time. Credit card balances and auto loans are examples of consumer debt. This type of debt is bad for your financial health because it is high-interest and encourages you to live beyond your means.

Consumer Price Index (CPI): The Consumer Price Index reports price changes, on a monthly basis, in the cost of living for such items as food, housing, transportation, health care, entertainment, clothing, and other miscellaneous expenses. The CPI is used to adjust government benefits, such as Social Security, and is used by many employers to determine cost-of-living increases in wages and pensions. An increase in prices is also known as **inflation**.

co-payment: The percentage of your medical bill that your health plan requires you to pay out of your own pocket once you've satisfied your annual deductible. A typical co-payment is 20 percent.

credit report: A credit report details your history of using credit and is the main report that a lender uses to determine whether or not to make you a loan. You must generally pay the lender to obtain this report.

debit card: Although they may look like credit cards, debit cards are different in one important way: When you use a debit card, the cost of the purchase is deducted from your checking account. Thus, a debit card gives you the convenience of a credit card without the danger of building up a mountain of consumer debt.

deductible: A new product from Keebler's elves, you may be thinking. Unfortunately, it is much more mundane. With insurance, the deductible is the amount of the loss that you pay if you file a claim. For example, say that your car sustains $800 of damage. If your deductible is $500, then the insurance will cover $300 and you'll pay $500 out of your own pocket for the repairs. The higher the deductible, the lower your insurance premiums and the less paperwork you will expose yourself to in filing claims (because small losses that are less than the deductible won't necessitate filing a claim). Take the highest deductibles that you can afford when selecting insurance.

deduction: An expense you may subtract from your income to lower your taxable income. Examples include mortgage interest, property taxes (itemized deductions), and most retirement account contributions.

derivative: An investment instrument whose value is derived from other securities. For example, an **option** to buy IBM stock does not have value in itself; the value is derived from the price of IBM's stock.

disability insurance: During your working years, you have a lot riding on your ability to earn an income. Without it, you would be in big trouble (unless a wealthy relative, wife, husband, or friend can support you). Disability insurance replaces a portion of your employment income in the unlikely event that you suffer a disability that keeps you from working.

discount broker: Unlike a full-service broker, a discount broker generally offers no investment advice and has employees who work on salary rather than on commission. Using a discount broker helps you avoid the conflict of interest that will inevitably come up with a so-called full-service broker. In addition to trading individual securities, most discount brokerage firms also offer no-load (commission-free) mutual funds.

diversification: You go out to eat Chinese food with four friends. The menu is a bit difficult to understand and you are not familiar with Chinese food. Is it prudent for all you to order the same dish? Probably not. If each person orders a different dish and you share the food, you have a much better chance of satisfying your palate. The same holds true when you invest your money. If you put all of your money into one type of investment, you're potentially setting yourself up for a big shock. If that investment collapses, so does your investment world. By spreading your money among different investments — bonds, U.S. stocks, international stocks, and so on — you'll ensure yourself a better chance of investing success and fewer sleepless nights.

dividend: Quotient, divisor, dividend? Forget elementary school math. The dividend is the income paid to investors holding an investment. With stock, the dividend is the portion of a company's profits paid to its shareholders. For example, if a company has an annual dividend of $2 per share and you own 100 shares, then your total dividend is $200. Usually, established and slower-growing companies pay dividends while smaller and faster growing companies reinvest their profits for growth. For assets held outside retirement accounts, dividends, except from tax-free money market and tax-free bond funds, are taxable.

Dow Jones Industrial Average (DJIA): A widely followed stock market index comprising 30 large, actively traded U.S. company stocks. The stocks in the DJIA are selected by senior editors at *The Wall Street Journal*.

down payment: The part of the purchase price for a house that the buyer pays in cash, up front, and does not finance with a mortgage. Generally, the larger the down payment, the better the deal that you can get on a mortgage. You can usually get access to the best mortgage programs with a down payment of at least 20 percent of the purchase price of a home.

earthquake insurance: Although the West Coast is often associated with earthquakes, other areas are also 'quake prone. An earthquake insurance rider (which usually comes with a deductible of 5 to 10 percent of the cost to rebuild the home) on a homeowner's policy pays to repair or rebuild your home if it is damaged in an earthquake. If you live in an area with earthquake risk, get earthquake insurance coverage!

Emerging Markets Index: The Emerging Markets Index is published by Morgan Stanley and tracks stock markets in developing countries. The main reason for investing in emerging markets is that these economies typically experience a higher rate of economic growth than developed markets. However, the potential for higher returns is coupled with greater risk.

equity: In the real estate world, this term refers to the difference between the market value of your home and what you owe on it. For example, if your home is worth $200,000 and you have an outstanding mortgage of $140,000, your equity is $60,000. Equity is also a synonym for **stock**.

estate: The value, at the time of your death, of your assets minus your loans and liabilities.

estate planning: The process of deciding where your assets will go when you die and structuring your assets so as to minimize likely estate taxes.

Federal National Mortgage Association (FNMA): The FNMA (or Fannie Mae) is one of the best known institutions in the secondary mortgage market. Fannie Mae buys mortgages from banks and other mortgage-lending institutions and, in turn, sells them to investors. These loan investments are considered safe because Fannie Mae buys mortgages only from companies that conform to its stringent mortgage regulations, and Fannie Mae guarantees the repayment of principal and interest on the loans that it sells.

financial assets: A property or investment, such as real estate or a stock, mutual fund, bond, and so on, which has value that could be realized if sold.

financial liabilities: Your outstanding loans and debts. To determine your net worth, you must subtract your financial liabilities from your financial assets.

financial planners: A motley crew that professes an ability to manage your money. Financial planners come with varying backgrounds and degrees: MBAs, Certified

Financial Planners, and Certified Public Accountants, to name a few. A useful way to distinguish among this mixed bag of nuts is to determine whether the planners are commission-, fee-, or hourly-based.

fixed-rate mortgage: The granddaddy of all mortgages. You lock into an interest rate (for example, 8 percent), and it never changes during the life (term) of your 15- or 30-year mortgage. Your mortgage payment will be the same amount each and every month. If you become a cursing, frothing maniac when you miss your morning coffee or someone is five minutes late, then this certain payment mortgage might be for you!

flood insurance: "When the flood waters recede, the poor folk start from scratch" (Richard Wright). They start from scratch unless they have flood insurance. If there's even a remote chance that your area may flood, having flood insurance is prudent.

401(k) plan: A type of retirement savings plan offered by many for-profit companies to their employees. Your contributions are usually exempt (yes!) from federal and state income taxes and compound without taxation over time.

403(b) plan: Similar to a 401(k) plan but for employees of nonprofit organizations.

full-service broker: A broker who gives advice and charges a high commission relative to discount brokers. But this is not the biggest problem with full-service brokers. Because the brokers work on commission, they have a significant conflict of interest: namely, to advocate strategies that will be of financial benefit to them.

future: An obligation to buy or sell a commodity or security on a specific day for a preset price. When used by most individual investors, futures represent a short-term gamble on the short-term direction of the price of a commodity. Companies and farmers use futures contracts to hedge their risks of changing prices.

guaranteed-investment contracts (GICs): Insurance company investments that appeal to skittish investors. GICs generally tell you one year in advance what your interest rate will be for the coming year. Thus, you don't have to worry about fluctuations and losses to your investment value. On the other hand, GICs offer you little upside because the interest rate is comparable to what you might get on a short-term bank **Certificate of Deposit**.

home equity: See **equity**.

home-equity loan: Technical jargon for what used to be called a second mortgage. With this type of loan, you borrow against the equity in your house. If used wisely, a home-equity loan can help pay off high-interest consumer debt or can be tapped for other short-term needs, such as a remodeling project. In contrast with consumer debt, mortgage debt is usually at a lower interest rate and is tax-deductible.

homeowner's insurance: Dwelling coverage that covers the cost of rebuilding your house in the event of fire or other calamity. The liability insurance portion of this policy protects you against lawsuits associated with your property. Another essential element is the personal property coverage, which pays to replace your damaged or stolen worldly possessions.

index: (1) A security market index, such as the **Standard & Poor's 500 Index**, is a statistical composite that measures the performance of a particular type of security. Indexes exist for various stock and bond markets and are typically set at a round number such as 100 at a particular point in time. See **Dow Jones Industrial Average**, **Russell 2000**, and **Wilshire 5000**. (2) The index also can refer to the measure of the overall level of interest rates that a lender uses as a reference to calculate the specific interest rate on an adjustable-rate loan. The index plus the margin is the formula for determining the interest rate on an adjustable-rate mortgage.

individual retirement account (IRA): A retirement account into which anyone with sufficient employment income or alimony may contribute up to $2,000 per year. Contributions may or may not be tax-deductible based on your eligibility for other employer-based retirement programs and which type of IRA you select (regular or Roth).

inflation: The technical term for a rise in prices. Inflation usually occurs when there is too much money in circulation and not enough goods and services to spend it on. Due to this excess demand, prices rise. There is a link between inflation and interest rates: Interest rates must keep up with inflation or no one will invest in bonds issued by the government or corporations. When the interest rates on bonds are high, it usually reflects a high rate of inflation that will eat away at your return.

initial public offering (IPO): The first time a company offers stock to the investing public. An IPO typically occurs when a company wants to expand more rapidly and seeks additional money to support its growth. A number of studies have demonstrated that buying into IPOs in which the general public can participate produces subpar investment returns. A high level of IPO activity may indicate a cresting stock market as companies and their investment bankers rush to cash in on a "pricey" marketplace. IPO could stand for *It's Probably Overpriced*.

interest rate: What lenders charge you to use their money. The higher the interest rate, the higher the risk generally entailed in the loan. With bonds of a given maturity, a higher rate of interest means a lower quality of bond — one that is less likely to return you your money.

international stock markets: Stock markets outside of the United States account for a significant portion of the world stock market capitalization (value). Some specific stock indices track international markets (see **Morgan Stanley EAFE** and **Emerging Markets Index**). International investing is one way to diversify your portfolio and reduce your risk. Some of the foreign countries with major stock exchanges outside the U.S. include Japan, Britain, France, Germany, and Canada.

junk bond: A bond rated Ba (Moody's) or BB (Standard & Poor) and lower. Historically, these bonds have had a 1 to 2 percent chance of default, which is not exactly "junky." Of course, the higher risk is accompanied by a higher interest rate.

Keogh plan: A tax-deductible retirement savings plan available to self-employed individuals. Certain Keoghs allow you to put up to 20 percent of your self-employment income into the account.

leverage: Financial leverage affords its users a disproportionate amount of financial power relative to the amount of their own cash invested. In some circumstances, you can borrow up to 50 percent of a stock price and use all funds (both yours and those that you borrow) to make a purchase. You repay this so-called margin loan when you sell the stock. If the stock price were to rise, you would make money on what you invested plus what money you borrowed. While this sounds attractive, remember that leverage cuts both ways — when prices decline, you lose money not only on your investment but also on the money you borrowed.

limited partnership (LP): Often promoted in a way that promises high returns, broker-sold limited partnerships generally limit one thing: your investment return. Why? Because they are burdened with high commissions and management fees. Another problem is that they are typically not liquid for many years.

load mutual fund: A sales load is the commission paid to brokers who sell commission-based mutual funds. The commission typically ranges from 4 to 8.5 percent. This commission is deducted from your investment money and thus reduces your returns.

marginal tax rate: The rate of income tax that you pay on the last dollars that you earn over the course of a year. Why the complicated distinction? Because all income is not treated equally: You pay less tax on your first dollars of earnings and more tax on the last dollars of your annual income. Knowing your marginal tax rate is helpful because you can analyze the tax implications of important personal financial decisions.

market capitalization: The value of all the outstanding **stock** of a company. It is the quoted price per share of a stock multiplied by the number of shares outstanding. Thus, if Rocky and Bullwinkle Corporation has 100 million shares of outstanding stock and the quoted price per share is $20, then the company has a market capitalization of $2 billion.

Moody's ratings: Moody's rating service measures and rates the credit (default) risks of various bonds. Moody's investigates the financial condition of a bond issuer. Its ratings use the following grading system, from highest to lowest: Aaa, Aa, A, Baa, Ba, B, Caa, Ca, C. Higher ratings imply a lower risk but also mean that the interest rate will be lower.

Morgan Stanley EAFE (Europe, Australia, Far East) index: The Morgan Stanley EAFE index tracks the performance of the more established countries' stock markets in Europe and Asia. This index is an important one for international-minded investors who want to follow the performance of overseas stock investments.

mortgage broker: Mortgage brokers buy mortgages wholesale from lenders and then mark the mortgages up (typically from 0.5 to 1 percent) and sell them to borrowers. A good mortgage broker is most helpful for people who will not shop around on their own for a mortgage or for people who have blemishes on their credit reports.

mortgage life insurance: Mortgage life insurance guarantees that the lender will receive its money in the event that you meet an untimely demise. Many people may try to convince you that you need this insurance to protect your dependents and loved ones. Mortgage life insurance is relatively expensive given the cost for the coverage provided. If you need life insurance, buy low-cost, high-quality **term life insurance** instead.

mortgage-backed bond (GNMAs and FNMAs): The Government National Mortgage Association (GNMA or Ginnie Mae) specializes in mortgage-backed security. It passes the interest and principal payment of borrowers through to investors. When a homeowner makes a mortgage payment, GNMA deducts a small service charge and forwards the mortgage payments to its investors. The payments are guaranteed in the case of a borrower not paying his or her mortgage. The Federal National Mortgage Association (FNMA or Fannie Mae) is a publicly owned, government-sponsored corporation that purchases mortgages from lenders and resells them to investors. FNMA mainly deals with mortgages backed by the Federal Housing Administration.

municipal bond: A loan that an investor makes to cities, towns, and states for public projects, such as building highways, parks, or cultural centers. What makes municipal bonds special is the tax-exempt status of their interest: They're exempt from federal taxes and, if you reside in the state where the bond is issued, state taxes as well. Municipal bonds are most appropriate for high tax-bracket people investing money outside of a tax-sheltered retirement account.

mutual fund: A portfolio of stocks, bonds, or other securities that is owned by numerous investors and managed by an investment company. See also **no-load mutual fund**.

National Association of Securities Dealers Automated Quotation (NASDAQ) system: An electronic network that allows brokers to trade from their offices all over the country. With NASDAQ, brokers buy and sell shares using constantly updated prices that appear on their computer screens.

negative amortization: Although it may sound like a description of the cause of dinosaur extinction, negative amortization occurs when your outstanding mortgage balance increases despite the fact that you're making the required monthly payments. Negative amortization occurs with adjustable-rate mortgages that cap the increase in your monthly payment but do not cap the interest rate. Therefore, your monthly payments do not cover all the interest that you actually owe. Avoid loans with this "feature."

net asset value (NAV): The dollar value of one share of a mutual fund. For a no-load fund, the market price is its NAV. For a load fund, the NAV is the "buy" price minus the commission.

New York Stock Exchange (NYSE): The largest stock exchange in the world in terms of total volume and value of shares traded. It lists companies that tend to be among the oldest, largest, and best-known companies.

no-load mutual fund: A mutual fund that does not come with a commission payment attached to it. Because of the lack of a load and generally lower management fees of these funds, they tend to have better returns than load funds. Some funds claim to be "no-load" but simply hide their sales commissions as an ongoing sales charge. You can avoid these funds by reading the prospectuses carefully and educating yourself.

open-end mutual fund: A mutual fund that issues as many shares as investors demand. These open-end funds do not generally limit the number of investors or amount of money in the fund. Some open-end funds have been known to close to new investors, but investors with existing shares can usually still buy more shares from the company.

option: The right to buy or sell a specific security (such as a stock) for a preset price during a specified period of time. Options differ from futures in that with an option, you pay a premium fee up front and you can either exercise the option or let it expire. If the option expires worthless, you lose 100 percent of your original investment. Use of options is best left to companies as hedging tools. Investment managers may use options as a hedging tool to reduce the risk in their investment portfolio. Like with futures, when most individual investors buy an option, they are doing so as a short-term gamble, not as an investment. For example: You have an option to buy 100 shares of Rocky and Bullwinkle Co. stock at $20 per share in the next six months. You pay $3 per share up front as the premium. During this time period, R&B's share price rises to $30 and you exercise your right to buy at $20. You then sell your shares at the market price of $30; you make a $10 profit per share, which is a return more than three times larger than your original investment.

pension: Also known as defined benefit plans, pensions are a benefit offered by some employers. These plans generally pay you a monthly retirement income based upon your years of service with the employer.

performance: How do you judge an investment's performance? Traditionally, by looking at the historic rate of return. The longer the period over which these numbers are tallied, the more useful. Considered alone, these numbers are practically meaningless. You must also note how well a fund has performed in comparison to competitors with the same investment objectives. Beware of advertisements that tout the high returns of a mutual fund, because they may not be looking at risk-adjusted performance or may be promoting performance over a short time period. Keep in mind that high return statistics are usually coupled with high risk and that this year's star could turn out to be next year's crashing meteor.

pre-certification: A health insurance requirement for benefit coverage that a patient get approval before being admitted to a hospital for nonemergency care.

preferred stock: Stock that offers a guaranteed amount of dividend to investors. Preferred stock dividends must be paid before any dividends are paid to the common stock shareholders. Although preferred stock reduces your risk as an investor (because of the more secure dividend and greater likelihood of getting your money back if the company fails), it usually also limits your reward if the company expands and increases its profits.

price/earnings (P/E) ratio: The current price of a stock divided by the current (or sometimes the projected) earnings per share of the issuing company. It's a widely used stock analysis statistic that helps an investor get an idea of how cheap or expensive a stock price is. In general, a relatively high P/E ratio indicates that investors feel that the company's earnings are likely to grow quickly.

prime rate: The rate of interest that major banks charge their most creditworthy corporate customers. Why should you care? Well, because the interest rates on various loans that you may be interested in are often based upon the prime rate. And, guess what — you pay a higher interest rate than those big corporations!

principal: No, not the big boss from elementary school who struck fear into the hearts of most eight-year-olds. The principal is the amount that you borrow for a loan. If you borrow $100,000, your principal is $100,000. Principal can also refer to the amount that you originally placed in an investment.

prospectus: Individual companies as well as mutual funds are required by the **Securities and Exchange Commission** to issue a prospectus. For a company, the prospectus is a legal document presenting a detailed analysis of that company's financial history, its products and services, its management's background and experience, and the risks of investing in the company. For a mutual fund, a prospectus tells you about the fund's investment objectives, costs, risk, and performance history.

real estate investment trust (REIT): Real estate investment trusts are like a mutual fund of real estate investments. Such trusts invest in a collection of properties (from shopping centers to apartment buildings). REITs trade on the major stock exchanges. If you want to invest in real estate while avoiding the hassles inherent in owning property, real estate investment trusts may be the right choice for you.

refinance: Refinance, or refi, is a fancy word for taking out a new mortgage loan (usually at a lower interest rate) to pay off an existing mortgage (generally at a higher interest rate). Refinancing is not automatic, nor is refinancing guaranteed. Refinancing can also be a hassle and expensive. Weigh the costs and benefits of refinancing carefully before proceeding.

return on investment: The percentage of profit that you make on an investment. If you put $1,000 into an investment, and one year later it's worth $1,100, you have made a profit of $100. Your return on investment is the profit ($100) divided by the initial investment ($1,000) — in this case, 10 percent.

reverse mortgage: A reverse mortgage enables elderly homeowners, typically those who are low on cash, to tap into their home's equity without selling their home or moving from it. Specifically, a lending institution makes a check out to you each month, and you can use the check as you want. This money is really a loan against the value of your home and thus is tax-free when you receive it. The downside of these loans is that they deplete your equity in your estate, the fees and interest rates tend to be on the high side, and some require repayment within a certain number of years.

Russell 2000: An index that tracks the returns of 2000 smaller-company U.S. stocks. Smaller-company stocks tend to be more volatile than larger-company stocks. If you invest in small-company stocks or stock funds, this is an appropriate benchmark to compare your performance to.

Securities and Exchange Commission (SEC): The federal agency that administers U.S. securities laws and regulates and monitors investment companies, brokers, and financial advisors.

simplified employee pension individual retirement account (SEP-IRA): Like other retirement plans, a SEP-IRA allows your money to compound over the years without the parasitic effect of taxes. SEP-IRAs are relatively easy to set up and allow self-employed people to put away annual contributions on a pre-tax basis.

Social Security: If you are retired or disabled, Social Security is a government safety net that can provide you with some income. The program is based on the idea that government is responsible for the social welfare of its citizens. Whether you agree with this notion or not, part of your paycheck goes to Social Security, and when you retire, you will receive money from the program.

Standard & Poor's (S&P) ratings: Standard & Poor's rating service is one of two services that measure and rate the risks in buying a bond. S&P's ratings use the following grading system, from highest to lowest: AAA, AA, A, BBB, BB, B, CCC, CC, C. See also **Moody's ratings**.

Standard & Poor's 500 Index: An index that measures the performance of 500 large-company U.S. stocks that account for about 80 percent of the total market value of all stocks traded in the U.S. If you invest in larger-company stock or stock funds, this is an appropriate benchmark to compare the performance of your investments to.

stock: Shares of ownership in a company. When a company "goes public," it issues shares of stock to the public (see also **initial public offering**). Many, but not all, stocks pay dividends — a distribution of a portion of company profits. In addition to dividends, the other way you make money investing in stock is via appreciation in the price of the stock, which normally results from growth in revenues and corporate profits. You can invest in stock by purchasing individual shares or by investing in a stock mutual fund that offers a diversified package of stocks.

term life insurance: If people are dependent upon your income for their living expenses, you may need this insurance.

Term life insurance functions simply: You determine how much protection you would like and then pay an annual premium based on that amount. Although it is much less touted by insurance salespeople than cash value insurance, it is the best life insurance out there for the vast majority of people.

Treasury bill: IOUs from the federal government that mature within a year. Other types of loans investors can make to the federal government are Treasury notes, which mature within one to ten years, and Treasury bonds, which mature in more than ten years. The interest that these federal government bonds pay is state tax-free but federally taxable.

underwriting: An insurance company's process for evaluating a person's likelihood of filing a claim on a particular type of insurance policy. If significant problems are discovered, an insurer will usually propose much higher rates or refuse to sell the insurance coverage.

will: A legal document ensuring that your wishes regarding your assets and care of your minor children are heeded when you die.

Wilshire 5000: Despite the name, this index actually tracks closer to 6000 companies of all sizes on major U.S. stock exchanges. If you invest in stock or stock funds of companies of all sizes, this is an appropriate benchmark.

zero-coupon bond: A bond that doesn't pay explicit interest during the term of the loan. Such bonds are purchased at a discounted price relative to the principal value paid at maturity. Thus, the interest is implicit in the discount. These bonds do not offer a tax break because the investor must pay taxes on the interest he would have received.

Index

WWW.DUMMIES.COM

YOUR ONLINE RESOURCE

Discover Dummies Online!

The Dummies Web Site is your fun and friendly online resource for the latest information about ...*For Dummies*® books and your favorite topics. The Web site is the place to communicate with us, exchange ideas with other ...*For Dummies* readers, chat with authors, and have fun!

Ten Fun and Useful Things You Can Do at www.dummies.com

1. Win free ...*For Dummies* books and more!
2. Register your book and be entered in a prize drawing.
3. Meet your favorite authors through the IDG Books Author Chat Series.
4. Exchange helpful information with other ...*For Dummies* readers.
5. Discover other great ...*For Dummies* books you must have!
6. Purchase Dummieswear™ exclusively from our Web site.
7. Buy ...*For Dummies* books online.
8. Talk to us. Make comments, ask questions, get answers!
9. Download free software.
10. Find additional useful resources from authors.

Link directly to these ten fun and useful things at
http://www.dummies.com/10useful

For other technology titles from IDG Books Worldwide, go to
www.idgbooks.com

Not on the Web yet? It's easy to get started with *Dummies 101*®: *The Internet For Windows*® *98* or *The Internet For Dummies*, 6th Edition, at local retailers everywhere.

Find other ...*For Dummies* books on these topics:
Business • Career • Databases • Food & Beverage • Games • Gardening • Graphics • Hardware
Health & Fitness • Internet and the World Wide Web • Networking • Office Suites
Operating Systems • Personal Finance • Pets • Programming • Recreation • Sports
Spreadsheets • Teacher Resources • Test Prep • Word Processing

IDG BOOKS WORLDWIDE
BOOK REGISTRATION

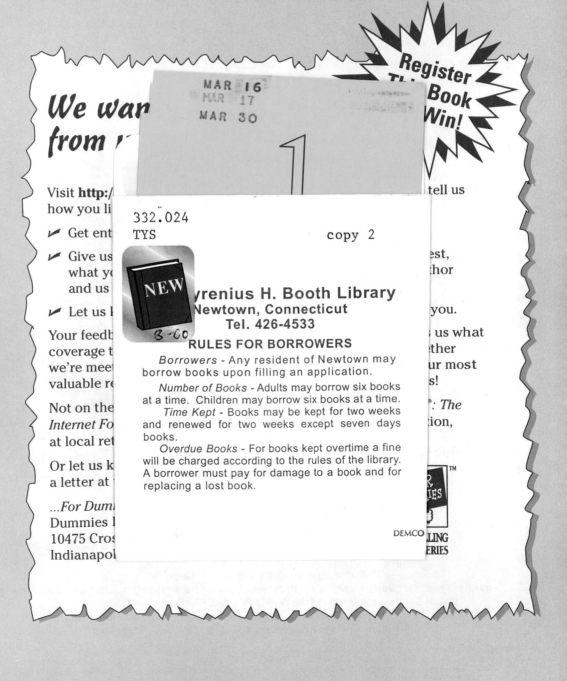